*For Leah and Emma,
the joys of my life*

Contents

Preface xi

Chapter   1.   An Unsound Operation of War 1

Chapter   2.   Steadfast and Loyal 26

Chapter   3.   Overture to Overlord 50

Chapter   4.   Night of Nights 92

Chapter   5.   Hitting the Silk 115

Chapter   6.   All-Americans 145

Chapter   7.   So This Is France 172

Chapter   8.   Get in There and Take Chances 230

Chapter   9.   Something to Behold 267

Chapter 10.   Proud of You 290

Chapter 11.   The First Day of a Long Struggle 309

Appendix I: Allied Casualties on Utah Beach
               and in Cotentin Peninsula, June 6, 1944 330

Appendix II: Medal of Honor and Distinguished Service
               Cross Awards for Valor on Utah Beach
               and in Cotentin Peninsula, June 6, 1944 332

Appendix III: First-Wave Units on Utah Beach 336

Appendix IV: Initial Parachute and Glider Assault,
               Cotentin Peninsula, 12:20–4:15 A.M.,
               June 6, 1944 338

Appendix V: Ninth Air Force, IX Troop Carrier Command,
               June 6, 1944 341

Appendix VI: Ninth Air Force, IX Bomber Command,
               Utah Beach Bombing Mission,
               6:09–6:27 A.M., June 6, 1944 343

Appendix VII: U.S. Navy Force U Bombardment Group 344

Appendix VIII: Capt. Frank Lillyman's Pathfinder Stick,
               June 6, 1944 346

Appendix IX: Uniform and Equipment of U.S. Army
               Paratroopers, 82nd and 101st Airborne
               Divisions, June 6, 1944 348

               Notes 350

               Bibliography 366

               Acknowledgments 372

               Index 375

Illustrations

1. General Sir Bernard Law Montgomery
   inspects U.S. Army troops 7

2. Lt. Gen. Omar Bradley and Maj. Gen. Joseph Collins 15

3. Maj. Gen. Raymond O. Barton 32

4. IX Troop Carrier Command C-47s towing gliders 38

5. A U.S. Navy signalman on Utah Beach on D-Day 57

6. Rear Adm. Don Moon 66

7. The 87th Chemical Mortar Battalion
   of VII Corps loads up 71

8. Gen. Dwight Eisenhower and Rear Admirals
   Morton Deyo and Alan Kirk. 79

9. Pilots from the 439th Troop Carrier Group assemble
   for D-Day. 100

10. Col. George Van Horn Moseley. 120

11. Col. Robert Sink 126

12. Lt. Col. Julian Ewell 131

13. Two U.S. paratroopers prepare for D-Day 135

14. Col. Howard Johnson. 138

15. 101st Airborne troops load a gun into a glider. 142

16. Paratroopers from the 82nd Airborne Division 148

17. Maj. James McGinity 159

18. Brig. Gen. James Gavin. 162

19. Ile de Terre under attack 175

20. Brig. Gen. Ted Roosevelt Jr. 178

21. Officers of the 8th Infantry 188

22. U.S. troops landing on beach. 195

23. A U.S. Army duplex drive tank 203

24. A heavy weapons company moves inland 223

25. Troops from the 87th Chemical Mortar Battalion 226

26. U.S. troops move through flooded area 235

27. Capt. George Mabry 242

28. Lt. Col. Erasmus Strickland. 253

29. American troops in front of church 255

30. 1st Lt. Turner Turnbull. 270

31. Two American paratroopers behind a hedgerow 272

32. Col. Edson Raff points out objectives on a map 279

33. A U.S. Army Sherman tank moves inland. 283

34. U.S. troops examine German miniature vehicles. 302

35. A 4th Infantry Division medic and two Norman children . . 318

Maps

1. The Strategic Situation, June 1944 6

2. SHAEF vs. COSSAC Overlord Plan 11

3. Cotentin Peninsula: German Deployment, June 1944 55

4. Force U: Exercise Tiger, April 28, 1944 60

5. Force U: Passage to Normandy, June 5, 1944 76

6. Force U: Utah Beach Bombardment, June 6, 1944 81

7. Ninth Air Force: Utah Beach Bombardment,
   June 6, 1944 86

8. 82nd and 101st Airborne Division Drop Zones 93

9. IX Troop Carrier Command, June 6, 1944 109

10. 502nd Parachute Infantry: Morning, June 6, 1944. 122

11. Drop Zone C: Morning, June 6, 1944 128

12. Drop Zone D: Morning, June 6, 1944 137

13. 505th Parachute Infantry: Morning, June 6, 1944 151

14. 507th and 508th Parachute Infantry: Morning,
      June 6, 1944 160

15. Utah Beach and Iles St. Marcouf: H-Hour, June 6, 1944. . . 174

16. Utah Beach: Second Wave, 7:30 A.M., June 6, 1944 198

17. Utah Beach: Third Wave, 8:00 A.M., June 6, 1944. 220

18. Utah Beach: Later Waves, 9:05 A.M., June 6, 1944 232

19. Utah Beach: Inland Penetrations, 10:00 A.M.,
      June 6, 1944 240

20. 501st Parachute Infantry: Afternoon, June 6, 1944 258

21. 502nd Parachute Infantry: Objective XYZ 263

22. 82nd Airborne Division: Afternoon, June 6, 1944. 269

23. Task Force Raff and Evening Glider Missions,
      June 6, 1944 281

24. 12th and 22nd Infantry: Afternoon, June 6, 1944 293

25. Utah Beachhead: Close of Day, June 6, 1944 304

Preface

A HEAVY BURDEN OF RESPONSIBILITY

Many of those who have experienced high command in war have described it as a lonely and burdensome job, and no man understood the weight of that responsibility better than Gen. Dwight D. Eisenhower. Ike's aides had observed their boss's inclination to chain-smoke during periods of stress, and by the end of May 1944, Eisenhower's addiction to tobacco had considerably worsened. The aides could not have known that on May 30, 1944, Eisenhower faced one of his toughest decisions of the war, a choice forced upon him by his senior air commander, Air Chief Marshal Sir Trafford Leigh-Mallory of the Royal Air Force. Just a few days before the initiation of Operation Overlord on D-Day, Leigh-Mallory had professed a near-total lack of confidence in the massive American airborne operation that was planned to support the Utah Beach invasion on D-Day. With the momentous invasion about to be launched, Ike would have little time to decide whether the proposed airborne venture behind Utah would lead to the slaughter of the U.S. Army's prized 82nd and 101st Airborne Divisions.

Good generals judge correctly when risks are worth taking in war and when they are not. Ike paced and smoked countless packs of cigarettes pondering the risks that could lead to disaster, but his ultimate endorsement of the American airborne mission on D-Day accentuated the incontestable truth that Operation Overlord was a highly risky undertaking, a detail that has been noticeably dimmed by the passage of more than six decades since the invasion. History has come to view D-Day as an inevitable Allied triumph. It was anything but. Several pillars of the D-Day plan posed significant risk, and first among them was the U.S. Army's proposed scheme of landing thousands of men by parachute and glider behind Utah Beach in the invasion's opening hours. As Ike noted in his World War II memoir, *Crusade in Europe,* "If [Leigh-Mallory] was right, it appeared that the attack on Utah Beach was probably hopeless, and this meant the whole operation suddenly acquired a degree of risk, even foolhardiness, that presaged a gigantic failure, possibly Allied defeat in Europe."

The U.S. Army Chief of Staff, Gen. George C. Marshall, had defined Eisenhower's role as Overlord's supreme commander as "a heavy burden of responsibility," and Ike's burden could be neatly summed up as ensuring that such an unthinkable defeat did not occur. As Thomas Paine had so eloquently noted in 1776 during an earlier period of acute uncertainty: Times such as these tried men's souls.

MONTY

When General Sir Bernard Law Montgomery arrived in Britain in January 1944 to assume the crucial role as Eisenhower's senior ground commander and chief planner for Operation Overlord, British and American soldiers regarded him with either adoration or abhorrence: There were no opinions in between. Then and now, Monty's critics have commonly categorized him as an excessively cautious commander, one who would wait for near-perfect conditions before initiating a military operation. However, the first three months of the Allied campaign in northwest Europe proved conclusively that this label is entirely invalid. Within a fifteen-week period from June to September 1944, Montgomery was in large measure the driving force behind two immense and highly risky military endeavors, both of which involved airborne operations on an unmatched scale: first, the June 6 seaborne and airborne assault against the Cotentin Peninsula, which included the Utah Beach invasion and the 82nd and 101st Airborne Divisions' air drop behind the Atlantic Wall; and second, Operation Market-Garden, a daring airborne thrust in September deep behind enemy lines that aimed to exploit the recent German rout in France and win the war in a single stroke. Neither of these two operations could have been devised by a commander who habitually practiced caution.

Monty's first look at the Operation Overlord plan on New Year's Eve 1943 had prompted him to demand greater resources, manpower, and time to enhance the invasion's chance of success. With the cool conceit for which he was renowned, Montgomery argued that D-Day would fail unless the proposed twenty-five-mile invasion front were doubled to fifty miles. Ike concurred, and the combined reputation of the two most celebrated Allied commanders of World War II carried so much weight with President

Roosevelt, Prime Minister Churchill, and the Allied Combined Chiefs of Staff that they granted almost all of what Monty asked for. True, the invasion would have to be postponed by one month, but when it came to pass, it would be considerably more ambitious than the old plan, with two new invasion beaches, thousands more assault troops, vastly greater numbers of ships and planes, and an airborne component that was four times the size of the D-Day parachute and glider force originally envisioned by Overlord planners.

One of those two new invasion beaches was Utah, and this book tells the story of that invasion. This story, however, is not simply one of American troops surging ashore in a secluded corner of Normandy at the crack of dawn on June 6, 1944. It is also a tale of U.S. Army paratroopers and glidermen, as well as Army Air Force Troop Carrier pilots who conveyed them to their objectives in the dead of night. It is a story of U.S. Navy, Coast Guard, and Royal Navy sailors who manned the landing vessels and warships that brought the combat troops across the English Channel and supported them once ashore. It is the story of Ninth Air Force B-26 Marauder bomber pilots who smashed the enemy defenses on Utah Beach immediately before the assault troops' arrival. Ultimately, it is a story of an incredibly complex military operation that was a brilliant success.

FROM THE SEA AND THE SKY

The addition of substantially more troops, ships, and planes to the D-Day invasion could hardly be viewed negatively by Allied generals, but to many strategists involved in Overlord planning, there was one troubling component of Monty's new plan—and that was Utah Beach. A glance at a map of the Normandy coastline called attention to their concerns. Utah Beach was the most isolated of the five Allied invasion sites on D-Day, and those generals who were well-versed in the German Army's proficiency at counterattack worried whether the American invasion force could hang on there before the Allied beachheads were united. Furthermore, the Germans had flooded the pasturelands behind the coastline, effectively turning Utah Beach into a barrier island rather than a contiguous part of the Normandy landmass. Only a few narrow and neglected causeways connected the beach with the interior, and as a result, American planners had to worry not only about getting on the beach, but also getting off it. Even such an optimist as Eisenhower fretted that without some sort of innovative assault plan, Utah Beach was a bottle waiting to be corked.

That innovation would be air power. The Allies' control of the sky in June 1944 was so complete that they resolved to include in Operation Overlord a type of military maneuver they had only rarely attempted before—and never on the massive scale they proposed for the Normandy invasion. The U.S. Army somewhat euphemistically referred to this novel maneuver as "vertical envelopment," and if it worked, more than 20,000 Allied troops would suddenly descend behind the German coastal defenses by parachute and glider early on D-Day. More than 13,000 of those would be Americans from the 82nd and 101st Airborne Divisions, landing in the hedgerow country beyond Utah Beach.

An operation of this kind was sure to trigger confusion on both sides, especially as it would be undertaken at night, but if the airborne troops could manage to seize key objectives, thereby blocking enemy counterattack routes and isolating the coastal defenders, the operation would certainly make the seaborne troops' job easier on June 6 and after. But airborne warfare was so new that no one could predict whether it would become an enduring part of military operations or just a passing trend. On one fact, however, all agreed: The D-Day airborne operation behind Utah Beach would be unpredictable and perilous, but what elements of Operation Overlord weren't?

Despite those perils, on D-Day American troops would cascade into that corner of Normandy from the sea and the sky and gain a military triumph that not only contributed mightily to the overall Allied success on D-Day, but also proved decisively that in modern warfare generals would thereafter have to think in three dimensions rather than two if they were to win.

Historians generally overlook the Utah Beach invasion in favor of the much larger and costlier Omaha assault. This is an oversight that twenty-first-century historians must rectify. The invasion of Utah Beach was one of the most successful American military operations of World War II. True, only about 21,000 men landed there on D-Day as opposed to 35,000 on Omaha, and although American casualties on Utah were fewer than those at Omaha, the Utah assault was hardly the "piece of cake" described by Gen. Omar Bradley in his memoir A Soldier's Story. Indeed, when one adds the 82nd and 101st Airborne components to the troops who landed on Utah, the Omaha and Utah invasions were comparable in size. Furthermore, when the casualties suffered by airborne units on D-Day are added to those suffered by VII Corps on Utah Beach, the sum is roughly three-quarters of the total loss endured by the Omaha assault force on June 6. Thus, when the invasion of the Cotentin Peninsula is viewed through a much broader lens than historians have generally applied, the facts are inescapable that the two major American contributions to the D-Day invasion, Omaha and Utah, were similar in both size and cost.

The combined seaborne-airborne invasion of the Cotentin on D-Day yielded a compelling legacy in the halls of power in Washington because the three principal general officers who led that invasion—Joseph Lawton Collins, Matthew Ridgway, and Maxwell Taylor—served consecutive terms as Chief of Staff of the U.S. Army from 1949 to 1959. As the U.S. Army's leading soldiers throughout that pivotal decade, these three men shaped the character of America's ground forces in the face of military threats entirely different from those of World War II. Although Collins, Ridgway, and Taylor had certainly achieved prominence before D-Day, the severe challenges of the Utah Beach invasion tested their military skills far more rigorously than anything they had experienced before in their careers. In fact, their impressive D-Day successes undeniably helped to place them in the upper reaches of the U.S. Army hierarchy after World War II.

In telling the story of the Utah Beach invasion, I follow the same methodology I used in my previous book, *Omaha Beach: D-Day, June 6, 1944,* relying overwhelmingly on primary sources generated by participants and U.S. Army historians shortly after the invasion—in many cases only days afterward. I adhered to this principle as far as possible simply because my career in military research, now thirty years in duration, has led me to appreciate that primary source materials, such as after-action reports, unit journals, and personal correspondence, provide far and away the most trust-worthy foundation for any historian who wishes to grasp the fundamental factors of a momentous military event. The Utah Beach invasion generated vast amounts of such materials, and although the process of perusing them all was protracted and at times exasperating, in the end it was an undeniable thrill to discover that many new and significant historical truths had emerged from the procedure, just as they had in *Omaha Beach.*

Since combat soldiers do not think like historians, I contend that without hearing soldiers' voices one cannot possibly fully understand a battle. In this book, readers will learn the story of the Utah Beach invasion from a military as well as an academic perspective. These two viewpoints are of course entirely dissimilar, but I expect that such a style is instinctive to me because of my historical schooling. I was certainly trained as an academic, but have spent most of my professional life imparting history not to conventional students, but to soldiers—both active and retired. Working with young and old warriors has profoundly influenced the methods I use to tell historical stories. Of all the themes touched upon by old soldiers who experienced the D-Day invasion, the most common and powerful is the chaos of war. From the perspective of the participants, seemingly nothing on D-Day went according to plan, and yet somehow or other, the invasion worked. That theme is touched upon repeatedly in this book.

On the other hand, the young members of today's military seek to become better combat leaders by searching for historical lessons providing evidence that war's chaos can to some extent be controlled. Indeed, the effort to control that chaos is another major theme of my books. During battlefield staff rides in Normandy that are part of some U.S. Army soldiers' military training, I regularly point out that memorizing the details and chronology of a battle is trivial. Rather, the significant moral of armed struggle is initiative. Soldiers must recognize the truly decisive moments of a battle, during which a small group of fighting men can seize the initiative—even against great odds—and impact the outcome out of all proportion to that group's size. This is another pillar of the *Utah Beach* story, as readers will soon discern when they grasp the significance of actions undertaken on D-Day by men such as Ted Roosevelt Jr., George Mabry, Julian Ewell, Benjamin Vandervoort, and dozens of others.

U.S. ARMY WORLD WAR II ORGANIZATION

The American invasion of the Cotentin Peninsula on D-Day involved an entire infantry division (the 4th), a small part of another (the 90th), two airborne divisions (82nd and 101st), and many specialized outfits, such as artillery, engineer, cavalry, signal, military police, and medical units, temporarily attached to those divisions for the landing. Under normal circumstances, an infantry division consisted of 14,300 men, and an airborne division, about 10,500, but those numbers swelled markedly on D-Day because of the profusion of units attached to those larger formations in the operation.

The primary components of a U.S. Army infantry division were its three 3,100-man regiments. In the 4th Division, these were the 8th, 12th, and 22nd Infantry. The 8th led the 4th Division ashore on D-Day and this narrative features that regiment prominently. According to a venerable army custom, the word "Regiment" is considered superfluous when referring to units of regimental size, and this book adheres to this practice. Hence, references to the "8th Infantry" or "12th Infantry" always imply regiments.

A conventional infantry regiment was configured into three 870-man battalions, designated simply 1st, 2nd, and 3rd. Battalions in turn broke down into companies: A, B, C, and D Companies in the 1st; E, F, G, and H in the 2nd; and I, K, L, and M in the 3rd. Companies D, H, and M were known as "heavy weapons" companies, because they employed more powerful machine guns and mortars than the other nine "rifle" companies. Each battalion also included a headquarters company.

As of D-Day, the organization of U.S. Army airborne divisions was still evolving. When the 82nd and 101st landed in Normandy, organizational tables indicated that they should have two parachute infantry regiments, each of about 2,000 men, but both divisions actually landed in the Cotentin with three parachute regiments apiece: the 505th, 507th, and 508th in the 82nd Airborne; and the 501st, 502nd, and 506th in the 101st Airborne. Each airborne division also possessed a single 3,100-man glider infantry regiment: the 325th in the 82nd; and the 327th in the 101st.

Parachute infantry regiments were configured somewhat differently than their conventional counterparts, since airborne commanders considered it unfeasible to drop heavy machine guns and mortars by air on a large scale. Therefore, parachute infantry regiments lacked heavy weapons companies. In a parachute regiment, the 1st Battalion consisted of Companies A, B, and C; the 2nd Battalion, Companies D, E, and F; and the 3rd Battalion, Companies G, H, and I. A headquarters company was also assigned to each battalion.

ALLIED COMMAND ECHELONS

The Utah Beach invasion was planned and executed by the U.S. Army's VII Corps, the command to which the 4th and 90th Divisions, as well as dozens of other diverse outfits, belonged. The VII Corps was a component of the U.S. First Army, which in turn was subordinated to the multinational 21st Army Group, led by General Sir Bernard Montgomery, Eisenhower's chief ground planner for the D-Day assault. The 82nd and 101st Airborne Divisions were directly subordinated to the First Army, but for practical purposes, they came under VII Corps control once the Utah beachhead was established by the close of D-Day.

CAST OF PRINCIPAL COMMANDERS

Gen. George Marshall, Chief of Staff, U.S. Army

Gen. Dwight Eisenhower, Supreme Commander, Allied Expeditionary Force

Gen. Bernard Montgomery, Commander, 21st Army Group

Adm. Harold Stark, Commander, U.S. Naval Forces, Europe

Lt. Gen. Omar Bradley, Commander, U.S. First Army

Lt. Gen. Lewis Brereton, Commander, U.S. Ninth Air Force

Lt. Gen. Frederick Morgan, Chief of Staff, to Supreme Allied Commander (COSSAC)

Rear Adm. Alan Kirk, Commander, Western Naval Task Force (Task Force 122)

Maj. Gen. Joseph L. Collins, Commander, U.S. VII Corps

Maj. Gen. Raymond Barton, Commander, 4th Infantry Division

Maj. Gen. Matthew Ridgway, Commander, 82nd Airborne Division

Maj. Gen. Maxwell Taylor, Commander, 101st Airborne Division

Maj. Gen. Paul Williams, Commander, IX Troop Carrier Command

Rear Adm. Donald Moon, Commander, Assault Force "U" (Task Force 125)

Brig. Gen. Henry Barber, Assistant Commander, 4th Infantry Division

Brig. Gen. Theodore Roosevelt Jr., Supernumerary General Officer, 4th Infantry Division

Brig. Gen. James Gavin, Assistant Commander, 82nd Airborne Division

Brig. Gen. Donald Pratt, Assistant Commander, 101st Airborne Division

Brig. Gen. James Wharton, Commander, 1st Engineer Special Brigade

Brig. Gen. Samuel Anderson, Commander, IX Bomber Command

Rear Adm. Morton Deyo, Commander, Naval Bombardment Group, Force "U"

Col. Russell Reeder, Commander, 12th Infantry, 4th Division

Col. Hervey Tribolet, Commander, 22nd Infantry, 4th Division

Col. James Van Fleet, Commander, 8th Infantry, 4th Division

Col. Roy Lindquist, Commander, 508th Parachute Infantry, 82nd Division

Col. George Millett, Commander, 507th Parachute Infantry, 82nd Division

Col. Howard Johnson, Commander, 501st Parachute Infantry, 101st Division

Col. George Van Horn Moseley, Commander, 502nd Parachute Infantry, 101st Division

Col. Robert Sink, Commander, 506th Parachute Infantry, 101st Division

Col. Eugene Caffey, Deputy Commander, 1st Engineer Special Brigade

Lt. Col. William Ekman, Commander, 505th Parachute Infantry Regiment, 82nd Division

Cmdr. M. H. Brown, Royal Navy, Commander, Force "U" Minesweeping Group

LANDING CRAFT

Any history of a World War II seaborne invasion demands frequent references to the diverse family of landing craft employed by the Allies to disembark troops and equipment ashore. To provide the reader a basic understanding of those landing craft, several of them are described here, from smallest to largest.

LCVP (Landing Craft, Vehicle, Personnel): Basic U.S. Navy and Coast Guard assault vessel, carrying thirty-one troops.

LCA (Landing Craft, Assault): Basic Royal Navy assault vessel, carrying thirty-one troops.

LCM (Landing Craft, Mechanized): Capable of transporting one tank, although on D-Day, LCMs typically carried about fifty engineers and their demolition equipment.

LCT (Landing Craft, Tank): Produced in many varieties, carried three or four tanks directly to the beach or for launching at sea.

LCT(R) (Landing Craft, Tank [Rocket]): LCT variant with more than 1,000 fixed rocket launchers added for close-in bombardment of the beach prior to the assault.

LCI (Landing Craft, Infantry): Large vessel, carrying 200 troops, considered too vulnerable to land under direct enemy fire.

LST (Landing Ship, Tank): Largest of the landing vessels, carrying up to twenty tanks and 200 troops, but considered too vulnerable to land under direct enemy fire.

ABBREVIATIONS

AAF	U.S. Army Air Force
Adm.	Admiral[a]
AWOL	absent without leave
BAR	Browning automatic rifle
Brig. Gen.	brigadier general
Capt.	captain[a]
CG	commanding general
Cmdr.	commander[a]
CO	commanding officer
Col.	colonel
CP	command post
Cpl.	corporal
DD	duplex drive (amphibious) tank
DZ	drop zone
Ens.	ensign[a]
ETO	European Theater of Operations
F.O.	field order (also forward observer, flight officer)
HQ	headquarters
Lt. Col.	lieutenant colonel
Lt. Cmdr.	lieutenant commander[a]
Lt. Gen.	lieutenant general
Lt. (jg)	lieutenant, junior grade[a]

LZ	landing zone
Maj.	major
Maj. Gen.	major general
M/Sgt.	master sergeant[b]
NCO	noncommissioned officer
PFC	private first class
Pvt.	private
RAF	Royal Air Force
S-1	adjutant or personnel officer
S-2	intelligence officer
S-3	operations officer
S-4	logistics officer
SHAEF	Supreme Headquarters, Allied Expeditionary Force
Sgt.	sergeant[b]
Sgt. Maj.	sergeant major[b]
S/Sgt.	staff sergeant[b]
T/Sgt.	technical sergeant[b]
T/3	technician grade 3[c]
T/4	technician grade 4[c]
T/5	technician grade 5[c]
XO	executive officer (second-in-command)
1st Lt.	first lieutenant
2nd Lt.	second lieutenant
1st Sgt.	first sergeant[b]

[a] U.S. Navy, U.S. Coast Guard, or Royal Navy rank. A navy captain was equal to an army colonel.

[b] The order of rank for World War II U.S. Army sergeants, from highest to lowest, was master sergeant, technical sergeant, staff sergeant, and sergeant (sometimes called "buck" sergeant). First sergeant and sergeant major were not ranks, but positions within a company, battalion, or regiment as its ranking NCO.

[c] Technician grades 3, 4, and 5 were equivalent in rank to staff sergeant, sergeant, and corporal, respectively, but technicians had no command authority.

CHAPTER 1

An Unsound
Operation of War

FIRST IMPRESSIONS

When Monty talked, people listened.

And now, on this first day of the year 1944, the individual listening intently to Monty was positively the most important man in the world among those millions of people dedicating themselves to the task of bringing Adolf Hitler's existence to a premature end. Senior American and British military commanders had lately been professing supreme confidence that Nazi Germany would no longer exist by the close of the new year, and now the most famous of those commanders, General Sir Bernard Law Montgomery—hero of El Alamein and conqueror of Rommel—was conferring with Prime Minister Winston Churchill to settle the issue of exactly how the hated Nazis must meet their end.

For an engagement between two of the most celebrated Englishmen of their day, the venue was decidedly un-English. Marrakech, the ancient Moroccan city of Berbers, Arabs, noisy souks, and labyrinthine casbahs, was considered by the prime minister as "the most lovely place in the world," a spot that he admitted "captivated" him. He cherished those rare opportunities when he could relax with brushes and paint to depict on his easel the nearby Atlas Mountains, topped with snow, in the glorious glow of a North African sunset, an experience that eleven months previously he had shared in hushed awe with President Franklin D. Roosevelt. In mid-

December, Churchill had come to Marrakech for a fortnight to recover from a grave case of pneumonia that had struck him down in Tunis while returning to Britain following the Tehran summit with Roosevelt and Stalin. At Tehran, the Big Three had agreed that the primary military operation of 1944 in western Europe must be the Anglo-American invasion of German-occupied France, scheduled for May—and that was precisely what the prime minister yearned to talk to Monty about.

To lead that invasion, the Allied top brass had just plucked Montgomery and the new supreme commander of the Allied Expeditionary Force, Dwight Eisenhower, out of the Mediterranean theater and ordered them to relocate to England posthaste. Invasion preparations must accelerate; the scheduled invasion date was little more than four months in the future, and countless details still had to be worked out. Monty would be Eisenhower's chief ground commander for the cross-Channel assault, and the two men had arranged a hasty get-together in Algiers on December 27 to talk over their command organization and ponder the existing invasion plan, christened Overlord, which Monty had never seen and Ike knew little about.

After a hasty return to the Italian front to say good-bye to his beloved Eighth Army, Montgomery had flown directly to Marrakech on December 31, 1943. His next stop would be London, but first he had a dinner date with the prime minister. Taking a seat at Churchill's dinner table could test the endurance of even the most robust soldiers, for the prime minister's power of eloquence and astonishing breadth of knowledge would invariably prolong a meal for hours; and the fact that this dinner would take place on New Year's Eve assured that Churchill's guests would not retire until the early hours of the next day.

Monty fully appreciated Churchill's insatiable appetite for conversation, as he had first dined with the prime minister in the summer of 1940 following the Dunkirk evacuation. At that meal, he had shocked Churchill by professing his aversion to alcohol and smoke. As a result of this abstinence, Monty declared, he was 100 percent fit—to which the prime minister swiftly retorted that he both drank and smoked and was 200 percent fit. Three and a half years later, neither's views had budged an inch on the subject of the vices of drink and smoke, but the war had changed dramatically since then, and now the two men had much weightier issues on their minds.

Situated 2,000 miles from London in a remote corner of Africa, Marrakech was hardly a suitable place to run a global war of such immense complexity, but Winston Churchill would nevertheless try. A few days before, he had wired the War Office in London to send out the very latest version of the Overlord invasion plan to Marrakech by courier, and as soon as Monty was ushered into the prime minister's presence on New Year's Eve, Churchill thrust the plan into the general's grasp and commanded him to read it. As Monty would soon be the chief executor of that plan, Churchill asserted, his observations of its merits—or lack thereof—were of the highest importance.

Monty was considered by some to be an immodest and ambitious man, but on this occasion, at least at first, he did not exhibit those traits. He confessed to the prime minister that this was hardly an appropriate time for him to air his views on so momentous a subject, for aside from conversing with Eisenhower about the invasion plan in a cursory way four days previously, he knew little about it and had not examined a copy. Furthermore, Monty had not consulted anyone who had been involved in generating the plan, nor had he discussed any of the highly complex naval and air aspects of the invasion with the chief sailor and airman who would be his equals on Ike's command team.

The prime minister, however, was a persuasive man, and in this case—Monty's supposed reluctance notwithstanding—the hero of Alamein did not need much persuasion to express his personal views directly to the world's most eminent statesman on a military operation that promised to be the most vital in the war so far. Here was an opportunity that Monty could not pass up: If Churchill wanted the general's judgment of the Overlord plan, Monty would surely give it. Besides, Monty could take this chance to excuse himself early from what promised to be a protracted Churchillian dinner. The celebrated general always liked to retire early, and with a copy of the Overlord plan under his arm, he gave his apologies to the prime minister and his wife and proceeded to his bedroom. Afterward, Churchill took a glass of punch to celebrate the new year, called in his staff and servants, and everyone joined hands in a circle to sing "Auld Lang Syne." The year 1943 was at an end.

The next morning, before New Year's Day breakfast, Churchill had a typed copy of Monty's "first impression" of Overlord.

General Sir Bernard Law Montgomery
Commander, 21st Army Group, "First Impression of Operation Overlord,"
January 1, 1944
The initial landing is on too narrow a front and is confined to too small an area. By D+12 a total of 16 divisions have been landed on the same beaches as were used for the initial landings. This would lead to the most appalling confusion on the

beaches, and the smooth development of the land battle would be made extremely difficult—if not impossible. . . . My first impression is that the present plan is impracticable. . . . The initial landings must be made on the widest possible front.

If the invasion scheme was "impracticable," Monty and Ike would have to make significant changes to the plan in a hurry. After a New Year's Day picnic with Churchill in the nearby Atlas Mountains, Montgomery boarded a plane for London, where he would immediately take charge of Overlord invasion planning.

The war was about to enter a new stage.

After Monty's departure, Churchill relaxed while listening to a gramophone recording of the Gilbert and Sullivan comic operetta *The Pirates of Penzance,* a Christmas gift from his daughter Mary. This was a good time to ponder Monty's harsh judgments of the current Overlord plan. The next day, Churchill cabled his chiefs of staff in England:

Winston Churchill
Prime Minister of Great Britain, Cable to British Chiefs of Staff,
January 2, 1944
I was encouraged to hear General Montgomery's arguments that many landing points should be chosen instead of concentration as at present proposed through one narrow funnel. . . . I hope that all expressions such as "Invasion of Europe" or "Assault upon the Fortress of Europe" may be eliminated henceforward. I shall address the President again on this subject shortly, pointing out that our object is the liberation of Europe from German tyranny, that we "enter" the oppressed countries rather than "invade" them and that the word "invasion" must be reserved for the time when we cross the German frontier.

LIKE A GOD FROM OLYMPUS

People may have listened when Monty talked, but many of them did not like what he said and most assuredly did not like how he said it. Montgomery was one of those generals whom soldiers either loved or hated; only rarely did military men hold mixed feelings about the hero of Alamein. In early 1944, however, one had to admit that many more people loved him than hated him, for his numerous military victories in the Mediterranean theater had undeniably inspired those millions who yearned for Hitler's downfall at so dark a time in the war when Nazi military power seemed irresistible. Were not a little arrogance and vanity a small price to pay for bestowing the Allies with hope?

But Monty was about to meet an audience that was distinctly less appreciative. Upon his arrival in London from Marrakech, he promptly scheduled a meeting for the morning of January 3 at St. Paul's School on the banks of the Thames in west London, where he had been educated as a boy. Here he would meet the staff that had prepared the Overlord invasion plan—and he would tell them, in a way that surely would rankle many members of that staff, exactly what he thought of it. On one point, however, all agreed: The upcoming invasion was a battle that the Allies could not afford to lose if they were to defeat Germany in 1944. And now the general who had experienced real war with phenomenal success would tell the textbook warriors who had sat behind desks for nine months precisely how the invasion should be carried out.

The Overlord planning team went by the name COSSAC, an acronym nominally applying only to the head of that team, Lt. Gen. Frederick Morgan of the British Army, whom the Anglo-Allied top brass had designated "Chief of Staff to the Supreme Allied Commander" in the spring of 1943. COSSAC's primary object was to determine for Churchill, Roosevelt, and the Anglo-American military chiefs whether an amphibious assault of German-occupied western Europe would be feasible in 1944; and if so, where that assault should be unleashed. Morgan's combined British-American team concluded in July 1943 that such an invasion was indeed feasible and recommended that it be launched against the region of northwestern France known as Normandy.

General Montgomery was in agreement—so far. But at the January 3 St. Paul's meeting, Monty promptly pounced on the method by which Morgan had suggested Overlord should be carried out. COSSAC's invasion outline had called for a simultaneous assault by one American and two British infantry divisions, plus two-thirds of a British airborne division. On that stretch of the Normandy coast known as Calvados, the infantry divisions would land on three separate beaches, which would later be known by their celebrated code names of Juno, Gold, and Omaha.

"The more I examined it, the more it became clear that the original plan was thoroughly bad," Monty noted somewhat caustically on January 3. He had seen enough of German military prowess in North Africa, Sicily, and Italy to know that the enemy would certainly react vigorously to the invasion, and if that vigor was not promptly suppressed, the invasion could fail and the war effort be set back by months, if not a year or more.

The obvious solution, as Monty asserted to the assembled officers at St. Paul's, was to intensify the violence and scope of the opening D-Day

The Strategic Situation, June 1944

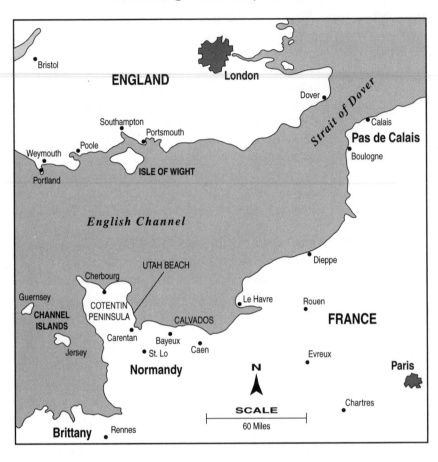

Bristol

ENGLAND

London

Dover

Strait of Dover

Calais

Pas de Calais

Boulogne

Southampton

Portsmouth

Poole

Weymouth

Portland

ISLE OF WIGHT

English Channel

UTAH BEACH

Dieppe

Cherbourg

Guernsey

Le Havre

Rouen

CHANNEL
ISLANDS

COTENTIN
PENINSULA

CALVADOS

FRANCE

Carentan

Bayeux

Caen

Jersey

St. Lo

Evreux

Paris

Normandy

N

Chartres

SCALE

60 Miles

Brittany

Rennes

*"Like a god from Olympus." General Sir Bernard Law Montgomery inspects
U.S. Army troops from the 8th Infantry, 4th Infantry Division, on April 21, 1944.*
COURTESY 8TH INFANTRY REGIMENT.

assault. The initial seaborne assault force for the July 1943 invasion of
Sicily, which had in large measure been planned by Montgomery, had been
roughly twice the size of the proposed Overlord force, and no one needed
to be reminded that the opening stages of the Sicilian campaign had been
remarkably arduous and costly. Given the fact that the legions of Germans
the Allies would face in Normandy would be far more robust than the
enemy garrison that had defended Sicily, Monty declared that under its current configuration, Overlord would have only a slender probability of success unless major revisions were made to the plan.

Furthermore, as Eisenhower's chief ground commander for the invasion, General Montgomery specified in a manner that no one could possibly misinterpret that he would be the person who would make those
revisions. Maj. Gen. Ray Barker, Morgan's chief American deputy at COS-
SAC, witnessed Monty's St. Paul's performance and later noted: "Monty
took the floor. In grandiose style, he said the plan was too restricted. . . . He
spoke as a god from Olympus. . . . It was quite clear that Montgomery was
the ground commander, [and he] was entirely within his rights."

Within the next several days, Monty spelled out precisely what Overlord would need to guarantee success. But he also understood that what he

needed would not be easy to obtain. The Allies were fighting over a vast expanse of the globe in 1944, and unlike World War I, which for the most part had been waged on the continent of Europe, this time amphibious operations constituted the essential means by which Anglo-American military forces must challenge and defeat their formidable German and Japanese opponents. If there were two hard lessons that American and British generals had learned so far in World War II, it was that amphibious warfare was extraordinarily risky and the resources to carry it out were in short supply. Monty had therefore to take his case directly to his boss, Eisenhower, who had returned to the United States for a two-week rest.

General Sir Bernard Law Montgomery
Commander, 21st Army Group, Cable to Gen. Dwight Eisenhower,
January 10, 1944
Urgent—Eyes only for Eisenhower: In consultation with [Admiral Bertram] Ramsay and [Air Chief Marshal Trafford] Leigh-Mallory [Eisenhower's chief naval and air commanders], I have made a close examination of the whole Overlord problem. In my opinion it is highly desirable that the extent of the initial assault area should be widened and that five divisions should be put on shore on the first tide, and a good build-up be possible. . . . Provided we can get what I recommend, then I consider Overlord has every chance of being a quick success so far as can be seen at present. . . . I suggest it is essential to make a really good lodgment in Northern France and that this must be given the necessary resources to ensure success. Time is very short. Will you hurl yourself into the contest and what we want, get for us?

Despite Monty's insufferable attitude, one of COSSAC's top British planners, Brig. Kenneth McLean, later remarked that "Monty's action was like a breath of fresh air."

Brig. Kenneth McLean
Assistant Chief of Plans, COSSAC, March 13, 1947
[Montgomery] said it must be a five division front or no show—give me this or get someone else. A wave of relief came over us. [Maj. Gen. Charles] West was extremely insistent on the three division assault. He and [Maj. Gen. Harold] Bull [COSSAC's chief British and American planners, respectively] made a last despairing visit to Monty at night [on January 5, 1944]. He chased them away. . . . We were now on our feet.

Among those members of COSSAC, however, McLean's favorable view of Monty was an exception. Morgan's planners had wrestled with the Overlord scheme for more than nine months, and throughout that period, their plans had been constrained by hazy information provided by their superiors concerning the number of landing craft and transport aircraft that would be available in Britain on D-Day to carry out the invasion. Consequently, Morgan's Overlord plan by necessity restricted the initial assault to only three infantry divisions and a fraction of an airborne division because those were the maximum number of units COSSAC presumed could be conveyed to Normandy by available landing craft and transport planes in the spring of 1944.

Furthermore, although Morgan may have been in charge of the COSSAC staff, he was not, strictly speaking, a military commander, for he controlled no combat troops. Rather, his role was limited to that of chief of staff to a supreme commander, but throughout most of COSSAC's existence that commander had not been named—and no one could inform Morgan when that person would indeed be identified and who he would be. Accordingly, in 1943, COSSAC had little clout in the highest Anglo-American political and military circles, and for Morgan to request additional resources for Overlord, which at that time was still an indistinct and controversial scheme, would have been in large measure fruitless. However, when Monty arrived on the scene in January 1944 and within a few days of his appearance imperiously demanded greater resources to bolster the cross-Channel invasion, COSSAC planners must have wondered how different their Overlord scheme would have been had they known with certainty that they would have enough shipping and transport aircraft to convey five infantry and three airborne divisions to Normandy on D-Day rather than the much smaller force that had constrained COSSAC's plans since its inception.

But in this crucial stage in the history of Operation Overlord, Monty repeatedly stressed, perhaps somewhat pompously, that his experience of war was thoroughly real, not theoretical, and his dissatisfaction with the COSSAC plan had just as much to do with the forthcoming postinvasion battle as it did with the supposedly feeble initial seaborne and airborne assault. According to Montgomery's 1958 *Memoirs,* he told Prime Minister Churchill at the Marrakech meeting on New Year's Day, "One of the lessons I had learnt in the war was the need to get experienced fighting commanders in on future operational plans early; if left too late it might be impossible to change the layout of the operation." Montgomery had planned, fought, and won more key battles against the German Army in the current war than any other British or American general. No one could deny the practical value of that experience; so when Monty declared, as he did to Eisenhower at a high-level staff conference on Friday, January 21, 1944, that "he did not consider that Overlord was a sound operation of war," people took notice.

If the operation was unsound, what would Monty do, beyond the straightforward expedient of throwing more men into the initial assault, to fix it? Montgomery's answer was prompt and unambiguous: He would double the length of Normandy shoreline upon which the Allies would storm ashore on D-Day—from COSSAC's twenty-five miles to about fifty miles. To achieve this extension of the front, two new invasion beaches would be added to COSSAC's original three: one at the eastern base of the Cotentin Peninsula, the other north of Caen, near the mouth of the Orne River. A more expansive invasion frontage, according to Montgomery, would achieve two objects essential to the success of any amphibious operation: First, the substantial size of the initial Anglo-American beachhead in Normandy would provide ample defensive security as the Allies poured troops and supplies ashore; second, no later than a few weeks after D-Day, the Allies should be able to seize a major Norman port—Cherbourg— which, when opened to Allied shipping, would substantially boost the flow of matériel into the battle zone.

Any Allied general who understood how the Germans practiced warfare expected that the enemy would react to the Normandy invasion with a swift and violent counterattack. They had done so at Sicily, Salerno, and Anzio, and the Allies anticipated that they would do so again. In those invasions, prompt German counterattacks had on occasion threatened to crush the Allied beachheads, and it was clear to the Allied top brass that if the Normandy enclave was to endure in the invasion's critical first few days, when it would be most vulnerable, the Allies must prepare for this kind of violent enemy reaction and do everything they could to repel it. If the Germans wished to throw the Allies back into the sea, Monty's broad invasion front would greatly complicate their task. Five distinct points of attack, plus several airborne drop zones, promised to diffuse whatever counterattacks the enemy could manage to launch after D-Day.

Furthermore, by extending the COSSAC assault front about six miles to the east—to a new invasion beach, which would soon be known as Sword—Monty's plan took advantage of the natural defensive barrier of the Orne River, which flowed roughly on a north-south axis from Caen to the sea. A successful assault against Sword Beach would enable the Allies

SHAEF vs. COSSAC Overlord Plan

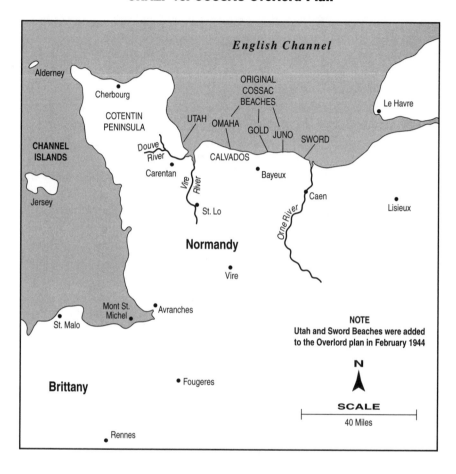

English Channel

Alderney

Cherbourg

COTENTIN
PENINSULA

CHANNEL
ISLANDS

Jersey

ORIGINAL
COSSAC
BEACHES

UTAH   OMAHA
GOLD   JUNO   SWORD

Le Havre

Douve
River

Carentan

CALVADOS

Bayeux

Vire River

St. Lo

Caen

Orne River

Lisieux

Normandy

Vire

Mont St.
Michel

Avranches

St. Malo

NOTE
Utah and Sword Beaches were added
to the Overlord plan in February 1944

N

Brittany

Fougeres

SCALE
40 Miles

Rennes

to secure the line of the Orne—and, with some luck, the key road junction at Caen. In this event, the left flank of the Allied invasion front would be nearly unassailable, since any German mobile reserve divisions deployed in central France would have to cross the Orne or pass through Caen to initiate a counterattack.

If, as the Allies contended, Anglo-Allied industrial production was so prodigious that Nazi Germany would sooner or later be overwhelmed by a deluge of bullets, shells, and bombs, Normandy would be the place to prove it. All Allied generals agreed that so much war paraphernalia must flow into Normandy in the wake of the invasion that the bewildered Germans would ultimately conclude it was only a matter of time. But under the COSSAC plan, according to Monty, a logistical buildup of this magnitude would be difficult to achieve. He pointed out that Morgan's three invasion beaches were distant from any sizable French port, and the Allies would certainly have to fight long and hard to seize one. By the time one of those ports was in Allied hands and functioning up to full capacity, the Germans in all likelihood would have piled so many troops into Normandy that it could take the Allies months to break out of their slender beachhead.

The original Overlord plan drawn up by COSSAC depended primarily on a manpower and supply buildup directly over the landing sites. To protect those invasion beaches from Normandy's capricious weather, two of them would be converted into artificial harbors by means of the ingenious but completely untested Mulberry design, which would use huge prefabricated concrete blocks and scuttled ships to form lengthy breakwaters enclosing two square miles of sheltered water. Monty did not have as much faith in the Mulberries as did the seamen who had dreamed them up, and at the January 21 staff conference, he bluntly summed up his feelings to Eisenhower: "The early capture of a port [is] important, in order that we should not remain totally dependent on 'Mulberry.'"

If the Allies must seize a port, there were only two logical choices: Le Havre or Cherbourg. As many formidable German units were deployed near Le Havre, including several mobile panzer divisions, Monty determined that it would have to be Cherbourg. Located at the northern tip of the Cotentin Peninsula, Cherbourg was a good choice. If the Allies could manage to cut the base of the peninsula, Cherbourg would be isolated and could be attacked without any fear of enemy reinforcement. To accomplish the quick capture of Cherbourg, Montgomery concluded to his boss Eisenhower, "It [is] desirable to extend the proposed area of assault so as to include an additional area on the eastern side of the Cotentin Peninsula."

A new landing site was therefore added to the burgeoning Overlord invasion plan. It would soon be known as Utah Beach.

NOT ENOUGH WALLOP

General Montgomery's position on Operation Overlord would be meaningless if his immediate superior, Eisenhower, did not endorse it. Had Ike said no, the name of Gen. Frederick Morgan probably would be much more prominent today than it is. But even someone with Eisenhower's clout could not simply say yes and hand over the invasion reins to Montgomery, for Monty's revisions could not be applied to Overlord without the addition to the operation of vast amounts of manpower and resources. Where they would come from, even Eisenhower did not know. Furthermore, obtaining those resources would most likely delay D-Day by up to one month, and that was something that only Churchill and Roosevelt could agree to. That Ike promptly approved of Montgomery's perception of the invasion undoubtedly bolstered Monty's standing among the Allied military chiefs, but from that moment forward, planning the military aspects of the invasion would be the easy part. The far more difficult piece of the Overlord puzzle would be to obtain the necessary sea and air resources that would enable the D-Day assault to be carried out as Monty had envisioned.

The hero of Alamein surprised no one by taking sole credit for the changes that gave Overlord new momentum. Such an attitude would markedly increase the already substantial number of people who despised him—but, as always, Monty simply did not care.

General Sir Bernard Law Montgomery
Commander, 21st Army Group, Letter to Adm. Lord Louis Mountbatten, February 24, 1944

Here in England I found everything and everyone just drifting along. Rather pathetic really. . . . The plan for Overlord was definitely quite impractical and could never have succeeded. It all had to be changed. I myself, of course, again became the bad man. . . . It is put on a sound basis now and everyone is cracking along on the revised plan.

Despite Monty's undeniably beneficial contributions to Operation Overlord, the historical evidence is overwhelming that he was not the first person to draw the conclusion that the COSSAC plan must be altered if the Normandy invasion would be, as President Roosevelt and Prime Minister Churchill had avowed, the primary Anglo-American military operation of

World War II. Even Monty's loyal longtime chief of staff, Maj. Gen. Francis de Guingand, admitted as much when he declared in 1947 that "any other trained soldier" would have reacted as Monty did to the initial scheme of Operation Overlord. Indeed, many trained soldiers did exactly that—and to their number could be added Winston Churchill.

Quebec (Quadrant) Conference
Conference Proceedings, the Citadel, August 19, 1943
The Prime Minister said that every effort should be made to add at least 25 percent strength to the initial [Overlord] assault. This would mean an increase in the landing craft necessary, but there are nine months available before the target date and much can be done in that time. The beaches selected are good, but it would be better if at the same time a landing were to be made on the inside beaches of the Cotentin Peninsula [the future location of Utah Beach]. The initial lodgment must be strong, as it so largely affects later operations.

General [George C.] Marshall [Chief of Staff, U.S. Army] agreed that an increase in the initial assault would greatly strengthen the Overlord operation.

General Eisenhower first examined a copy of COSSAC's Overlord plan on October 27, 1943, in the Algiers hotel from which he was then directing Allied forces in the Mediterranean theater. At that time, Ike had no idea that in a little over one month, President Roosevelt would select him as the Allied supreme commander, whose fundamental mission would be to carry out Overlord. One of Eisenhower's aides, U.S. Navy Commander Harry Butcher, noted in his diary his boss's initial reaction to the COSSAC plan: "Ike said that there's not enough wallop in the initial attack."

Two decades later, Eisenhower elaborated his views on the original Overlord scheme:

Gen. Dwight Eisenhower
Supreme Commander, Allied Expeditionary Force
I examined [the COSSAC plan] carefully. . . . The big point I made was that the plan visualized a front that was too narrow. I thought it should be expanded above the planned three-division assault to five or six. Later I was informed of my appointment to Overlord and soon thereafter Montgomery left for England as my Deputy. I told him of my doubts of the plan as drawn up and told him to represent me to this effect in all planning prior to my arrival in London.

The point of view of the man who would directly command all the American ground forces committed to the invasion, Lt. Gen. Omar Bradley,

"We wanted a broader landing." Lt. Gen. Omar Bradley, commander of First U.S. Army, and Maj. Gen. Joseph Lawton Collins, commander of VII Corps.
U.S. ARMY SIGNAL CORPS, NATIONAL ARCHIVES.

coincided with Eisenhower's. Bradley had come to England from the Mediterranean theater in October 1943 to organize and train the U.S. First Army for the D-Day invasion, and as his troops would carry the essential responsibility of seizing the port of Cherbourg, he had a profound interest in where those forces would be put ashore in Normandy and how they would be expected to accomplish their mission.

Lt. Gen. Omar Bradley
Commander, First U.S. Army, Interview with U.S. Army Historian, October 14, 1946
When [Bradley] arrived [in England] he was given the original COSSAC plan, which involved a landing with three divisions, then a shift to the [right, or west],

cutting the [Cotentin] Peninsula near Coutances and turning northward to take Cherbourg. Bradley never liked this plan. It gave the Germans time to build up opposition. He wanted an attack on [what would later be known as] Utah Beach. He was told there were not enough landing craft. [Bradley said] numerous people had wanted a broader landing . . . Monty had been told of the Overlord plan in December, and that Monty had been given instructions. Much of what [Montgomery] said upon reaching London he had been told to say. He was carrying out Eisenhower's orders.

After the war, Monty ungraciously referred to the COSSAC staff as the "displaced strategists" and emphasized that he had "discarded" their plans. Predictably, several former COSSAC planners reacted harshly to such disparaging remarks. The distinguished Royal Navy Captain John Hughes-Hallett, an iron-willed commander whose nickname among his sailors was "Hughes-Hitler," was Monty's most vociferous critic. Hughes-Hallett spoke with authority, for he was a veteran combat leader who had commanded Allied naval forces in the August 1942 Dieppe raid, played a major role in the destruction of the German battlecruiser *Scharnhorst* in December 1943, and contributed heavily to the Mulberry artificial harbor concept, which was such a prominent feature of Overlord plans.

Capt. John Hughes-Hallett
Naval Chief of Staff, COSSAC, February 12, 1947
Monty gives the impression that the [Overlord] plan was very much changed. He had the nerve to send me a copy of his book [*Normandy to the Baltic*] in which he virtually says we didn't do anything he could keep. Actually [the two plans] were very much alike. . . . In my letter to the Admiralty in May 1943, I had allowed for the Cotentin landing, which was not a new idea at all despite Monty. However, [the Cotentin landing] had great disadvantages. Not only did it involve getting extra landing craft, but also [necessitated] training an extra U.S. division in an assault role. It also meant that we had to postpone the invasion [from May 1] to June 1.

Within senior Allied command circles in England in early 1944, whispers began to circulate that General Montgomery was unworthy of the lofty reputation he had gained in the Mediterranean over the past fifteen months. These whispers swelled steadily; until after the war, Monty was openly defined by his critics as a general with an absolute aversion for risk. One senior RAF airman, Sir Arthur Coningham, said of Monty, "He wouldn't fight until he had everything." General Bradley agreed with this sentiment.

Eisenhower's chief of staff, Lt. Gen. Walter Bedell Smith, remarked after the end of the European war, "Bradley last night said that Monty never won a battle anyone else couldn't have won."

But if Monty's direction of the Overlord planning process in 1944 was typical of his generalship, these criticisms were overly harsh. Even if Montgomery was not the first general to conclude that the COSSAC invasion scheme must be modified, his self-styled role as the chief proponent of a revamped Overlord—viewed by many witnesses as arrogant—put his reputation as a great military leader on the line. With arrogance comes risk: Had only a single one of his changes to the invasion plan failed to work in actuality, Monty would have had to shoulder most of the blame.

Furthermore, many of Monty's revisions to the COSSAC plan were certainly risky, and in displaying a determination to take these risks, he exhibited at least one of the qualities of great generalship. Of all the changes to Overlord instigated by Montgomery, the most perilous by far was his resolve to add an invasion beach to the plan at the eastern base of the Cotentin Peninsula—the beach that has since been known as Utah. The fact that in reality the Utah assault was carried out successfully, with comparatively light casualties, has obscured the vital point that many Overlord planners in the spring of 1944 considered the Utah Beach invasion an extremely chancy and uncertain operation of war. Some, in fact, thought it would fail. The original COSSAC plan declared: "An attack with part of our forces in the Cotentin and part on the Caen beaches is . . . considered unsound. It would entail dividing our limited forces by the low-lying marshy ground and intricate river system at the neck of the Cotentin Peninsula; thus exposing them to defeat in detail."

True, Monty's insistence that COSSAC's "limited forces" must be augmented would help—but would a heftier assault force be sufficient to overcome the obvious isolation of Utah Beach that COSSAC had defined as its greatest risk? No one, including Monty, knew; but everyone realized that the geography of that sector of Normandy would be the crucial factor.

For the troops who would assault Utah, the principal predicament would be not getting on the beach, but getting off it. The terrain beyond Utah for more than a mile is very flat and low, little more than five or six feet above sea level at its highest; and by astute manipulation of the locks along the rivers and streams of the lower Cotentin watershed, the Germans had managed to flood the pasturelands behind Utah to a depth of a few feet. The U.S. Army's terrain study of this locale warned that the flooding "is especially obstructive to movement . . . and travel is restricted to established routes (causeways), which can easily be obstructed by blocks or demolitions."

At the site the Allies planned to invade, only a few such causeways existed, none of which could be classified as anything more than a narrow country road. If the Germans could seal those causeways and on D-Day bottle up the Utah Beach assault force in a slender enclave no more than several hundred yards deep, the Allies would be in trouble. With nowhere to go, troops and vehicles could pile up on the beach in such density that it would be a German artillerist's dream.

In that event, the nearest invasion beach that could provide help to Utah was Omaha, which was so distant—twenty-seven miles by road— that it could take days or even weeks for a rescue force to traverse that interval against appreciable enemy opposition. Even worse, much of the ground between Utah and Omaha was boggy and wholly unsuited to the movement of a mechanized army. The Germans would certainly exploit the many river-crossing sites and narrow causeways running only a few feet over the surrounding meadowlands along the Allies' route of advance. Unless someone came up with something new, the troops assaulting Utah Beach would definitely be on their own for a few days.

Monty came up with something thoroughly new. Instead of employing a small airborne force in the Caen area, as the COSSAC scheme had intended, Montgomery resolved to drop at least two airborne divisions along the base of the Cotentin and in the area directly behind Utah Beach. An airborne operation of this kind, if executed flawlessly, could unlock the dreaded causeways leading off Utah; help open up the coveted link to Omaha Beach; cut off the Cotentin from enemy reinforcement; and help ensure that Cherbourg could be captured quickly.

But the skills of Anglo-American invasion planners would be severely tested if they added such an airborne maneuver to the Overlord repertoire. The Allies had been thrashing out the revolutionary tactic of "vertical envelopment" for years, but they had not attempted an airborne operation before on the scale envisioned by Monty, and those smaller airdrops that had already been tried had hardly been flawless. In truth, given the disposition of enemy forces in the Cotentin and the harsh Norman terrain, several senior Allied officers were convinced that an airborne venture in support of the Utah landing would fail and cost an alarming number of casualties.

Montgomery and Bradley nevertheless firmly contended that Utah's isolation from the rest of the Overlord invasion beaches justified the acknowledged risk of the airborne operation. Vertical envelopment had been debated long enough. Could there ever be a better time to put it into practice than this, perhaps the most crucial moment of World War II, even if air crews, paratroopers, and gliderists were still working zealously to learn the right way to do it? Thus to lessen the risk of one key Overlord operation, Monty would initiate another that in all probability would be even riskier.

Perhaps Monty was not so cautious after all.

STAKES INCALCULABLE

No one, not even his harshest critics, doubted General Montgomery's self-confidence. On matters over which he had control, all agreed that Monty would strive passionately to make his new Overlord plan work. But his revisions to the COSSAC plan would oblige the Allies to add large numbers of new troops, ships, and aircraft to the Overlord equation—and even a military man in a position as lofty as Monty's would have no control over that.

Finding assault troops for Monty's new invasion sites at Utah and Sword was not the problem. The Allies, particularly the Americans, had a profusion of fresh outfits primed and ready for combat, and plenty of time remained before the May 1944 invasion target date to enhance their amphibious warfare skills. Unhappily for Monty, however, hasty calculations by Overlord planners concerning precisely how many additional ships and aircraft would be required by the new and enlarged invasion design revealed beyond any doubt that there would not be sufficient numbers of those items in Great Britain by May to carry out Montgomery's revised plan.

The principal items in short supply in the Allied camp were landing craft and troop carrier aircraft, including gliders. Anglo-American planners had been plagued by these deficiencies for years, and by this point in the war, they possessed a solid grasp of exactly what it would take to convey to Normandy the extra assault infantry and airborne troops demanded by Monty. The planners' numbers pointed to the inevitable conclusion that if the inflated Overlord invasion was to be carried out, it would have to be delayed from early May until early June, and even with that one-month delay, time would be tight for the Allied military chiefs to find the additional ships and planes Monty demanded and deploy them to Britain in time for D-Day.

A postponement of only a single month would also raise potentially momentous issues that would reach the highest levels of the Anglo-American chain of command. At the Tehran summit in November 1943, President Roosevelt and Prime Minister Churchill had promised Stalin that the Western Allies would launch Overlord in May, and a pleased Stalin had replied that the Soviet Army would launch a simultaneous offensive on the Eastern Front, a double blow that Allied leaders hoped would trigger Nazi Germany's collapse within a few months. To postpone Overlord until June, however, might cause "Uncle Joe," as Roosevelt and Churchill privately referred to Stalin, to lose faith in the Western leaders' word.

After hearing Monty's critical view of the COSSAC invasion plan in Marrakech on New Year's Day 1944, Churchill believed that the invasion's deferment until June was inevitable. Such a delay, Churchill maintained, would be insignificant politically and could even offer some military advantages.

Winston Churchill
Prime Minister of Great Britain, Cable to President Roosevelt,
January 7, 1944
In conversation with U.J. [Uncle Joe] we never mentioned such a date [for the invasion] as May 5 or May 8, but we always spoke to him around [May] 20. Neither did we at any time dwell upon the exact phase of the operation which should fall on any particular day. If now the Y date [early June] is accepted as final, I do not feel that we shall in any way have broken faith with him. . . . [Also] the ground will be drier for U.J.'s great operations by Y. We shall make a much heavier attack and with much better chances of success.

Roosevelt at first disagreed.

Franklin D. Roosevelt
President of the United States, Cable to Prime Minister Churchill,
January 14, 1944
It is my understanding that in Tehran, U.J. was given a promise that Overlord be launched in May. . . . I think the psychology of bringing this up at this time would be very bad in view of the fact that it is only a little over a month since the three of us agreed on the statement in Tehran.

Unlike Churchill, however, FDR typically deferred to the views of his military commanders. Indeed, that FDR soon accepted a short delay for Overlord was due to the influence of those men, primarily Eisenhower and Marshall.

Gen. Dwight Eisenhower
Supreme Commander, Allied Expeditionary Force, Cable to General
Marshall, January 22, 1944

There is a very deep conviction here, in all circles, that we are approaching a tremendous crisis with stakes incalculable. Every man with whom I have so far dealt is definitely sober and serious but confident of the outcome if all of us do our very best. . . . Altogether we need five divisions assault loaded. This means additional assets in several lines but chiefly naval, with special emphasis on landing craft. . . . I fervently hope that we can . . . still get here the minimum strength necessary to reasonable prospects of success even if we have to wait until the end of May [or early June], although this will cost a month of good campaigning weather.

And so all ultimately agreed: D-Day would be in June, on a date set by Eisenhower as early as possible in the month with suitable lunar and tidal conditions.

Monty had talked—and people had listened. True, his ideas for enlarging and broadening the Normandy invasion were little different from what many generals, including some from COSSAC, had been saying for months. The crucial difference was that Monty's celebrated reputation as a military champion enabled him to successfully influence those who held the reins of power in the Anglo-American command hierarchy, whereas others in the past had failed. As his chief of staff, Francis de Guingand, later noted, Montgomery was "a commander who could bang the table and say what he wanted"—and, even more important, get it. If Utah and Sword Beaches were to be added to Overlord's list of invasion sites, Monty's principal requirement would be more landing craft, and when he banged his fist on the table, those additional craft would eventually appear.

To sailors, landing craft were hardly as glamorous as battleships and aircraft carriers. At one point in 1942, in fact, landing craft production had dropped to twelfth place in construction precedence in American naval shipyards. But those men responsible for administering American and British naval construction had foreseen that Allied global strategy would sooner or later depend on the manufacture of vast quantities of landing craft and had worked tirelessly to fulfill what amounted to highly ambitious production goals. "Landing craft [are] the most important single implement of war from the point of view of the European theater," declared the chairman of the U.S. War Production Board, Donald Nelson, in September 1943. Nelson added that "25,000 or more lives" would depend on having adequate numbers of landing craft when the decisive moment of the European war arrived.

By May 1944, that moment had unquestionably arrived. And without the surge in American and British landing craft production that had taken place in late 1943 and early 1944, Monty's vision of the Normandy invasion would have been just a dream. So when the Allies went searching for the additional landing craft they needed for the new Overlord, to their satisfaction they discovered more than adequate numbers. The major obstacle was that those landing craft were spread all over the world, and the obvious problem was how to redeploy them somehow to Britain in time for D-Day without totally paralyzing future amphibious operations in other theaters.

A redistribution of this kind was a complex and delicate balancing act that at times severely strained relations between the American and British military chiefs, and even Roosevelt and Churchill, who habitually bickered over how and where the limited amphibious assets should be used. But in the end, Monty's bang on the table had resounded piercingly in the conference halls of the Anglo-American top brass. Presently, naval officers received their sailing orders, made their diverse assortment of landing craft ready for a long journey at sea, and like children being summoned home to dinner by their mother's call, headed with all possible speed for England. There was an important job to do there, and from everything the sailors had heard, it would be a job that they would tell their grandchildren about.

If the congregation of such a large number of Allied landing craft in Britain for the Normandy invasion was such an impressive achievement, the assembly of American troop carrier aircraft for D-Day must be considered phenomenal. Because of the limited number of transport aircraft available in England for the foreseeable future, the original COSSAC invasion plan drawn up in the summer of 1943 had restricted the involvement of airborne troops to just two-thirds of an airborne division, or little more than 6,000 men. Presumably these troops would be British, as there were then only meager numbers of American transport aircraft in Britain.

When Montgomery arrived in England in January 1944, the estimated level of airborne involvement on D-Day was hardly any better. According to Eisenhower's senior airman, Sir Trafford Leigh-Mallory of the RAF, there would be only enough air transport on D-Day to drop one Allied airborne division behind German lines. Monty resolved to drop this division behind Utah Beach, not near Caen, as the COSSAC plan had specified. But he insisted upon much more airborne punch in the invasion than that.

SHAEF Conference
Minutes, Room 105, Norfolk House, St. James's Square, London, 1000 Hours, January 24, 1944
General Montgomery discussed the desirability of having two airborne divisions land or be dropped simultaneously in two different places. Air Chief Marshal Leigh-Mallory stated that this was impossible with the aircraft at present allotted for the operation, but that the second airborne division would be delivered within twenty-four hours after the first.

For the Utah Beach invasion to succeed, that was not good enough, and General Bradley, the man responsible for ensuring that the Utah invasion would work, told Montgomery so at a January 1944 commanders' conference. An attendee noted in his diary: "During a discussion of the airborne plans, General Bradley stated emphatically that the employment of the two U.S. airborne divisions [82nd and 101st] was absolutely essential to the success of the invasion."

In early 1944, IX Troop Carrier Command of the U.S. Ninth Air Force, the organization responsible for conveying American airborne troops into combat in Normandy, operated only about 100 C-47 transport aircraft in England. As a C-47 typically carried only seventeen paratroopers at a time, that number of C-47s could not carry even a single American parachute infantry regiment of approximately 2,000 men. For Bradley to find sufficient C-47s to convey two entire airborne divisions to Normandy, he would have to increase the current number of C-47s in England by a factor of ten in the next few months—seemingly an impossible task, given that Troop Carrier air and ground crews would need considerable time before the invasion to make the lengthy journey to England, settle into their new airfields, absorb their vital D-Day mission, and train with the paratroopers and gliderists they must convey to Normandy.

Air Chief Marshal Sir Charles Portal
Chief of Air Staff, British Chiefs of Staff, Memorandum, February 6, 1944
The very highly organized system of assembly, take-off, maneuver, and approach has to be learned and practiced. . . . All this training at present takes two months and is then dependent on weather. No cut [in training] is possible without risking failure.

If, as the American military chiefs had long insisted, the invasion of Europe would be the decisive operation of World War II from the Western

Allies' standpoint, they must now demonstrate their resolve by providing Eisenhower and Montgomery with the air assets they needed to make D-Day work. Dozens of Troop Carrier squadrons in the United States had been waiting for this moment for months, and when orders arrived from Gen. Henry "Hap" Arnold, chief of the U.S. Army Air Force, to deploy to England, the air and ground crews knew with certainty that all the rigorous training they had just endured would soon be put into practice against a live and very dangerous enemy. A remarkable migration of aircraft was about to take place: In the first three months of 1944, more than 600 C-47s, the legendary transport aircraft known as the "Gooney Bird" by its devoted crews, would be flown in a steady stream to Baer Field, just outside Fort Wayne, Indiana, where the airmen would receive detailed instructions for their journey, a lengthy transoceanic passage that promised to be the most challenging mission the crews had flown in their short army air force careers. Meanwhile, ground crews and headquarters personnel prepared to embark for England by sea with all the military paraphernalia a Troop Carrier squadron would need to function in a war zone.

Flying orders dictated that each Troop Carrier squadron proceed south to Florida to begin a circuitous voyage of more than 10,000 miles to Puerto Rico, Brazil, Ascension (a speck of an island in the South Atlantic), West Africa, Morocco, and finally England. Some of these Troop Carrier units had been in existence only five months, and none of their crews had seen any combat, but they did not need to be reminded that the last leg of this journey to England would be in a combat zone. The C-47 airmen knew that they would soon have a chance to put their thorough flight training into practice. What the Allied commanders had in mind for them was anybody's guess, but whatever it was, it would in all likelihood make history.

Meanwhile, the army air force initiated a corresponding redeployment of its Troop Carrier units that currently were operating in the Mediterranean theater. Unlike their comrades who were crossing the Atlantic to England for the first time, the veteran Troop Carrier airmen in the Mediterranean had seen combat in the skies over Sicily and Italy, and they knew from their harsh experiences in that theater that many aspects of airborne operations must be refined and practiced if paratroopers and glider infantry were to contribute appreciably to the upcoming invasion of western Europe. But, as the crews reasoned on their long flights to England via Gibraltar, that was what training was for—and for the next several months, there would be plenty of time for that.

The influx of the Americans suddenly transformed fifteen quiet English airfields, with names like Upottery, Cottesmore, and Spanhoe, into bustling centers of Troop Carrier activity. So many C-47s had suddenly appeared in the sky, roaring over the verdant fields of Lincolnshire, Devon, and Berkshire, that the astonished English locals marveled at the Americans' seemingly limitless supply of aircraft: If all these Yanks will help us finish off Hitler more quickly, they declared, bring us more of them.

By April 1944, when the Ninth Air Force tallied up its order of battle in England, it revealed the astonishing sum of more than 1,000 Troop Carrier C-47s and about 1,100 air crews to fly them. True, some crews were much more experienced than others, and it would not be easy for IX Troop Carrier Command to prepare them all, for the difficult nighttime parachute and glider operation Bradley envisioned for D-Day. Nevertheless, Bradley would have his two airborne divisions for the invasion after all, and suddenly the Utah Beach assault did not seem as hazardous as the Allied military chiefs had once thought. But for Troop Carrier airmen, much work remained if they were to contribute substantially to the success of that invasion.

In the end, Monty and Ike had in large measure managed to acquire the additional troops, ships, and airplanes they had sought to improve the chances that the Overlord invasion would succeed. Furthermore, with the assault delayed until early June, they would have one extra month to brace the troops for an operation that promised to be grueling. No one imagined that additional troops, equipment, and time alone would guarantee victory. Rather, the foundation of success for the assault troops would be superlative training and unshakable confidence. But as the bleak English weather of January and February 1944 faded into spring, the troops had much more work to do before they could consider themselves ready for the momentous task they would face on D-Day. There was not much time left.

CHAPTER 2

Steadfast and Loyal

LIGHTNING JOE

Ike had many crucial issues on his mind in his first month as supreme commander, and one of them was obtaining generals of the highest caliber to lead the D-Day invasion. But what Eisenhower wanted would not be easy to obtain, and on February 9, 1944, he noted to his boss, General Marshall, "I am just a bit uneasy about our failure to get a greater leaven of combat experience among our formations."

The decision had been made and approved to widen the Normandy invasion to include a combined seaborne and airborne assault on the southeastern base of the Cotentin Peninsula against that stretch of coast soon to be known as Utah Beach. That operation would be conducted almost entirely by American forces, and Ike's immediate challenge would be to locate an American general with the essential combat experience, preferably of the amphibious kind, and to put him in charge of the U.S. Army corps that would be designated to execute that assault.

According to Ike and Bradley, the VII Corps would do nicely for the Utah operation. Its staff had been functioning continuously since before Pearl Harbor and had made the trans-Atlantic journey to Great Britain in October 1943. In early February 1944, Bradley assigned to the VII two superb infantry divisions, the 4th and 9th, both of which were thoroughly primed to enter combat in Normandy. Ike could find no better outfits in the

U.S. Army to carry out the Utah invasion, but did the VII Corps's current commander, Maj. Gen. Roscoe Woodruff, inspire in the supreme commander that same kind of confidence?

Apparently he did not. The fifty-three-year-old Woodruff had been one of the most esteemed cadets in the West Point class of 1915, the same class that had brought his friends Eisenhower and Bradley into the U.S. Army as fresh second lieutenants. After America's entry into World War II, West Pointers would hail the 1915 graduates as the "class the stars fell on," and indeed, those stars speedily fell upon Woodruff's shoulders. He possessed a firm leadership style and was apparently well suited for high command. After raising and training the 77th Infantry Division in the States, the army had shoved Woodruff upward by one command step and designated him the commander of VII Corps in 1943. In the fall of that year, Woodruff and his staff waited patiently in Britain for the profound challenge, and perchance everlasting fame, that the upcoming cross-Channel invasion would soon bring him and his outfit.

Woodruff so far had not led men in an active combat theater, and if there was one lesson Ike had learned in the Mediterranean, it was that actual battle promptly brought out facets of generals' personalities that training never had. The fact that those facets were on occasion unquestionably negative confirmed for Eisenhower that for Operation Overlord—potentially the U.S. Army's most critical moment of World War II—he could not entrust the Utah landing to a commander who had not yet proved that he could function effectively under the strain of combat.

That there were in early 1944 hardly any major generals in the U.S. Army who had demonstrated exceptional combat leadership discouraged neither Ike nor Bradley. There were at least a precious few, and to lead the Utah invasion, Eisenhower yearned for one in particular: Maj. Gen. Lucian Truscott. He had already participated in four amphibious operations in World War II, and his outstanding leadership of the 3rd Infantry Division in the Mediterranean theater had impressed even Chief of Staff Marshall. Ike's predicament was to snatch Truscott from Italy, where he had just assumed command of the VI Corps in the Anzio beachhead to salvage what had so far been a dreadfully fruitless and costly campaign. From the highest reaches of the Allied high command, however, came the message that Truscott would not be available. Ike would have to find someone else in a hurry.

Eisenhower settled on forty-seven-year-old Maj. Gen. Joseph Lawton Collins, a 1917 graduate of the U.S. Military Academy. Collins's classmates included many notable soldiers, among them Mark Clark, Matthew

Ridgway, Ernest Harmon, Norman Cota, and Charles Gerhardt. Collins and Clark, both of whom would rise to the rank of four-star general, shared the same birthday of May 1, 1896, and were the class of 1917's youngest members.

Joe Collins was an affable if somewhat immodest man who had adroitly led the 25th Infantry Division in the 1943 battles on Guadalcanal and New Georgia in the south Pacific. He carried with him to England the nickname "Lightning Joe," derived from the 25th's "Tropic Lightning" shoulder patch. He also brought a nasty malaria infection he had contracted on Guadalcanal, which still troubled him occasionally in early 1944; but perhaps this was sufficient evidence for Ike that Collins was used to the rigors of active combat. Like Eisenhower and Bradley, Collins had not served overseas in World War I, and for him, this had not only been a profound disappointment, but a potentially devastating impediment to promotion in the stagnant U.S. Army of the interwar years. However, befriending Col. George C. Marshall, assistant commandant of the Infantry School at Fort Benning in the late 1920s, did not hurt. Furthermore, during prewar maneuvers under the scrutiny of Marshall and other top army leaders, Collins's customary display of superior managerial skills—ironically as chief of staff of the same VII Corps he would later command on D-Day—gave him an assured ticket to high command in World War II.

Collins's experience in the Pacific theater, where amphibious warfare was the norm, may have led Ike and Bradley to the mistaken impression that he had plenty of practice in seaborne invasions and would therefore be an obvious choice to lead the Utah Beach assault. Collins's 25th Division, however, had joined the Guadalcanal and New Georgia campaigns well after their initial assault stages, and his command skills were practiced almost entirely in the inhospitable inland jungles on both islands. No matter: During his first interview in England with the two men who would determine whether he would lead VII Corps on D-Day, Bradley turned to Ike and said, "He talks our language"; so much so, in fact, that Bradley named him VII Corps commander on February 12, 1944.

The troops who would assault Utah Beach had their leader. Later, Maj. Gen. Maxwell Taylor, the commander of the 101st Airborne Division, professed the opinion that Bradley's choice for VII Corps command had been perfect. "General Collins was a great corps commander because he did not interfere with the details of the work of a division," declared Taylor. So what if some thought Collins was a little immodest? One needed only to behold Monty to see that most great generals were hardly humble men. In his postwar memoirs, however, Collins would follow a modest road. "I was just lucky to be in the right place at the right time," he noted of his takeover of VII Corps from Woodruff.

Collins's pressing duty was to prepare for an invasion that was very much a late addition to the Overlord plan—and he would have to move fast to do it. Thanks to the COSSAC staff, Collins had plenty of information about that coastal sector of Normandy's Cotentin Peninsula that VII Corps must assault. Unhappily for Collins, as Overlord's stepchild he would have to develop a Utah invasion scheme with a substantially smaller naval component, particularly in large troopships and small assault landing craft, than Eisenhower's command team had allocated to the three original D-Day beaches, Omaha, Gold, and Juno. Collins's counterpart for the Omaha invasion, Maj. Gen. Leonard Gerow of V Corps, would be capable of opening the D-Day assault in a big way by hurling nine infantry companies, totaling more than 1,550 men and supported by 112 Sherman tanks, against Omaha Beach across a front nearly four miles in length. In contrast, Collins would be forced to initiate the Utah invasion with only four infantry companies, supported by 56 tanks, on a beach frontage of little more than one mile.

Given Utah's isolation from the other four invasion beaches and the prompt counterattacks the enemy could be expected to launch against any vulnerable Allied enclaves, some VII Corps planners surely wondered whether their more modest invasion scheme left only a slender margin for success. Good generals, however, are paid to be confident, and if Collins ever harbored any doubt about his imminent duty, he never spoke a word of it.

Bradley had promised support in the shape of a major airborne operation behind Utah Beach, but in February it was too early for anyone to say how big this operation would be and what it could be expected to accomplish. Nevertheless, it would be help that Collins desperately needed. Four years later, Collins remarked, "From the point of view of General Bradley and myself, the operation of the airborne divisions was vital to the success of the overall operation."

IVY MEN

As the primary fighting force of the world's greatest democracy, the U.S. Army in World War II prided itself on its homogeneity. As long as soldiers with dark skins were not added to the mix, the army stirred the legendary American melting pot with obvious enthusiasm: Southern boys whose grandfathers had fought under Lee were obliged to mix effortlessly with Italians from the North End who knew nothing of the Civil War; farmers' sons from Iowa were expected to share barracks with Poles from Greenpoint and Mexicans from El Paso, Texas. The blend was supposed to yield an army composed of outfits equally well trained and, even more important, interchangeable.

By and large it worked. In a homogeneous army, however, one would not have expected U.S. Army divisions of more than 14,000 men to develop highly unique characteristics and temperaments—but that is exactly what they did. A division's distinctive flavor stemmed to some extent from its commanding general, who may have been a polo-playing traditionalist from the Old Army or a former enlisted man who had joined the regulars before World War I. That flavor could also have been drawn from the region in the United States where the division drew recruits and draftees or from its training record and combat performance, if any, so far in the war. A division patch stitched onto the left shoulder of a GI's uniform indeed said a lot about that soldier's spirit, particularly in the early days, before combat turned over personnel at an alarming rate and dulled that spirit considerably.

In late February 1944, when General Collins began to solidify his Utah invasion plan, those soldiers wearing a square, olive drab shoulder patch with four green ivy leaves had so far experienced a pretty easy war. Those GIs belonged to the 4th Infantry Division, a unit that will forever be linked to the D-Day invasion of Utah Beach. The 4th had just made the trans-Atlantic journey to England after more than three years of interminable training for active operations that never seemed to materialize. For two of those years, the 4th had absorbed hundreds of trucks and trained as an experimental "motorized" division, but the army shelved that trial in 1943, much to the regret of 4th Division men, who would thereupon have to do a lot more marching.

The division trained for so long in the States that its members had almost convinced each other that the 4th would never go overseas. Things have a way of changing fast in the army, however, and by the spring of 1944, the Ivy Division—the "I-V" pronunciation a suggestion of the roman numeral for the number 4—found itself bivouacked in the verdant countryside of Devon, England, preparing energetically for the invasion the GIs hoped would mark the beginning of the end for Nazi Germany.

War is a young man's pastime, but the U.S. Army's top brass must have considered the members of the 4th Infantry Division as extraordinarily mature. On the eve of D-Day, the comparatively advanced average age of 4th Division personnel, from commanding general down to the most humble privates, yielded the impression that the 4th must have contained the U.S. Army's oldest fighting men. In the innocent months before Pearl Harbor, when America had briskly mobilized for a war in which it was not yet involved, word had come down from the top that draftees reaching the age of twenty-eight could be discharged if they wished to return to civilian life. The advent of war changed that; but after so many years of stateside training, many 4th Division GIs could not shake their conviction that their outfit was too old to enter combat. In early 1944, a rumor of impending overseas movement swept through the 4th Division, but to many GIs, those rumors were entirely implausible.

22nd Infantry, 4th Division
History of the 22nd Infantry, 1945
The officers and men believed it highly improbable, if not impossible for the [22nd] Regiment to be committed. . . . They laughed at the very idea because it was a known fact the average age of the troops was over twenty-eight, and they thought, "Old troops don't fight—they're not physically capable." Suddenly the laughs changed to serious thinking. The CO of the regiment, Col. Hervey Tribolet, held a closed meeting with all the officers informing them that within the next month the regiment would be on its way overseas.

When the 4th Division arrived in England in late January 1944, Ike and Bradley did not take long to deduce that it would probably do well when it first entered combat. Such a lengthy period of solid of training had infused the division with steady confidence, and although by 1944 the division was composed overwhelmingly of draftees, the noticeably high morale of those men was in part sustained by the deep-rooted Regular army traditions of the three infantry regiments—8th, 12th, and 22nd—forming the 4th's fighting core. Cynical GIs habitually regarded U.S. Army divisional mottos as meaningless, but the 4th's slogan, "Steadfast and Loyal," seemed to define the Ivy Division's true character.

The U.S. Army had seen to it that the 4th would be primed for D-Day even before it shipped out to Britain. For more than two months in the fall of 1943, the division had thoroughly practiced amphibious warfare techniques in the waters of the Gulf of Mexico at Camp Gordon Johnston, Florida. Marksmen kept a sharp lookout for alligators during landing exercises, although it was obvious to all that the European shoreline could hardly resemble the southeastern coast of the Florida Panhandle. Nevertheless, when the 4th Division settled into its English cantonments, General Bradley's inventory of divisions with superior amphibious training was increased from three to four.

The 1st and 29th Infantry Divisions would carry out the Omaha Beach invasion, leaving the 4th and 28th Divisions as candidates for the Utah

"Training discipline must be strict."
Maj. Gen. Raymond O. Barton,
commander of the 4th Infantry
Division. COURTESY 8TH INFANTRY REGIMENT.

assault. There would be only enough shipping to convey one division to Utah on D-Day, so Bradley would have to choose one division or the other—not both. The 28th, an old Pennsylvania National Guard outfit that Bradley himself had commanded for eight months until his transfer to North Africa in February 1943, was acknowledged to have excellent amphibious training. According to Bradley, the 4th must have been just as good, if not better, and consequently the Ivy Division would soon have an appointment to keep in Normandy on D-Day.

If the 4th Division was indeed "steadfast and loyal," those characteristics stemmed in part from its commander, Maj. Gen. Raymond O. Barton. A native of the Oklahoma Territory, Barton had graduated in the West Point class of 1912, three years ahead of his superiors Ike and Bradley and five years before his immediate boss, Collins. Barton did not see combat in World War I, but he served for four years in Europe in the postwar occupation forces and, in fact, commanded the last American military post in Germany prior to the departure of the U.S. Army from its occupation zone in 1923. By 1944, at fifty-four years old, Barton had perhaps reached the age at which Chief of Staff Marshall did not believe men should be commanding combat outfits, but despite his thoroughly unmilitary nickname of

"Tubby," his former West Point sports of boxing and wrestling had helped produce an extraordinarily tough and confident soldier.

Given the harsh and lengthy training regimen GIs in an infantry division were forced to endure, it was highly unlikely that they would worship their commanding general. This was particularly true of Barton, who was described by one 4th Division colonel as "a very strict disciplinarian who commanded his division with an iron hand." Barton, however, did at least command respect. During exercises, he was so frequently near the fighting men that it was easy for the troops to recognize his weather-beaten face with its clipped mustache and bushy eyebrows. Shortly after he took command of the 4th in 1942, a member of the 22nd Infantry noted: "His manner was firm and brisk, but not sour or stiff. The rank and file are strongly impressed with the ability and energetic leadership he has exhibited in the short time since he took command of this division."

Maj. Gen. Raymond O. Barton
Commander, 4th Infantry Division, speech to 22nd Infantry, July 3, 1942
I am your leader. I want to know what you think. In the not too distant future we will be in battle. When bullets start flying your minds will freeze, and you will act according to habit. In order that you develop the right habits, training discipline must be strict. I know 90 percent of you want to cooperate. I will take care of the other 10 percent.

To carry out a successful invasion against a coastline the enemy had occupied for almost four years, VII Corps commander Collins would have to do much more than simply hurl Barton's 4th Division ashore. Amphibious tanks must support the initial assault; demolition troops would be required to clear lanes through German beach obstacles; engineers would have to prepare the beach for the influx of vast amounts of matériel. The Ivy Division did not possess the resources that would enable them to perform these kinds of tasks, and consequently, Bradley augmented Collins's VII Corps in the months before D-Day with dozens of independent units as small as twelve-man squads, each of which was issued scrupulously prepared and top secret orders spelling out its part of the grand military choreography that would soon take place on Utah Beach on D-Day. Collins was fortunate to have under his command some of the U.S. Army's most experienced organizations for these types of specialized tasks.

To the uninitiated, the opening phase of a seaborne invasion did not seem a suitable moment to employ tanks, but on Utah and Omaha Beaches,

Bradley resolved to surprise the Germans by deploying them in the open-ing wave by means of secret duplex drive (DD) amphibious technology. Only three U.S. Army tank battalions in England were trained to operate DD tanks, which were designed to launch from large landing craft about three miles offshore, swim toward the beach under their own power, and then operate conventionally on land. To some observers, DD tanks sounded like a questionable idea, and in truth, they had never been tested in combat, but that would change on D-Day when the VII Corps' 70th Tank Battalion surged ashore at H-Hour with Barton's GIs. Simultaneously, two other tank battalions would do the same at Omaha. Some who had profound faith in DD tanks hoped that the supposedly second-rate enemy defenders of the Normandy coast would take off for the rear the moment they saw these Allied secret weapons for the first time.

If anyone could make DD tanks work, it would be the men of the 70th. The outfit had been established in the summer of 1940 in response to the U.S. Army's mad rush to copy the noticeably successful methods German panzers had used to carry out their new form of warfare called "blitzkrieg." But the 70th must eventually do something that German panzers had never done, and that was to participate in an amphibious landing. The tankers practiced seaborne invasion techniques as early as March 1942 and became sufficiently proficient to join Operation Torch, the invasion of North Africa that took place in November of that year. The 70th also participated in the invasion of Sicily in July 1943. By early 1944, no one could call the 70th green, but when the tankers transferred to England and got their first look at the DD tanks they would use on Utah, even those grizzled veterans must have felt a twinge of apprehension.

General Collins's first and most vital task was to make the Utah inva-sion work. But that was only a first step, the start of a vast land battle in which VII Corps and all other Anglo-American combat units would, if post-D-Day plans developed as Monty had hoped, destroy the German Army in Normandy and lead to the liberation of western Europe. To play his part in this battle, Collins had to swiftly establish a prodigious flow of matériel ashore, as all Overlord studies pointed out that for the Allies to prevail in this critical campaign, they must build up troops, equipment, and supplies in Normandy faster than the Germans could.

Luckily for Collins, he had on his VII Corps troop list the ideal unit to manage the Utah beachhead. Created in June 1942 as a model organization to support the many future seaborne invasions the U.S. Army hoped to launch in both Europe and the Pacific, the 1st Engineer Special Brigade (ESB) embodied modern amphibious warfare. The 1st ESB was a unit of astonishing diversity, whose soldiers and sailors displayed most of the varied military skills that America had to teach its servicemen if it was to contribute to victory in World War II. Its dozens of specialized outfits, amounting to more than 10,000 men, included port companies, U.S. Navy beachmaster outfits, firefighting platoons, bomb disposal squads, graves registration units, and amphibious truck companies, equipped with the army's renowned swimming truck, the DUKW (pronounced "duck"). But the soul of the 1st ESB was the veteran 531st Engineer Shore Regiment, a unit of nearly 2,500 men who were superbly trained to prepare the beachhead for the arrival of reinforcements and supplies and to ensure that the men and equipment that arrived on the beach could thereupon get off it. This type of work certainly did not generate headlines, but the GIs who would be fighting the war in the front lines could not get along without it.

Another notable outfit in Collins's VII Corps was the 4th Cavalry Group, whose troopers would be the first seaborne Allied soldiers to walk on French soil on D-Day. In 1944, Americans might regard any U.S. Army unit with the word "cavalry" in its designation as absurdly archaic, but the army had separated the 4th Cavalry from its beloved horses in the summer of 1941 and converted it to a cutting-edge mechanized unit focused on scouting missions. Utah Beach hardly seemed the place for such a unit, but Collins had another important mission in mind: the seizure before dawn on D-Day of the Iles St. Marcouf, two tiny islands about five miles northeast of Utah. This was an extraordinarily tough job, as the 4th Cavalry would learn on June 6.

The Utah invasion was an operation of immense complexity, and Collins had at least one outfit under his command to cover every facet of modern warfare. The 377th Anti-Aircraft Artillery Battalion would protect the beachhead from the Luftwaffe; the 87th Chemical Mortar Battalion held orders to provide hasty fire support for the infantry in the critical opening stage of the assault before the arrival of artillery; the 237th and 299th Engineer Battalions, with help from U.S. Navy demolition teams, were assigned the exceptionally dangerous task of blasting gaps through the enemy's beach obstacles; the 746th Tank Battalion would land and race inland toward enclaves held by American airborne troops; the 65th Armored Field Artillery Battalion, a unit with combat experience in North Africa and Sicily, was thoroughly trained in the difficult procedure of firing its self-propelled howitzers while loaded aboard landing craft.

All these units and more held top secret orders as bulky as a Manhattan telephone book, so methodically prepared by Collins's staffers that even the army's many pessimists might be convinced that this time, at last, the U.S. Army knew what it was doing—and this time, undeniably, it did. But thorough planning did not ensure success; execution was the key. On D-Day, every one of Collins's units must fulfill its tasks in a timely manner; otherwise, the entire plan could fall apart and the invasion would fail. And then there were the Germans: Collins's many veterans who had fought them in the Mediterranean understood that the enemy was a cunning and ruthless foe who would not allow the Americans to hold the initiative forever. In Normandy, the Germans would be sure to have some surprises in store, and the GIs must be ready for whatever the enemy had to offer.

General Collins himself was a combat veteran who had witnessed war's harsh realities in the Pacific, but Normandy would be infinitely more complex than Guadalcanal and New Georgia. On D-Day, he would be a director, guiding his vast array of units on an immense stage of war that the world would watch intently. How would the show turn out? The confident Collins had no doubts, and if he was to confirm beyond any doubt to Ike and Bradley that he indeed was the renowned "Lightning Joe," this would be the stage on which he must prove it.

VALOR WITHOUT ARMS

The men of the VII Corps would not be alone. Before dawn on D-Day, Bradley had promised an airborne operation of unparalleled immensity in the marshy lowlands behind Utah Beach and the tangled bocage of the Cotentin interior. The two American airborne divisions that would carry out this innovative maneuver, the 82nd and 101st, would for the moment be under Bradley's direct command, not Collins's, but from the start, the airborne mission was designed to make the VII Corps' job easier on D-Day and afterward. In the Overlord planning stage, therefore, Collins exerted pronounced influence on how the airborne mission should be carried out.

Like most military plans the Americans' combined airborne-seaborne assault on the Cotentin Peninsula looked thoroughly neat on paper. According to the VII Corps planning staff, if the parachutists and glider troops could achieve the undeniably tough tasks that were expected of them, the enemy would surely stagger from the blow, and the Utah beachhead would thereupon swell like a balloon filling rapidly with air.

Many harbored the disturbing thought that an airborne operation of this magnitude had never been attempted before. Indeed, when it had been tried on a smaller scale during the first two days of the Sicily invasion in July 1943, its execution had been anything but smooth. On the opening night of that assault, a long overwater flight by 226 C-47s, by the dim light of a crescent moon, had triggered navigational problems, and most of the 82nd

Airborne Division's paratroopers had missed their drop zones in southeastern Sicily by a wide margin. Much worse, on the second night, a fleet of 144 C-47s conveying paratrooper reinforcements to drop zones within the American beachhead, a mission that should have been unopposed, was slaughtered by friendly antiaircraft fire from both ground units and offshore warships. Twenty-three C-47s were shot down and another thirty-seven severely damaged, with great loss of life among both paratroopers and air crews. If friendly troops and sailors had proved such deadly antiaircraft gunners in Sicily, what would the Germans do in Normandy?

That there was much room for improvement was obvious to anyone who had observed the Sicily operation. If the American airborne mission in Normandy was to succeed—and ultimately it would be more than four times the size of the Sicily drop—air navigation techniques would have to be considerably improved, drop and landing zones must be marked more clearly, and friendly ground and naval units should be trained to hold their fire when assemblies of C-47s passed overhead. Launching the D-Day parachute and glider missions on a night with a full moon would help. What was required above all was a firm conviction that the Sicily operation could be improved upon, and only constant practice would help achieve that goal.

The somewhat euphemistic official U.S. Army term for an airborne assault was "vertical envelopment," and the Ninth Air Force men responsible for dropping soldiers vertically behind enemy lines were IX Troop Carrier Command's pilots and crews, who had been flooding Britain with their C-47 transports and CG-4A Waco gliders since January 1944. The airmen certainly appreciated the value of practice. In the war's early days back in the States, the enthusiastic crews had tried to do just that with entirely inadequate numbers of aircraft. Later, once America's booming production lines had peaked, plentiful C-47s suddenly filled training airfields, and Troop Carrier slowly blossomed into a vital branch of the army air force that was just as accomplished as any other. To Troop Carrier air crews, however, practice could be just as dangerous as the real thing. True, flight exercises did not involve enemy gunfire, but only a highly skilled pilot could fly at night in an exceptionally tight multiship formation, as the Normandy mission would require him to do, with adjacent C-47s flying at 150 miles per hour twenty feet from his wingtips on either side—all under strict radio silence. It did not take an aviation expert to determine that this sort of flying was hazardous, and when C-47s plunged into unanticipated cloud banks, as they would on D-Day, the experience became downright alarming. It was a tough skill to master, but a 439th Troop Carrier Group pilot, 1st Lt. Adam

"Every pilot in IX Troop Carrier Command on D-Day was well qualified."
IX Troop Carrier Command C-47s towing gliders over Normandy.
U.S. ARMY SIGNAL CORPS, NATIONAL ARCHIVES.

Parsons—a former paratrooper—noted, "Every pilot in IX Troop Carrier Command on D-Day was well qualified."

Dropping paratroopers was hard enough, but Troop Carrier's mission was further complicated by its equally hazardous responsibility for glider operations. A C-47 pilot had to learn the art of taking off and flying with an attached glider, sometimes two, and then cutting them loose at precisely the right time over a designated landing zone. Furthermore, some pilots were trained in specially equipped C-47s to fly in at an astonishingly low altitude over a landing zone and pick up parked and fully loaded gliders with a hook, grabbing the gliders' 300-foot nylon tow ropes and abruptly hauling them into the air. This "snatch" procedure obviously was treacherous, but it was the fastest way to return gliders to their home bases after combat and get wounded men in inaccessible battle zones straight to the hospital.

Gliders seemed incongruous in a war noted for its remarkable technology. Their lack of engines was understandable, but their obvious fragility amazed all who saw them for the first time. Aside from its wooden wings, tail, and floor, the American CG-4A Waco was nothing more than a frame of steel tubes encased with canvas and capped by a Plexiglas nose. When they cut loose from their tow planes and eventually floated down to earth in what pilots bluntly referred to as a "controlled crash," the Waco hardly seemed capable of surviving that landing. In Normandy's difficult hedgerow country, many did not.

The glider pilot's job was not alluring, and the army air force struggled to induce men to try it. Once gliders landed in a combat zone they would not leave it any time soon, a certain indicator that their pilots would join and sometimes fight with the infantrymen they had just flown into battle. This was not a suitable incentive to become a glider pilot, but most of the men who did so swiftly became adept at their jobs despite the low standing of the glider branch in the army air force and the undeniably uncertain future of glider warfare.

Troop Carrier airmen wondered why they alone seemed to grasp the fact that their organization was unquestionably a *combat* outfit. That Troop Carrier pilots and crews endured mortal danger during an airdrop seemed obvious given that C-47s were slow and vulnerable and flew in large groups at exceptionally low altitudes directly over enemy territory. As for glider pilots, once they cut loose from their tow planes, gravity's indissoluble pull would in due course bring them down to earth, and when it did, the pilots' skill would determine whether they and their embarked passengers would live.

The supreme commander himself once accidentally reinforced the Troop Carrier identity crisis. Ike was reviewing a Troop Carrier outfit in England in August 1944 when he mistakenly referred to it as a part of the Air Transport Command, a noncombat organization that hauled supplies, not combat troops. The dismayed and disbelieving Troop Carrier men promptly booed their commander. When he realized his mistake, Ike had to admit that they had a point.

U.S. Army Field Manual 100-5
Field Service Regulations, Operations, June 1944
Troop Carrier forces are air forces, which are specially organized, trained, and equipped to transport airborne troops and supplies into combat. They should not be confused with elements of the Air Transport Command.

No one denied that a C-47 was a wonderful machine, but when it flew within small-arms range of the enemy, it had its drawbacks. It had no armor whatsoever, and its fuselage could be pierced by every weapon the German Army possessed. Even worse, most C-47s in England were not equipped with that marvelous American invention of plastic and rubber, the self-sealing fuel tank. The celebrated fighters and bombers of the Eighth Air Force had such tanks, but not the transport aircraft, which seemingly had an even more pressing need for them. Consequently, Troop Carrier crews had to learn to live with the alarming fact that one bullet penetrating a fuel tank could lead to their C-47's instant destruction. So too could a single enemy hit on a "parapack" slung beneath a C-47 during an airdrop, which usually contained ammunition intended for paratroopers on the ground. C-47s could not hit back at the enemy because they were unarmed, and strict army air force regulations prohibited Troop Carrier crew members from using weapons onboard for fear of hitting paratroopers. Living with these kinds of dangers made Troop Carrier men understandably sensitive. But if one affair could convince nonbelievers that Troop Carrier was indeed a combat outfit, it would be the Normandy invasion.

Lt. Gen. Lewis Brereton
Commander, U.S. Ninth Air Force, diary, May 20, 1944
I have no illusions as to the extreme difficulty of this operation. We have, however, the best Troop Carrier Command in the world, and its morale could not be higher.

Brig. Gen. James Gavin
Assistant Division Commander, 82nd Airborne Division
Concerning the C-47 crews: They were brave men. When we arrived at the point of jumping, we were usually in the thickest of the fight, and we had to get out of those crates. The crews knew how to fly them through heavy flak, and they almost invariably did. They were brave men, and I couldn't speak too highly of them.

RENDEZVOUS WITH DESTINY

One could hardly imagine that the villainous German Army in World War II was worthy of emulation, but in the months immediately following Pearl Harbor, there was probably not a single U.S. Army general who would not have agreed with the contention that the Allies had to study and learn from the enemy if they were to win the war. Blitzkrieg, that revolutionary method of war Hitler had used to conquer most of Europe, must be turned upon its originators with a vengeance. American land forces must be hastily mechanized with prodigious numbers of tanks, trucks, and jeeps, while U.S. Army generals learned how battles could be won with concentrated ferocity followed by swift exploitation. "I believe we can lick the Hun only by being ahead of him in ideas as well as material resources," Ike noted to Marshall in February 1944.

But a few imaginative U.S. Army officers recognized that the lesser-known ingredient of German blitzkrieg—airborne operations—offered the Americans the opportunity to transform completely the way modern battles were fought, particularly assaults from the sea. All Allied generals agreed that amphibious operations were hazardous but must be eventually mastered if Germany and Japan were to be defeated. Even Gallipoli, the 1915 seaborne invasion of Turkey universally noted for its futility, probably would have worked, according to airborne advocates, if the enemy had been struck simultaneously from the air as well as the sea. Further, there was solid proof of the value of airborne operations. On the first day of the German attack on Belgium, May 10, 1940, a mere seventy-eight German gliderists had neutralized the fortress of Eben Emael, near Liège, while paratroopers seized the very bridges the fortress was supposed to guard. Eben Emael was renowned for its modernity and supposedly was capable of holding off any form of conventional attack, even by a panzer division.

And then there was Crete. The German conquest of that enormous Greek island in less than a week in May 1941 by 17,000 airborne troops— a combination of paratroopers, gliderists, and conventional infantry landed by transport planes at captured airfields—had astonished military conformists. The enemy had managed to accomplish this feat without a supporting assault by sea and despite being outnumbered two-to-one by Commonwealth forces.

The American visionaries were watching, and images of what the U.S. Army could do given more and better airborne resources danced through their heads. For the moment, those images were merely fantasies, as only a single American parachute battalion of a few hundred men had existed when the Germans' daring air assault seized Crete. But Chief of Staff Marshall was a true believer, and he opened up the army's coffers so liberally that in the next three years, an airborne force of men and machines would be spawned on a scale so immense that the German effort would look puny in comparison. What had been only a single, small parachute unit in May 1941 would by D-Day be transformed into a force of so many parachute and glider battalions that no one bothered to count them anymore.

General Marshall, however, might not have been so confident in airborne operations had he known that the Germans had suffered heavy losses of men and machines on Crete, about one-third of the 17,000 troops and 530 aircraft they committed. Even a man so unmindful of human suffering as Adolf Hitler observed that the Crete victory was not worth the loss of so many elite troops. Thus, while the American neophytes plunged enthusiastically into the airborne domain, heading irrevocably to their D-Day appointment in Normandy, the enemy proceeded precisely in the opposite direction and would never again launch an airborne assault of consequential size.

By 1944, the Americans were ready. In Normandy, their two best airborne divisions, the 82nd "All-Americans" and 101st "Screaming Eagles," would attempt to inflict upon the Germans what the Germans themselves had inflicted upon the British on Crete in 1941. But the vertical envelopment concept was so new that no Allied soldier could say with certainty how airborne divisions should carry it out. If parachute and glider units would both serve in the same division, what was the proper mix and how would they work together? Would the paratroopers follow the German example on Crete and focus solely on seizing airfields so that subsequent waves of infantry could be transported into battle by air? Or could parachute forces be relied upon to fulfill more ambitious objectives on their own?

In the spring of 1944, no one knew for sure; there simply had not been enough previous airborne combat missions to articulate any convincing answers. In August 1942, when the U.S. Army created the 82nd and 101st, its first two airborne divisions, divisional glider troops outnumbered paratroopers by a sizable margin. But from that moment forward, the trend in American airborne doctrine unambiguously favored the more glamorous paratroopers over their glider comrades, who received less pay than those who jumped out of airplanes and always seemed to suffer from a shortage of Waco gliders and men to fly them. When the 82nd deployed overseas in April 1943, the army doubled the number of parachute infantry battalions on its roster while cutting the number of glider battalions in half. Furthermore, when the 82nd hurled several of its parachute units into Sicily in the opening stage of that July 1943 invasion, its single glider infantry regiment did not even participate in the assault.

The D-Day airborne mission would prolong this trend. As configured for the Normandy invasion, parachute infantry battalions outnumbered their glider counterparts in both the 82nd and 101st by a three-to-one ratio. Moreover, the Cotentin hedgerow country was so cramped, and the enemy so thick on the ground, that several senior Allied airmen hypothesized that American gliders would be shot out of the air like clay pigeons at a shooting range if they attempted to land in daylight on the morning of D-Day. Gen. James Gavin, the 82nd's assistant division commander, agreed, noting in his diary, "Until we devise a better way to carry glider infantry, they are not worth much to us airborne." Consequently, the 82nd and 101st would open the D-Day assault almost entirely with paratroopers, although the plan called for about 100 gliders, packed with much-needed antitank guns and their crews, to land just before dawn. More ambitious glider missions would take place that evening and the following day; but on June 6, the Cotentin would primarily be the paratroopers' arena.

Today the enduring fame of the 82nd and 101st Airborne Divisions obscures the fact that in early 1944, the airborne division concept was so hazy and unsettled that the many diverse units that such divisions comprised did not at first mesh with as strong a sense of divisional esprit as the U.S. Army's more conventional and stable outfits, such as the 1st or 4th Divisions. As influential a figure as Eisenhower noted in a September 20, 1943, cable to General Marshall: "I do not believe in the Airborne division. I believe that airborne troops should be organized in self-contained units comprising infantry, artillery, and special services, all of about the strength of a regimental combat team."

But Ike's opinion swayed no one. Divisions, rather than smaller regimental combat teams, endured as the U.S. Army's fundamental airborne units for the rest of World War II, although their tables of organization were hardly as settled as standard infantry divisions. When the veteran 82nd Airborne transferred from the Mediterranean to Northern Ireland in December 1943 for the imminent D-Day mission, the U.S. First Army radically transformed it by adding to its rolls two complete parachute regiments and a single glider battalion. None of those outfits had combat experience, nor had they any previous affiliation with the legendary "All-Americans." Initially the 82nd's distinctive "Double-A" divisional patch was foreign to the new men, who knew nothing of the 82nd's remarkable combat career in the Mediterranean theater.

But regardless of the unit patches they sewed onto their uniforms, American paratroopers saw themselves as a special breed, somehow set apart from the U.S. Army's more conventional foot-sloggers. Even a casual observer of army ways could instantly detect this sentiment by discerning the sometimes swaggering off-duty behavior of those men who wore the distinctive over-the-ankle parachute boots. "We like to think of ourselves as a *corps d'élite,* and we are," declared Gen. William Lee, the originator of American airborne doctrine.

Furthermore, a paratrooper's training was vastly different than that of a standard infantryman. When the U.S. Army raised its first parachute battalions in 1940 and 1941, airborne divisions existed only in planners' imaginations, and consequently the paratroopers trained in isolation and acquired a fiercely independent spirit. Only the stroke of Marshall's pen in Washington in August 1942 triggered the transfer of parachute regiments to the newly formed airborne divisions, which in their initial configurations contained far more glider troops than parachutists. An enduring anecdote from the early days of the 82nd Airborne alleged that a parachute officer once blurted to the astonished division commander that his paratroopers desired to "cooperate" with the 82nd Division during training.

To Lt. Gen. Lesley McNair, chief of army ground forces and one of Marshall's principal deputies, the creation of the U.S. Army's first two airborne divisions was merely a matter of shuffling soldiers. In August 1942, McNair selected the 82nd Infantry Division, currently in training at Camp Claiborne, Louisiana, for an extraordinary transformation. The 82nd, which had once been the outfit of the legendary World War I hero Sgt. Alvin York, had been trained to a high standard by Omar Bradley and was now led by the charismatic Maj. Gen. Matthew Ridgway. McNair split the 82nd in two and attached a separate parachute regiment to each half. The 82nd Airborne Division, which remained under Ridgway's command, and the 101st Airborne Division, led by Maj. Gen. William Lee, had come to life.

The two divisions were virtually identical twins, but their commanders were anything but. Bill Lee was as modest and gentle as a major general could be. A graduate of North Carolina State and a veteran of the 81st Division in World War I, Lee returned to the States in 1919, determined to embark on a career in the U.S. Army. As an observer and military attaché in France and Britain in the interwar period, he embraced mechanized warfare and ultimately became one of the U.S. Army's most prominent tankers. To Lee, mobility was the key to any successful military operation, a concept that the Germans had already adopted and would soon refine into their legendary blitzkrieg.

After observing early German airborne techniques in the late thirties, Lee recognized that airplanes were even more mobile than tanks and trucks, and he soon became the U.S. Army's first proponent of what he labeled "air infantry." In 1939, Lee was assigned to the War Department in Washington, and he worked fervently to convince Marshall and McNair that the substantial monetary and training investment required to establish a powerful striking force of air infantry in the form of airborne divisions would be worth it. Lee had learned to parachute at age forty-seven, but his career almost came to an abrupt end after a devastating jump accident in late 1941. He would recover, but his operations officer, Col. James Gavin, noted, "I don't think Bill was ever the same man." Nevertheless, Lee was the perfect choice to take command of the 101st upon its inception, and he promptly told his troops, "The 101st Airborne Division has no history, but it has a rendezvous with destiny." He was right: Lee would lead the 101st to England in September 1943 and wait there for the crucial assignment in the invasion of Europe that everyone suspected would occur sometime soon.

In contrast, Matthew Ridgway had just made his first parachute jump in the summer of 1942 and knew virtually nothing about airborne warfare. Even so, he set out to learn it without delay, and given his reputation within the army as an exceptionally dynamic soldier, he was destined to master it thoroughly. Ridgway, like Joe Collins of the VII Corps, was one of those esteemed members of the West Point class of 1917 who had benefited greatly from a close association with George Marshall, with whom Ridgway had first served in China in 1925. But much to his disappointment, Ridgway had missed out on overseas combat duty in World War I, a trait he shared with Eisenhower, Bradley, and Collins—the three men who would shape his division's future in Normandy. Fortunately for Ridgway, George Marshall obviously did not consider combat experience in 1918 as a prerequisite to high command in World War II.

After months of incessant stateside training under Ridgway, the 82nd finally deployed in May 1943 to North Africa, which by then had been cleared of the enemy. In the July 1943 Sicily invasion, Ridgway and his paratroopers gained the combat experience they had sought so eagerly. Two months later, in the opening stages of the Italian campaign, the 82nd was thrown into battle once again in the Salerno beachhead. After a hard fight, the Germans withdrew northward toward Rome, and Ridgway pushed the All-Americans ahead toward Naples. The 82nd reaped countless headlines on the home front by capturing that great port city on October 1, 1943.

Minus one of its veteran parachute regiments, the 82nd headed for Northern Ireland in December 1943. When it arrived, its members suspected that even the memorable liberation of Naples would be eclipsed by the invasion that rumors proclaimed was about to occur.

Maj. Shields Warren
Executive, 1st Battalion, 508th Parachute Infantry,
82nd Airborne Division
My first contact with General Ridgway was shortly after the 508th Parachute Infantry arrived in Nottingham, England from Northern Ireland. All field grade officers of the regiment were assembled to meet General Ridgway, who gave us a short talk welcoming us to the 82nd Airborne Division. While the entire talk could not have lasted longer than five or ten minutes, I have never been more impressed by any individual's personality as much as that exhibited by General Ridgway. His personality could truly be called magnetic, since I found myself hanging on each

word he spoke. I said as much to my friend and classmate [Lt. Col.] Tom Shanley [CO, 2nd Battalion, 508th] afterward, who agreed wholeheartedly with my opinion.

In February 1944, General Lee suffered a heart attack, and Eisenhower was compelled to choose a successor to command the 101st. Surprisingly, Ike's selection, Brig. Gen. Maxwell Taylor, was drawn not from the 101st, but the 82nd. Taylor had been one of Ridgway's chief subordinates in the 82nd even before its transformation into an airborne division, and like Ridgway, Taylor, a noted artilleryman, had been thrust by that sweeping doctrinal change into the completely unfamiliar world of airborne warfare. He had parachuted out of an airplane only once, and of that occasion, jumpmaster Julian Ewell—whom Taylor would meet again in Normandy early on D-Day—noted: "I was watching him as he landed, and a brisk breeze snatched him up in the air, and he hit with a terrible crash, head first I think. . . . He bounced up, apparently unhurt."

A 1922 graduate of West Point, Taylor was a brilliant officer, celebrated for his ability to speak French, Spanish, and Japanese fluently. He did not, however, possess Ridgway's extraordinary charisma and drive, and many of the men with whom he served saw him as somewhat strict and formal, with a tendency to chew out soldiers for comparatively minor transgressions.

Taylor's forthcoming paradrop into Normandy would not be his first trip behind enemy lines. In September 1943, a group of Italians loyal to those men who were currently negotiating their country's surrender to the Allies had secretly conveyed him and a companion, disguised as captured pilots, to Rome. Taylor met with senior Italian leaders to discuss arrangements for an 82nd Airborne air assault on the capital just as the Italians announced their surrender to the Allies. But Taylor judged the Italian commitment as too feeble to offer the daring plan any chance of success, and he radioed Eisenhower with the advice that the 82nd's assault should be canceled. It was, and Ike later noted, "The risks [Taylor] ran were greater than I asked any other agent or emissary to undertake during the war . . . every minute [he] was in imminent danger of discovery and death."

If the Normandy invasion would involve many more airborne troops than originally envisioned, particularly American ones, General Marshall sensed that the Overlord planners in London needed a knowledgeable American officer to advise them on airborne matters. Ridgway recommended Bill Lee's former chief planner, James Gavin, who at the age of thirty-six had just gained his first star as the 82nd's deputy commander.

Even in this period of rapid-fire promotions, achieving general officer rank at thirty-six was extraordinary, but all who knew "Slim Jim" Gavin appreciated that he fully deserved the honor.

Maj. Gen. Matthew Ridgway
Commander, 82nd Airborne Division, official evaluation of Gavin, 1944
Gavin possesses to a superior degree self-possession regardless of pressure in and out of battle, loyalty, initiative, zeal, sound judgment, and common sense. His personal appearance and dignity of demeanor are in keeping with these high qualities, and to them all he adds great charm of manner. He is a proven battle leader of the highest type.

Gavin had raised the 505th Parachute Infantry, which would be the only American parachute regiment with combat experience to drop into Normandy on D-Day, and led it in two costly campaigns—Sicily and Salerno. If anyone could advise the Overlord planners what airborne units needed to succeed on D-Day, it would be him. But after his arrival in England in late November 1943, Gavin noted in his diary: "There is a feeling that the proposed plans for the employment of the airborne troops in the coming operations lack vision and boldness. As General [William] Butler [of the Army Air Force] put it, 'It is like having Michelangelo paint a barn.'"

General Bradley's insistence that the Utah invasion could not succeed without a supporting airborne operation, a resolve that Montgomery fully supported, would later add "vision and boldness" to Overlord's airborne planning, but achieving that goal was anything but easy. Gavin was impatient to fulfill the role Marshall had assigned to him and demonstrate that American airborne forces were ready to participate in the imminent invasion on a large scale. The American airborne faction, however, was highly suspicious of Air Chief Marshal Sir Trafford Leigh-Mallory, who, as Ike's senior air force officer at SHAEF, was responsible for Overlord's airborne operations. Even worse, a key advisor on Leigh-Mallory's staff was the British Army's senior airborne officer, Lieutenant General Sir Frederick Browning, a man in whom Ridgway and Gavin had little faith. According to those two officers, Browning was scheming to divert the Allies' limited airlift resources for British purposes on D-Day. Furthermore, the Americans could not gracefully accept Leigh-Mallory's control over an area of military operations that even he admitted to knowing little about. The matter came to a head at an airborne meeting in London on February 18, 1944.

Brig. Gen. James Gavin
Assistant Division Commander, 82nd Airborne Division

Leigh-Mallory said to me, "Now, General, tell me about these things. I want to understand how you make these parachute operations work." So I went over the whole thing. I soon began to realize that he was very cold to the whole idea. He didn't believe a word I was saying. . . . He didn't think it was possible for the Americans to carry out an airborne operation. . . . On the other hand, I had worked closely with General Bradley, and he had told me he would not go into Normandy without the airborne divisions in front of him.

Airborne missions demanded close cooperation between soldiers and airmen, but in planning for D-Day, teamwork between senior army and air force commanders was occasionally rocky. That the debates over the use of airborne forces were not carried out according to national lines was clearly demonstrated by General Montgomery, who steadfastly supported Bradley and the Americans on every Overlord airborne issue and repeatedly demonstrated more enthusiasm than Leigh-Mallory about audacious airborne missions. In truth, this contentious relationship continued even after D-Day, when Montgomery and Leigh-Mallory became embroiled in a dispute over Monty's bold plan to drop British airborne forces near Caen on June 10. Leigh-Mallory was categorically opposed to the idea, triggering Monty's caustic riposte that Leigh-Mallory was "a gutless bugger who refuses to take a chance"—an opinion with which Gavin certainly would have agreed.

In a few months, however, Leigh-Mallory would die in an airplane crash, and he would never have a chance to respond to this scorn. He was responsible to Ike for carrying out the D-Day airborne operation, but from his perspective, no Allied airborne mission in the past had yielded confidence that it would work. Indeed, as Leigh-Mallory later pointed out, Normandy's hedgerow terrain was unfavorable for airborne, particularly glider, operations; and the density of enemy troops near the few decent drop zones in the Cotentin Peninsula made it probable in his view that an airborne assault would be dreadfully costly in both men and aircraft.

These were crucial issues that would be decided later that spring, but from Gavin's standpoint, these high-level military dialogues were not for him. He was a fighting soldier above all else, and he observed in his diary, "My future is with the [82nd] Division." He was right: Ridgway would make sure that when the 82nd Airborne jumped into Normandy, Gavin was with it.

Gavin's vigor and self-confidence epitomized the American airborne character. Youth was their hallmark. Of the eighteen American parachute infantry battalions that would drop into Normandy on June 6, half were commanded by men who had graduated from West Point less than ten years previously. One of those soldiers, Lt. Col. Louis Mendez of the 508th Parachute Infantry, had graduated only in 1940. For men in their twenties, leading 600 paratroopers into combat in the most challenging of military maneuvers was a vast responsibility. But all the plans and preparations that went into the airborne assault boiled down to one fixation: engage the reviled enemy at close quarters and kill him. To the modern observer, the passage of more than sixty years has dimmed the truth that many of the paratroopers earnestly looked forward to those acts.

If that is the fastest way home . . . let's get it over with.

Col. Howard Johnson
Commander, 501st Parachute Infantry, 101st Airborne Division, briefing, June 5, 1944
I'm proud of you. You've shown me what you can do. . . . Tomorrow you'll be fighting Germans. Are you ready? [Johnson was answered by an affirmative roar.] We've worked together, sweated together, trained together. But what we do tonight will be written in history! [Johnson then removed his ankle knife from its casing and raised it.] I swear to you that before the dawn of another day, this knife will be stuck in the foulest, black-hearted Nazi bastard in France! Are you with me? [The troops rejoined: "We're with you!"] Then let's get 'em! Good hunting!

The paratroopers then filed past Colonel Johnson, and he shook hands with every one.

CHAPTER 3

Overture to Overlord

SOLDIERS OF THE REICH

If James Gavin represented the American Army's spirit, the mood of the enemy was typified by Karl-Wilhelm von Schlieben. Von Schlieben was a forty-nine-year-old major general who had witnessed enough combat in two world wars to satiate even the most bloodthirsty warrior. By December 1943, he found himself in command of the 709th Division, a pitiable outfit in which no one could take much pride, guarding Normandy's Cotentin Peninsula. It was a backwater thousands of miles from the Russian front, the place where most Germans thought the war would be decided. Like most German generals in 1944, von Schlieben's energy had been sapped by the proud German Army's catastrophic defeats and the führer's incessant demands to accomplish the impossible. As a case in point, von Schlieben's 709th Division held orders to defend nearly fifty miles of the Cotentin's east coast with 12,000 men whose average age was thirty-six, some of whom would probably run away the moment they first spotted the enemy.

Even worse, word had come down from the top that starting in 1944, the führer would focus his ruthless spotlight on von Schlieben and his fellow commanders in occupied France because of his belief that the Anglo-American invasion would come sometime that spring. Hitler had assigned the celebrated Field Marshal Erwin Rommel to northwest Europe to ensure that the coastal defenses were in top-notch condition, and Rommel quickly broadcast his theory to von Schlieben and his colleagues that the only way to defeat the enemy's imminent invasion was to concentrate as many troops as possible into coastal defenses. There, as the enemy stormed ashore, the defenders could direct their firepower against Allied troops in the surf and on the beach, when they would be most vulnerable. Furthermore, according to Rommel, the resolve of even unsteady divisions like von Schlieben's 709th would be bolstered by vast minefields, belts of beach obstacles, swaths of barbed wire, and concrete pillboxes so thick they would be almost indestructible.

It was an interesting theory, but von Schlieben and his superiors in Normandy knew that it could not be accomplished unless the high command could assign substantial reinforcements and a much greater amount of matériel to the theater. Von Schlieben's army commander, Gen. Friedrich Dollmann—a gentlemanly old soldier nicknamed "The Last Knight"—remarked, "In view of the thin line of coastal defense, we will scarcely be able to prevent the enemy from establishing a beachhead." As for von Schlieben, whose 709th Division covered that sector of the eastern Cotentin that would soon be known as Utah Beach, the hollowness of Rommel's scheme was even more clear. He noted, "If one had called the coast a 'line of security,' which indeed it was, instead of a 'main line of resistance,' probably the old principle would have been remembered that attempting to defend everything results in no defense at all."

Von Schlieben's 709th Division was not an appropriate representative of an army that prided itself on its military prowess. Neither its firepower nor its morale approached those of the superbly trained American outfits it would soon fight; and as for its mobility, von Schlieben lamented, "It did not even have horses." The 709th had been engaged in garrison duties in occupied France since the summer of 1941, months before America was involved in World War II. The comforts of garrison life in a prosperous region of western Europe inevitably softened the division's military edge, a condition that was worsened by recurring transfers of young and fit soldiers to the Russian front. To replace them, the Wehrmacht invariably provided older men, those recovering from wounds, recalcitrant recruits from regions occupied by the Nazis—even former Soviet prisoners of war, whose loyalties to Hitler were entirely suspect.

The 709th's principal job was to defend the Cotentin's east coast against an Allied amphibious assault, but von Schlieben had neither the manpower nor the resources to fulfill that task. To guard the peninsula's southeastern shoreline, covering six miles and forming the 709th's extreme right flank, he could manage to deploy little more than a battalion of

700 men from his 919th Regiment, supported by some thoroughly unreliable Georgian troops who were obviously unhappy that fate had brought them thousands of miles from their homes in the Caucasus Mountains to serve Adolf Hitler. A continuous defensive line along the beachfront was out of the question; the best the Germans could do in this sector was to erect nine *Widerstandsnest* (strongpoints), each of which was supposed to be a semi-independent island of resistance consisting of at least one concrete pillbox; a few mortars, heavy cannons, and antitank guns; and several fighting positions for machine-gun teams. Strands of barbed wire encircled each strongpoint, but von Schlieben grumbled, "The distance between the [strongpoints] varied from 1,000 to 4,000 meters." Minefields could have sealed those wide gaps, and according to von Schlieben, "Rommel had promised explicitly that 'millions of mines' would be supplied." However, they never showed up. In von Schlieben's case, the "Atlantic Wall" that Hitler had promised would stop the Allied invasion was more like a sieve.

It was squarely in the center of this part of the Cotentin that the 4th Infantry Division would soon surge ashore on a beach the GIs knew simply as "Utah." Unlike Omaha Beach, which was backed by dominating heights that offered the defenders a profound combat advantage, the Cotentin shoreline presented almost no terrain that was useful to the Germans. Aside from some undulating sand dunes behind a low coastal seawall, the terrain behind Utah Beach was as flat as a tabletop. Consequently, von Schlieben's *Widerstandsnest* were positioned for the most part not on commanding ground, but directly on the beachfront, inadequately concealed and with poor fields of fire. As von Schlieben would soon learn, anything Allied warships and aircraft could see, they could hit.

Nevertheless, Rommel asserted to von Schlieben and his fellow commanders that German manpower and matériel deficiencies could to some extent be alleviated by the expedient of obstructing potential landing beaches with basic and readily obtainable objects, such as logs or steel rails. Starting in February 1944, 709th Division troops complied, and within a few weeks, the Cotentin's beaches had sprouted hundreds of impediments that Allied air photographs could hardly miss. Despite their seemingly archaic appearance, the obstructions were deadly: When topped with mines and submerged by Normandy's legendary tides, they could destroy dozens of unsuspecting Allied landing craft as they approached the beach and, as Rommel maintained, would therefore be well worth the intense labor required to erect them. However, as von Schlieben later recalled, "This work left no time to train the troops, and it actually exhausted them." Furthermore, even Rommel's celebrated resolve was no match for nature's immense power, as the dismayed German workers watched the surging surf continually pound the logs and rails, jolting them loose or burying them half deep in sand. Consequently, when the Allies launched the Utah assault on June 6, the enemy's obstacle belts on the Cotentin beaches were more meager than the Americans had expected and ended up causing little trouble. In contrast, the thick belts of obstacles on Omaha Beach, fifteen miles to the east, had survived nature's pounding—probably because work on them had not started until April—and the perplexed American invaders there learned the effectiveness of Rommel's scheme.

Above all, Rommel needed fresh troops in the Cotentin, and in May 1944, he got them. Two high-quality units, the 91st *Luftlande* (Air Landing) Division, comprising about 8,000 men, and the 6th *Fallschirmjäger* (Parachute) Regiment, of about 3,500, moved into the region, a clear sign to concerned Allied intelligence officers, who swiftly picked up the movement, that the Germans may have figured out that something momentous was about to happen. Given Rommel's well-known penchant for coastal defense, the Allies were concerned that these two units were deployed not on the shoreline, but in reserve positions well inland—some of them, in fact, almost right in the middle of 82nd Airborne Division drop zones that Generals Bradley and Gavin had chosen earlier that year. Even worse, as both German units were supposedly familiar with airborne operations, they presumably also knew proper techniques to counter them. Could it be that the Germans had been tipped off? No one knew for sure, but Bradley, Gavin, and the other American airborne planners now faced a predicament that could change the whole course of the invasion.

A POOR PLACE TO FIGHT

If any part of a region's topography offered military benefits, the Germans were sure to notice, and when they arrived in Normandy in the summer of 1940 and took their first look at the Cotentin Peninsula, they indeed noticed many benefits. True, nothing about the Cotentin shoreline afforded the Germans any pronounced defensive advantages, but the peninsula's diverse terrain still presented several opportunities for them to frustrate their opponents' plans.

The Cotentin's southeastern corner is dominated by a watershed that includes two major rivers, the Douve and Merderet, countless minor streams, and several canals dating back to the Napoleonic era. Because all these waterways flow through lowlands, they are remarkably sluggish, so much so that tidal surges from the sea can back up the rivers' flow, forcing salt water upriver for fifteen miles. Such backups, especially in rainy seasons, invariably triggered inundations in the wide, flat floodplains adjacent to the rivers' banks. The locals solved this problem in the late nineteenth century by building a sturdy stone dam across the Douve near its mouth, with six arched gates that could be closed during high-tide periods so that the sea could not force its way upriver. They called this dam La Barquette, and as soon as the Germans—and later the Americans—figured out what it did, they became intensely interested in what it could do for them.

In November 1942, the Germans decided to recruit the sea as an ally. They reversed the times at which La Barquette's lockkeeper normally opened and closed his six floodgates, and consequently the tide began to gush upriver freely—and stay there. Over the next several months, the Douve-Merderet watershed became a series of interconnected lakes, up to ten feet deep and more than one mile wide in places. The flooding profoundly affected potential military operations within that locale. It was almost as if the Germans had transformed the Cotentin's southeastern corner into an island. If Collins wished to push his VII Corps south and west out of the Utah beachhead—something he must do if he was to fulfill his two essential goals of linking up with the 29th Division from Omaha and capturing Cherbourg—his troops could cross the Douve and Merderet only in a few places, so few that the Germans surely would defend each of them resolutely. Even worse, these crossing sites were a tactical nightmare for the attacker, since they were nothing more than narrow roads up to a mile long, raised just a few feet above flooded meadows on either side. For the GIs to launch an attack straight down those lengthy causeways could be as suicidal as the charge of the Light Brigade. Finally, the Americans had positioned some 82nd and 101st Airborne Division drop zones perilously close to the floodplain, so paratroopers faced the unpleasant prospect of a night landing in water whose depth they could only guess at.

In the southeastern Cotentin's coastal sector, the Germans again proved that they knew exactly what they were doing when it came to influencing topography to suit their purposes. Immediately behind the beach the Allies had secretly labeled "Utah" lay a nearly flat plain with a width of more than a mile, and by the simple expedient of damming up with boulders and tree limbs the seven or eight tiny rivulets that carried rain and groundwater down to the sea, the Germans managed to transform that plain into a giant lake, whose depth varied depending on how recently rain had fallen. This clever manipulation virtually isolated Utah Beach from the Cotentin interior. The only way for vehicles to leave Utah Beach was by means of four narrow stone-surface roads that were built up to an elevation scarcely higher than the flooded pastures that bordered them—and Allied air photos

Cotentin Peninsula: German Deployment, June 1944

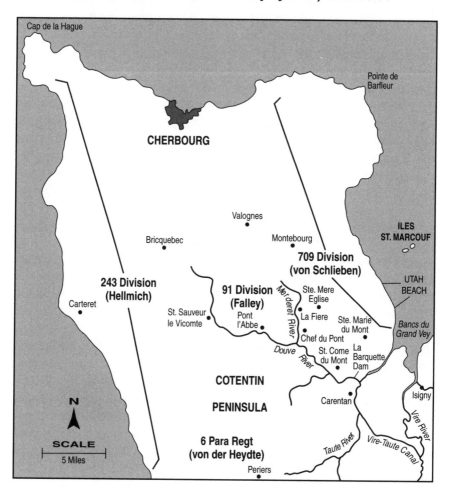

Cap de la Hague

Pointe de Barfleur

CHERBOURG

Valognes

Bricquebec

Montebourg

ILES
ST. MARCOUF

**709 Division
(von Schlieben)**

UTAH
BEACH

**243 Division
(Hellmich)**

Carteret

St. Sauveur
le Vicomte

**91 Division
(Falley)**

Pont
l'Abbe

Ste. Mere
Eglise

La Fiere

Ste. Marie
du Mont

Bancs du
Grand Vey

Merderet River

Chef du Pont

Douve River

St. Come
du Mont

La
Barquette
Dam

COTENTIN

Isigny

PENINSULA

Carentan

Vire River

**6 Para Regt
(von der Heydte)**

Taute River

Vire-Taute Canal

Periers

N

SCALE

5 Miles

had discerned that even those roads were occasionally underwater. American foot troops just might be able to pass inland through the flooded fields, but no one knew for sure what the conditions would be on D-Day. Resolute German resistance on the shoreline coupled with rainy weather prior to the invasion could contain the Americans within the Utah beachhead like the proverbial ship corked in a bottle.

The Normandy coast is renowned for its tides, which surge back and forth with an intensity matched in just a few places in the world. Twice in any given twenty-four-hour period, the tide recedes so far from the coast that a person at the water's edge appears as a mere speck when viewed from the dunes beyond the beach. Then, little more than five hours later, the sea is lapping up almost as far as those dunes, and the beach has been reduced to a strip of sand no more than a few yards wide.

The Germans would make every effort to exploit this natural phenomenon, and when Field Marshal Rommel arrived in France in early 1944, he figured out precisely how to do it. By distributing a diverse array of mined beach obstacles on the tidal flat on the Cotentin's beaches, Rommel attempted to narrow the Allies' invasion options considerably. Unless the Allies could figure out how to destroy those obstacles before the invasion, they would have to land their first assault waves at near low tide—otherwise, Allied landing craft could wreck themselves upon the treacherous impediments, which would be submerged at higher tides. For American troops to land at low tide on the eastern Cotentin—which under some conditions exposed a beach flat of more than 800 yards—would be a German machine gunner's dream and could result in a slaughter worse than in no-man's-land in the previous war. And even if American troops could succeed in getting ashore, they would have to figure out some way of blasting gaps through the German obstacle belts so that landing craft could approach shore safely as the tide rose with its customary celerity.

Unhappily for Rommel, his Cotentin beach obstacles were much too sparse to have a significant impact on the Americans' Utah invasion on D-Day, a condition he blamed on his own troops' indolence. All too often on inspections, Rommel had to deal with apathetic troops whose attitude proclaimed: Of all the beaches in France, why will they come here? To which Rommel asserted: They will come someplace, and when they do, we must be ready or the war is lost. On June 6, they came to Utah Beach—and the Germans were far from ready.

Even with all the measures the Germans had taken to ensure that the Cotentin's terrain would be an invader's nightmare, there was probably not a single soldier in the 709th Division who considered his shoreline position

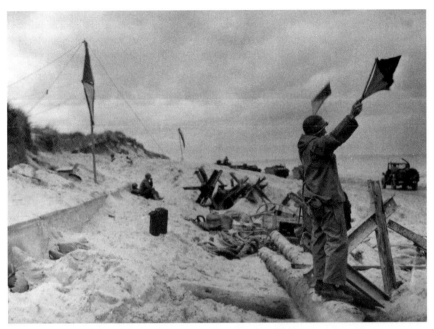

"Low lying, without distinctive terrain features." A U.S. Navy signalman on Utah Beach on D-Day. The signalman is standing on and adjacent to German beach obstacles recently bulldozed by U.S. engineers. Note the masonry seawall at the base of the dunes. U.S. NAVY, NATIONAL ARCHIVES.

defensible. If the Allies invaded here, the Cotentin's interminable sand dunes offered the German defenders scant hope that they would survive a combined sea, air, and land onslaught by the enemy host. About the only thing the Germans could do was to build as many coastal pillboxes as possible, using concrete that was inadequately supplied because every unit in occupied France was clamoring for it, and then pray that the Allies would choose someplace else to invade.

Utah Beach
Top Secret "Bigot-Neptune" analysis, April 21, 1944
"Utah" Beach, 9655 yards long. Low lying and without distinctive terrain features, is composed of compact gray sand between high and low water marks. . . . The beach is backed for its entire length by a masonry seawall, with the exception of a stretch of piling 210 yards in length. Behind the wall, from approximately the center of the beach and extending southward, sand dunes approximately 10 to 25 feet high extend inland nearly 150 yards. Inland of the entire beach area are inundated

lowlands. Numerous exits in the form of ramps exist off the beach for its entire
length. However, as these exits lead through gaps in the seawall, all of them have
been blocked. Normally a good network of roads leading into the interior exists,
but because of the inundated area, the interior can be reached only by three roads
at present.

DRESS REHEARSALS

Time is a prized military commodity, and as the winter of 1943–44 drew to
a close, General Collins apparently did not have enough of it. The Utah
Beach assault was a late addition to the Overlord invasion scheme, and
Collins's VII Corps staff would have to work swiftly to draw up a realistic
and effective plan to storm that small part of Normandy on D-Day. In terms
of training, no one doubted that the 4th Infantry Division and its partners
were already primed for combat, but would there be enough time to practice the incredibly intricate tasks associated with an amphibious assault on
such an immense scale?

The invasion plan would keep U.S. Army and Navy staff officers pounding away at typewriters for weeks, and the resultant mountain of paperwork
would specify thousands of tasks large and small that every outfit must fulfill flawlessly if the VII Corps was to achieve its D-Day goals. Each soldier
had to be assigned to a marshalling area near the English coast, sealed off
from the outside world, and wait for the word to board the navy transport
that would carry him across the Channel to Normandy as just one small part
of a huge convoy. Warships must protect those convoys; minesweepers must
clear safe lanes through heavily mined waters; fighters must provide air
cover in case the Luftwaffe made an appearance. Planners had to prepare
invasion timetables more dense than a Grand Central Station train schedule
at rush hour, specifying landing times for dozens of different units on Utah
Beach down to the minute. And theoretically, this was the easy part: The real
difficulty would come when the GIs took their first steps in France—and the
enemy opened fire. The operation's success depended entirely on perfect
timing; and perfect timing could not be achieved without thorough practice.

The Anglo-American top brass ordered Collins to conduct a VII Corps
dress rehearsal for the Utah invasion, designated Exercise Tiger, from April
22 to 30, 1944. If there were flaws in the invasion plan, this would be the
time—the only time—to reveal and correct them. The exercise's initial
stage was carried out smoothly. Troops from the 4th Division and all the
outfits that would support it on Utah Beach assembled in the marshalling
areas they would use for the actual D-Day operation and loaded up on the

same transports that would convey them across the Channel for the real invasion. So far, so good: GIs were hardened to the interminable waits that made up U.S. Army life, and for the first five days of Exercise Tiger, waiting was virtually all they did.

Eventually the convoys put out to sea and maneuvered with military precision in Lyme Bay, just off the English coast, aiming to deposit the VII Corps on a picturesque and secluded Devon beach named Slapton Sands, which would act as a surrogate Utah Beach on the simulated "D-Day," April 28, 1944. British authorities had emptied entire seaside parishes of their residents in December 1943, and consequently the mock invasion could be accompanied by naval and air bombardments using live ammunition, providing the assault troops a feel for the sights and sounds of real battle. The 4th Division stormed ashore on Slapton Sands with Ike, Bradley, and Collins as witnesses, and despite a few timing problems, the exercise was carried out in a manner that was as orderly as the top brass could have hoped. Indeed, had it not been for a thirty-minute period shortly after midnight on April 28, the nine days of Exercise Tiger would have been considered a striking success, generating confident notions in invasion planners' minds that amphibious warfare was not so difficult after all. But in those thirty minutes, the exercise suddenly turned into an unmitigated disaster and taught the Americans the same lesson they had already learned several times in the current war: Never underestimate the Germans.

The Germans who demonstrated their prowess to their enemies on the morning of April 28 were the crews of about a dozen *Schnellboote* (literally "fast boats," known as "E-boats" by the Allies), which operated out of Cherbourg and preyed on Allied shipping at night in the English Channel. These sleek 100-foot craft had engines so powerful that they could speed through the water at forty knots with a roar that sounded like an airplane's motor. They carried two torpedoes and small-caliber guns, and Allied sailors had learned long ago that *Schnellboote* captains were thoroughly aggressive in putting those weapons to good use.

After dark on April 27, the *Schnellboote* slipped into Lyme Bay, and their crews immediately perceived that they had stumbled into something big. At about 2:00 A.M. on April 28, they spotted a convoy of eight U.S. Navy LSTs heading south, escorted by a single Royal Navy warship. It was Convoy T-4, carrying GIs from the 1st Engineer Special Brigade to Slapton Sands, where they would land behind the 4th Division—just as they were supposed to do on D-Day on Utah Beach. Rumors had circulated at Allied headquarters that the enemy's speedy torpedo boats had come out of Cher-

Force U: Exercise Tiger, April 28, 1944

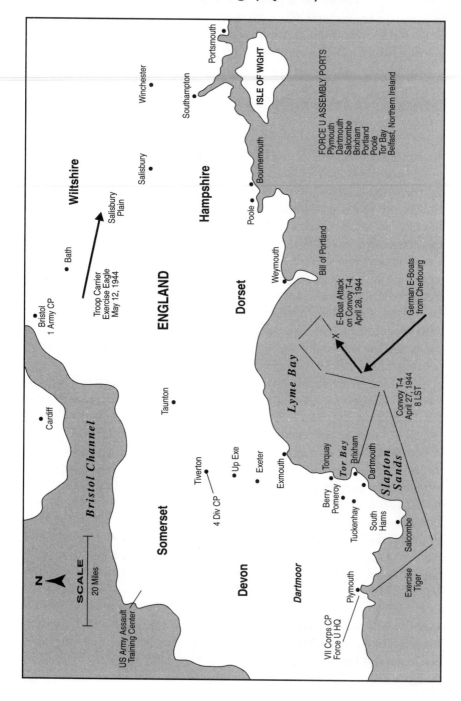

bourg and were on the prowl that night, and several peculiar radar contacts had hinted that that rumor was true. Nevertheless, only HMS *Azalea,* a tiny Royal Navy corvette with a top speed of just fifteen knots, escorted Convoy T-4 toward Slapton Sands. A second escort, the more nimble destroyer HMS *Scimitar,* had recently suffered a collision and was in Plymouth undergoing repairs. A replacement escort, HMS *Saladin,* had been sent out to T-4, but it had not arrived by the time the *Schnellboote* announced their presence with flares and crackling gunfire.

For *Azalea* to protect its flock of eight American LSTs was like a mother sheep trying to protect its lambs from a pack of hungry wolves. It could not be done. By the time *Azalea* realized anything was amiss and had turned to deal with the threat, the *Schnellboote* had brazenly closed to point-blank range, unleashed salvos of torpedoes and barrages of gunfire, and disappeared. *Azalea* did not have an opportunity to fire a single shot, and even had it done so, it would not have been able to stop the enemy attack.

Oberleutnant Günther Rabe
Schnellboot Captain, German Kriegsmarine
Shortly before 0200 [April 28] we saw in the southeast indistinct shadows of a long line of ships that we did not immediately identify as LSTs. . . . At 0207 [after firing two torpedoes] we saw that we had hit the target [LST-507]. Fire was spreading from bow to stern rapidly, and a dense cloud of smoke rose from the ship.

The *Schnellboote* were nearly invisible in the darkness—only a few witnesses actually saw them—but the destruction they inflicted was obvious to all. Two LSTs packed with 1st Engineer Brigade soldiers were turned into flaming wrecks and later sank. A third LST was badly damaged but managed to make it back to Dartmouth, looking as if something had smashed it with a giant hammer. The loss of three LSTs, which had already been in short supply, was a blow to the Allies. But far worse was the loss of life. The *Schnellboote* attack killed about 550 U.S. Army soldiers and 200 U.S. Navy sailors, and injured about 300 more. Two U.S. Army companies, the 3206th Quartermaster Service Company and the 557th Quartermaster Railhead Company, were nearly annihilated, leaving only a few dazed survivors, men who at one time had considered themselves fortunate to be members of outfits that were not expected to fight in the front line. But on April 28, 1944, Lyme Bay was itself the front line, and it could be again during the actual D-Day invasion.

LST-511
"Report of Action 28 April 1944," May 3, 1944
First heard were the [*Schnellboote*] motors, which were initially reported to be an airplane, as it sounded much like one. . . . The boat approached at about 40 knots on a course heading from port to starboard, passing directly in front of the ship by no more than 15 yards. At this point none of our guns were able to depress sufficiently to fire on it. . . . The boat then disappeared from view. No description of the craft can be given due to the darkness of the night and its coloring. [*Schnellboote* were sometimes painted black.] Only the wake and its gunfire were seen.

Lt. Cmdr. George Geddes
Captain, HMS Azalea, *Action report, April 28, 1944*
At approximately 0210 tracer was observed being fired to port by an LST. "Action Stations" was sounded, *Azalea* closed the convoy, but nothing further was observed and no contacts were obtained. At approximately 0215 an LST in the rear of the convoy [LST-507] was torpedoed and set on fire and tracers were fired by LSTs to starboard. Within a minute or two a second LST was torpedoed and set on fire. *Azalea* zig-zagged down the starboard side of the convoy. I was uncertain from which side the convoy was attacked. . . . During the time *Azalea* was on the starboard beam, tracer was fired across my bows by an LST, and the convoy was beginning to scatter.

For a while, the Allied military chiefs fretted that some of the missing soldiers and sailors, a few of whom knew Overlord plans and may even have been carrying top secret papers, may have been picked up out of the water—alive or dead—by the enemy. In that event, Exercise Tiger would be remembered not as an ordinary military disaster, but as a calamity of ruinous proportions to the Allied cause, for the Germans could well have been the lucky recipients of an intelligence bonanza almost unparalleled in the history of warfare. However, as more and more bodies were recovered from Lyme Bay and staffs made sense of what had transpired that terrible night, planners' anxiety that the invasion plan had been compromised slowly subsided. That the enemy in all probability had not gained any vital D-Day secrets was reassuring; but if they had managed to deal such a devastating blow to Exercise Tiger with just a few *Schnellboote,* what did Rommel have in store on D-Day?

If the U.S. Army and Navy needed to practice landing troops on Utah Beach, the army air force's IX Troop Carrier Command had an even more pressing need to rehearse its D-Day role. No one doubted that most of Troop Carrier's C-47 crews were well trained and high-spirited, but none had participated in an operation as vast and momentous as the airborne invasion of Normandy — in fact, the majority had not seen any combat at all. To carry out this operation correctly, navigation, timing, and tight formation flying at night would have to be mastered. Since nothing at this scale had ever been tried before, Generals Bradley and Collins yearned to know whether the operation was indeed feasible.

Exercise Eagle proved that it was. This Troop Carrier exercise on May 11–12, 1944, which was the most ambitious training flight for airborne movement in World War II, was designed to duplicate as closely as possible IX Troop Carrier Command's challenging D-Day mission. In full darkness, Troop Carrier crews flew tight formations amounting to more than 900 C-47s, including many with attached gliders, following dogleg flight paths across the breadth of England to drop zones marked with lights on Salisbury Plain.

Upon its completion, senior Allied commanders were satisfied that Troop Carrier could indeed carry out such an enormous combat mission; but one element of the exercise diverged from reality in a significant way. It seems that gliders and the men who flew them were so scarce that, according to strict instructions, glider pilots could not perform the risky procedure of nighttime landings in the countryside. Instead, they had to follow the much safer procedure of bringing their aircraft to earth only at airfields designated in orders. To anyone who was supposed to participate in the invasion of Europe by glider, this was an ominous order. If the U.S. Army considered it too dangerous to practice one's craft in a flight exercise, the real thing definitely was not going to be easy.

U.S. Air Force Historical Division
"Airborne Operations in World War II, European Theater," John Warren,
September 1956
The effect of Eagle was to induce a mood of optimism as far as Troop Carrier capabilities were concerned. [Maj. Gen. Paul] Williams [CG, IX Troop Carrier Command], who had already declared that, barring unexpectedly heavy flak or failure by the pathfinders, 90–100 percent of the paratroops in IX Troop Carrier Command's Normandy mission would land in the correct area, was confirmed in his opinion. Even Leigh-Mallory stated that he was highly impressed.

For Troop Carrier air crews, an exercise as grandiose as Eagle was a challenge that had many of the dangers of a real combat mission. That Eagle was carried out with only one accident verified that Troop Carrier's training procedures had indeed been effective. But the one accident that did occur, a midair collision between two C-47s returning to Cottesmore air-field after dropping their paratroopers, cost the veteran 316th Group twelve men, including the group commander, Lt. Col. Burton Fleet, and the leader of one of the 316th's four squadrons, Maj. James Farris.

1st Lt. John Johnson
Pilot, 316th Troop Carrier Group, IX Troop Carrier Command
Major Farris was leading our squadron, the 36th, approaching March [a Cambridgeshire village] where we were to make almost a 180 degree turn to set up our final descent and landing approach at Cottesmore. Suddenly I saw a single aircraft about ten degrees to our right and headed toward us. He appeared to be about 100 feet lower than we were. . . . To my consternation, slowly turning to horror, he continued to climb and was closing fast. Applying full right rudder and full right aileron, I pushed the wheel forward and cut back my engines, rolling downward to the right away from Major Farris. Within two seconds the collision occurred [between Farris's C-47 and another piloted by 1st Lt. Joseph Sharber]. The flash temporarily blinded me. Regaining some vision, I watched burning parts fall all around me. . . . The next morning several of us were driven to the site of the crash. I remember being asked if I could identify one of the bodies, still lying on the ground, naked, with the head missing. I could not.

A MAN CALLED MOON
A cardinal principle of amphibious warfare as practiced by the Americans and British in World War II was that sailors were in charge of all matters related to the movement of soldiers by water, including the ultimate phase of a seaborne invasion: the assault on an enemy-occupied coastline. Army officers often did not submit to this arrangement smoothly and at times attempted to persuade, inveigle, or even bully a naval officer to do what made the most sense from a soldier's point of view. But the rule was clear. Army commanders could not wield unfettered authority over their troops until they set foot on shore. For this arrangement to work, senior army and naval officers had to establish solid bonds and learn to work together effort-lessly, overcoming all of the petty suspicions and rivalries between the services that had persisted for generations. An imminent battle of profound importance to the future of the free world had a way of narrowing these differences to the point of irrelevance, a theme General Collins grasped immediately when he took over command of the VII Corps in February 1944.

The man Collins must get to know intimately was Rear Adm. Don Moon, the U.S. Navy commander of the 865 ships and landing craft known as "Force U," which would convey Collins and his troops to Utah Beach on D-Day. A graduate of the U.S. Naval Academy's class of 1916, in which he ranked fourth, Moon was renowned within the U.S. Navy hierarchy for his brilliance. But those who worked directly with him noticed something else: a solemn, aloof man who commonly labored at his desk eighteen hours per day, a job requirement that his staff did not enjoy.

A factor that contributed to Moon's grim personality was his intimate knowledge of the enemy's aggressive methods of making war. Twice before D-Day, Moon had been involved in episodes disastrous to the Allied cause. The first occurred in the summer of 1942, when a group of U.S. Navy warships under Moon's command had escorted Convoy PQ-17 from Iceland, destined for north Russia. German U-boats and bombers saw to it that most of PQ-17's merchant ships never made it, and there was nothing Moon could do to stop the slaughter. Nearly two years later, the devastating attack on Convoy T-4 during Exercise Tiger by German *Schnellboote* reminded Moon that the enemy would attempt to inflict the same terrible damage to Force U on its way to Utah Beach. A member of Moon's staff recalled that in the aftermath of Exercise Tiger, Moon was called to the flagship of his boss, Rear Adm. Alan Kirk, to explain what had transpired to the unfortunate convoy.

Capt. John Moreno
Staff Officer, Force U, Western Naval Task Force

We went in to see [Rear Adm. Arthur] Struble [Kirk's chief of staff]. He was looking out the porthole and initially didn't even turn around to acknowledge our arrival. A British submarine went by with a broom lashed to the periscope, signifying that she had made a clean sweep during her last patrol. Struble remarked, "Well, I see *somebody* did his duty." Then he turned to Moon with the coldest glance I've ever seen and said, in an unfriendly tone of voice, "All right, Moon, tell me what happened." I think that is when Moon really broke down.

Less than two months after D-Day, onboard his flagship *Bayfield* at anchor in Naples harbor, Moon grabbed a pistol and shot himself through the head.

But that was in the future. Five months before his suicide, Moon was in Algeria planning an amphibious assault against the French Riviera, an operation code-named Anvil that was supposed to take place simultaneously with the Normandy invasion. When, in March 1944, Anvil was postponed, Moon got word to shift to England to take command of Force U. Thus, like everyone else involved in the Utah operation, Moon got a late

"He is certainly pleasant to do business with." Rear Adm. Don Moon, commander of the U.S. Navy's "Force U."
U.S. NAVY, NATIONAL ARCHIVES.

start on invasion planning and did not even set up his headquarters until D-Day was less than three months away. At that critical time, Force U was little more than a figment of someone's imagination. Overlord planners had transmitted to the U.S. Navy high command the number of ships needed to carry out the Utah invasion, but with all the campaigns the Americans were currently carrying out around the world, no one expected it to be easy for the navy to fulfill those requirements. The most alarming deficiency was in warships, which would be tasked to bombard the beach prior to the assault. Without more firepower at his disposal, the troubled Moon worried that Utah Beach could turn into another Gallipoli.

Moon's command post for the next eleven weeks would be Plymouth, a city that the Luftwaffe had been making every effort since 1940 to reduce to rubble—with considerable success. Plymouth's vast harbor and rich maritime heritage made it a perfect place for Moon's headquarters, and in mid-March, the Force U staff set up a command post near the waterfront, close by the steep bluff known as the Hoe, where, according to legend, Sir Francis Drake had calmly played at bowls as frantic messengers announced the imminent arrival of the Spanish Armada. Nearby, too, was the Barbican, the ancient Elizabethan district whence the Pilgrims had commenced their journey to America.

One of Moon's first visitors in Plymouth was General Collins, who befriended the cheerless admiral immediately. They must have made an odd pair: Collins was the celebrated "Lightning Joe," but Moon was hardly the type of man to whom the moniker "Lightning" could be applied. Nothing in Moon hinted to Collins that the admiral would later take his own life. Collins, however, noted one strange thing: On rainy days, Moon wore galoshes to protect his shoes. For a soldier immersed for decades in rough army life, Collins found this puzzling. Nevertheless, Collins noted, "He is certainly pleasant to do business with and is genuinely cooperative in every way"—so cooperative, in fact, that Collins moved VII Corps headquarters 130 miles from Hampshire to Plymouth to be by Moon's side as the details of the upcoming invasion were worked out. If the U.S. Army and Navy must work together to make the Utah invasion work, the operation had gotten off to a good start.

Moon would get his ships—hundreds of them—and despite the trauma of Exercise Tiger, the crews who manned those ships would have a crash course in the next two months in how to invade a beach occupied by an enemy army that was supposedly the world's best. At the end of May 1944, when there was no further time for training, the admirals judged the sailors primed for the great event that was about to occur. Many skeptical sailors did not agree, but that was hardly surprising, given that the Utah operation had been dreamed up only a few months previously. Besides, who could ever be fully ready for an invasion of this magnitude? The sheer size of it, and some good luck, should far outweigh any elements of the invasion plan that were still imperfect. Furthermore, if the Allies could preserve the invasion secret until the last moment, they would have the advantage of catching the Germans by surprise.

For all of Admiral Moon's challenging tasks, he knew he would be judged only by the measure of his ability on D-Day to deliver ground troops to Utah Beach on time and on target. In contrast, for VII Corps commander Collins, the invasion would be only a beginning, as no one expected the Germans to throw their hands up at sunset on D-Day and allow the 4th Division to march inland with impunity. Utah Beach would certainly be tough, but capturing Cherbourg could be tougher. And after that, the total obliteration of the German Army in Normandy and setting out on the road to Berlin would probably be the toughest job of all.

Regardless of their dramatically different perspectives on the current war, the time was rapidly drawing near when Moon's sailors and Collins's soldiers would have to come together to focus all their energies on fulfilling that tricky military operation known as amphibious warfare. To hardly anyone's surprise, General Eisenhower initiated that process in the latter half of May by ordering all troops involved in Operation Overlord to proceed at once to their coastal marshalling areas. For Collins's VII Corps, this meant that the 4th Division and all the diverse units attached to it for the Utah operation must depart their barracks in Devon for the last time and head down to the sea for their ultimate appointments with the navy.

Ike's order instantly triggered the formation of endless convoys of U.S. Army trucks, tanks, and jeeps, which commenced their journeys to the coast, roaring southward along the pastoral country roads of the beautiful South Hams region like freshets gushing downhill to the ocean after a thunderstorm. They passed through thatch-roofed villages seemingly older than Shakespeare, with names like Berry Pomeroy, Tuckenhay, and Up Exe; and as usual, the Ivy Division's infantrymen had to march on foot, burdened with equipment so heavy that the columns looked like battalions of humpbacks. By this stage of the war, if an infantryman was not thoroughly used to lengthy route marches, he didn't deserve to be in the infantry.

If one had to fight a war, this was the time to do it. For months, the distressed Yanks had wondered whether the sun ever made an appearance in England, but the opening of Operation Overlord proved that it indeed did. The South Hams area of Devon was famous for its gentle climate, and its ubiquitous roadside hedgerows had abruptly sprouted Queen Anne's lace, foxglove, and countless other flowers in a variety of colors, releasing fragrances so potent that one could hardly imagine that the incessant columns of vehicles and marching men were heading into combat. By now the GIs had trained so often on the damp and dreary moors that the English countryside no longer had much appeal, but spring had suddenly transformed the landscape into beautiful checkerboard patterns of green and gold—the England that 4th Division men had read so much about but had so far never seen. If the troops must now depart for Normandy, perhaps never to return, this would be the way to remember England.

In the roadside fields, quartermaster outfits had stockpiled war supplies in immense dumps, a sure sign to passing GIs that when the fighting started, they would have sufficient quantities of everything they needed to pummel the enemy into a hasty extinction. How could the worn-out German Army compete with such a display of logistical might? The supplies were heaped into such mountainous piles, however, that most observers thought it inconceivable that the enemy would not figure out what was about to happen.

The invasion for which the 4th Division had prepared for so long was imminent. The Ivy Division men piled by the thousands into their coastal marshalling areas, which would be their homes for . . . who knew how long, with the actual invasion date such a closely guarded secret? During Exercise Tiger, the GIs had resided in these same camps, which they called "sausages" because they looked like links of sausages when their boundaries were drawn on a map. This time, however, the extraordinary security measures practiced in the camps suggested to the men that what was about to happen was no exercise, but a real military operation with profound consequences—so profound that even jovial company pranksters were silenced by the quiet contemplation of their fate.

22nd Infantry, 4th Division
History of the 22nd Infantry, 1945
On May 18 the Regiment moved once more to the marshalling areas of Torquay, Brixham, Plymouth, and Dartmouth. The quarters consisted of tents and only a few frame buildings. All civilians, if found talking to a soldier, were immediately impounded. . . . When the troops were assembled, outgoing mail ceased and all connections with the outer world were terminated. Briefing of all field grade officers began at once. Special maps, photographs, sand tables, and sponge rubber terrain plots were sent down for study and planning. All of these covered the area on the eastern edge of the Cherbourg peninsula from Utah Beach north. While the troops were here, Maj. Gen. Collins, VII Corps commander, came to the marshalling area of the 3rd Battalion and had dinner with Company K, in which he had previously served as a 2nd lieutenant.

For weeks, Eisenhower and his staff had been pondering the day the invasion should be launched, and by early May, they had narrowed the options down to three: June 5, 6, or 7. From Ike's lofty perspective, if D-Day was to work, two natural conditions must coincide: First, there must be a full moon, or close to it, so that the dangers of nocturnal flying would be eased; second, at dawn, the tide off Normandy must be low so that the navy could deposit first-wave assault troops on the beaches below the formidable German obstacle belts, before the rising tide submerged them and made the coxswains' jobs hazardous. After polling his commanders, including Collins, Ike finally selected June 5 as D-Day.

For Force U to fulfill a June 5 appointment off Normandy, it would have to get an early start. Its ships and landing craft were based in southwestern England, some as far away as Belfast, Northern Ireland, and their passage to Normandy would be longer than the armadas heading to the other invasion beaches. Of Force U's twelve convoys, some were so slow that they made headway little faster than a soldier on a routine jog. To make it to Utah Beach at H-Hour, these sluggish convoys would have to depart England in late afternoon on June 3.

Despite the undeniable dangers of the imminent invasion, being locked in tight for more than a week in a marshalling area was about the limit of endurance for the men of the 4th Division. It was therefore a relief when the top brass finally opened the gates on June 1 and ordered the GIs down to the harborsides to embark on the transports that would convey them to Utah Beach. Both soldiers and sailors had already mastered these complex loading procedures in Exercise Tiger, and when their appointed sailing times approached, each of Force U's convoys was ready.

Brig. Gen. Theodore Roosevelt Jr.
Supernumerary General Officer, 4th Division, letter to his wife, Eleanor,
June 3, 1944
Well Bunny Dear [Roosevelt's wife, Eleanor], We are starting out on the great venture of this war, and by the time you get this letter, for better or for worse, it will be history. We are attacking in daylight the most heavily fortified shore in history, a shore held by excellent troops. We are throwing against it excellent troops, well-armed and backed by superb air and good naval support. We are on transports, buttoned up. Our next stop, Europe. . . . The men are crowded below [on USS *Barnett*] or lounging on deck. Very few have seen action. They talk of many things, but rarely of the action that lies ahead. If they speak of it at all it is to wisecrack. . . . Most generals are afraid to battle for what they believe with superiors who hold the power over their advancement. One of the reasons I'm so fond of Tubby Barton is that he is not. He will never, wittingly, let his men down.

War is an endeavor that many people try to forget, but the sight of Force U's steady procession of countless ships leaving Plymouth and other Devon ports on June 3 and 4, 1944, was something that witnesses could never eradicate from their memories. General Bradley echoed the thoughts of thousands when he murmured to his aide, "It's hard to believe that we are really on our way." Admiral Moon faced a daunting task: He had to get 865 ships and landing craft safely across a body of water that in 1944 was one of the most dangerous places in the world. Soon after its convoys entered the open waters of the English Channel, however, Force U's first difficulty derived not from the enemy, but from General Eisenhower. At a staff meeting early on the morning of June 4, a definitive prediction of bad

"We are starting out on the great venture of this war." The 87th Chemical Mortar Battalion of VII Corps loads up for the journey to Normandy under the Royal Albert Bridge, spanning the Tamar River near Plymouth.

U.S. ARMY SIGNAL CORPS, NATIONAL ARCHIVES.

weather for June 5 forced Ike to postpone D-Day by twenty-four hours, to June 6. By that time, however, four of Force U's twelve convoys had already put to sea with strict orders to maintain radio silence until they arrived off Utah Beach.

Moon's staff managed to recall all of the convoys except one. This unfortunate armada, known as Convoy U-2A, amounted to more than one-quarter of Force U's ships. Oblivious to Ike's postponement, it plowed ahead toward Normandy at a steady speed of six knots and by midday on June 4 had covered more than 125 miles. Moon sent a speedy destroyer, USS *Forrest,* to catch U-2A and bring it back home; and just to make sure, a British admiral in Portsmouth sent over a scout plane to signal the convoy to turn back. It worked, but in the words of a U.S. Navy action report, "Had this not been done, it was possible that the force would shortly have been detected by the enemy's radar, and this would most probably have increased his vigilance for the next few days."

The saga of Convoy U-2A was only beginning. If the invasion was to take place on June 6 as Eisenhower had ordered, U-2A would not have time to return to its home base of Plymouth. Instead, it would have to seek shelter from the rough Channel weather in nearby Portland harbor, currently reserved for Force O, the Omaha Beach invasion fleet. But fuel, not shelter, was the real problem. For Convoy U-2A's 247 vessels to reach Utah Beach before dawn on June 6, most would have to be refueled, and the Force U staff was frantic that Portland would have neither adequate facilities nor fuel to shoulder this immense extra burden in the short interval before U-2A would have to sail again. If Force U could not reach Utah Beach in time, Ike would again have to postpone the entire D-Day operation by another twenty-four hours. That would be a blow to Admiral Moon's pride that would exceed even the Exercise Tiger fiasco.

Convoy U-2A would have a respite of no more than about four hours in Portland, and if the invasion was to take place on June 6, a lot of work would have to be done in a hurry. According to an official U.S. Navy report, it was Adm. John Hall, the U.S. Navy commander of Force O, who, by remaining on the telephone nearly constantly over that critical four-hour period with Royal Navy authorities on Portland Bill, "somehow achieved the impossible" and, with the exception of eight or nine vessels, got Convoy U-2A to sea again just a little bit late. Thanks to Hall and the Royal Navy, Force U was back on track again. According to Moon's official action report, this accomplishment "was close to a miracle."

Crossing the English Channel southward to Normandy was supposed to be the toughest part of Moon's task, but compared with Convoy U-2A's missed recall order it turned out to be easy. All of Moon's sailors assumed that the farther Force U sailed away from the English coast, the greater the chance they would stumble into a hornet's nest. Moon's route to Normandy would pass straight through a minefield in which, according to Allied intelligence, the enemy had planted naval mines by the thousands. Furthermore, as Force U approached Normandy, German radar stations would surely detect it, and when they did, it would not be long before the same dreaded *Schnellboote* that had inflicted so much harm during Exercise Tiger would suddenly make an appearance. Moon's fleet was particularly vulnerable in this regard, because it was the westernmost of the five Allied invasion fleets and therefore was closest to the enemy naval base at Cherbourg. If Force U was to avoid attack, the Germans must be caught unawares—a possibility that seemed remote, given the enemy's reputation.

U.S. Navy

"The Invasion of Normandy," U.S. Naval Forces Europe, administrative history, 1945

On the night of 5/6 June nothing particularly disturbed the normal routine of the German Naval Group Commander West, Admiral [Theodor] Krancke, until well after midnight. At about 1 AM on the morning of June 6, he was informed that the BBC had broadcast an announcement that the invasion would be launched very soon. Krancke assumed that it was "hardly likely that the invasion would be announced in advance over the radio," and made no further disposition of his forces. At 0130 the paratroop landings near the Orne were reported to him. This induced him to put his [forces] on alert, but he still did not consider a large landing probable. At 0200 large vessels were reported to seaward of Port-en-Bessin. This, together with further reports of airborne landings, at last persuaded Krancke that a sizeable operation was in progress.

It was too late. By the time the Germans realized what was going on, Allied transports were already anchoring off the Normandy coast, protected by a thick screen of warships the enemy could never hope to penetrate. If the *Schnellboote* attempted to sortie regardless of the Allies' show of strength, American and British warships and aircraft would pounce on them at dawn like hungry lions on a herd of antelope.

Lt. Gen. Lewis Brereton

Commander, U.S. Ninth Air Force, diary, June 5, 1944

The stupidity of the enemy is simply incredible. Throughout the last 24 hours there has been no enemy reconnaissance of the shipping areas. . . . During this time hundreds of ships left ports in the west of England, and some of them were in the Channel and headed for the invasion coast when they were ordered to turn back.

SILENT KILLERS

If Field Marshal Rommel favored one weapon above all others, it was the mine. He had employed them on land by the hundreds of thousands in North Africa, and in 1944, he ambitiously intended to swell that number into the tens of millions. Since the anticipated Allied invasion of northwest Europe must come by sea, Rommel resolved to add sea mines to his repertoire. In truth, according to Rommel, sea mines would be the Germans' first line of defense, inert sentinels of the French coast that would never sleep and, unlike humans, could never be caught by surprise.

Had the German Navy been able to carry out this plan with abundant resources, unfettered by Hitler's customarily irrational whims, dozens of Allied transports and warships could have been sunk or damaged during the cross-Channel trip. This effect could have been appreciably magnified, perhaps to the extent of crippling the Allied invasion armada, had Hitler allowed his admirals to use "pressure" mines, new German wonder weapons that were activated with devastating effect by the change in water pressure triggered by the passing of enemy vessels overhead. Pressure mines were proclaimed by their inventors as unsweepable, a fact that Allied navies soon learned was true. Ultimately, however, German sailors guarding the Normandy coast would get no pressure mines, as Hitler would not risk the chance that one could fall into Allied hands intact before the invasion. The best the German Navy could do to help out Rommel was to lay a belt of their more conventional sea mines in the English Channel and Strait of Dover starting in March 1944. Any Allied invasion fleet heading for Normandy or the Pas de Calais would have to traverse this barrier.

Most of Rommel's overly ambitious schemes for the defense of northwest Europe were compromised by factors beyond his control, and naval mines were no exception. Although solid historical evidence pertaining to the German mining effort in the English Channel is still scanty sixty years after D-Day, ironically the Germans themselves appear to have been responsible for neutralizing their own mine barrier by setting deactivation timers on their mines for late May or early June 1944, thereby rendering most of the mines harmless by the time the Allies embarked for Normandy. In retrospect, such a tactic appears senseless, but German admirals apparently held concerns that the minefield would seriously obstruct their own naval movements and prevent their *Schnellboote* and U-boats from undertaking future offensives against Allied shipping in the Channel. If the Allied invasion did not cross the English Channel by June 1, the Germans erroneously surmised, it probably would not come in that locale at all.

Later, some Allied sailors hypothesized that the enemy's mine barrier was neutralized not by deactivation timers, but by the impact over a two- or three-month period of the Channel's notoriously volatile currents, which severed mines from their mooring cables and caused them to drift clear of potential shipping lanes. However, in a 1946 interview with Allied interrogators, Vice Adm. Friedrich Ruge, Rommel's chief naval advisor, demurred. The German minefield failed to impede the Allied invasion fleets, Ruge declared, simply because "comparatively few mines were laid before [D-Day]. When the invasion was felt to be imminent, it was no longer possible to do much in this respect."

Whatever the truth may have been concerning the state of the German minefield in the Channel on June 5, 1944, it turned out to be nothing more than a nuisance to the immense Allied convoys that had to traverse it en route to Normandy. Still, Moon and all the other admirals guiding their fleets across the Channel on the day before the invasion could not have known that. They had to assume that what Allied intelligence had told them about the enemy's formidable field of sea mines was true. Moon knew that these mines could wreak havoc on Force U on a scale that would make the loss suffered in Exercise Tiger seem insignificant in comparison. Like all American and British admirals in charge of Overlord invasion fleets, therefore, Moon took extraordinary precautions to avoid mine damage.

Seventy-seven minesweepers, thirty-two of them American, the rest British and Canadian, would precede Moon's convoys, clearing enemy mines and marking safe routes with buoys illuminated in colors distinctive to Force U. The real challenge for the minesweepers would come after Force U had turned south from the English coast toward Normandy. The worrisome enemy mine barrier lay dead ahead, and to transit it, the plan called for Force U to conform to two narrow corridors, one for fast ships, the other for slow ones. These corridors must be absolutely cleared of enemy mines or disaster could result.

Admiral Moon's inclination to worry was surely accentuated when he learned what happened to the minesweeper USS *Osprey* at 5:57 P.M. on June 5.

U.S. Navy Mine Squadron 7, Force U
War diary, 1757 hours, June 5, 1944

USS *Osprey* [Lt. Charles Swimm, captain] was struck by an underwater explosion, under forward engine room, explosion is believed to be from a moored contact mine. Position 50° 12.9N, 01° 20.4W—about 35 miles south of the Isle of Wight. USS *Chickadee* came alongside *Osprey* to assist. Fire that broke out onboard *Osprey* was under control in 3 to 5 minutes and extinguished in 10 minutes. . . . In view of list and irreparable damage and lack of watertight integrity, as a result of the blast, the order to abandon ship was given at 1815. *Chickadee* took all survivors onboard. [Casualties were six dead, twenty-nine wounded.]

The loss of the *Osprey,* a veteran of the North African invasion and one of the U.S. Navy's most venerable sweepers, occurred in daylight twenty miles north of the alleged position of the enemy's minefield. If enemy mines were already demonstrating their potency before Moon's ships had

Force U: Passage to Normandy, June 5, 1944

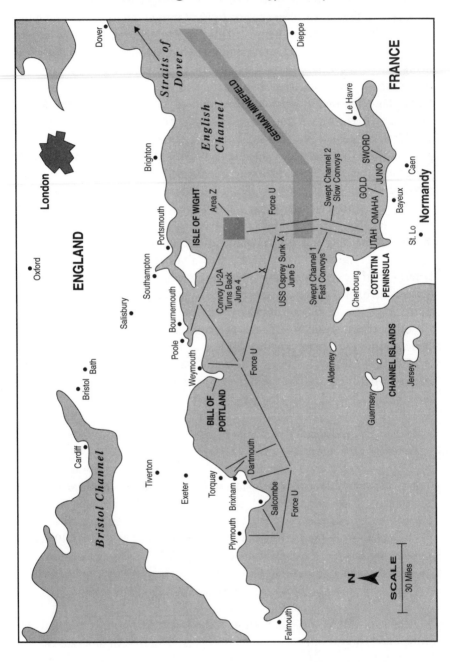

even approached the dangerous zone, what would happen when the sweepers plunged into the belt as darkness fell?

Happily for Moon, the answer to that question was . . . nothing. Moon's chief minesweeping officer, Cmdr. M. H. Brown of the Royal Navy, led a group of British sweepers into the supposed minefield shortly after dark and noted in a report, "As the Lady Godiva of the party who had to lead the parade, I felt remarkably naked at this time." For the remainder of June 5, the astonished Brown encountered not a single enemy mine in the danger zone, nor anyplace else for that matter. In the end, *Osprey* was the first and only Allied vessel lost as a result of mines in the cross-Channel passage. For Moon, this was indeed a relief; but on D-Day, Moon's mine worries would suddenly be rekindled by an unexpected band of deadly German mines just off Utah Beach that lay directly across the lanes American landing craft must follow to reach the shore. Moon did not yet realize it, but those mines would trigger the supreme crisis of his career.

IN HARM'S WAY

Operation Overlord depended on perfect timing, and that challenging requirement prompted thousands of nervous glances at clocks and watches among the Allied soldiers, sailors, and airmen who began to carry out the invasion on the night of June 5, 1944. The clocked ticked on, and finally it was midnight: D-Day—the day for which these men had focused their lives over the past several months—had arrived.

The main body of Force U carefully followed the paths swept through the enemy's mine belt by the ever-vigilant minesweepers. No trouble yet—but the next stop was Utah Beach. Unlike Moon and Collins, most of the sailors of Force U and the soldiers embarked on its ships had never heard a shot fired in anger. However, as Moon's vessels anchored off Utah Beach starting at about 2:30 A.M., there were immediate and obvious reminders to all that a lot of good men would not live to see another sunset, for intense German antiaircraft fire had started to burst on the western horizon. The greatest airborne operation in history had apparently begun just a few miles away; and if that operation did not work, regardless of how well Moon and Collins did their jobs, an aggressive enemy could seal off Utah with little difficulty.

There were little more than six hours of darkness in Normandy at this time of year, and if Force U wished to take position off Utah covered by night's veil, it would have to move fast. The plan assigned every one of Moon's 800-plus warships, transports, and landing craft to an offshore location, specified as precisely as the starting positions of pieces on a chessboard, and virtually all of those vessels managed to find their designated spots with little difficulty and, remarkably, no interference from the enemy. That Admiral Moon had accomplished the first stage of his Overlord task was announced by the roar of dozens of anchor chains through hawseholes as his ships took position for the amazing event that was about to occur.

If Moon's ships were chess pieces, then his four large troop transports were his kings, for if the enemy could destroy them, the game was over. *Barnett, Bayfield, Joseph Dickman,* and the British *Empire Gauntlet* were so vital to the upcoming task that Overlord orders dictated that each ship must anchor more than twelve miles off Utah Beach, out of range of the formidable coastal defense guns that the enemy had deployed so profusely throughout the Cotentin Peninsula. In total, the four transports embarked close to 5,000 troops of the 4th Division and its attached units, and the bulk of those GIs were scheduled to land within the invasion's first ninety minutes. Furthermore, *Bayfield* was Moon's flagship as well as Collins's VII Corps and Barton's 4th Division command posts. A lucky hit by a heavy German shell could kill hundreds of GIs, paralyze the invasion's army-navy nerve center, and deal the assault a fatal blow from which it could not recover; and therefore Moon and Collins would display no imprudence in this instance. But the seasick GIs who would soon be forced to travel three hours or more to Utah Beach on the Channel's famously rough waters, packed like cattle into diminutive landing craft, perhaps wished that their commanders would be a little more bold and anchor the transports closer inshore.

If the invasion was to succeed, Allied warships must sooner or later follow the adage of John Paul Jones and "go in harm's way." A group of eighteen vessels under the command of Rear Adm. Morton Deyo held orders to do exactly that. Deyo's staff had pored over air photographs of the Cotentin and identified more than fifty targets on the east coast that were worthy of Allied attention: heavy guns in concrete casemates, pillboxes, machine-gun nests, flak towers, and more. Planners had drawn up explicit orders for each ship to engage one or more of those targets starting at 5:50 A.M., the earliest moment when there would be sufficient light to open fire with precision. The first waves of the 4th Division would be touching down on Utah only forty minutes later, so the "beach drenching" that had been discussed so frequently during planning could hardly be achieved in so short a time. In the Pacific, naval bombardments of much greater length had accomplished little, and the Germans were considerably more skilled than the Japanese in building fortifications. Orders were orders, and at the very least, the naval bombardment would lift the morale of those infantrymen who were about to enter France.

"A grand seigneur.*" Rear Adm. Morton Deyo (on right), commander of Force U's naval bombardment group, standing with Gen. Dwight Eisenhower and Rear Adm. Alan Kirk.* U.S. NAVY, NATIONAL ARCHIVES.

The fifty-seven-year-old Deyo had graduated in the Naval Academy's class of 1911, five years ahead of his current boss, Admiral Moon. One of his fellow admirals described Deyo as a *grand seigneur*—a great gentleman—whose courtliness and intellect were celebrated throughout the fleet. Deyo's bombardment group was a melting pot. It encompassed the battleship USS *Nevada*; five cruisers, including three from the Royal Navy; ten destroyers; a nineteen-year-old Dutch gunboat, HNMS *Soemba*; and the ancient British monitor *Erebus,* a curious crossbreed vessel with a hull little bigger than a destroyer, but packing the biggest weapons in Force U: two 15-inch guns mounted on a forward turret so lofty that it seemed as if the ship would tip over from too much topside weight.

But Deyo's most notable ship was surely *Nevada,* which had gained immortality as the only U.S. Navy battleship to get under way during the infamous Pearl Harbor attack. The crew of *Nevada,* which was tied up just behind USS *Arizona* on Battleship Row, hastily cut her loose from her moorings as the devastation produced by the surprise Japanese air raid unfolded around them, including the obliteration of the unfortunate *Arizona*. Crippled by an enemy torpedo hit, *Nevada* had plodded down the channel toward the harbor exit, but several bomb hits cut her effort short. *Nevada*'s crew had then purposely run her aground to prevent her from blocking the channel. In 1942, Adm. Chester Nimitz had at first considered writing her off, but then decided that repairs and a full overhaul were worthwhile. The work took more than a year, but in spring 1943, *Nevada* rejoined the fleet for the Aleutian Islands campaign; and now, against a new enemy, she was about to commence her third battle.

At about 5:15 A.M., apprehensive German defenders in their coastal pillboxes peered out to sea in the gloomy predawn light and promptly discerned what they were about to receive. They could not possibly stop it, but nevertheless they would try. At about 5:30, their heavy batteries opened fire on the Allied ships, seemingly so numerous that the Germans did not have enough shells to engage them all. But the Germans were good shooters, and near misses set off enormous geysers of foaming white seawater near the cruisers USS *Tuscaloosa*, USS *Quincy,* and HMS *Black Prince*. Ultimately, however, the Germans accomplished nothing except to induce the Allied warships to initiate their coastal bombardment at 5:36, fourteen minutes early.

U.S.S. *Quincy*
Heavy cruiser CA-71, Bombardment Group, Force U, Action report,
June 6, 1944
At 0452 anchored in position in fire support area in 10 fathoms of water. No mines were encountered, and it is believed that surprise was complete. The minesweepers did an excellent job of buoying the channels. At 0530 the ship was taken under fire by shore battery 13A. [First Army intelligence reports designated 13A as four 105-millimeter guns at Fontenay-sur-Mer; but *Quincy* was probably under fire from the much more formidable 210-millimeter guns at Crisbecq, one mile southeast of Fontenay.] Four [enemy] salvos landed 2,000 to 2,500 yards short. . . . At 0604 5-inch battery fired 464 rounds at Targets 70 and 72 [German strongpoints on the shoreline at Utah Beach]. At 0550, main battery commenced fire on Target 20, artillery headquarters; fired 48 rounds.

To the GIs who were about to land in the first wave, any display of force that might hurt the enemy would be encouraging, and the sight of Deyo's eighteen warships crashing into action had precisely that effect.

Force U: Utah Beach Bombardment, June 6, 1944

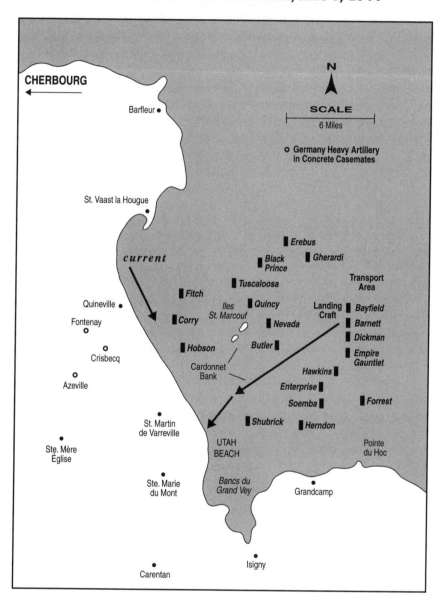

Foot soldiers had been trained for close-range warfare, and the vast panorama of war at sea was new and impressive. When they observed the warships go into action, the troops were invariably surprised by the long interval between the sight of a gun opening fire and the thunderous reverberation produced by that blast; but when the bombardment reached a crescendo, in truth those aftershocks came so fast that they meshed into one continuous, booming roar. Particularly astonishing to the soldiers in close proximity to *Nevada* or *Erebus* was the discharge of one of their mammoth 14- or 15-inch guns, a blast so powerful that the resulting concussion of air seemed like a physical force almost strong enough to overturn passing landing craft. With effects such as these on nearby friendly troops, what would the Germans feel like on the receiving end? One could only guess; but the 4th Division troops set to land on Utah Beach within the hour were about to find out.

Maj. Gerden Johnson
Executive, 1st Battalion, 12th Infantry, 4th Division
We were running about 850 yards astern of a battleship, and as I asked the skipper which it was, *Nevada* fired a broadside at the coast. The concussion of those naval guns was so great that our little LCI heeled over perilously near to the water. The skipper was white; my men were white and green. I was scared skinnier than my normal 135 pounds.

Capt. D. A. Farquharson-Roberts
Royal Marines, gun captain, HMS Erebus
The fire bell rang out and the left gun fired, to be followed after 30 seconds by the right gun. We could fire four rounds per minute. . . . The 43rd round was rather noteworthy. The left gun was at the ready and I was looking through the viewing slit as it fired. I saw at once some splashes ahead of the ship and reported to the bridge that we were under fire. I was told this was not so and to have a look at the turret. I did, and to my utter amazement the crew of both guns were reeling around dazed. I yelled "Still!" and ordered the right gun to cease fire. . . . The initial shock of discharge had caused the shell to explode in the barrel, hence the splashes I had seen. The force of the charge had forced the bits of the shell out of the barrel. Thank God the breech had held. . . . The captain [Capt. J. S. Colquhoun] then reported to the force commander that we were no longer capable of firing.

Every sailor who manned a gun off Utah Beach on D-Day was primed to use it, and on June 6, 1944, there would be no repeat of the Exercise Tiger fiasco. Any German vessel or aircraft that dared to approach the fleet would be blasted out of the water or sky. Given the gunners' eagerness to use their weapons, however, one of the most notable of Force U's many D-Day achievements was its fire discipline. On two occasions on D-Day morning, large bodies of friendly aircraft passed close by or directly over the fleet, and trigger-happy gunners on Moon's ships could easily have shot many of them down—but held their fire.

In the first instance, hundreds of Troop Carrier C-47s passed overhead at very low altitudes en route to their English airfields after dropping paratroopers and towing gliders into the Cotentin to open the invasion shortly after midnight. Based on the disastrous fratricide incident that had occurred in the July 1943 Sicily airdrop, Troop Carrier crews had good reason to be uneasy on D-Day, especially as they approached Force U in the dark, flying in the same direction that German bombers might take if they attacked the fleet. However, despite a strong temptation to use their weapons, a Force U action report noted, "All hands had been warned, so none [of the C-47s] was taken under fire."

The second occurrence took place at about 6:10 A.M., when nearly 300 Ninth Air Force B-26 Marauder bombers came roaring down the coast of the Cotentin from the north at less than 5,000 feet, aiming to soften up the enemy's Utah Beach defenses with a deadly cascade of bombs. By the time the Marauders arrived, the sun was up, the bombers were visible and recognized as friendly, and their intentions were immediately obvious to all. Again Force U's eager antiaircraft gunners held their fire, a notable display of restraint for which the anxious bomber crews were thankful.

Careful preinvasion briefings and the simple expedient of painting the fuselages and wings of the C-47s and Marauders with alternating white and black stripes had provided the shipboard antiaircraft gunners with sufficient evidence that the swarms of aircraft were not German. There would be no repeat of Sicily here.

MARAUDER MEN

By 1944, any sensible Allied commander would have agreed with the sentiment expressed by a new U.S. Army Air Force manual: "The gaining of air superiority is the first requirement for the success of any major land operation." By June of that year, that superiority had certainly been achieved, and the Allies would carry out the Normandy invasion with the confident expectation that the enemy air force would be powerless to interfere. The air battle over Europe had been won prior to D-Day, thanks to the efforts of RAF Bomber Command and the U.S. Eighth and Ninth Air Forces, which had regularly pummeled Germany's war industry and inflicted grievous losses on Luftwaffe fighters. By the time Eisenhower was ready to launch Operation Overlord, the German Air Force was stretched so thin that even Hitler harbored little hope that airpower alone could deter the Allied invasion.

Every facet of the Overlord plan depended on air superiority. Had the Allies not gained dominance of the skies over northwest Europe, the Germans would have detected their foe's strategic intent much earlier than they actually did, and indeed might have been able to forestall the invasion by launching their bombers against Allied landing craft, packed tightly into ports along England's south coast and highly vulnerable to air attack. Given that Eisenhower was chronically short of landing craft, powerful German air attacks against Allied shipping would certainly have reduced the Allies' transport capacity sharply.

All seamen agreed that the phase of the invasion in which the Allies were at most risk was the Channel crossing. Ships confined to narrow channels, strung out in columns of immense length, were highly vulnerable to torpedo and bomb attacks by German aircraft; but thanks to Allied air superiority, those attacks never materialized. Allied dominance of the air also enabled the Americans to launch nearly 1,000 C-47s in the Cotentin airborne operation with little fear that enemy night fighters could penetrate defenseless Troop Carrier formations and shoot the C-47s down, paratroopers and all, with impunity.

One of the most significant consequences of the Allies' air superiority over Normandy was the airmen's freedom to support their infantry brethren who must storm the five invasion beaches. Allied airmen did not normally look favorably upon the ground commanders' periodic attempts to use aircraft as supplements to conventional artillery, for conventional air doctrine proclaimed that there were much better ways to use aircraft to help win ground battles. But D-Day was an exception; and even those senior air force officers passionately devoted to bringing down Germany with airpower alone agreed that Allied heavy bombers could be momentarily diverted to aid ground troops in establishing footholds in Normandy. In this war and the last, the Germans had nearly perfected their ability to make fortifications resistant to their opponents' artillery, and if the Allies wished to dent the Germans' formidable coastal defenses of Normandy, Monty and Bradley resolved to call upon Allied bombers to strike the enemy on a massive scale immediately prior to the assault. The senior generals considered the inclusion of airpower in the "beach-drenching" procedure as particularly vital, because the naval bombardments of the five invasion beaches were of comparatively short duration.

The preinvasion air bombardment could be the key factor that transformed an otherwise bloody assault into a walkover. But could the bombers take out pinpoint targets as small as machine-gun nests? For years, American airmen had boasted about precision bombing, even from high altitudes, but the reality of air combat in western Europe had proved that perfect bombing accuracy was virtually impossible to achieve. Had precision bombing really worked, German coastal defense targets in Normandy, all clearly identified on air photographs, should have been easy for bombardiers to hit. To hit them, however, those bombardiers had two key prerequisites: daylight and decent weather.

The Overlord plan hinged on initiating the invasion as soon as possible after dawn so that the Allies could maximize the number of troops brought ashore on D-Day in preparation for the enemy's inevitable violent response. Accordingly, American bombers would be forced to make difficult nighttime assemblies over England and undertake their attacks on the enemy's coastal defenses in an early-dawn light so dim that pilots could scarcely pick out their targets. Furthermore, conditions were overcast throughout much of Normandy on the morning of June 6, a remnant of the stormy weather of the previous two days, and bombing from above that overcast would not be easy.

What seemed like an uncomplicated aerial attack against German beach defenses was in actuality exceptionally difficult—and what happened in the skies over Omaha Beach on D-Day proved it. For the Omaha mission, the Eighth Air Force dispatched about 450 B-24 Liberator heavy bombers with orders to strike the enemy's coastal positions shortly after dawn, just minutes before the first assault waves would land, when friendly landing craft were only a few thousand yards offshore. A deadly deluge of thousands of bombs would have rained down on the stunned defenders had the mission worked. But it did not work, despite the Liberators' masterful nocturnal assembly in the skies over England and their timely arrival over their targets. The B-24s approached Omaha from the north, perpendicularly, directly over the invasion fleet, above a cloud layer that completely blanketed the earth. At the Liberators' 16,000-foot altitude, they would be forced to bomb blindly through the overcast. Under those conditions, bombing errors could cause considerable friendly casualties, and consequently the airmen had orders to delay the release of their bombs from five to thirty seconds after passing over their targets. Of the thousands of bombs released, virtually none landed anywhere near Omaha Beach. The mission accomplished nothing, and in its aftermath, the airmen blamed the ground commanders for

Ninth Air Force: Utah Beach Bombardment, June 6, 1944

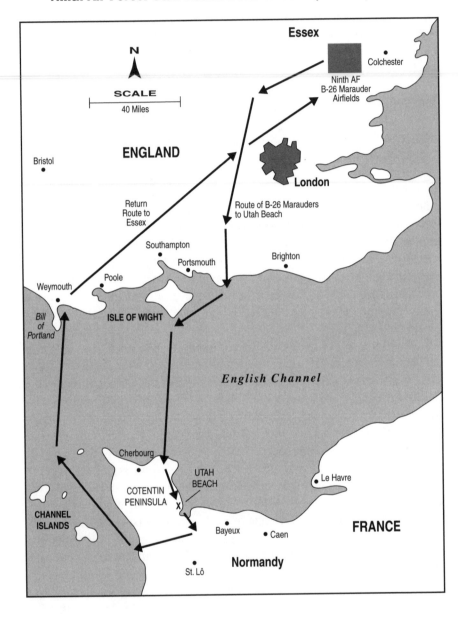

developing an invasion plan with such a close margin for safety, and the ground commanders blamed the airmen for their timidity. That something had gone terribly wrong was obvious to the first-wave troops on Omaha Beach, who had been promised unparalleled levels of air support.

In stark contrast, the Ninth Air Force simultaneously carried out a highly successful bombing mission over Utah Beach with much fewer—and smaller—bombers, following wholly different attack procedures than the Eighth used over Omaha. This achievement was especially impressive because on Utah, the chance of inflicting accidental casualties on friendly troops was far higher than at Omaha. The Eighth Air Force's bombardment preceded the Omaha invasion, but in the Cotentin Peninsula, American paratroopers and gliderists were already fighting close behind Utah Beach when the Ninth's B-26s approached their coastal targets. Consequently, Marauder crews fully understood when they dropped their bombs that thousands of American GIs lay somewhere to the west beyond the coast, carrying out their vital D-Day airborne missions. Furthermore, Force U's 865 ships were positioned just east of Utah Beach, and as the B-26s made their bomb runs, hundreds of landing craft packed with assault troops were rapidly approaching the coast. If the B-26 bombardiers did not know their jobs, errant bombs could kill both airborne and amphibious assault troops by the hundreds.

Using the Eighth's heavy bombers to attack pinpoint targets was like using a howitzer on a rifle range: The howitzer might achieve a bull's-eye, but a smaller weapon would do the job better. On Utah, that weapon was the Ninth Air Force's legendary B-26 Marauder medium bomber, which accomplished bombing results on D-Day so obviously superior to what the heavies achieved on Omaha that, in retrospect, General Collins and his VII Corps GIs were exceptionally fortunate that Bradley teamed them for the Normandy invasion not with the Eighth Air Force, but with the Ninth. Unlike the Eighth, which resolved to bring Germany to its knees by destroying its industrial base, the Ninth Air Force existed specifically to support American field armies in the imminent land war in France. It would fulfill this role by knocking out bridges, neutralizing enemy air-fields, cutting rail lines, attacking enemy reinforcements, and dropping bombs directly on German frontline positions. The commander of all Ninth Air Force bombers on D-Day, Brig. Gen. Samuel Anderson, noted that among his airmen, "Enthusiasm was always highest when the mission was in direct cooperation with ground operations."

When in 1939 aeronautical engineers sketched their first blueprints of the B-26 Marauder at the Glenn L. Martin plant in Baltimore, they seemingly envisioned a combat role for their new medium bombers strikingly similar to the mission they would carry out on D-Day at Utah Beach. No one doubted that the Marauder was a cutting-edge design, but the first two years of its existence proved that it was a tough airplane to fly, and even tougher for ground crews to maintain. Early models were frequently over-loaded, and that lapse combined with pilot and ground crew slipups yielded an accident rate high enough that some of its cynical aviators labeled it "The Widow-Maker." A Missouri senator named Harry Truman investi-gated the issue, and in July 1942, he counseled the AAF to halt B-26 pro-duction. The Martin Company waged a dynamic campaign to save its Marauder line, suggesting that most B-26 training crashes were avoidable, and designers added several improvements to 1942 Marauder models.

Martin's persuasive arguments saved the B-26, but still senior air offi-cers could not fathom how the Marauders' medium bombing capability fit into the AAF's repertoire. B-26s had neither the range nor the payload to join with B-17s and B-24s in their effort to destroy German industry with precision bombing from high altitudes; yet early attempts at low-level attacks had yielded inordinately high losses. Eventually the AAF learned that Marauders functioned best when attacking ground targets from an alti-tude of 10,000 to 12,000 feet, a tactic the Martin Company had recom-mended since the aircraft's inception.

According to Ninth Air Force orders, six and a half B-26 bomb groups, a total of 341 aircraft, would participate in the Utah Beach bombardment from 6:09 to 6:27 A.M. on D-Day. Most aircraft were armed with sixteen 250-pound bombs with instantaneous fuses, ordnance that would not form craters upon impact and impede the inland movement of American vehicles once the beach was secured. However, some particularly sturdy German pillboxes required special attention, and therefore sixteen B-26s were loaded with two 2,000-pound "blockbuster" bombs apiece, the heaviest ordnance in the Ninth Air Force's inventory. Even if one of those weapons missed its tar-get, the Germans would not fail to be impressed by its colossal blast.

As every American serviceman in England appreciated in the spring of 1944, D-Day would be so pivotal to the Allied war effort that all partici-pants must perform their duties with extra effort to ensure the operation's success. At Ninth Air Force premission briefings shortly after midnight on June 6, when the astonished Marauder men were finally let in on the D-Day secret, the top brass informed all B-26 units that their upcoming bombing missions were so essential to the success of the Utah Beach inva-sion that they must carry them out even if, as weather reports indicated, fly-ing conditions were poor.

Col. Wilson Wood
Commander, 323rd Bomb Group, Ninth Air Force, premission briefing,
June 6, 1944

This is the day we have all been waiting for—this is it! This is D-Day, and our men will be going ashore. To get ashore, the defenses we are scheduled to attack have to be knocked out. So the order is that we are to go in at any altitude necessary to strike the targets visually and effectively. I repeat: You will go in at any altitude necessary to get the job done. . . . Let's kick the hell out of everything Nazi that's left! [As Wood ended his briefing, a witness noted that "cheers and whistles vibrated through the air."]

The B-26 crews may have reacted enthusiastically to the news of the invasion, but when they assembled on the runways at about 3:00 A.M. near the aircraft that would fly them to Normandy, they knew immediately that this mission would be no milk run. Any time orders dictated that hundreds of aircraft must assemble in the dark in tight formations with nothing but tiny wing lights to warn of the proximity of nearby planes, the lives of men would depend on how well pilots had learned their jobs and their ability to focus intently on the current task. Furthermore, that warning about going in at any altitude to attack was ominous: In the past, when Marauders had bombed from low levels, German antiaircraft fire was deadly. Crews were hardly cheered by hazy intelligence reports detailing expected enemy resistance: "Weak to moderately heavy flak may be encountered."

Takeoff was around 4:00 A.M. Each bomb group, typically consisting of fifty-four Marauders, gathered in the night sky a few thousand feet over Earls Colne, Great Saling, Chipping Ongar, and other Essex airfields about thirty miles northeast of London where the Ninth Air Force's bombers were based. The hazards of a nighttime assembly were demonstrated when two 394th Bomb Group Marauders collided in flight over Boreham, with the loss of all twelve crew members. Nevertheless, by sunrise, hundreds of B-26s had successfully congregated in boxes of eighteen aircraft apiece and were heading south for Normandy. The commander of the 386th Bomb Group, Lt. Col. Sherman Beaty, recalled, "How we ever managed to take off and form fifty-four ships under those conditions, I will never know—but we did." As the Marauders flew out over the English Channel, the aviators caught sight of the spectacle of thousands of ships heading for France, a vision that B-26 airmen with a feel for history surely resolved to relate to their progeny—assuming those airmen survived the war.

The Marauders' carried out their attack on Utah Beach following two entirely different methods than the Eighth Air Force used over Omaha.

First, the B-26s approached their coastal targets parallel to the shoreline, not perpendicular to them as the B-24s did at Omaha. Second, the Marauders attacked their targets from the comparatively low altitudes of 4,000 to 6,000 feet—more than 10,000 feet lower than the B-24s at Omaha, and about half the altitude recommended by the Martin Company for prudent use of its Marauders.

Both procedures put Marauder crews at obvious risk. By following the east coast of the Cotentin to Utah Beach, the Marauders would fly continuously over enemy territory and could be subjected to nearly incessant antiaircraft fire. Furthermore, at those low altitudes enemy ground fire would be both widespread and potentially deadly, as even light machine guns could join in the barrage. That such a flight route was hazardous was obvious to all; but on this day of days, the Marauders must clearly see their enemies, regardless of the risk, in order to destroy them. At such a low height, there would be no cloud cover to obstruct views, and targets should be readily discernible. Perhaps most important of all, bombardiers' anxiety over accidentally hitting friendly troops would be greatly lowered.

Ninth Air Force
Report, "Tactical Bombing of Beach Defenses by IX Bomber Command Marauders," September 1944
The attacking planes should not make a run directly over the assault forces if this can possibly be avoided. On a straight coast, the axis of attack should be parallel to the coast. The danger of bombing the assault forces on a perpendicular attack appears to be great enough to justify an attack parallel to the coast even if this involves passing over a defended area.

On that night in June 1944 when the Allies suddenly appeared in Normandy, any German soldier who spared a moment to ponder the war's outcome knew immediately that Hitler could never win. In the early hours of June 6, dismayed German troops could perceive thousands of Allied aircraft of all types flying with impunity all over the front with no interference whatsoever from the renowned Luftwaffe. Relying on antiaircraft fire alone to stop the horde of Allied planes from reaching their targets was as effective as trying to deter a swarm of angry hornets with a flyswatter.

Despite the Marauders' low altitude and vulnerable flight path, German ground fire brought down only two. One 323rd Bomb Group pilot, 2nd Lt. John Moench, noted: "It was the first time I encountered tracer fire from the ground. The damn things come up at you and you swear: every one of those is going to hit me." Forty-six more B-26s failed to bomb Utah as a result of mechanical problems or their crews' inability to locate their proper targets on the first pass—and Ninth Air Force orders specified that B-26s must not make second passes because of fears of midair collisions in the crowded skies over Normandy. Of the 341 B-26s that had set out from England to bomb the beach defenses, 293 dropped their bombs almost exactly on schedule.

Brig. Gen. Theodore Roosevelt Jr.
Supernumerary General Officer, 4th Division, letter to his wife, Eleanor, June 11, 1944
Suddenly we heard the drone of planes [at about 6:10 A.M.], and silhouetted against the colored clouds of dawn, formations of planes swept by and passed toward shore. Flight after flight dropped its bombs on the German emplacements. There'd be a ripple of thunder, blazes of light, clouds of dust, and the planes would pass us again on the way home. One fell by me, flaming like a meteor.

According to a Ninth Air Force study, those 293 Marauders dropped 4,414 bombs on Utah Beach, totaling more than 1 million pounds of explosives. Fifty-nine percent of those bombs detonated within 500 feet of their targets, including 16 percent that were direct hits, or very nearly so. The cascade of bombs from the Marauders raised so much smoke and dust on Utah Beach that Admiral Deyo's bombarding warships momentarily lost sight of their targets, and sailors bringing their landing craft to shore could no longer pick out coastal landmarks, a development that in all probability triggered Force U's mislanding a mile south of its intended beach a short time later. Those were small prices to pay, however, for the demoralizing effect on the German defenders that the B-26 Marauders had provided. As a direct result of the Ninth Air Force success at Utah, the burden of the troops who were about to pour ashore on Utah Beach was greatly eased.

Nobody was calling the Marauders "Widow-Makers" anymore.

Robert M. Snow
Operational research consultant, IX Bomber Command, Ninth Air Force, September 22, 1944
It is difficult to make any comparison of the effectiveness of the bombing on this beach with that of the other beaches. However, it is understood that on the other beaches, many of the bombs fell far behind the beach, and that stiffer resistance was encountered there than on Utah Beach. There is not necessarily a connection between these two facts, if they are facts, but at least they are suggestive.

CHAPTER 4

Night of Nights

ANOTHER LITTLE BIG HORN?

If, as General Bradley asserted, the success of the Utah Beach invasion depended on a simultaneous airborne operation beyond the Cotentin shore-line, he must have been thankful in the spring of 1944 that Gen. Hap Arnold's deployment of abundant Troop Carrier groups to England from the United States would allow him not one, but two American airborne divisions for this vital purpose. True, Air Chief Marshal Leigh-Mallory was definitely cool to this idea, but General Montgomery's support of Bradley had never wavered: The Americans must get their airborne operation if Utah Beach was to be a part of the Overlord invasion plan. Leigh-Mallory, however, had pointed out that Normandy's inscrutable bocage terrain was wholly unsuited for glider operations, a detail that Monty and Bradley could not deny. As a result, in the initial D-Day airborne assault, the vast majority of Troop Carrier C-47s would be devoted to dropping only the parachute echelons of the 82nd and 101st Divisions. Most of the divisions' glider troops would enter the battle later, by both air and sea.

When he had arrived in London in the fall of 1943, Brig. Gen. James Gavin had decried the lack of "vision and boldness" in Overlord's airborne plan as it then existed. By May 1944, however, he could hardly make that criticism. Bradley's initial scheme of airborne operations in the Cotentin on

82nd and 101st Airborne Division Drop Zones

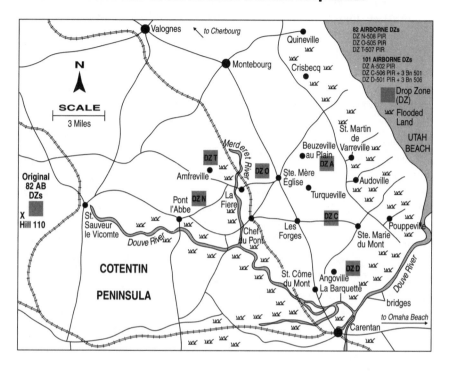

D-Day was probably the boldest airborne operation ever conceived. Indeed, as the Allies unexpectedly learned in late May, it was *too* bold. The First Army plan called for the 101st Airborne to support the 4th Division's landing at Utah, first by seizing the critical causeways leading inland from the coast over the inundated pastures behind the beach, and second by capturing the key crossroads town of Ste. Mère Église. The 82nd Airborne would land fifteen miles to the west in the environs of one of the Cotentin's most dominating heights, known as Hill 110, near the village of St. Sauveur-le Vicomte. Here the paratroopers would seal off the base of the Cotentin Peninsula, thereby isolating the critical port of Cherbourg. Airborne missions didn't come any more challenging than this: The 82nd's drop zones were so far away from Utah Beach that every paratrooper understood that the division would have to hang on without help for several days.

Had this plan actually been carried out, the D-Day history of the 82nd Airborne Division would have been characterized not by the struggles around Ste. Mère Église and the La Fière causeway, but by even tougher fights at St. Sauveur and Hill 110. In retrospect, the 82nd was fortunate that the St. Sauveur plan was abandoned, for in all probability, the isolated division would have been subject to the enemy's habitually prompt and vigorous counterattacks, forcing the airborne troops to fight tenaciously for days just to retain the ground they had seized on D-Day. Indeed, it is conceivable that the Germans would have inflicted the same brutal punishment on the 82nd that they later would wreak on the British 1st Airborne Division in Holland during Operation Market-Garden. During the preparation for that daring September 1944 airborne mission, General Browning would lament, "I think we might be going a bridge too far." Overlord planners were plagued by similar skepticism over the 82nd's risky D-Day mission, and ultimately Bradley did something about it.

For a military plan so scrupulously prepared as Operation Overlord, 82nd Airborne GIs must have been astonished at how radically their D-Day mission changed just ten days before the scheduled invasion date. This change was triggered by the top secret work of cryptographers at Hut 3, Bletchley Park, the old Victorian mansion situated fifty miles outside London, where for years Allied intelligence teams had been decrypting and analyzing intercepted radio messages at the highest levels of the German military command. Bletchley Park's decrypts were so confidential that not a single man in the 82nd, including Ridgway, had any idea that the Allies held such an intelligence edge over the enemy, an edge so vital that it was about to save countless American lives.

On May 24, 1944, Hut 3 decrypted a bombshell from the enemy's high command in France: The German Army's 91st Division, a new outfit that had been stationed in eastern France as recently as late April, had moved to Normandy. This piece of news alarmed those few senior Allied officers, including Bradley, who were privileged to receive Bletchley Park decrypts, for the 91st apparently had deployed directly into that area of the Cotentin where the 82nd Airborne was scheduled to drop on D-Day. Even worse, when Allied air photographs of that locale were developed in late May, they revealed that the new German unit was energetically preparing defenses against Allied airborne landings. As proof, the drop zones near Hill 110, which had formerly been clear, had suddenly sprouted hundreds of wooden poles about ten feet high, known by the Germans as *Rommelspargel*, "Rommel's asparagus," which would make glider landings and parachute drops on those zones exceptionally hazardous.

Bradley ordered Ridgway to change his plans—and fast. For 82nd Airborne troopers, this was a shock. They had been diligently studying their mission for weeks, only to be told at the last minute that an entirely new scheme must be carried out. Harried airborne and troop carrier staffs had to work out hundreds of fresh details in a matter of days, creating lingering doubts in many minds that the invasion's airborne mission would succeed. Was there enough time to formulate workable plans? For such a vital military operation, there had to be.

Brig. Gen. James Gavin
Assistant Division Commander, 82nd Airborne Division, diary,
May 26–27, 1944
Neptune has been changed, and we are now to jump astride the Merderet River with the mission of seizing the crossings, protecting the flanks of the corps, securing a bridgehead over the Merderet, and being prepared to advance to the west to the Douve. Gen. Ridgway was called down to Bristol [First Army headquarters] yesterday and given the new plan. . . . Since we are now dropping much closer to the amphibious troops, our chances of survival are greatly improved. . . . [The next day there was a] meeting of the regimental COs [505th, 507th, 508th Parachute Infantry] at which time the new situation was outlined to them. Lots of work. These damn changes. Complete sets of plans, terrain memory classes, plastic models—all wasted. . . . At this stage of the planning, the new drop looks like a real snafu.

Maj. Gen. J. Lawton Collins
Commander, VII Corps, "Change in Plan for Operation Neptune,"
May 30, 1944

On May 26, 1944 VII Corps received intelligence reports indicating the strength of the enemy had been enhanced in the Cotentin Peninsula, necessitating alterations in the tactical plan for Operation Neptune. . . . The following solution was proposed by the commander, VII Corps: . . . To shift the whole area of operations of the 82nd Airborne eastward, approximately eight miles, compressing its area of operations in close proximity to the 101st Airborne, and likewise compressing the sphere of activity of the 101st, enhancing its mission of securing a bridgehead over the Douve, linking up with V Corps in order to secure a route of supply from Omaha Beach to the VII Corps, should this route be needed. The 82nd would now be dropped astride the Merderet River, one regiment [the 505th] to the east; capture Ste. Mère Église and one strongpoint southwest of Beauzville-au-Plain and seize various crossings of the Merderet and Douve. . . . The 101st would land east and south of Turqueville with its mission unchanged. [During Overlord planning, both airborne divisions were under Bradley's direct command, not Collins's. Bradley had at first proposed a different revision to the airborne plan, but in the end concurred with this scheme suggested by Collins.]

For the men of the 82nd and 101st, changing plans at such a late date was difficult enough; but their troubles would have intensified had they realized that on the day the new airborne plans were circulated, the entire American airborne operation on D-Day had come into question at the highest levels of the Anglo-American command hierarchy. Air Chief Marshal Leigh-Mallory, Ike's chief air officer, had been skeptical of the Cotentin airborne mission for months, and as the commander of Allied tactical air forces in Operation Overlord, he was nominally in charge of all airborne operations. Previously he had expressed compelling arguments that the D-Day mission devised by Bradley in the Cotentin would be extraordinarily risky. In late May, Hut 3's shocking identification of the 91st Division's presence directly astride Troop Carrier air routes into Normandy heightened Leigh-Mallory's reservations considerably. To Leigh-Mallory, Bradley's last-minute changes in the plan made no difference. In the opening stage of the invasion, nearly 1,000 C-47s carrying paratroopers and towing gliders would be overflying terrain packed with Germans, apparently focused on defeating just what Bradley was determined to try.

Air Chief Marshal Sir Trafford Leigh-Mallory
Commander, Allied Expeditionary Air Force, letter to Eisenhower, May 29, 1944

I hesitate to increase your problems at the present difficult time, but I feel I should be failing in my duty to you if I did not let you know that I am very unhappy about the U.S. airborne operations as now planned for the night of D-Day. . . . I have discussed the new [airborne plan] with [Bradley], and have explained to him the very unsatisfactory nature of this operation from the air point of view, in particular that I cannot guarantee the safe arrival of any definite percentage of troops or equipment, and that in my opinion, a large proportion of the force will be lost. [Bradley] stated he was prepared to accept this loss, as he considers this airborne operation of vital importance to the Utah seaborne assault. . . . The factors which cause me concern are as follows: The arrival of a sufficient number of paratroops in a condition fit to fight in the Ste. Mère Église area . . . is stated to be absolutely vital to the beach assault. I consider there is no certainty that even 50% of the force will be effective. . . . [Troop Carrier C-47s] will have to fly across the Cotentin Peninsula from west to east at less than 1,000 feet in full moonlight and over country in which German troops are now known to be concentrated. The early groups may reach their objectives without severe casualties, but later groups . . . are likely to suffer heavily. . . . Whilst it is not my province to advise on the military aspects of the operation, my opinion is that, in view of the confined and small size of the fields and the probability of scattered landings, there will not be sufficient cohesion between the paratroops after landing to overcome the beach defences before the sea assault has to be made. My conclusion, therefore, is that the airborne operation is likely to yield results so far short of what [Bradley] expects and requires that, if the success of the seaborne assault in this area depends on the airborne, it will be seriously prejudiced.

No one disagreed with Leigh-Mallory that the airborne operation was risky—almost everything about Overlord entailed some risk. The significant issue, however, was whether the risks faced by the 82nd and 101st Airborne Divisions were worth the benefits they would yield to the 4th Division's Utah invasion and the VII Corps's subsequent drive to take Cherbourg.

Gen. Dwight Eisenhower
Supreme Commander, Allied Expeditionary Force, letter to Leigh-Mallory,
May 30, 1944
You are quite right in communicating to me your convictions as to the hazards involved, and I must say that I agree with you as to the character of those risks. However, a strong airborne attack in the region indicated is essential to the whole operations and it must go on. Consequently, there is nothing for it but for you, the Army Commander [Bradley] and the Troop Carrier Commander [Maj. Gen. Paul Williams] to work out to the last detail every single thing that may diminish these hazards. It is particularly important that air and ground troops involved in the operation be not needlessly depressed. . . . I am of course hopeful that our percentage losses will not approximate your estimates because it is quite true that I expect to need these forces very badly later in the campaign.

No more changes. D-Day was less than one week away, and now that the planning and training had come to an end, according to Ike the Allies' most important quality, from general to private, was confidence.

Brig. Gen. James Gavin
Assistant Division Commander, 82nd Airborne Division, diary,
May 25–27, 1944
Either this 82nd Division job will be the most glorious and spectacular episode in our history, or it will be another Little Big Horn. There is no way to tell now, but we are going in and we will, I am certain, do a hell of a good job. . . . [Bradley] is still as confident as ever that we will swamp the German. It is difficult to fully share his optimism, although one really wants to.

LIGHTING THE WAY

It was up to Troop Carrier now. The lives of American soldiers, and General Bradley's reputation as a responsible commander, depended on how well Troop Carrier's aviators had learned their jobs. It all came down to depositing 82nd and 101st Airborne paratroopers on or near their Cotentin drop zones before dawn on D-Day in a reasonably compact manner. But this seemingly straightforward task was actually incredibly difficult. Drop zones looked neat on maps, but finding them in the dark, even on a night with a full moon, could challenge even the best pilots and navigators — and maps did not shoot back. Furthermore, from the comparatively low altitude of 700 feet, the Cotentin's jigsaw bocage had a sameness that was utterly baffling. But worst of all, while searching for their murky drop zones, C-47 pilots had to keep a sharp lookout for friendly aircraft: Compact parachute drops required tight wingtip-to-wingtip formations, demanding constant pilot attention if midair collisions were to be avoided.

Compared with what the airborne troops were about to endure in Normandy, Troop Carrier's moment in the spotlight would be brief. But Troop Carrier Command's Field Order 1, issued to all crews on June 2, emphasized that that moment was critical, and like all other Allied servicemen involved in the D-Day assault, Troop Carrier airmen must put their lives on the line to make that assault work.

Maj. Gen. Paul Williams
Commander, IX Troop Carrier Command, Field Order No. 1, June 2, 1944
Pilots of aircraft will be held responsible for the delivery of paratroop loads or gliders to the DZs [drop zones]. Evasive action prior to delivery of troops will not be tolerated. In the event a DZ or LZ [landing zone] is missed on the initial run-in, troops will be delivered within the combat area. In the event that the [Cotentin's eastern] coastline is reached and troops have not been delivered, aircraft will execute a right turn and deliver troops in DZ "D." [Williams's implication was that pilots must not return to England with any paratroopers onboard their C-47s.] Attention is directed to the fact that excessive jump speeds produce high casualty rates among paratroopers. Jump speeds of 100 mph or less will be complied with.

Planners pored over air photographs of the Cotentin and pinpointed six drop zones, each of which corresponded to one of the three parachute regiments subordinated to both the 82nd and 101st Divisions. Designated by a single letter, each drop zone was an oval about one and a half miles long and one-half mile wide, sited as close as possible to the objectives each regiment must seize on D-Day. The airborne plan also specified landing zones for two predawn glider missions, one in support of each airborne division.

If the pilots' toughest task was finding their drop zones at night, many new additions to the airborne repertoire would make this job easier in Normandy. The shaky parachute drops in Sicily had demonstrated to soldiers and airmen alike that it was eminently sensible to drop a small party of paratroopers equipped with lights and navigation aids to mark a drop zone prior to the principal airdrop. The U.S. Army labeled these men "pathfinders," and if they did their job correctly, what had in the past been nearly invisible to a Troop Carrier pilot would now beckon to him from far afield, drawing his C-47 and its embarked paratroopers to their proper drop zone as a lighthouse's beacon lures a ship on a dark sea. But even the best pathfinding teams would be useless to their comrades unless they themselves could find their drop zones.

*"It was up to Troop Carrier now." Pilots from the 439th Troop Carrier Group
assemble for their D-Day mission at Upottery airfield in England.*
U.S. ARMY SIGNAL CORPS, NATIONAL ARCHIVES.

Clearly the job would not be easy. Dropping alone into enemy territory
and announcing one's presence in the open countryside with bright lights
and radio beacons seemed almost suicidal. But that driving force behind so
many U.S. Army airborne precepts, James Gavin, worked out sensible
pathfinder techniques for the 82nd Airborne after the Sicily campaign, and
to ensure that Troop Carrier crews would be as skilled as the men they
would convey into combat, he collaborated extensively with Lt. Col. Joel
Crouch of Troop Carrier Command, an eminent prewar United Airlines
pilot. Only one month after Gavin and Crouch worked out pathfinder procedures, 82nd Airborne pathfinders and their C-47 crews successfully put
their freshly learned expertise into practice in a September 1943 combat
jump within the Salerno beachhead.

However, the pathfinders' early work in Italy was trifling compared
with what would be expected of them in Normandy. The D-Day drop
would be so large that the number of pathfinders and trained aircrews must
swell by a considerable factor, and as a result, IX Troop Carrier Command
established a Pathfinder School under Crouch's direction at the immense

North Witham airbase in Lincolnshire. Each Troop Carrier group sent three of their best pilots and crews to Crouch with orders to learn how pathfinding techniques should be practiced. Also, both the 82nd and 101st Airborne dispatched teams of parachutists to North Witham under Captains Neal McRoberts and Frank Lillyman. All attendees, both soldiers and airmen, were volunteers. The instructors had to accomplish a lot of teaching in a short time, and their training techniques were vigorous enough to severely test the endurance and skill of even the most confident men.

Crouch whipped pilots into shape by forcing them to fly three missions per day. He purposely disoriented navigators so that they could function effectively under severe stress; awarded substantial prize money and a forty-eight-hour pass to London to the crew that could drop a dummy by parachute closest to a marker on a drop zone; and insisted that his pilots make at least one jump to learn the rigors of the pathfinders' job. Crouch himself made nine jumps, a detail that displeased the Ninth Air Force's top commanders because of their fear that jump injuries could incapacitate dozens of pilots. But according to Pathfinder School legend, on official reports, Crouch declared that the inordinate number of sprained ankles among his pilots was caused by accidents when they leaped off the backs of trucks on their way back to barracks after training missions.

Crouch used cutting-edge technology to enhance the already considerable talents of his pupils. Nocturnal missions and those in poor weather could strain the skills of even the finest pilots, but thanks to a radar set known as SCR-717, a device developed by the U.S. Navy to search for small objects such as lifeboats, his C-47 pilots could discern topographical features on a scope even at night or through clouds. Furthermore, a British radio navigation device called "Gee" enabled pathfinder navigators onboard C-47s to fix their locations during a mission with a high degree of accuracy. Crouch reasoned that with tools such as these in the hands of experienced aviators, Troop Carrier crews should have no difficulty placing their pathfinders on their drop zones.

Invasion orders dictated that Crouch's C-47s must convey twenty pathfinder teams to Normandy to initiate the airborne assault shortly after midnight on D-Day. This was surely the most critical part of the Americans' airborne mission: If the pathfinders had learned their jobs well, each of the six drop zones would be marked by three teams, one for each of the 600-man battalions making up the regiment that would descend onto that zone shortly after the pathfinders' arrival. Two additional teams held orders to mark a landing zone for a 101st Airborne glider mission at 4:00 A.M. Everything about pathfinder doctrine emphasized redundancy: If one or two teams missed their drop zones or were annihilated by the enemy, the remaining team—even a portion of it—could call in the incoming C-47s on its own.

A pathfinder team consisted of eighteen paratroopers: two officers, twelve men to carry and operate lights and navigational equipment, and four riflemen to provide security. Each team would fit into a single C-47, which would fly in close formation with the two others assigned to the same drop zone. After parachuting from their aircraft and reaching the ground, the pathfinders would locate their objectives and immediately mark the drop zone by setting up lights and a twenty-eight-pound battery-powered transmitter known as "Eureka," whose radio signal on a pre-arranged frequency could be picked up on corresponding receivers called "Rebeccas" onboard approaching C-47s. If the procedure worked as expected, incoming waves of C-47s should have no trouble homing in on the pathfinders' lights and Eureka beacons.

Supreme Headquarters Allied Expeditionary Force
"Navigation and Employment of Pathfinder Units," March 13, 1944
The standard night marking for each DZ will consist of lights forming a *"T"*, with at least 4 holophane lights across the top, and at least 3 holophane lights forming the stem, all lights being 25 yards apart. [A "holophane" light used glass reflectors to enhance its beam.] Lights were to be red, green, or amber [depending on the drop zone on which they were deployed]. [The lights' beams projected very low toward the horizon in the direction from which the incoming C-47s would approach, although each light also had a frosted pane on its top, making it visible from above.] The tail light of the *"T"* will also be the code light [meaning that it would blink a Morse code signal corresponding to its drop zone letter]. The Eureka will be placed within a radius of 100 yards from the head of the *"T"*.

The enemy's arrival could make life very uncomfortable for pathfinders occupied in such involved work. But in truth, the pathfinders' principal challenge was time: They needed to work fast because they would arrive on the ground only thirty minutes before dozens of C-47s were scheduled to appear over their drop zones. If the pathfinders could not deploy their colored lights and Eurekas on time, reasonably close to the places they had picked out on maps in England, incoming Troop Carrier pilots would be challenged by having to locate their drop zones by dead reckoning—an imprecise method, as the Sicily airdrop had proved. Could the pathfinders accomplish their mission under combat conditions? No one knew, but on D-Day they would find out.

If they were pathfinders, they must lead the way; and on D-Day, their teacher, Colonel Crouch, would be at the forefront, guiding the vast Troop Carrier air fleet into battle in the largest airborne operation ever attempted. When orders came down from Ike's headquarters that the invasion was on for June 6, Crouch passed the word around North Witham that the time everyone had been waiting for had come. Shortly before 10:00 P.M. on June 5, when there was still plenty of daylight, he and his three-ship flight of C-47s roared into the sky, followed in close succession by the six additional pathfinder flights that would guide follow-on waves to their respective drop zones. They flew south, heading for the distinctive Bill of Portland on England's south coast, which symbolically pointed like a finger straight to Normandy.

When they reached the Channel, the C-47 pilots dropped to astonishingly low altitudes to avoid German radar, so low that a pilot who let his mind slip for more than a second risked hitting the masts of the countless ships below that were also headed for Normandy. Two Royal Navy patrol boats occupied preset points in the Channel, and they kept Crouch's C-47s on track by displaying green holophane lights and transmitting navigational beacons. When they flew over the last boat, the pilots turned 90 degrees to their left. Normandy was sixty miles dead ahead.

Now there would be no more guide ships, and the pilots were on their own. Their immediate challenge was to avoid antiaircraft fire from the German-occupied Channel Islands, a task that could be accomplished only by carefully slipping the C-47s between the islands of Guernsey and Alderney. Only minutes after midnight on June 6, Crouch's C-47 made landfall on the west coast of the Cotentin Peninsula. He, his crew, and his passengers were the first Americans over Normandy on D-Day.

But one of Crouch's aircraft did not make it.

1st Lt. Harold Sperber
Copilot, IX Troop Carrier Command Pathfinder Group, Drop Zone C
[We flew] at a very low altitude and maintaining radio silence. As darkness approached the only lights on the aircraft were four small blue lights on the surface of each wing and the top of the fuselage, and a faint glow from flame suppressors on the engine exhausts. Shortly after passing the islands of Jersey and Guernsey, all hell broke loose. There was an explosion in the left engine [probably caused by antiaircraft fire from Alderney]. [Capt.] Clyde [Taylor, the pilot] immediately feathered the left propeller and started a right turn. At that point I pushed the nose down to avoid a collision with [Lt. Dwight] Kroesch [piloting an adjacent C-47]. It was a close call. . . . The C-47 was a fantastic and forgiving airplane, but

it was not designed to fly on one engine with 16 fully loaded paratroopers and a crew of 5. And all we had in front of us was ocean—cold, cold ocean. . . . Suddenly we saw a ship. . . . We passed the word to get ready to ditch, and turned away from the ship. With landing lights on, we descended and then hit the water—and I mean hit. Suddenly all I could see was bright green water. [All airmen and paratroopers were rescued by HMS *Tartar,* a Royal Navy destroyer.]

The Troop Carrier pathfinder crews no longer worried about enemy radar; if the Germans did not see them now, they never would. Mission orders prescribed a climb to a higher altitude once the C-47s reached Normandy, but as soon as the pilots did that, they ran unexpectedly into a cloud bank hugging the coast of the Cotentin Peninsula. For aviators who flew tight formations, clouds generally meant trouble, especially ones like these that seemingly appeared out of nowhere at such a low altitude. For Crouch's three-ship pathfinder flights, however, the clouds were less of a problem than they would be later to the much larger follow-on formations. Still, with less than twenty miles to go before the drop zones, a distance that a C-47 could traverse in about ten minutes, the pilots had to think and act fast when they broke free of the clouds.

Normally jumpmasters did not sound the commands "Stand up—Hook up—Equipment check!" to their paratroopers until the pilot had turned on the red cabin light above the door, a warning that the drop would be in four minutes. But on this drop, several jumpmasters ordered their men to hook up and get ready as soon as their C-47s passed over the Normandy coast. This was an extraordinary moment, and everyone must be ready.

When all eighteen heavily encumbered pathfinders stood up and hooked their static lines to the anchor cable running down the length of the C-47's cabin, the resulting line of men ran all the way from the door at the left rear of the aircraft to the pilot's cockpit. No one could ever say that a C-47 was built for its passengers' comfort: With dimmed lights the cabin was dark and gloomy, and the blast of air and reverberating engine noise through the open door made conversation almost impossible. But those who cared to peer outside noticed something that would be common in the sky over the Cotentin Peninsula for the next four hours: enemy antiaircraft fire. If the Germans had been caught by surprise, obviously they had gotten over it.

Green light—Go! The pilot momentarily pulled back the throttle on the left engine to reduce prop blast, and the leading paratrooper crouched and promptly disappeared out the door into the black void. After so much waiting, the jump seemed remarkably abrupt. As each man leaped out of the airplane, the column of paratroopers running down the length of the cabin swiftly shortened, those at the rear of the line shuffling clumsily forward, jostling those to their front as if to encourage them to get out the door as fast as possible. Suddenly no one but the Troop Carrier crew chief and radio operator were left, whose shouts of "All out!" signaled to the pilot that he could head for home.

It was still a long way back to England, but as the crew chief and radioman hauled the static lines back into the cabin, the C-47 crews finally had a moment for reflection. Crouch had trained his Troop Carrier crews hard, and in Normandy it paid off. At postmission briefings, Crouch and his staff pieced together the pathfinder mission and concluded that although their D-Day drops were not perfect, they were entirely creditable. Of the nineteen C-47s that made landfall, the majority landed on or within a mile of their drop zones; and most important, none of the drops were flagrantly off their marks.

The rest of the job was up to the paratroopers. After floating down to earth and cutting free of their chutes, their immediate task was to locate their comrades and get to work setting up the holophane lights and Eurekas. There was no time to lose. In training, team commanders habitually had gathered their men with the blow of a whistle, but in the perplexing Norman bocage, somehow that didn't seem to be a good idea. The Germans had been alerted, and now they were prowling the countryside trying to locate the Americans.

1st Lt. John Joseph
Pathfinder Leader, 3rd Battalion, 507th Parachute Infantry,
82nd Airborne Division, 1947

As the men left the planes they could hear plainly the nervous peppering noise of small arms fire coming from the ground. Upon landing most of the men were too startled to know exactly what to do other than to protect themselves. . . . It was quickly decided that the best plan of action was to walk along the line of flight to the east in an effort to contact other members of the pathfinder team. In case they were unsuccessful in finding more men, they knew that the one Eureka carried by Sgt. [James] Thore would be sufficient to guide all three serials of the 507th [117 C-47s scheduled to arrive at 2:30 A.M.] to the drop zone. . . . Inasmuch as the drop zone was a series of small fields, the Eureka was set up in the corner of the main field, where advantage could be taken of fair cover and concealment. The search for other members of the pathfinder team was abandoned. It was better to be sure of having one Eureka operating on time than to try to find a light or two and risk losing everything. Immediately after it was set up the Eureka "triggered in" on the first serial ten minutes prior to its scheduled arrival. It was a relief to know that contact had been made.

PFC Frederick Wilhelm
Pathfinder, 1st Battalion, 502nd Parachute Infantry, 101st Airborne Division
Coming into the jump field, they [Crouch and copilot Capt. Vito Pedone] slowed the ship up so our opening shock was almost nothing. We had some trees and woods about, but our drop was almost in the center of the field. Our job was to set lights up to guide the incoming troops in. We had very strong lights with us. As it was very dark, I had some doubts whether or not the light would work, so in enemy territory I turned my light on to see. I guess at the time it was an incredibly stupid thing [to do]. [One of Wilhelm's fellow 502nd pathfinders, PFC Francis Rocca, noted, "We set up all right and succeeded not only in attracting our planes to our DZ—but also the fire of half the German Army."]

Three unfortunate 508th Parachute Infantry pathfinder teams scheduled to land on Drop Zone N dropped right into the middle of an alerted enemy unit from the 91st Division. Many GIs were killed while still in their chutes; still more were wounded or captured. When the teams later took the time to count up their losses, they amounted to two-thirds of their members. Even so, the pathfinders managed to get two holophane lights and a Eureka set working.

The three C-47s carrying 501st Parachute Infantry pathfinders missed Drop Zone D, but the pilots realized their mistake when they passed over the Cotentin's east coast. Circling right for another pass, they eventually deposited the pathfinders onto their zone on the second try. But there was another hornet's nest of enemy troops in that locale, and unlike the other five zones, this one was mostly low, open ground with few good hiding places and even fewer sites that were suitable for setting up lights. Almost half the pathfinders on this drop zone became casualties.

In training, some cynics had referred to pathfinding as a suicide mission—and maybe they had been right.

FLYING LIKE A GOSLING WITH A MOTHER GOOSE
The pathfinders were merely the first raindrops of a typhoon; and when that tempest arrived in Normandy, the stunned Germans would soon deduce that their occupation of that beautiful land would probably not endure

much longer. Crouch's twenty aircraft would be followed by so many more C-47s and Waco gliders that even Rommel himself could not fail to draw that conclusion. They would come in waves of thirty-six aircraft, sometimes more, known by Troop Carrier crews as "serials," composed of tight three-ship building blocks called "Vees," three of which combined into larger nine-ship formations the airmen called a "Vee of Vees." Starting at about 12:35 A.M. on D-Day, twenty serials, totaling 800 C-47s, would begin roaring in over the Cotentin's west coast at 1,500 feet, flying 140 miles per hour, and they would come, wave after wave, for nearly the next two hours. Later 104 more C-47s towing CG-4A Waco gliders would follow. Col. Robert Sink of the 506th Parachute Infantry had told his regiment, "Tonight is the night of nights"—and now his men knew why.

The airborne's essential fighting unit for D-Day was the 600-man parachute infantry battalion, eighteen of which were about to descend on the unfortunate enemy. Each Troop Carrier serial hauled a single battalion, augmented in some cases by additional aircraft carrying specialists such as headquarters troops, engineers, and medical personnel. One unique serial from the 436th Troop Carrier Group conveyed the 101st Airborne's 377th Parachute Artillery Battalion, one of only four U.S. Army parachute artillery battalions in the European theater. The 377th's commander, Lt. Col. Benjamin Weisberg, was a prewar gunner from the New York National Guard who had aspired to be a pilot, but his imperfect eyesight barred him from that goal. Now, instead of piloting an airplane, he was jumping out of one. Once on the ground, Weisberg's men had the daunting mission of congregating in the dark, locating twelve disassembled 75-millimeter pack howitzers dropped in bundles, assembling them, and supporting the 502nd Parachute Infantry on its drop zone with artillery fire. Another unusual serial, consisting of twenty-four C-47s from the 314th Group, carried 82nd Airborne headquarters personnel, including Brig. Gen. James Gavin, the assistant division commander.

Unhappily for Troop Carrier crews, their flight paths took them straight into the same cloud bank that had disrupted Crouch's pathfinders. It came up so suddenly in the dark that there was nothing they could do to avoid it, and since Field Order 1 had ordered that "radio silence will be maintained except in case of extreme emergency," Crouch's radio operators could not warn their comrades of the imminent cloud menace. Flying at 1,500 feet, many Troop Carrier serials plunged right into the middle of it. Pilots could only hope that it would dissipate before they reached their drop zones. Fortunately it did—but in retrospect, this cloud bank would affect IX Troop Carrier's performance on D-Day more than all the enemy's antiaircraft fire.

1st Lt. Robert Ingram
Pilot, 91st Troop Carrier Squadron, 439th Group,
carrying 506th Parachute Infantry

Suddenly [Capt. James] Corgill's C-47 disappeared [in the clouds], even though I was holding position right up next to him. [Lt. James] Hurley's airplane was gone too. [Corgill was flight leader in a three-ship 'Vee,' with Hurley on the right, Ingram on the left.] Just when I had about decided that I was invading France alone, their blue lights came back into sight, and we were still in proper formation. I was relieved. Only the flight leaders carried navigators and radar receivers, so the rest of us depended on them to guide us to the DZ and home again. As our orders were to drop the paratroopers in France no matter what the situation, I was as intent on staying with Capt. Corgill as a Canada goose's gosling is when flying with its high-flying mother. My relief, however, didn't last long. He and Hurley went out of sight again when he went into a second, thicker layer of clouds. . . . I was determined to stick with my mother goose because I had no desire to be on my own so close to the climax of our mission. So, hoping that Corgill was holding a constant rate of descent and airspeed, I began easing closer to where his C-47 should be. I believed I had a good chance to pick up his blue formation lights before my C-47 hit his. We came out of the clouds in a tighter formation than would be considered safe under the best of conditions. Hurley must have been thinking like me, and had eased closer to our leader, too. When we broke out his left wing must have been less than three feet from my right wing tip, and smack in between them was Corgill's rudder.

Luckily, Ingram avoided a midair collision, but when his three-ship Vee emerged from the clouds over the Cotentin Peninsula, only minutes from Drop Zone C, amazingly no other C-47s from his forty-five-ship serial were visible. Where were they? No one could tell, but there was nothing for Ingram to do now except search for the correct pathfinder T-lights and Eureka transmission and head to his drop zone on his own.

When the serials charged into the clouds over the Cotentin, flight formations that had been perfect suddenly became something much less. Every good pilot realized that this effect was unavoidable: In flying conditions like this, especially with strict radio silence, nature was a greater hazard than the enemy. It was simply impossible to fly wing-to-wing formations in the dead of night, in a fog so thick that General Gavin remarked that he could not even see the wingtips of his own C-47 from the cabin door. Even under the best conditions, tight formation flying required so many constant adjustments by pilots to hold their positions, particularly those flying the left and right ships behind a leader in a Vee, that it seemed almost impossible to

IX Troop Carrier Command, June 6, 1944

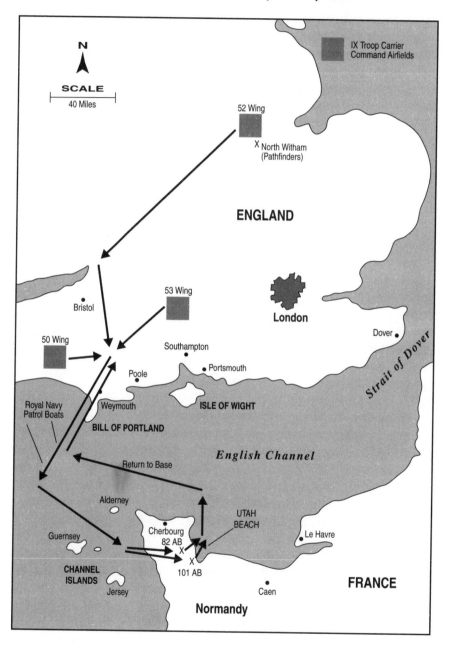

maintain the essential Vee of Vees when the pilots could not even see their neighbors' blue wing lights. An alarming number of catastrophic midair collisions could occur under those conditions, so many that the success of the American D-Day airborne drop could be imperiled before the enemy had even opened fire in earnest.

But the show must go on—no matter what. Some flight leaders climbed through the clouds and broke through the top layer at about 2,000 feet. Their visibility improved dramatically, but with only a few minutes to the drop zone, they would have to pass over the clouds or search for a hole in them, then quickly descend to the proper drop altitude of 700 feet if they were to make it to their objectives on time. Meanwhile, they could only hope that the other eight C-47s in their formation had stuck by them.

Lt. Col. Charles Young
Commander, 439th Troop Carrier Group, D-Day Mission Report,
June 6, 1944

On approaching the west coast of the peninsula, there was a layer of clouds or haze that made us think it was land. . . . It was not apparent until it was too late to avoid it. I had to make a quick decision as to whether to try to climb up over this cloud bank or go down beneath it, and I decided to climb up over it. . . . About 11 miles inland I found a hole through the clouds and went down on instruments again. I broke out through the cloud just past the first railroad [running up the west side of the Cotentin through St. Sauveur-le Vicomte].

Other flight leaders decided to drop when they hit the cloud bank, hoping to get under it and allow pilots to maintain visual contact with other C-47s en route to the drop zone. The overcast bottomed at about 1,100 feet, only 400 feet above the altitude prescribed by Field Order 1 for the drop. Consequently, the pilots would have good observation of the ground as they approached their objectives, but their C-47s would now be visible and highly vulnerable to alert German antiaircraft gunners.

Regardless of how a pilot maneuvered as his C-47 rushed into the cloud bank, he could not read his fellow pilots' minds, nor could he contact them by radio; so he had no way of knowing whether his actions would be matched by others. Although most paratroopers remained blissfully unaware of the abrupt danger posed by the clouds, these were gut-wrenching moments for Troop Carrier crewmen. Ultimately, although some serials managed to hold their formations by avoiding the worst of the overcast, the clouds forced most formations to spread out like buckshot from a shotgun blast.

1st Lt. William Hitztaler
Pilot, 14th Troop Carrier Squadron, 61st Group, D-Day Mission Report,
June 22, 1944

Coming in low over the coast we received machine gun fire. Then we hit low clouds. Trying to follow Capt. Harruff, leader of the first flight, we pulled up and then down through the clouds, veering to the right slightly so as not to run into them. I could not find them upon emerging, so I took up the proper course heading. In approaching the DZ, our aircraft encountered flak, which hit toward the rear and the tail. One paratrooper was badly hurt and was believed dying. [Hitztaler's C-47 was shot down after its paratroopers jumped. He bailed out and evaded capture until rescued by American troops on June 19, 1944.]

On to the drop zones—but where were they? Those serials that stayed tight despite the clouds would have the least trouble finding them. Pathfinders had set up at least one Eureka beacon on each of the six drop zones, and flight leaders in nine-ship formations picked up the signals on the frequencies corresponding to their objectives on their Rebecca sets, in some cases at a range of more than fifteen miles. The leaders could then adjust their headings to home in on the Eurekas, hoping that accompanying C-47s could observe those course corrections and follow suit.

Serials that broke up in the clouds experienced much more trouble finding their targets. Those pilots who had lost their flight leaders in the clouds were on their own—and they had to think fast, for Field Order 1 dictated that "pilots will be held responsible for continuing to the combat area even though they may become detached from the main formation enroute [*sic*]." For fear of flooding the airwaves with transmissions, orders also specified that only "one Rebecca [on the flight leader's C-47] will be operating in each nine-ship flight." Lost pilots could always search for their pathfinders' T-lights, but less than half the teams had managed to place complete sets on their drop zones by the time the main C-47 serials arrived. Moreover, pilots could see the lights' low, focused beams only if they approached them head-on, or nearly so, and as a result most pilots who searched for those elusive shafts of light looked in vain. To reorient themselves, several lost pilots turned on their Rebecca sets despite orders to the contrary—a sensible choice, as it turned out, since the feared oversaturation of the airwaves by beacon transmissions did not occur. Others used GEE radio navigation to figure out their locations, although pinpointing a drop zone by this system was exceptionally difficult. When all else failed, pilots relied on the old-fashioned method of visual observation, searching for the many distinctive ground landmarks, such as rivers, towns, and railroad lines, that they had memorized back in England from Ninth Air Force reconnaissance photographs.

Wherever the pilots were, they must now focus their undivided attention on finding their drop zones. Beneath them, however, the Germans were creating an alarming distraction by throwing up such a considerable barrage of bullets and shells that it seemed almost impossible to fly through it without getting hit. One member of the 506th Parachute Infantry on a 439th Troop Carrier Group C-47 observed, "Tracer bullets whizzed everywhere angrily, criss-crossing the sky in crazy, striking patterns." Here, at last, was the enemy reaction that Leigh-Mallory had glumly predicted to Ike would slaughter the C-47s and render the entire airborne operation ineffectual.

93rd Troop Carrier Squadron, 439th Group
Postmission interrogation with 1st Lt. Edward Beauregard, June 1944
Intense anti-aircraft fire was taking place at this time. . . . A few seconds later the bottom of Lt. [Marvin] Muir's plane was hit, near the companionway, and the baggage compartment was immediately filled with flames which could be seen through the astral dome and the radio operator's window. [Muir was leading a three-ship Vee, with Beauregard's C-47 on his right wing.] . . . The flames got worse and spread to the cabin very quickly. Almost immediately paratroopers began coming out the door. I was unable to estimate the number, but it looked like the usual stick. I was unable to tell whether any of the crew jumped. The plane then rose 50 feet on the left wing and seemed to stall. Then it dropped over on the right wing into my path. I dropped under and slid to the left. From then on I saw nothing until the flash of the explosion when the plane hit the ground. [Muir and his four-man crew were killed, but seventeen of the eighteen paratroopers onboard exited successfully. The U.S. Army awarded Muir the Distinguished Service Cross posthumously, noting that he tried "to get above the formation and give his paratroopers, and crew if possible, an opportunity to jump."]

1st Lt. Charles Santarsiero
Company I, 506th Parachute Infantry, 101st Airborne Division
One of our planes [probably from 441st Group] went down and exploded. The explosion shook our plane. Someone asked: "What the hell was that?" I said one of our fighter pilots had just shot down a Kraut. They cheered! For their morale, I thought it best that way. How does one tell their men that their buddies were just blown to hell? [A Troop Carrier pilot, 1st Lt. Donald Orcutt, noted: "I remember my peripheral vision revealed the tremendous blast of light when he took the hit. There were no survivors from that one."]

A steady stream of 820 Troop Carrier C-47s passed over the Cotentin Peninsula from midnight to 3:00 A.M. on June 6, and of these, the Germans managed to shoot down 21. This loss rate of less than 3 percent hardly amounted to the catastrophic thrashing that Leigh-Mallory had predicted. However, Troop Carrier losses certainly would have been much more severe had the C-47 not been such a remarkable piece of machinery. Hundreds of C-47s returned to their English airfields with holes in their bellies, punctured fuel tanks, severed cables, flat tires, and dead hydraulic lines. Although some were written off as irreparable, ground crews promptly restored most of them to a serviceable condition within a few days.

In the aftermath of D-Day, several paratroopers commented unfavorably on the supposed inability of Troop Carrier pilots to adhere to proper jump speeds and altitudes of 110 miles per hour and 700 feet, as well as their inclination to take evasive action against orders during their run-ins to drop zones. During an August 13, 1944, 82nd Airborne debriefing in England, Lt. Col. Thomas Shanley, a battalion commander in the 508th Parachute Infantry, stated, "A lot of jumpmasters said the planes took evasive action, and that may be the reason for the dispersion on the jump." Even the U.S. Air Force's 1956 official history of the D-Day airborne drop noted, "Although the pilots had been warned against evasive action many of them did indulge in it."

In truth, however, many of these allegations were overstated and misleading—and in some cases untrue. In an isolated C-47 passenger cabin, paratroopers could not see what the pilot could see. They could not know that an unforeseen cloud bank had caused their pilot to lose sight of neighboring C-47s and probably forced him to climb or drop precipitously to get out of the blinding fog. They did not realize that when their pilot emerged from the clouds, he may have been separated from his flight leader and had little idea where he was, with only a few minutes to find his drop zone. What paratroopers interpreted as "evasive action" and "excessive speeds" were in many cases abrupt maneuvers and throttle adjustments that the pilot had been forced to initiate to reach his objective in the limited time available. With bullets and shells whizzing throughout the sky, however, the alarmed passengers viewed these sudden jinks and banks as something entirely different. But the overwhelming dedication of most Troop Carrier pilots to complete their job as closely as possible to the stipulations of Field Order 1 was epitomized by the fact that some who initially missed their drop zones, or whose drops were incomplete for some reason, made 180-degree turns in the midst of the enemy's intense antiaircraft barrage to try again.

14th Troop Carrier Squadron, 61st Group
Postmission interrogation with Capt. Gene Franscioni, June 9, 1944

At 0226 Franscioni, now directly over the DZ, gave the troops in his aircraft the green jumping light. The gunfire from the ground kept streaking in and around the vicinity of the airplane but no hits were received. Franscioni . . . held his ship in the jump attitude for approximately 15 seconds, leveled it off, and still in formation, increased his speed to get out of enemy territory. . . . The ship's navigator, 2nd Lt. W. Lyon, then informed Franscioni that there were still some paratroops left in the airplane. . . . The 11th man in the stick had gotten jammed in the door, causing those [eight] behind him in line to fall so that all were rendered unable to jump on the target. Franscioni asked them whether they would jump if he would take them all the way back over the DZ. Their answers were all in the affirmative. . . . Franscioni made a 180 degree turn to his right and flew in on the deck. . . . [He] recognized the DZ by the hail of tracers coming up from around it. At 0234 hours, exactly 9 minutes after he had dropped the first batch, Franscioni gave the remaining 8 troopers the green light.

What Air Chief Marshal Leigh-Mallory had told Ike could not be done had indeed been done, thanks to the high level of teamwork between IX Troop Carrier Command and the 82nd and 101st Airborne Divisions. The invasion of the Cotentin Peninsula was working—so far. The rest was up to the paratroopers.

CHAPTER 5

Hitting the Silk

FOG OF WAR

If all World War II battles were to some extent chaotic, what transpired in the Cotentin Peninsula in the opening hours of the D-Day invasion can only be described as absolute bedlam. In the middle of the night, Troop Carrier pilots had just dropped more than 13,000 heavily armed and highly motivated paratroopers into Normandy, directly in the midst of two unsuspecting enemy divisions and a slumbering civilian population. No neat battle lines emerged from the ensuing pandemonium until after sunrise; and in fact, this entire early phase of the operation nearly defies description, because the military actions that took place were isolated and unconventional, carried out by individuals or small groups of GIs who collided with the enemy while wandering the claustrophobic bocage in search of their comrades.

Where was everyone? To answer that question, a lost paratrooper first had to figure out where he was, but unless he was lucky enough to have landed right in the middle of his drop zone next to a recognizable landmark, that was an exceptionally difficult task. There were not many visible landmarks in the bocage, at least ones that could be discerned in the dark. It would take time—and daylight—to sort out the mess. In the meantime, hundreds of ferocious small combats erupted in and around the Norman towns and villages whose names would soon be renowned as the places where the liberation of Europe from Nazi domination began: Ste. Mère Église, Ste. Marie du Mont, Angoville au Plain, St. Martin de Varreville, and more.

No historical account of this early fighting amid the dark, threatening hedgerows can ever be complete, since so many participants did not survive and so many more had no idea where they were. But from the perspective of the high command, the important issue was whether the airborne units could fulfill the critical missions prescribed by the Overlord plan. On his VII Corps command ship *Bayfield*, anchored twelve miles off Utah Beach, General Collins waited anxiously for word that these missions had been accomplished. The 4th Division's inland push from Utah Beach on June 6 and afterward hinged, first, on the paratroopers' control of the four causeways leading off the beach; second, on their capture of key crossroads towns, such as Ste. Mère Église and Carentan, which would help secure the vulnerable beachhead from the enemy's counterattacks that were sure to come within the next forty-eight hours; and third, on their seizure of the two causeways traversing the flooded Merderet River at La Fière and Chef du Pont, the only routes by which Collins's troops could attack westward and cut the Cotentin Peninsula in two.

These would be challenging tasks, especially as those airborne outfits that had managed to assemble after the harrowing airdrop were mere skeletons of their former incarnations at last roll call at Troop Carrier airfields in England. But slowly, inexorably, those rare paratroopers who were born to lead fathomed their whereabouts correctly, gathered lost members of their outfits—and anyone else who cared to join—and headed straight to the places that orders dictated they must attack and hold. At those sites, and dozens more like them throughout Normandy, the outcome of the D-Day invasion would be determined.

If the airdrop of 13,000 paratroopers triggered confusion among the Americans, the effect on the Germans was total bewilderment. So far, the Allies had made no seaborne landings anywhere in Normandy. If these paratroopers signified that the Allied invasion of Europe had begun, where would the rest of the invading forces land? And even more important: How should the German high command respond to those first frantic reports that enemy paratroopers were spread all over the Cotentin Peninsula?

Maj. Friedrich Hayn
Chief of Military Intelligence, German LXXXIV Corps, 1947
At 1:11 AM—an unforgettable moment—the field telephone shrilled. [This was 2:11 A.M. to the Allies, as their clocks were set one hour ahead of the Germans.]

Something seemed to be in the air. Hearing the message, the General's body stiffened [Lt. Gen. Erich Marcks, commander of the German LXXXIV Corps], his right hand clutched the edge of the table, and with a jerk of his head he beckoned to his chief of staff to listen in. . . . "Enemy paratroopers jumped south of St. Germain de Varreville and near Ste. Marie du Mont. Another group observed west of highway [between] Carentan and Valognes on both sides of the Merderet and along the road [between] Ste. Mère Église and Pont l'Abbé." Our army corps command post [just outside St. Lô] was humming like a beehive. At last it was over, this long suspense, this everlasting circle of alert, standby, and readiness for action, which since April had kept our soldiers on their feet and was beginning to have a numbing effect on them.

Brig. Gen. James Gavin
Assistant Division Commander, 82nd Airborne Division, 1947
Standard German anti-airborne measures included static posts at key points such as bridges, towns, road crossings. These were augmented by highly mobile patrols as soon as landings took place. On the night of the attack, the experience of the defenders was that when these patrols went out they became engaged all over the place. . . . Higher German headquarters ordered troops to different points on the basis of information that reached them; and these too became engaged either en route to or at their objectives. Soon small units were fighting all around and in all directions. [German] unit commanders apparently lost control of everything except the troops right around their headquarters.

That there were no front lines in the initial stage of an airborne attack became obvious to the unfortunate Maj. Gen. Wilhelm Falley, commander of the German 91st *Luftlande* Division, in a chance encounter with American paratroopers at about 3:30 A.M. Those Americans, led by 1st Lt. Malcolm Brannen of the 508th Parachute Infantry, had just unknowingly landed close to the 91st's headquarters at an ornate eighteenth-century chateau named Bernaville, near Pont l'Abbé. As Brannen's little group of paratroopers pondered their next move, Falley's staff car abruptly roared around a bend of the road. Brannen and his accomplices opened fire, killing Falley and triggering a crash that threw the general's aide out of the car and onto the roadbed. The stunned aide could see the instigators of this ambush, and he repeatedly bellowed in heavily accented English, "Don't kill!" But according to Brannen, the German simultaneously reached for his pistol, and the Americans promptly shot him dead. The GIs figured their prey was someone important, and Falley's fancy general's cap corroborated that assumption.

Later, when Brannen excitedly related the gruesome details of Falley's death to his own division commander, General Ridgway replied, "Well, in our present situation killing division commanders does not strike me as being particularly hilarious—but I congratulate you."

325th Glider Infantry, 82nd Airborne Division
POW interrogation with Gefreiter Baumann, General Falley's driver,
June 11, 1944
General Falley, accompanied by his aide, left his headquarters about 1800 June 5 in his car for a conference at Rennes. [They turned around when they heard news of the invasion.] About fifty yards from his headquarters at a castle near Pont l'Abbé, the vehicle was ambushed by six paratroopers. The General was killed instantly, and his aide, after firing a few pistol shots, was killed immediately afterward. [The driver] jumped out of the car after having received a wound in his right shoulder. The paratroopers walked him off as a prisoner and took him wherever they went.

To the German high command, the American airborne drop demanded a vigorous reaction, but some of the orders issued by General Marcks at his remote command post in St. Lô in response to the alarming reports from the Cotentin were impulsive and would later have dire consequences. At about 4:50 A.M. Marcks directed three first-class battalions of German troops in reserve near Bayeux, amounting to more than 2,000 men, to move toward Carentan, about twenty miles distant, to deal with the supposed threat in that sector posed by the American airdrop. These troops were the enemy's only force capable of counterattacking Allied seaborne landings on the Calvados shoreline north of Bayeux. The German units had been on the road toward Carentan for only ninety minutes when American and British troops slammed into that coast on Omaha and Gold Beaches. It was not until after 8:00 A.M. that Marcks realized his error and ordered the movement halted. By that time, however, the Germans had marched in precisely the wrong direction from the coastal defenses where they were desperately needed. They had to turn around, retrace their steps, and head as swiftly as possible toward the coast. But by the time they arrived, the situation on both Omaha and Gold Beaches was irreparable.

Although the Allies did not yet realize it, the acute worry instilled in the enemy's high command by the American airdrop had already yielded solid benefits. At a critical moment in the battle, the confusion that swept through the German command hierarchy on the morning of June 6 severely hampered the enemy's ability to react effectively to the invasion, not only on Utah Beach and in the Cotentin Peninsula, but all across the invasion front. In this new type of warfare called vertical envelopment, it seemed that it would take both the invaders and the defenders days to figure out what was going on.

THE HEINIES WERE CHAGRINED

If the mountain of papers constituting the VII Corps invasion plan actually amounted to a practical operation of war, 4th Division troops surging over the causeways heading inland from Utah Beach would be greeted not by German fire, but by comrades in the 101st Airborne Division. The men who planned the Utah landing assumed that the flooded meadowlands behind Utah would not be passable on D-Day, and if they were right, 4th Division troops would be obligated to stick to the causeways if, as invasion orders demanded, they were to push swiftly into the Cotentin interior. But those causeways were a tactical nightmare, running westward from the beach for more than a mile over flat, featureless grassland with virtually no places for advancing GIs to take cover from enemy fire. At the causeways' western extremities, the terrain rises by about twenty-five feet, and on this prominent north-south ridge, the Germans had set up several powerful artillery batteries and defensive positions for the entirely sensible reason that those places offered commanding views not only of the adjacent flatland behind the beach, but also of the sea beyond. What the enemy could see, they could kill; and if the 101st did not manage to seize the causeways from behind on the morning of D-Day, the Germans could turn them into killing zones worse than no-man's-land in World War I.

The two northernmost causeways, designated 3 and 4, were critical. According to the 4th Division plan, these would be the first routes by which infantrymen would head inland from the beach on D-Day, an event that could occur as early as 7:30 A.M. if the invasion was proceeding smoothly. But Allied intelligence had pinpointed a powerful enemy battery of four captured Russian 122-millimeter howitzers just west of the village of St. Martin de Varreville, a tiny commune with an ancient Romanesque church, situated on the critical high ground between the western limits of Causeways 3 and 4. Just a few German machine guns positioned in and around this village could hold up an American advance from the beach, so General Collins could only hope that the paratroopers would already hold St. Martin when the 4th Division started to move inland. There would surely be trouble if they did not.

To clear the Germans out of the St. Martin area, General Taylor of the 101st selected the 502nd Parachute Infantry, a regiment that had been with

"He could strike terror in the heart of God." Col. George Van Horn Moseley, commander of the 502nd Parachute Infantry, 101st Airborne Division, known as "Old Moe" to his men. COURTESY MARK BANDO.

the division since the 101st's inception in August 1942. One 502nd para-trooper recalled, "You could write a book on the characters who comprised the 502nd: In twenty years of service I have never seen such brave men, nor such funny characters." So many characters, in fact, that in 1943 the regiment typically had four times more men AWOL than any other unit in the 101st. The characters started at the top. Col. George Van Horn Moseley, the 502nd's thirty-nine-year-old commander, was a 1927 West Point gradu-ate who, a subordinate noted, "could strike terror in the heart of God." By June 1944, "Old Moe" had led the regiment for more than two years, but the limit of his combat experience was little more than one day, as a result of a broken ankle Moseley suffered on the D-Day jump. His departure from Normandy, however, may also have been related to his peculiar con-duct. The officer who took over the 502nd after Moseley's relief, Lt. Col. John Michaelis, later noted that his boss was "crazy" and once drew a weapon on him to enforce a controversial order on D-Day.

Compared with the other parachute outfits that dropped into Normandy on D-Day, the 502nd had the advantage of being carried in the airborne mission's first four Troop Carrier serials. Consequently, when the 502nd passed over the Cotentin, the Germans had not yet opened the fierce anti-aircraft barrage they would achieve in the next few hours. But when the first thirty-six C-47s from the 438th Group flew toward Drop Zone A at 12:44 A.M., the 502nd pathfinders had yet to deploy their T-lights and Eurekas, and it was difficult for Troop Carrier pilots to discern their objectives in the gloom. Even after those finding aids were finally set up, the last serial flown by the 436th Group, fifty-four C-47s carrying the 377th Artillery Battalion and the 502nd's Company C, got so separated and disoriented in the clouds that every stick missed Drop Zone A by at least three miles, and in rare cases by nearly twenty. As a result, men of the 377th would be able to get only one of their twelve howitzers into action by the end of the day.

502nd Parachute Infantry, 101st Airborne Division
D-Day Action Report, July 1944
At 0048 the red light came on and jumpmasters electrified into action. "Stand up! Hook up! Check equipment! Sound off for equipment check!" Now the jumpers were tense, every man alert for the next command. "Stand in the door!" Crowd forward, reach forward, listen, tense, excited now. Green light—"Let's Go! Bill Lee!"[On instructions from General Taylor, 502nd troops shouted the name of the 101st's former commander while jumping.] With the cry of "Bill Lee!" the 502nd "hit the silk" and descended like Hitler's doom on occupied France.

The first chore for the agitated men of the 502nd was to head to their objectives in and around St. Martin. This was no easy task, as many sticks had landed a mile or more off target, and in the dark, most paratroopers did not know in which direction to initiate their movement to reach those objectives. As the vanguard of the American airborne assault, however, the men of the 502nd had a head start in sorting out the confusion, and even as some 82nd Airborne units were still jumping shortly before 3:00 A.M., small groups of 502nd men were already stealthily moving toward St. Martin from all points on the compass.

They would have to fight to get there. For the many 502nd troops who landed north of their drop zone, a narrow country road paralleling the Cotentin's east coast less than two miles west of the shoreline pointed south straight toward their objective and would be the obvious conduit that would lead them where they needed to go. Just east of this road, near the hamlet of Ravenoville, the paratroopers stumbled into the enemy at a sturdy Norman farm complex called Marmion.

Maj. John Stopka
Executive, 3rd Battalion, 502nd Parachute Infantry, August 11, 1944
The lead scout, S/Sgt. [Robert] O'Reilly, was fired upon and he immediately hit the dirt and fired back. Lt. [Ernest] Harris and Lt. [Howard] Collins, who were behind O'Reilly, saw the situation at hand and relayed the information back to me,

502nd Parachute Infantry: Morning, June 6, 1944

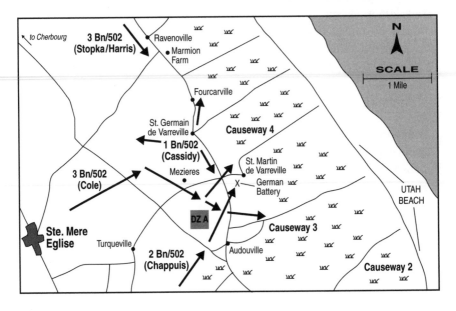

saying that it appeared to be a strongpoint of some sort. . . . I shouted to Lt. Collins to move across the road, take two men and try to flank the position from the left; and for Lt. Harris to take two more men and do the same thing from the right. Collins and Harris had not been gone more than ten minutes when I heard the chatter of several machine pistols and machine gun fire coming from the direction where Harris had gone. . . . I heard some carbine firing and yelling by Harris, and about one minute later I saw Harris come out of the [building] with a group of the enemy with their hands up and somewhat worse for wear. There were 24 enemy prisoners. Harris said he had gotten behind their position, and as they came out he picked them off and made so much noise that the enemy apparently thought he had a small army with him. After losing six of their own, the rest gave up. After turning the prisoners over Harris said he was going back to mop up the trenches. . . . [Later] I heard the chatter of machine guns, carbine fire, and shouting by Harris. I could see Harris jumping a trench, shouting, firing his rifle, and generally making quite a scene. Following him at about 50 yards were his two men, creeping and crawling on their stomachs, looking rather timid and afraid to get out and move, but on seeing Harris jump up and fire, yell and carry on like he did, they got up and did the same thing.

The army awarded Harris, a native of Missouri, the Distinguished Service Cross for this action, but as he lived only five more days, he never even knew of the paperwork Major Stopka submitted on his behalf for this prestigious award. In January 1945, Stopka, too, was killed in action.

The 101st Airborne had allocated 2,000 paratroopers to fulfill the critical D-Day missions in and around St. Martin de Varreville, but shortly after sunrise, a small fraction of that number would accomplish the two most important of those goals: the seizure of the western exits of Causeways 3 and 4, and the capture of the German battery east of the village. Luckily for the 502nd, the enemy resisted with much less resolve than anticipated, a circumstance attributable in part to the heavy pounding RAF heavy bombers had recently delivered to this area. Indeed, the bombing had been so severe that when the paratroopers arrived at the battery they had studied on photographs for so long, they noted that most of the battery's gun positions had been destroyed, and the guns, along with their operators, had moved to an unknown location.

The outfit holding orders to take the St. Martin battery was the 502nd's 2nd Battalion, commanded by Lt. Col. Steve Chappuis, a native of Cajun country and a 1936 Louisiana State University graduate. Chappuis had climbed the army's hierarchy in an unusual way: Although he had learned his military skills at LSU's reserve officer training program, he nonetheless had been offered a commission in the U.S. Regular Army—a rare opportunity that Chappuis had eagerly accepted. Among 101st Airborne Division field grade officers, Chappuis was comparatively elderly: At age thirty-one, he was one of the oldest parachute battalion commanders to land in Normandy.

Chappuis later recalled that after the D-Day drop, his battalion "was pretty well spread, and we were as much as three or four miles from our drop zone." Even worse, he had injured his leg badly in the jump, but like so many others with similar aches, he managed to hobble to the objective, gathering his own and many other paratroopers along the way.

1st Lt. Legrand Johnson
Commander, Company F, 2nd Battalion, 502nd Parachute Infantry
I had about 30 men, who, as far as I know, comprised the force that was to destroy the guns. . . . [We] took off in approved infantry school fashion, swarming over the area with no opposition. Col. Chappuis was there with several men—by 0700 we had less than 200 men assembled. . . . Col. Chappuis and Capt. Hank Plitt [2nd Battalion S-3] were "accepting" surrender of the German troops in the underground area, which was a huge affair, like subway tunnels with ammunition and food. The Heinies were sure chagrined when they came out with their hands up and learned that they outnumbered the hell out of us.

The man responsible for seizing Causeways 3 and 4, Lt. Col. Robert Cole, had commanded the 502nd's 3rd Battalion for more than two years. A graduate of the West Point class of 1939, Cole's first active-duty assignment in the U.S. Army was with the 15th Infantry at Fort Lewis, Washington, which had recently returned from twenty-six years of service in Tientsin, China—and whose executive officer was a lieutenant colonel named Dwight Eisenhower. In October 1944, Ike remembered Cole as a "top-notch officer," but by then Cole was dead, a casualty of Operation Market-Garden in September. Cole's exploits in Normandy, particularly his instigation of an audacious bayonet charge outside Carentan five days after D-Day, made him a legend within the 101st Airborne, and his superiors recommended him for a Medal of Honor. The U.S. Army awarded that decoration to Cole posthumously in October 1944.

On D-Day, Cole landed at about 1:00 A.M., closer to Ste. Mère Église in the 82nd's sphere than to his own objectives near St. Martin. But he made his way eastward across the seemingly impenetrable bocage for three miles, doing what every bold airborne leader did that night: gathering stray paratroopers and leading them on to an objective, regardless of their unit affiliations. Shortly after sunrise, Cole's group finally reached the ridge overlooking the flooded pasturelands behind Utah Beach, but there were virtually no signs of the enemy. Strange . . . If the Germans were as skilled at warfare as everyone said they were, they should have fought for this critical ground like tigers.

Cole had accomplished his mission, and the western extremities of Causeways 3 and 4 were in American hands. Suddenly the 4th Infantry Division's job had become a lot easier.

JUST A KID

They had to find the church steeple at dawn. The men knew that the distinctive tower could be seen from miles away, and the sooner they could locate it, the sooner they could move there and open up Causeway 2 to Utah Beach and, one mile beyond that, Causeway 1. In a land where even the most minuscule villages possessed squat Romanesque churches 800 or more years old, the Église Notre-Dame was something special. It was situated three miles southwest of Utah Beach, squarely in the middle of a typical Cotentin village named Ste. Marie du Mont. The church was ancient, dating to the twelfth century, but on June 6, 1944, its remarkable steeple was the focus of the invaders' attention. Unlike the somber Romanesque church towers characteristic of Normandy, the Église Notre-Dame's domed upper steeple, topped by a cross, was a soaring Renaissance monument to the glory of God. It was hard to miss, and come daylight, nearby GIs would be drawn there like the local worshippers to one of its Sunday masses.

The liberation of this ancient Norman parish was the job of the 101st Airborne's 506th Parachute Infantry, commanded by Col. Robert Sink. The 506th took its regimental slogan, "Currahee," from the mountain at Camp Toccoa, Georgia, that 506th recruits had sprinted up more times than they cared to remember during 1942 training. That steep and extremely strenuous climb was the inspiration of Lt. Adam Parsons, then a paratrooper and the 506th's physical conditioning officer, but on D-Day a Troop Carrier pilot with the 439th Group, who with his commanding officer, Lt. Col. Charles Young, would fly in Sink and his command group in C-47 Number 159, the lead aircraft for Drop Zone C.

Lt. Col. Charles Young
Commander, 439th Troop Carrier Group, diary, June 6, 1944
At our pilot briefing, which [Col. Sink] attended, I had bet Col. Sink that I could put him within 300 yards of the spot he pointed to on the DZ, "T" or no "T." The

"A good combat man, a good fighter." Col. Robert Sink, commander of the 506th Parachute Infantry, 101st Airborne Division. COURTESY MARK BANDO.

pathfinders had left no T lit, but had a [Eureka] radar in operation. I believe I put him within 200 yards.

A 1927 graduate of West Point, Colonel Sink had a mustache and a weather-beaten face that made him appear older than his thirty-nine years. Sink did not consider that a soldier would be effective unless he was in superb physical condition, and back in the States, people had taken notice of that philosophy when he once marched the 506th 110 miles in three days. General Gavin, who served for two years with Sink in the Philippines, recalled: "They used to call him 'Bourbon Bob,' but he wasn't a big drunk like some of them. . . . He was a good combat man, a good fighter." The 101st's commander, Maj. Gen. Maxwell Taylor, felt the same way: "Sink displayed exceptional skill in preparing his unit for combat and exceptional tactical ability during the invasion of Normandy."

As Sink prepared to exit Colonel Young's C-47 over the drop zone, he remembered a nearby GI shouting, "I should have my head examined!"—a sentiment wordlessly endorsed by hundreds of paratroopers on D-Day as they peered out the open door of their transports into the shadowy abyss below, a place where they and many of their comrades might die in the next few hours, or even minutes.

Once on the ground in the middle of Drop Zone C, the perplexed Sink wondered: Where are my men? It was the same question that every airborne commander asked himself that night. Sink should have had more than 1,000 troops to capture Ste. Marie du Mont and open up Causeways 1 and 2, but two hours after coming to earth, he had only about 75 men at his disposal, most of whom were from Sink's own headquarters group and his regimental reserve, Lt. Col. William Turner's 1st Battalion. There was little Sink could accomplish with such a small group, so he, Turner, and their followers marched off to a nearby farm named Caloville, about a mile west of Ste. Marie du Mont. Until matters cleared up, this would be the 506th's command post.

1st Lt. Salve Matheson
Adjutant, 506th Parachute Infantry, 101st Airborne Division, 1949
It had been an old story during training jumps, particularly at night, for the situation to be extremely confusing initially. We used to say: "They were confused, and so were we—only we were more used to it." The enemy's failure to take advantage of the scattering of the 506th and other regiments was the principal reason for the success of the airborne operation. . . . Caloville was discovered to be a large farm consisting of a courtyard, barns, and a large house, all of masonry construction. Upon interrogation of the French inhabitants by Capt. John Maloney [the 506th's chaplain], a Frenchwoman merely kept shaking her head and stating *"Les grands canons,"* and pointing on the map to the vicinity of Holdy [a farm about one-half mile northeast of Caloville]. Her meaning was to be clear later in the day.

Col. Robert Sink
Commander, 506th Parachute Infantry, 101st Airborne Division
At our first command post after landing [Caloville], the CO of my headquarters company, Capt. Edward Peters, said that he knew where a sniper was near the command post and was going out to get him. He himself got it, between the eyes.

Sink's immediate concern was the location of Lt. Col. Robert Strayer's 2nd Battalion, the outfit that held the key mission of moving without delay into Ste. Marie du Mont and the nearby hamlet of Pouppeville to open up the two causeways from Utah Beach. Sink, however, detected no sign of Strayer's men anywhere near Caloville. If they failed to show up soon, someone would have to find enough men and hastily produce a new plan to fulfill Strayer's mission.

Strayer's men would not show up soon, because most of them were three to four miles to the north on other drop zones that their Troop Carrier

Drop Zone C: Morning, June 6, 1944

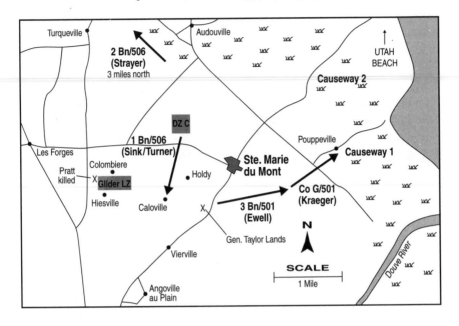

pilots had apparently mistaken for the 506th's objectives near Ste. Marie du Mont.

Lt. Col. Robert Strayer
Commander, 2nd Battalion, 506th Parachute Infantry
We were glad to get the hell out of the plane and into action since the idea of sitting on our duffs and getting shot at without fighting back was not our style. . . . A panel split on my chute and consequently I landed very hard. Both ankles and my right knee were injured. I started hearing noises near a hedgerow. I tried to get my squirt gun assembled, but I was in such a position that this was difficult. I took my cricket from around my neck, then clicked it [as a means of identifying him as an American], when to my surprise instead of an answering click I heard a loud "Moo." Was I relieved! My first sight of dead soldiers—Americans—was an uncanny feeling. My first reaction was and still is, "How stupid wars are," but I didn't have time to think much about it as I was too busy. My battalion's initial objective was capturing the towns of Ste. Marie du Mont and Pouppeville, thus securing the causeways for the advance of the seaborne forces. [But] our battalion was scattered over a distance of seven miles and consequently was far away from the objective.

Someone else would have to fulfill the mission. It was hardly a division commander's job to carry out a task of this kind personally, but airborne warfare was definitely unconventional; and in the predawn darkness of June 6, Maj. Gen. Maxwell Taylor realized that if his 101st Airborne Division was to accomplish its difficult D-Day missions, he himself must fulfill Strayer's task with as many men as he could gather in the bocage around Ste. Marie du Mont.

Taylor was an unenthusiastic parachutist, but by coincidence, one of the first 101st soldiers he encountered in Normandy was Lt. Col. Julian Ewell, who had been the jumpmaster on Taylor's first jump at Fort Benning in 1942.

Maj. Gen. Maxwell Taylor
Commander, 101st Airborne Division, February 1946
I landed alone in a field surrounded by the usual high hedges. . . . It took me about 20 minutes to find anyone. . . . Gradually I picked up a few men of the 501st and later contacted Gen. [Anthony] McAuliffe [the 101st's artillery commander], who had a group of artillery personnel with him. Still under the cover of darkness, we worked eastward for about one-quarter mile and finally halted in an enclosed field where we began to gather up stragglers. It was here that I first ran into Colonel

Ewell. We did not know exactly where we were until first light. Looking to the north through the tree-line which protected our field, we spotted the church tower of Ste. Marie du Mont. I had studied this so many times on the air photograph that I recognized it at once.

Portrayed by one of his men as "the finest officer with whom I ever served," the twenty-eight-year-old Ewell was one of the U.S. Army's first paratroopers and now commanded the 3rd Battalion, 501st Parachute Infantry, designated by Taylor as the 101st's divisional reserve. Ewell's outfit had suffered from a particularly severe enemy antiaircraft barrage as it approached the drop zone, and two fully loaded C-47s had been shot out of the sky, killing forty paratroopers and airmen.

Pvt. Arthur Morin
Company G, 501st Parachute Infantry, 101st Airborne Division, August 1944

Our plane was hit twice by anti-aircraft fire, the first time in the radio compartment, and resulted in two casualties to the parachute echelon. The ship was on fire as a result of the first hit, as well as the two men near the radio compartment door. The second hit was near the tail of the plane. Right after the first hit the jumpmaster, S/Sgt. [Charles] Word, hollered, "Let's Go!" and I bailed out. To get out it was necessary for me to climb up toward the door over other members of the stick who were lying on the floor of the plane and then dive out the door. The crew chief [T/Sgt. Melvin Isserson] did not have a chute on, and to the best of my knowledge none of the crew members got out of the plane. Immediately after I landed, the plane crashed in flames approximately 250 yards from me and exploded.

In spite of these disasters, Colonel Ewell had to gather his men on Drop Zone C west of Ste. Marie du Mont and fulfill his mission as Taylor's reserve, waiting for word from his commander to commit his battalion to the battle because of some unforeseen emergency. The astonished Ewell did not even have time to collect one-tenth of his outfit before Taylor informed him that that emergency was at hand.

Maj. Gen. Maxwell Taylor
Commander, 101st Airborne Division, February 1946

It was apparent by first light that the 506th, which had the task of securing the two southernmost causeways, had received a bad drop. I do not recall having encountered a single 506th soldier, although there were many of the 501st and a few of the 502nd. Recognizing that Sink's regiment was probably not in a position to execute its primary mission of securing the south causeways, I decided to move all available personnel on that mission myself. Because of the weakness of the force [about eighty-five men, mostly Ewell's], it seemed unreasonable to go for both exits, so I picked the south one at Pouppeville. I deliberately left cleaning up of Pouppeville to Ewell. He was in obvious danger of getting too much supervision from all the "brass" which he had around him. Furthermore, it was apparent from the way he went about his business that he didn't need much advice.

Ewell's men, drawn mostly from Capt. Vernon Kraeger's Company G, warily approached the village from the west on a narrow road lined by tall hedgerows. Situated on the high ground overlooking the western end of Causeway 1, Pouppeville was held by about seventy Germans from the 91st *Luftlande* Division, who immediately demonstrated a manifest determination to hold their ground. Several of them unexpectedly opened fire as the paratroopers came around a gentle curve in the road, but the astonished enemy quickly ascertained that the Americans wanted Pouppeville badly and were obviously willing to take great risks to take it.

"The finest officer with whom I ever served." Lt. Col. Julian Ewell, commander of the 3rd Battalion, 501st Parachute Infantry, 101st Airborne Division. COURTESY MARK BANDO.

Cpl. Virgil Danforth
Company G, 501st Parachute Infantry, 101st Airborne Division
Captain Kraeger insisted on walking down the center of the road toward the town, carrying his carbine, which was almost as big as he was. . . . We kept telling the

captain to get back where he belonged, but he kept telling us to mind our own business. He had almost lost his whole company—two plane loads had crashed— and he was just plain mad.

The Germans resisted fiercely for a time, inflicting eighteen casualties on the Americans, including six dead, but yielded in the end to Ewell's unrelenting attack. Ewell himself nearly became one of those casualties: A sniper's bullet glanced off his helmet and dented it, but he was unhurt.

Maj. Lawrence Legere
Assistant S-3, 101st Airborne Division
I was shot through the right leg while dashing across a road intersection [just west of Pouppeville]. The bullet entered just above the knee and exited the outside-middle of the thigh, shattering the bone it had passed through. I was wearing a small regulation entrenching shovel from the right side of my pistol belt, and my first sensation was not one of pain, but of hearing a loud "clang" as the bullet passed through the blade of the shovel. . . . Only a few seconds after I had been shot, a little medic with red crosses prominently displayed on his arms and helmet rushed in the middle of the road and knelt down to help me. While he was reaching into his satchel, the German put one rifle bullet through his head and he died immediately, his body falling over mine. . . . Since the war I have on several occasions tried to find out who this medic was, but without success. [It was T/5 Edwin Hohl of Buffalo, New York, who was remembered by General Taylor's radio operator, T/5 George Koskimaki, as "just a kid." The U.S. Army awarded Hohl the Silver Star posthumously.]

T/4 Raymond Geddes
Company G, 501st Parachute Infantry, 101st Airborne Division
Legere was yelling in pain; and Hohl went right out there, as he was trained to do, wearing a big Red Cross on his helmet and another on his arm. The sniper fired, and Hohl just sort of did a somersault. He never said a word. I called out to him to see if he was all right, but he never answered. I hope somebody got the bastard who shot him. There was no doubt that he was shooting a medic.

Pouppeville was in American hands; and despite the confusion of the nighttime airdrop, General Taylor now had the satisfaction of controlling three of the four coveted causeways leading off Utah Beach shortly after sunrise. The fourth, Causeway 2 at Ste. Marie du Mont, would follow before long. The German defenders of Utah Beach had no escape now, and more important, the 4th Division would be able to exit the beach securely after its seaborne landing. The original plan was in tatters, but somehow the most vital part of the 101st Airborne's mission had worked.

DYING AS MEN WOULD DIE

The area where the Douve River meets the sea is one of the most desolate places in Normandy. At the southeastern corner of the Cotentin Peninsula, that sluggish waterway empties into the English Channel at a vast sand bank known locally as *Bancs du Grand Vey*, which at low tide extends almost as far as the eye can see from the coastline. The region bordering the river mouth looks more like Holland than France, with miles of Napoleonic-era earthen dikes surrounding thousands of acres of soggy land the locals had reclaimed from the sea over the course of centuries. Aside from a sliver of high ground near the hamlet of Brévands, the entire area is just a few feet above sea level, a windy, lonely land crisscrossed by countless drainage ditches, with only rare signs of human habitation.

In this vast emptiness known by the natives as *le marais* (swampland), Colonel Sink's 3rd Battalion, 506th Parachute Infantry, commanded by West Virginia native Lt. Col. Robert Wolverton, had to fulfill an arduous D-Day mission. The enemy had built two modest bridges over the Douve near Brévands, about two miles upstream from its mouth. These, along with the nearby La Barquette dam, were the only places where military units could cross the Douve in the six-mile stretch between Carentan and the sea. If the Germans maintained control of these critical crossing points, they could use them to move reinforcements over the river after D-Day to counterattack the vulnerable southern flank of the Utah beachhead.

Wolverton must ensure that the enemy never got that chance. Orders spelled out his outfit's D-Day mission: He had to gather his men in the dark on Drop Zone D and hasten more than two miles eastward over the *marais* to seize the two bridges. If the Germans threatened to cross the bridges to attack Utah, the twenty-four-man demolition team accompanying the 3rd Battalion was to blow them up. If the enemy made no moves on the Brévands front, Wolverton must preserve the bridges for later use by Collins's VII Corps.

A 1938 West Point graduate, Wolverton was highly esteemed by his men. On the day before the invasion, he had gathered his battalion for some final words near the runways of the Exeter airfield from which it would soon depart for Normandy.

Lt. Col. Robert Wolverton
Commander, 3rd Battalion, 506th Parachute Infantry, June 5, 1944
Although I am not a religious man, I would like all of you to kneel with me in prayer. . . . That if die we must, that we die as men would die, without complaining, without pleading, and safe in the feeling that we have done our best for what we believed was right.

Col. Frank Krebs, commander of the 440th Troop Carrier Group at Exeter, conveyed Wolverton and his command team to Normandy on *Stoy Hora*, the lead C-47 of a forty-five-ship serial. A BBC reporter named Ward Smith accompanied Wolverton's stick and filed a report when he returned to Exeter with Krebs that morning.

Ward Smith
Reporter, BBC, June 1944
I shall never forget the scene up there in those last fateful minutes, those long lines of motionless, grim-faced young men burdened like pack-horses so that they could hardly stand unaided. . . . So young they looked, on the edge of the unknown. And somehow, so sad. Most sat with eyes closed as the seconds ticked by. They seemed to be asleep, but I could see lips moving wordlessly. . . . The time had come. We were over the drop zones. I wish I could play up that moment, but there was nothing to indicate that this was the supreme climax. Just a whistling that lasted for a few seconds — and those men, so young, so brave, had gone to their destiny.

Wolverton's combat career lasted only an instant. According to comrades who jumped from his C-47, the enemy shot him as he descended just east of St. Côme du Mont, and he was dead by the time his chute deposited him on the ground. That Drop Zone D was a particularly perilous place for a parachute landing on D-Day was corroborated by the nearly identical fatalities suffered by many of Wolverton's men, including his second-in-command, Maj. George Grant, and the CO of Company G, Capt. Harold Van Antwerp. Furthermore, shortly after the drop, the Germans captured Wolverton's three remaining company commanders, including Capt. John McKnight of Company I.

Capt. John McKnight
Commander, Company I, 506th Parachute Infantry, 1947
Apparently the Germans anticipated that the invaders might use this area for just such a purpose, and they ringed it with machine guns and mortars, and were sit-

"Safe in the feeling we have done our best for what we believed was right."
Lt. Col. Robert Wolverton (at right), commander of the 3rd Battalion, 506th
Parachute Infantry, 101st Airborne Division, preparing for the D-Day jump with
one of his men at Exeter airfield in England. U.S. ARMY SIGNAL CORPS, NATIONAL ARCHIVES.

ting at their arms in readiness when the 3rd Battalion came in. . . . Floating down
into this well-lit and fire-covered area, the battalion lost about twenty men from
enemy action before its first groups could collect themselves.

Roused into action by the earlier arrival of American pathfinders,
enemy troops swarmed all over the high ground on the western fringe of
the drop zone near St. Côme du Mont. The Germans had set a barn alight
in the middle of the marsh, and that blaze enhanced the light of a full moon
to provide the Germans with a clear view of the paratroopers tumbling out
of Krebs's C-47s and floating so vulnerably to the ground. With such effective enemy observation of the *marais*, movement of any kind on the part of
the paratroopers was exceedingly risky, and consequently only a small
fraction of Wolverton's unit, led by operations officer Capt. Charles Shettle, was able to assemble and head across the marsh to the two Brévands
bridges before sunrise, as orders demanded.

3rd Battalion, 506th Parachute Infantry, 101st Airborne Division
D-Day Action Report, June 27, 1944

Captain Shettle with one man met Lt. [Rudolph] Bolte with six men and Lt. [Frank] Rowe with six more men near the assembly area. . . . Along the route [to the bridges], sixteen more men were picked up with Lt. [Frederick] Broyhill and an engineer officer. [They] reached the [bridges] at 0430. Immediate resistance was met from the east bank of the river, but the battalion managed to secure and hold the west bank and control the bridges. At this time Lt. [Richard] Meason and Lt. [Joseph] Doughty arrived at the site with three officers and fifteen additional men. Captain Shettle decided to cross the river at Bridge 37 [the southernmost of the two bridges]. . . . Two volunteers crossed the bridge, although they were subjected to heavy machine gun fire. [These were PFC Donald Zahn, followed by Sgt. George Montilio, both of Company H. The U.S. Army awarded both men the Distinguished Service Cross for valor during this action.] . . . At this time the battalion was still without communications, short on ammunition, and had only one ration for only about two-thirds of the men. . . . For the remainder of the day the position was held on the riverbank. [That afternoon] word was received that Col. [Howard] Johnson and a group from the 501st Parachute Infantry were fighting at the locks of La Barquette [one mile to the west]. Captain Shettle made his way to the locks, but found this unit in much the same situation as the 3rd Battalion.

Shettle's little band fulfilled its D-Day mission and held on to the bridges throughout June 6 and for two days after that, not only denying the enemy the use of the spans, but also controlling the site for a river crossing by the 327th Glider Infantry on June 10 and 11, a vital part of the 101st Airborne's attempt to encircle the critical German stronghold in Carentan. During his three days at the Brévands bridges, contact between Shettle and his regimental commander was nonexistent, and Colonel Sink had presumed that most of his 3rd Battalion was destroyed. Even worse, on June 7, friendly P-47 fighter-bombers mistakenly attacked the bridge sites, inflicting several casualties on Shettle's men and destroying both spans.

Wolverton's 3rd Battalion shared the deadly Drop Zone D with Col. Howard Ravenscroft Johnson's 501st Parachute Infantry. The 501st was something of an orphan outfit, as it did not arrive in England until late January 1944 and was not officially attached to the 101st Airborne Division until shortly before the invasion. Even so, Colonel Johnson's reputation within the paratrooper community was legendary. A dropout from the U.S. Naval Academy in his early twenties, Johnson ultimately found a home in the airborne forces after the U.S. Army rejected him in the interwar years for pilot training because of a vision problem. His edgy personality and

Drop Zone D: Morning, June 6, 1944

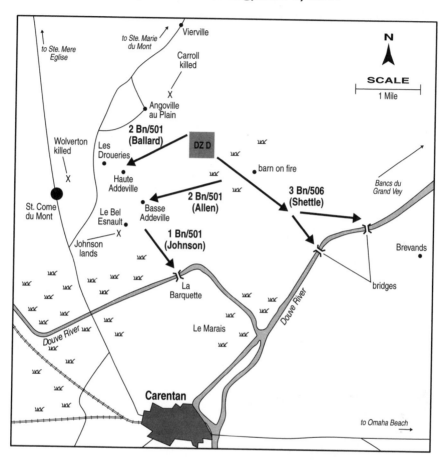

100-plus practice parachute jumps had earned him the nickname "Jumpy," and day after day at Camp Toccoa, Georgia, he would bellow at his troops, "Who's the best?"—a question that was invariably answered, "We are!" On D-Day, he was two weeks shy of his 41st birthday, but his boyish face made him appear much younger. Any subordinate who mistook that youthful appearance for vulnerability would not make that mistake again.

The Germans in St. Côme du Mont and on the fringes of the featureless marsh inflicted the same kind of brutal punishment on Johnson's troops that they had wreaked on Wolverton's unfortunate men. Johnson himself, however, had a comparatively lucky landing in an area sheltered by trees near a majestic chateau named Le Bel Esnault. As soon as he came down to earth, he was fired upon wildly by an enemy sentry opposite the chateau's front gate. Johnson jerked out his .45 pistol and replied with two shots, after which, as he reported to a U.S. Army historian, "[I] heard a scream, followed by silence."

Johnson decided to head for the La Barquette dam, about a mile upstream from the two Douve River bridges that Shettle's men were about to seize. Although he did not yet know his location with certainty, Johnson's decision turned out to be the right thing to do, as the 501st's 1st Battalion, which held orders to seize La Barquette, had been badly dispersed and mauled by the Germans upon landing. Shortly after dropping on the edge of the swamp near Angoville au Plain, the 1st Battalion's twenty-eight-year-

"Who's the best?" Col. Howard Johnson, commander of the 501st Parachute Infantry, 101st Airborne Division, known as "Jumpy" to his men.
Courtesy Mark Bando.

old commander, Lt. Col. Robert Carroll, and two of his staff officers had been killed, the second battalion commander from the 101st to die that night on this fatal drop zone. Shortly afterward, Carroll's second-in-command, Maj. Phillip Gage, was severely wounded and captured. But in the next several hours, Johnson gathered up more than 100 paratroopers, and as the sun rose, they carefully worked their way south across the marshy low ground toward what they hoped would be the Douve River—and with any luck, the La Barquette dam.

Suddenly there it was up ahead: the distinctive stone dam with its six arched floodgates, which the paratroopers recognized at once from air photographs they had examined in England. Were there any Germans on the lock or in the three adjacent cottages who would defend it? Apparently not, as the enemy did not respond to the fifty paratroopers who dashed across the gravel roadway atop the dam to the east side. As at St. Martin de Varreville, Pouppeville, and the Brévands bridges, the Germans had yet again failed to safeguard a site of critical military importance, and the GIs had snatched it before the enemy could react. If this pattern of unpreparedness was typical of all enemy outfits in the Cotentin Peninsula, the American D-Day invasion would certainly succeed. But Johnson knew that the Germans had not conquered most of Europe by luck. And anyone who made the mistake of underestimating their military abilities would be in for a surprise.

PFC Adrian Doss
Company B, 501st Parachute Infantry
About 0630 June 6 I tumbled into a deep ditch covered by a large hedgerow, and to my surprise I fell against a man who I first thought was a Kraut. But after appraising his haggard, disheveled appearance I saw I was looking at my regimental commander [Johnson], who naturally displayed everything but dignity; and after a moment he asked me, "Where is my regiment?" He was a great commander, and his actions eventually cost him his life. [Johnson was killed in October 1944 in Holland.]

Just north of the Le Bel Esnault chateau, situated on a nose of high ground overlooking the Drop Zone D marshland, are three tiny Norman farming hamlets: Angoville au Plain, Haute (Upper) Addeville, and Basse (Lower) Addeville. Most of the paratroopers belonging to the 501st's 2nd Battalion, commanded by a former Floridian dairy farmer named Lt. Col. Robert Ballard, came to earth in this lethal locale, and they immediately discerned that the enemy populated those three villages in force. Ballard's job was to capture St. Côme du Mont on D-Day and destroy the several bridges lying between that town and Carentan. If he succeeded, the enemy's anticipated counterattack against Collins's VII Corps in the critical days after the invasion would be thwarted. But at dawn on June 6, Ballard concluded that his disorganized battalion could get nowhere near St. Côme du Mont unless his men could knock the Germans off the high ground and clear out those three villages.

Given the large number of Germans in the area and their considerable terrain advantages, Ballard's task would be almost impossible. Yet two separate forces of paratroopers set out to accomplish it: the first, comprising about 100 men under the leadership of the 501st's operations officer, Maj. Richard Allen; and the second under Ballard himself, consisting of more than 200 paratroopers. Allen's force got caught up in ferocious close-in fighting at Basse Addeville, which a trooper recalled was "scarcely even a village, [with] houses of brick and rotting plaster, with red-tiled roofs." At least for the moment, St. Côme du Mont would not be reached by that route. Meanwhile, Ballard instigated an attack about one-half mile to the north against Haute Addeville but got no closer to his objective than Allen.

2nd Battalion, 501st Parachute Infantry, 101st Airborne Division
U.S. Army Historical Division, Interview with Lt. Col. Robert Ballard,
July 1944

Dawn was cracking as the companies moved out of the fields and down the hedgerows toward St. Côme du Mont, which Ballard proposed to assault immediately. . . . Ballard had reached the conclusion that there was a much larger [enemy] force there than he had bargained on. . . . The attack order was issued at 0430 by Capt. William Pelham, the S-3. The plan was that they would move against Les Droueries [a farm west of Haute Addeville] with two companies abreast. Company E on the right with 30 men was to go after the farm buildings and the road crossing on that side while Company F with 30 men was to attack toward the crossroads on the left. . . . Company E had already worked forward as far as the bend in the road when rifle and automatic fire, seeming to come from enemy positions grouped closely around the houses, broke all around it and stopped the advance. The bullet fire ranged down both sides of the road and was also picking away at the embankment of the forward hedgerows. A curtain of mortar fire dropped down on both roads and the field lying between them. The men of Company E went flat in the ditches almost instantly, and remained there, inert. . . . Company F got no farther than Company E. . . . By 0800, Ballard had felt out the pressure sufficiently that he was certain the enemy force intended to stand its ground. . . . He felt that his attack thus far had been largely futile. A few of the enemy in the dug-in positions between Ballard's force and the first house had been killed but there had been no abatement of the fire.

On the high ground overlooking the marsh east of St. Côme du Mont, the Germans were displaying the tenacity in combat for which their army was renowned. They would not be pushovers after all.

A RECIPE FOR DISASTER

General Bradley had vehemently disagreed with Air Chief Marshal Leigh-Mallory's gloomy prophecies about the American airborne operation in the Cotentin, but with at least one of Leigh-Mallory's points, Bradley ostensibly concurred. Given the newly discovered presence in the Cotentin of the German 91st *Luftlande* Division, First Army planners considered major American glider landings at dawn on D-Day exceptionally risky. With the Germans alerted by the parachute landings, and the paratroopers in all probability still fighting for their drop zones, as dawn broke the enemy would surely shoot the vulnerable gliders out of the sky like ducks in hunting season. Consequently, Bradley limited the initial glider landings early on D-Day to two lifts totaling only 104 CG-4A Wacos, split evenly among two landing zones: one for the 82nd Airborne, the other for the 101st. Bradley consented to much larger glider landings shortly before sunset, but by then the landing zones would supposedly be under firm American control.

What astonished American glider pilots assigned to the morning mission was not its small size, but its scheduled arrival time. D-Day orders specified landing times for the 101st and 82nd lifts as 4:00 and 4:07 A.M., two hours before sunrise. American glider pilots had not trained extensively for nighttime landings, and in the bocage, a terrain type every glider pilot knew would be particularly tough, the plan, according to one pilot, "sounded like a recipe for disaster." Thus, in order to avoid German antiaircraft fire, orders demanded that the glider pilots carry out nighttime landings that potentially could inflict more damage on the Wacos than the enemy ever could. The glider mission appeared to be shaping up as a classic army snafu.

The 101st Airborne glider mission consisted of fifty-two C-47s from the 434th Troop Carrier Group, which were to tow their gliders toward a village named Hiesville, a little more than a mile west of Ste. Marie du Mont. There the glider pilots would cut their Wacos loose and drift silently downward to meet their fate on a landing zone that would be clearly marked by 101st pathfinders, assuming they had successfully fulfilled their part of the mission. The gliders carried a total of 155 troops, mostly medical personnel, including surgeons, as well as crews for sixteen 57-millimeter antitank guns. Occupying the 434th's leading glider was the 101st's second-in-command, Brig. Gen. Donald Pratt, together with his aide and a command jeep. General Taylor recalled: "Pratt was very superstitious. The night before the operation we were sitting around talking about it when someone came in and tossed a hat on his bed. He immediately threw it off and said something about it being bad luck." But Pratt had the good fortune of drawing the best glider pilot in the army air force, Lt. Col. Mike Murphy, an expert in aerial acrobatics from the old barnstorming days, whose Waco was labeled "The Fighting Falcon" and was adorned with a large 101st "screaming eagle" emblem.

Towed by their mother ships, and meeting the same cloud banks and enemy antiaircraft fire that had disrupted the earlier Troop Carrier flights, the 434th's gliders passed over the Cotentin's west coast about an hour after the last of the C-47 serials carrying 82nd Airborne paratroopers.

"A recipe for disaster." 101st Airborne Division glider troops load a gun into a Waco glider in preparation for the D-Day mission. U.S. ARMY SIGNAL CORPS, NATIONAL ARCHIVES.

When the glider pilots cut loose over Hiesville at about 450 feet, they immediately gathered that this nighttime landing in the middle of enemy territory was going to be as perilous as they had anticipated.

Flight Officer George Buckley
Glider Pilot, 74th Squadron, 434th Troop Carrier Group

As soon as the rope disconnected from our glider, I started a 360-degree turn to the left, feeling my way down into the darkness, holding the glider as close to stalling speed as I could. . . . You know the ground is down there, but you can't see it; you don't know if you're going to hit trees, ditches, barns, houses, or what, and all this time the flak and tracers are coming up all around you. . . . We still couldn't see a thing, and I knew that we were about to run out of altitude. Finally, out of the corner of my eye, I noticed a faint light patch that looked like an open field surrounded by trees. It was. By this time we were so low that we had no choice in the matter. . . . We flared out for a landing just above the stalling speed and touched down as smooth as glass. But just when we thought we had it made, there was a tremendous bone-jarring crash. We had hit one of those damn ditches that the Germans dug across the fields. . . . We plunged down into the ditch, and when the nose slammed into the other side, the glider's back broke as it slid up over the opposite bank. The floor split open, and we skidded to a halt in the field on the other side. . . . For a split second we sat in stunned silence, and I breathed a sigh of relief because none of us seemed to be injured. We then bailed out fast because there was rifle and machine gun fire going off in the fields around us.

But for the glider pilots and their passengers, the war had only just begun. Now that they had survived their alarming "controlled crashes" in Normandy, they must begin carrying out the tasks they had trained for so long to fulfill.

T/5 Emil Natalle
Surgical Technician, 326th Airborne Medical Company, 101st Airborne Division, November 30, 1944

One of the five [passengers] said, "Anybody hurt?" The reply came back a resounding and unanimous "No!" Imagine a landing that left a glider a total loss, looking more like a pile of cardboard cartons impaled on poles than an aircraft, and no one really injured! We tumbled out of the glider quickly after releasing our safety belts. . . . [Later], returning to the scene of the landing, Maj.[Albert] Crandall, senior surgical officer, was there attempting to gather his surgical team together in order to get his hospital into operation. [The 101st hospital was to be set up in a chateau named Colombière, near Hiesville.]

There had been many skeptics—but the 434th Group had done well. Of the fifty-two gliders participating in the mission, forty-nine made it to the Cotentin, about two-thirds of which landed on target or within two miles of Hiesville. Only one C-47 and its towed Waco had been shot down by the antiaircraft fire that Leigh-Mallory had so dreaded. A high percentage of the gliders, however, were damaged beyond repair as a result of their rough landings, and the airmen and gliderists suffered about thirty casualties, including twelve dead.

One of the fatalities was the fifty-one-year-old General Pratt. Colonel Murphy's glider had made a good landing at about sixty miles per hour, but even the wing spoilers and Murphy's full weight applied to the brakes could not stop the heavily loaded "Fighting Falcon" on the wet grass for more than 200 yards. Ultimately what halted Murphy's aircraft was not the brakes, but one of the huge hedgerows so typical of Normandy. A piece of machinery as flimsy as a Waco glider stood no chance against the solidity of a Norman hedgerow, and the resulting crack-up broke both of Murphy's legs and killed his copilot, Lt. John Butler. Murphy glanced back into the passenger cabin to check on Pratt: The general was sitting in his jeep as if asleep, drooped over the steering wheel. He was dead, apparently of a broken neck. The man who was so strongly superstitious had been killed by a stroke of bad luck.

CHAPTER 6

All-Americans

FROM THE FRYING PAN TO LA FIÈRE

The Americans could accomplish nothing without Ste. Mère Église. That typical Norman town, with its eleventh-century church located in the central square, was a focal point for those many natives of the Cotentin Peninsula who made their living by farming or raising livestock. But in 1944, Ste. Mère Église was also a critical military objective, for six major roads cutting through the heart of the peninsula passed through it. If German forces deployed to the north or west of Utah Beach were to launch a counterattack designed to drive the Americans back into the sea in the days following the invasion, they would have to use those roads to do it. If, however, American paratroopers held the town, that counterattack could be foiled before it had gotten anywhere near the sea.

Alexandre Renaud, the 1944 mayor of Ste. Mère Église, remembered that the senior German Army officer in town was an unenthusiastic Austrian who seemed more engrossed by the piano than by his military responsibilities. According to Renaud, this indifferent soul was always forgiving when only a small fraction of the forty-man workforce of Ste. Mère Église natives the Germans required the mayor to provide daily actually showed up for work to erect antiglider obstacles in the nearby fields. The Austrian would merely say over and over again, "Try and have one or two more tomorrow." He had no idea that his peaceful garrison life was about to be shattered by the arrival of thousands of Americans in the environs of Ste. Mère Église; and even worse, an entire U.S. Army parachute regiment, consisting of 2,000 men thoroughly imbued with a longing to kill their enemies, had a firm intention of seizing the town almost before the Germans realized that the invasion had begun.

The 505th Parachute Infantry was the only one of six parachute regiments to land on D-Day that had combat experience. Col. James Gavin had trained the 505th to a fever pitch in 1942, and that grounding had paid off in the regiment's brutal initiation to war, when it fought off German panzers at Biazza Ridge in Sicily with no antitank weapons larger than bazookas. Two 1943 combat jumps within a span of little more than two months instilled in the 505th's paratroopers a feeling that they were something special, and when they shipped out to Northern Ireland in December 1943 to prepare for D-Day, they let everyone know it. Under a new commander, Lt. Col. Herbert Batcheller, discipline lapsed, AWOLs soared, and Gavin, now a general, blamed it on the new man's "inadequate and unforceful supervision of the regiment." When he learned of this situation, General Ridgway shipped Batcheller off to the 508th Parachute Infantry, reducing him to a battalion commander, and brought in Lt. Col. William Ekman, formerly the 508th's second-in-command, as the 505th's new leader. The thirty-one-year-old Ekman, who had served a two-year hitch as an enlisted man in the early thirties, was a West Point graduate from the class of 1938. For such a young man to lead more than 2,000 troops, mostly hardened combat veterans, into the most momentous military operation of World War II was a considerable challenge.

Troop Carrier's 315th and 316th Groups, both of which had extensive flying experience in combat in the Mediterranean, gave the 505th the best drop of any American parachute outfit in Normandy. Somehow the fliers avoided the cloud bank on the Cotentin's west coast that had perplexed earlier serials, and they arrived over Drop Zone O, just northwest of Ste. Mère Église, in reasonably tight nine-ship formations. Even better, the 505th pathfinders had deployed their T-lights almost flawlessly, so for pilots approaching on the proper course, the drop zone was easily recognizable. Within two hours of the drop, all three battalions of the 505th had at least partially assembled in the dark, forbidding bocage, and their leaders had figured out their correct locations. True, many men were still missing, no doubt lost in the hedgerows; they could find their way to their objectives later. But for now, enough paratroopers had been gathered that the 505th could start fulfilling its D-Day missions. As for the Troop Carrier crews, the mission had gone so smoothly that one 316th Group radio operator, S/Sgt. Michael Ingrisano, later remembered it as "a milk run."

The responsibility for seizing Ste. Mère Église rested with Ekman's 3rd Battalion, commanded by Lt. Col. Edward Krause. Nicknamed "Cannonball" by his men, Krause had successfully led his outfit in July 1943 through the tough fight at Biazza Ridge, where he had witnessed German military prowess far superior to what he was about to behold in Ste. Mère Église. Krause had exhibited such forceful leadership during airborne training that among 3rd Battalion paratroopers, he held a fearsome reputation. One private remembered, "Krause was a very abrasive personality, and I doubt if many people would have nice things to say about him." A senior 82nd Airborne officer labeled Krause a "psycho," and some had whispered that the strains of combat in Sicily had caused him to snap. Whatever the truth of those allegations, Krause led his outfit straight into Ste. Mère Église on D-Day, fulfilling his orders more promptly than any other U.S. Army parachute battalion commander in Normandy. The unfortunate Austrian garrison commandant in Ste. Mère Église would have no opportunities to play the piano for a considerable time.

Lt. Col. Edward Krause
Commander, 3rd Battalion, 505th Parachute Infantry, August 13, 1944
We [gathered] close to 200 men in about an hour an a half of assembling. . . . It was just before 4 AM when I made the decision to move out to Ste. Mère Église. We moved in from the northwest [following a secluded path, guided by a Frenchman who, Krause noted, was "inebriated"]. I would say we arrived in town just before light [about 5:15 A.M.] and had no opposition at all, mainly due to the covered route by which the civilian took us; but in the center of town there were spasmodic shots that increased as we moved in. . . . The remaining enemy troops were apparently scared out of the town. The force we had was just a jumbled group, and in order to secure the town as quickly as possible we endeavored to establish roadblocks around the town as hastily as possible—which we did.

With the town secure, Krause proceeded straight to a flagpole in front of the Ste. Mère Église *Hôtel de Ville* (town hall), removed an American flag from a haversack, and raised it, noting that it was the same flag the 3rd Battalion had raised over Naples in October 1943. He then sent a courier to provide Colonel Ekman with the brief but thoroughly noteworthy message: "I have secured Ste. Mère Église." Krause had achieved a decisive victory,

"We like to think of ourselves as a corps d'élite, *and we are." Paratroopers from the 82nd Airborne Division in Normandy.* U.S. ARMY SIGNAL CORPS, NATIONAL ARCHIVES.

but it was one that the enemy would vigorously strive to reverse on this and the next day. At about 9:30 A.M. the Germans launched the first of many counterattacks to retake Ste. Mère Église, this one from the south astride the main road to Carentan, but Krause's paratroopers repulsed it. The presence of the enemy in such force south of Ste. Mère Église, however, alarmed the Americans, as in just a few hours 176 Troop Carrier gliders carrying more than 400 82nd Airborne troops and several vital pieces of ordnance and equipment were scheduled to land in the fields east of this road. If the Germans controlled the terrain surrounding the glider landing zone, they would surely destroy the gliders before they hit the ground. Accordingly, instead of being content to hold what they had, the 505th must sooner or later launch its own assault if the glider mission was to succeed.

    The 82nd Airborne's invasion planners actually feared German counterattacks from the north more than enemy action from the south. The 101st Airborne was supposed to take care of the Carentan area, thereby denying German movement toward Ste. Mère Église from a southerly direction. But the flank north of Ste. Mère Église was wide open, and if the

Germans reacted to the invasion with their customary zeal, substantial enemy forces, including tanks, could come barreling down the Cherbourg road toward Ste. Mère Église on D-Day. Given the paratroopers' light weaponry, it would be difficult for the 82nd to prevent a forceful attack from this direction from breaking through. As a result, the 82nd's invasion plan ordained that the 505th's entire 2nd Battalion, commanded by Lt. Col. Benjamin Vandervoort, must move out promptly after its drop to establish a defensive line about one and a half miles north of Ste. Mère Église, centered on the hamlet of Neuville au Plain. Given the 505th's July 1943 experience at Biazza Ridge, its troopers feared German tanks more than anything else the enemy could offer, but if Vandervoort's men could hang on for just a few hours, help was supposed to arrive in the form of plentiful antitank guns landed by gliders just before dawn.

Gavin later said the twenty-nine-year-old Vandervoort "was probably the best battalion commander I had." General Ridgway concurred, calling Vandervoort "one of the bravest, toughest battle commanders I ever knew." Vandervoort had joined the Maryland National Guard as an enlisted man at sixteen years of age and was commissioned into the Regular army seven years later upon graduation from college. He volunteered for the fledgling U.S. Army parachute forces more than a year before Pearl Harbor, and by the time of the July 1943 airborne invasion of Sicily, he was one of Gavin's most trusted staff officers in the 505th Parachute Infantry.

Unhappily for Vandervoort, on D-Day he landed in Normandy on a 45-degree slope with such force that he broke his left shinbone about an inch above the ankle. Every step triggered excruciating pain, so he injected himself with morphine and hobbled onward to gather his men. A few hours later, he located the battalion surgeon, Capt. Lyle Putnam, and had him take a look at the injury.

Capt. Lyle Putnam
Surgeon, 2nd Battalion, 505th Parachute Infantry
Luckily it was a simple rather than a compound fracture. He insisted on replacing his jump-boot, laced it tightly, formed a very makeshift crutch from a stick, and moved with the outfit as an equal and a leader without complaint. . . . The man did not lose two hours active duty in our thirty-three days in Normandy. He thoroughly convinced every man of his battalion of his merits and qualities.

In early June 1944, the 315th Troop Carrier Group at Spanhoe airfield in England received orders to convey a special passenger to Normandy as part of the 82nd Airborne's D-Day airdrop. The 315th had to provide a top-notch pilot and crew for this mission, for that passenger was none other than the 82nd's commander, Maj. Gen. Matthew Ridgway, accompanied by a party of five officers and five enlisted men. This would be the forty-nine-year-old Ridgway's fifth jump of the war—but his first into combat. He would not fail to notice an inaccurate drop, and in that unfortunate event, the highest reaches of Troop Carrier Command would surely hear about it. The 315th Group had to put Ridgway right in the middle of Drop Zone O, and at about 2:00 A.M. on June 6, it achieved that goal. Two days later, Ridgway composed a short letter to Brig. Gen. Paul Williams, the chief of IX Troop Carrier Command: "Please express to all elements of your command who brought this Division in by glider or parachute . . . our admiration for their coolness under fire, for their determination to overcome all obstacles, and for their magnificent spirit of cooperation." The oldest paratrooper, from whom praise did not come easily, was clearly pleased.

Like almost every other American who jumped into Normandy that night, however, Ridgway drifted alone for some time in the bocage's tiny pastures, walled in by towering hedgerows, wondering where everyone was. He landed close to Vandervoort's 2nd Battalion, and indeed, as the nearly crippled Vandervoort started to assemble his outfit, the first officer he met was Ridgway.

Lt. Col. Benjamin Vandervoort
Commander, 2nd Battalion, 505th Parachute Infantry
I was sitting against a hedgerow having people put up green flares and lights to assemble the battalion. Someone came up and said, "General Ridgway is over there and wants to see you." I said: "Tell him I have a broken leg." The General came over and asked how I was. He wanted to know how the assembly was coming along and seemed to find it all right. We looked at a map with a flashlight, and that's all the detail of our meeting that I remember.

Maj. Gen. Matthew Ridgway
Commander, 82nd Airborne Division, November 12, 1948
I, with a nucleus of my headquarters, small as it was, began the exercise of direct command over all divisional elements with which it was in contact before daylight on D-Day. This direct personal control was extended as rapidly as possible, and in a remarkably short time included all major divisional units. It was never interrupted during the entire thirty-three days of the division's participation [in the Normandy campaign].

505th Parachute Infantry: Morning, June 6, 1944

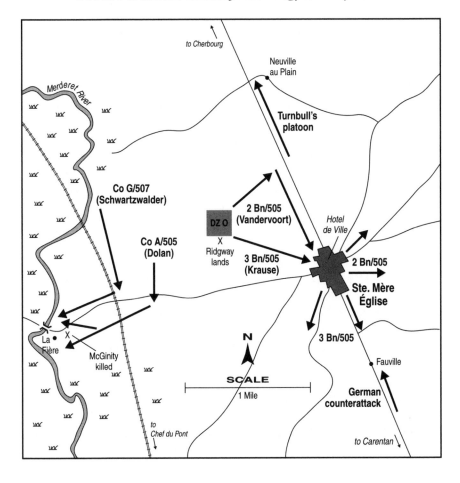

to Cherbourg

Neuville
au Plain

Turnbull's
platoon

Merderet River

Co G/507
(Schwartzwalder)

2 Bn/505
(Vandervoort)

DZ O

X
Ridgway
lands

Co A/505
(Dolan)

3 Bn/505
(Krause)

Hotel
de Ville

2 Bn/505

Ste. Mère
Église

La
Fière

X

McGinity
killed

N

3 Bn/505

Fauville

SCALE
1 Mile

German
counterattack

to
Chef du Pont

to Carentan

Troop Carrier pilots from the 316th Group gave the 2nd Battalion an extraordinarily tight drop; and lured by the flares fired into the sky, it came together quickly, almost in its entirety, ready to move out toward Neuville au Plain to block the Cherbourg road.

Lt. Col. Benjamin Vandervoort
Commander, 2nd Battalion, 505th Parachute Infantry, August 13, 1944
I think it was about 0410 when I felt I had completed the assembly sufficiently so that I could move out on our mission and take the town of Neuville au Plain. In the meantime . . . the news from Ste. Mère Église was so vague to the regimental commander [Ekman] that he had me stand by. General Ridgway happened to be in my CP during that period, and he also directed me not to move without consulting him. It was not until daylight that I received orders to move. We actually started moving at 0600.

Vandervoort's men had just started toward Neuville when their D-Day mission abruptly changed. Somehow the runner Krause had dispatched to announce the seizure of Ste. Mère Église had failed to reach Ekman, so no one outside of the 3rd Battalion knew whether the capture of that vital objective had occurred. If Ste. Mère Église remained in German hands, occupying Neuville would be of no value. Therefore, Ekman ordered Vandervoort to divert his battalion to the south, rather than move north toward its original target, to ensure that the 505th's major D-Day goal would be accomplished in a timely manner. Vandervoort promptly complied, but on his own initiative, he detached a forty-three-man platoon from Company D, led by 1st Lt. Turner Turnbull, to move north and occupy Neuville. That decision, as events later proved, was entirely sensible.

As the 2nd Battalion men moved into Ste. Mère Église, they detected no live Germans—but many dead ones. Krause's troopers apparently had matters well in hand. But the grisly scene in the town square adjacent to the ancient church was a profound shock to the newcomers.

Capt. George Wood
Chaplain, 2nd Battalion, 505th Parachute Infantry
Lt. Col. Vandervoort asked me to do something about the men [paratroopers from the 505th and 506th Parachute Infantry] hanging dead in the trees down in the village square. There were six of them, and it was affecting the morale of the men to see their buddies' lifeless bodies hanging there. I had no burial detail, so I got a detail of six men with an officer from the front line [south of town]. There was much anger among the men over the killing of their buddies in trees, but I

explained that this was what we could expect in our kind of outfit. [This was thirty-three-year-old "Chappie" Wood's third combat jump. He would make a fourth in September.]

Two miles west of Ste. Mère Église, one of the main roads radiating from that town crosses the Merderet River at a bridge adjacent to an aged stucco manor house named La Fière. In June 1944, the 82nd Airborne focused considerable amounts of staff time on seizing that modest bridge, and the ferocious fight that swirled around it on D-Day and for three days thereafter would in the end define the division's combat achievements in Normandy.

The La Fière bridge is small enough that nowadays one hardly even notices it. Indeed, the span seems so insignificant that it is difficult to comprehend why the paratroopers considered it so vital. A crucial fact that the modern observer invariably fails to notice, however, is that for a distance of about 600 yards west of the bridge, the road is slightly elevated above the surrounding pastureland. By June 1944, the Germans had inundated those pastures by shrewd manipulation of La Barquette's locks near Carentan, and they looked more like shallow lakes than farmers' fields. Consequently, that elevated road, which the plan books referred to as a "causeway," was vital because it was the only location where troops and vehicles could cross the swollen Merderet for miles on either side of the La Fière bridge.

The 505th's Company A, led by 1st Lt. John Dolan, held the job of taking the bridge. Troop Carrier crews from the 315th Group furnished Dolan's men with a first-rate drop, and by dawn, he had assembled his outfit and was on the move toward the bridge, following the road running west out of Ste. Mère Église. His immediate problem was a group of twenty-eight Germans occupying defensive positions in and around the La Fière manor house. The enemy troops had been alerted by the earlier arrival of some 507th Parachute Infantry GIs under the command of Capt. Ben Schwartzwalder and Lt. John Marr, and unlike many other enemy units on D-Day, these Germans were prepared to fight.

1st Lt. John Dolan
Commander, Company A, 505th Parachute Infantry
About 700–800 yards from the bridge we came upon a dirt road running southeasterly from the road to the bridge. . . . Beyond it in the direction of the bridge was an open, flat field about 100 yards deep and 75 yards wide. I directed Lt. Donald Coxon [leader, 3rd Platoon] to send his scouts out. This he did, and he also went out with them. He had plenty of personal courage, but he didn't have the

heart to order them out without going with them. A few moments later a German machine gun opened up, killing Coxon and one of his scouts, [PFC Robert] Ferguson. [Another member of Company A noted that Coxon's death "was a blow for some of us, as he had been with us since our days in the 'Frying Pan' at Fort Benning."] I directed Lt. [George] Presnell [leader, 2nd Platoon] to recross the road and attack along the northerly side down to the bridge. This was done, and the 2nd Platoon didn't meet with any fire until they arrived at the bridge. . . . We cut back toward the road, traveling in a northerly direction. Major [James] McGinity [XO, 1st Battalion] was leading, and I was about three or four paces behind. . . . When we had traveled about two-thirds of the way up the hedgerow, they opened up on us. . . . Major McGinity was killed instantly. I returned the fire with my Thompson submachine gun at a point where I could see leaves in the hedgerow fluttering.

Schwartzwalder's and Dolan's men were pinned for about an hour, but the GIs continually worked around the Germans' flanks and finally routed them. To complete the victory, Schwartzwalder's paratroopers rooted out twenty-five Germans from the La Fière manor house and its adjacent farm buildings.

The coveted bridge was in American hands. As to what was happening on the causeway's western end, 600 yards distant—it was anybody's guess. No paratrooper could rest easy until that vital part of the objective was also secured. But so far on D-Day, the 505th Parachute Infantry had done as well as even the optimists had predicted, if not better.

SACRED GROUND

The little cluster of stone buildings called Cauquigny on the far side of the La Fière causeway was the key. Paratroopers from the 505th around the La Fière manor house were peering intently across the Merderet floodplain at this hamlet, wondering who, if anyone, was there. All eyes were drawn to Cauquigny's most distinctive edifice—its forsaken chapel, with its three arched clerestory windows. If the Americans could gain control of this little corner of Normandy, Collins's VII Corps would soon surge across the causeway over the formidable Merderet River and cut the Cotentin Peninsula in two. In that event, the Germans in Cherbourg would be finished. But in actuality it would take more than three days and hundreds of casualties for the 82nd Airborne to call Cauquigny its own.

The responsibility for seizing Cauquigny fell to the 507th Parachute Infantry, an outfit that was new to the 82nd Airborne and, unlike the 505th, had never been in combat. Normandy would be the only World War II campaign in which the 507th was a component of the All-American division, and regimental veterans later regularly lamented that they were in truth a "bastard" outfit on D-Day.

Col. George Millett, nicknamed "Zip" by his comrades, had commanded the 507th since its inception in 1942. Like Gavin, the forty-year-old Millett had graduated in the West Point class of 1929, but in his role as the 82nd's assistant division commander Gavin displayed not the slightest school loyalty to his classmate. In a February 1944 diary entry, Gavin noted, "I wish that someone had had the moral courage to relieve him before he had come this far." Gavin later recalled: "Millett was awful. Very overweight. . . . Mentally I don't think he was ready for what he got into."

The 61st and 442nd Troop Carrier groups in large measure overshot the 507th's drop zone by about a mile, which hardly would have been disastrous to the paratroopers in ordinary terrain. However, the area immediately to the east of their drop zone encompassed the Merderet's wide floodplain, and as a result, many 507th sticks landed right into the middle of what amounted to a shallow lake. A water landing so far from the sea was a shock to the paratroopers, for preinvasion photographs of this region had not revealed extensive flooding. But the photos turned out to have been deceptive: Entire areas of the Merderet valley actually were inundated, masked by tall marsh grass protruding from the water. Furthermore, the same torrential storm that had forced Eisenhower to postpone the invasion by one day had dumped a considerable amount of water in this neighborhood, and the Germans had ensured that it would not run off soon. Among those 507th men who landed in this desolate locale, several were pulled beneath the water's surface by the extraordinary weight of their equipment, and if they could not swiftly cut themselves free, they drowned. Most of the survivors were soaked, lacked much of their vital equipment, and were unable to find their leaders.

One of those who landed in the flooded meadows was the commander of the 507th's 2nd Battalion, Lt. Col. Charles Timmes, who only narrowly avoided drowning. At nearly thirty-seven years of age, Timmes—who had been born in Austria and held a law degree from Fordham University—was ancient compared with other airborne battalion commanders. Gavin later characterized Timmes as "quiet as a mouse, but a terror in combat." At a debriefing two months after D-Day, Timmes understated the case when he reported that after his drop, he "had a lot of difficulty in assembling." With only about two dozen men, less than 5 percent of his battalion, he moved straight south to Cauquigny. Not a German was in sight. Gunfire was erupting to the northwest, however, seemingly from the location of a key 507th D-Day objective, a village called Amfreville. At dawn, Timmes's paratroopers proceeded in that direction, only to discover that Amfreville was so firmly in the enemy's hands that it could be captured only with a much larger group than Timmes currently possessed. Timmes and his men retreated eastward into the bocage, where they could catch their breath and wait for more GIs to emerge from the Merderet marshlands. Meanwhile, Timmes detached Lt. Louis Levy with ten men to secure the western end of the La Fière causeway at Cauquigny.

As Levy's squad tramped southward, they ran into a small band of paratroopers led by Lt. Joseph Kormylo of the 507th's Company D. The two officers conferred and decided to set up a perimeter defense around the derelict Cauquigny chapel. Like most areas of the bocage, this was an excellent place to establish a defensive strongpoint. The ubiquitous hedgerows provided perfect concealment; and the church itself, although it currently lacked a roof, had ancient stone walls so thick that they would surely withstand even the largest rounds the Germans could throw at them. Somehow, little more than a dozen 507th paratroopers had taken a vital 82nd Airborne objective; and with the coveted La Fière causeway in American hands, if the 4th Division would show up soon, it could cross the Merderet without a shot fired in opposition. But at that time, the 4th was just beginning to push inland from Utah Beach, and its leading columns were still miles away, with hundreds of Germans standing between them and La Fière.

Suddenly a startling clamor from the west roused Levy and Kormylo: Germans. A large part of the noise apparently was being generated by the distinctive clank of metal tracks on pavement, revealing beyond any doubt that the enemy was rapidly approaching Cauquigny with several of those weapons paratroopers feared most—tanks.

Company D, 507th Parachute Infantry, 82nd Airborne Division
U.S. Army Historical Division, Interview with Lt. Joseph Kormylo,
July 1944
The tanks [captured French Hotchkiss H-39 light tanks from the 100th Panzer Training Battalion] were already moving along the main road, and Kormylo could see their turrets above the hedgerows as they came on at a distance of about 50 yards. [Kormylo and a private] fired a few rounds with their rifles and then beat it back. They passed Levy, and he yelled: "Go on!" But he stayed there [hidden in a hedgerow]. The Germans set up a machine gun within five yards of Levy where he waited in the indented embankment. Levy could hear them laughing and talking. . . . He took out a grenade, pulled the pin, counted three, and gave it a little toss. It exploded between the two Germans and wounded both. He took a few steps and

dispatched them with rifle fire. . . . The tanks were already up and shelling the church. . . . The German infantry by this time had closed right up on the road, and what remained of the American force was fighting it out with them with just the edge of the hedgerow separating them. They were throwing grenades at one another, but the enemy numbers were piling up so that it became perfectly clear that the position had no chance to hold. Kormylo saw a German come up over the hedgerow at two feet distance. He emptied the carbine into him and blew the top of his head back. . . . The men then withdrew. [Levy would be killed on July 5.]

After a short pause to reorganize, the German tanks and infantry pushed on, racing past the chapel onto the causeway and heading straight for the La Fière bridge, 600 yards distant, covered by a furious mortar barrage and ripping bursts of machine-gun fire. But the enemy did not realize that Cauquigny had merely been the first level of what amounted to an American defense in depth of the entire La Fière position, for waiting behind the Merderet was an amalgam of paratroopers, mostly the 505th's Company A under Captain Dolan. The Germans were about to learn what the Americans already knew: Even with plentiful covering fire, any attack straight down the elevated roadway, with no possibility of maneuver into the adjacent marshlands, had little chance of success. True, the Hotchkiss tanks' armor could stop rifle and machine-gun bullets, but not bazooka rounds; and waiting on the far bank where the Merderet made an S-turn, two Company A bazooka teams were lying prone, waiting for the right moment to rise up and fire.

Sgt. William Owens
Company A, 505th Parachute Infantry
We placed our anti-tank mines right up on top of the road where the Germans could see them, but not miss them with their tanks. We placed our two bazooka teams where they had a good field of fire. There were two men to a team. One team was under PFC [Lenold] Peterson [noted by an interviewer as "a voluble Scandinavian who still speaks with a very broken accent"] and the other under PFC [John] Bolderson, good reliable men who had been through the mill before. [The other two team members were Privates Marcus Heim and Gordon Pryne.] . . . We let the tanks come on: It was an armored column along with trucks of infantry. When the lead tank got approximately 40 feet from the mines, the tank commander saw them and the tank stopped. Then our bazooka teams let loose and both got direct hits, disabling the first tank. This blocked the road [and] the other tanks could only retreat. They then tried to get the infantry through to knock us out, but our small arms fire drove them back.

Pvt. Marcus Heim
Company A, 505th Parachute Infantry,
Distinguished Service Cross Citation, July 26, 1944

Pvt. Heim, assistant bazooka gunner, was stationed at the end of a bridge over the Merderet River to repel attacks by enemy troops who controlled the other end of the bridge. This position was subject to incessant rifle, machine gun, mortar, and artillery fire. After an artillery preparation the enemy sent an assault force supported by three tanks over the bridge. Though part of the troops withdrew, Pvt. Heim remained at his position until the enemy tanks approached to within 30 yards. In spite of the intense fire, Pvt. Heim rose from his position and with the gunner fired rockets into the three tanks. Pvt. Heim remained with his [bazooka] and fired it until it was put out of action.

1st Lt. John Dolan
Commander, Company A, 505th Parachute Infantry

[The bazooka teams] were under the heaviest small arms fire from the other side of the causeway, and from the cannon and machine gun fire from the tanks. To this day I'll never be able to explain why all four of them were not killed. They fired and reloaded with the precision of well-oiled machinery. Watching them made it hard to believe that this was nothing but a routine drill. . . . [Later, they] called for more ammunition. Maj. [Frederick] Kellam [CO, 1st Battalion, 505th] ran up toward the bridge with a bag of rockets followed by Capt. [Dale] Roysden [S-3, 1st Battalion, 505th]. When they were within 15 or 20 yards of the bridge, the Germans opened up with mortar fire. Major Kellam was killed and Captain Roysden was rendered unconscious from the concussion. He died later that day.

The bold bazooka teams ensured that the La Fière bridge would remain in American hands for good. But within a period of just a few hours at La Fière, Captain Dolan had seen many of his comrades die, including the 1st Battalion's two highest-ranking and most esteemed officers: the commander, Maj. Fred Kellam, known to the troops as "Jack of Diamonds," and his executive, Maj. Jim McGinity, nicknamed "Black Jack." Over the next three days, the enemy pounded this seemingly inconsequential bridge with mortars and artillery, and it cost the lives of dozens more good Americans than just those two—so many, in fact, that those 82nd Airborne GIs who survived the La Fière maelstrom would come to regard this battle as the division's defining moment in Normandy.

One of the salient aspects of D-Day, from the American perspective, was how willing U.S. Army generals were to put their lives at risk to ensure that this historic operation developed as Overlord plans had intended. No

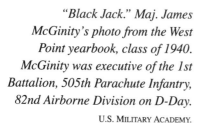

"Black Jack." Maj. James McGinity's photo from the West Point yearbook, class of 1940. McGinity was executive of the 1st Battalion, 505th Parachute Infantry, 82nd Airborne Division on D-Day.
U.S. MILITARY ACADEMY.

one needed to be reminded that this was an extraordinary day, and to assure the GIs that they were not alone, most of those Americans who wore stars on their helmets made certain that the fighting troops saw their leaders at the front. That this was an inherently perilous thing to do was proved by the death of General Pratt in one of the invasion's first glider landings. Indeed, combat in Normandy on D-Day was a great leveler of rank: On that first day of the invasion, more than a dozen American general officers entered France by sea or air, and as a rule, they were in just as much peril as any other soldier. It hardly seemed sensible for the U.S. Army to risk losing such a vast store of military knowledge and experience, but ultimately the generals proved their point: If generals could face enemy bullets and shells and still get a vital job done, privates could too.

The thirty-seven-year-old general known to all 82nd Airborne troopers as "Slim Jim" Gavin was about to demonstrate that truth to his men. Conveyed to Normandy in a special 314th Troop Carrier serial accompanying the 508th Parachute Infantry, Gavin missed his drop zone by a mile and landed at about 2:15 A.M. on the edge of the Merderet marsh north of La Fière. Generals are trained to make quick decisions, but making the right ones consistently is the hallmark of a brilliant leader. Gavin had experienced the chaos of airborne warfare during the 82nd's jump into Sicily the previous summer, and he fully understood that in this new type of combat

507th and 508th Parachute Infantry: Morning, June 6, 1944

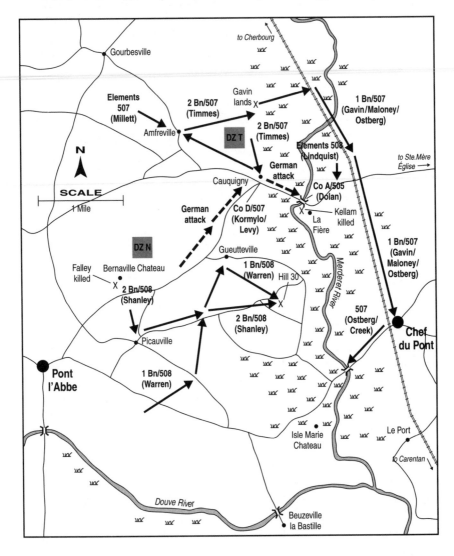

operation, reality would diverge from design the moment his paratroopers' chutes billowed open over enemy territory. To Gavin, the initial stage of the Normandy airdrop corroborated that truth. After gathering close to 200 paratroopers and discerning his location, Gavin deduced that if all the 82nd's difficult D-Day objectives were to be fulfilled by sunset, the original plan must be modified directly. That deduction was the easy part. Gavin's toughest challenge would be to determine exactly what those modifications should be.

Brig. Gen. James Gavin
Assistant Division Commander, 82nd Airborne Division, August 16, 1944
At about 0430 Col. [Arthur] Maloney [XO, 507th Parachute Infantry] and Lt. Col. [Edwin] Ostberg [CO, 1st Battalion, 507th], with about 150 men, had reported to me, and I decided to move as soon as possible to seize the west end of the La Fière bridge. I considered it necessary to accomplish this before daylight because of the impracticability of fighting through the swamps in the face of any German automatic weapons.

Lt. Col. Arthur Maloney
Executive, 507th Parachute Infantry
As I reached a corner in the hedgerows, I was stopped in my tracks by an authoritative "Halt!" Right then I forgot the password, and in a voice far from commanding I answered, "Dammit, don't shoot, it's Maloney!" "OK, Colonel, come on over here, General Gavin and Colonel Ostberg are gathering men to go out and save a glider which has an anti-tank gun in it." . . . When asked how things were going, I replied: "Not so good. We haven't enough people assembled here to take our first objective" [the western end of the La Fière bridge].

Gavin and his 507th group headed south, following the Carentan-Cherbourg railroad line, toward La Fière. They found the modest yet vital bridge there under the control of a group from the 505th Parachute Infantry under Captain Dolan. With that objective seemingly in good hands, Gavin led his band nearly two miles farther south down the railroad to the village of Chef du Pont, an objective that Gavin knew was just as essential as La Fière. About 1,000 yards southwest of Chef du Pont, another apparently inconsequential bridge traversed the Merderet, and the 82nd Airborne had to control this span if Collins's VII Corps was to move west and cut the Cotentin Peninsula in two as Overlord orders prescribed. But as Gavin approached Chef du Pont, he immediately discerned that the Germans would give up neither the town nor the bridge without a fight.

Brig. Gen. James Gavin
Assistant Division Commander, 82nd Airborne Division, August 16, 1944
Lt. Col. Ostberg went ahead with the point to Chef du Pont. I accompanied Lt. Col. Maloney and followed up. . . . Upon arrival at the railroad station at Chef du Pont, it was observed that there was considerable small arms fire. It could be expected from any direction. There was considerable firing at the bridge where Ostberg was evidently engaged. . . . Maloney moved up to join Ostberg and the situation appeared pretty well in hand . . . and I figured that Maloney would have the bridge at any moment, or within an hour or two.

"He is a proven battle leader of the highest type." Brig. Gen. James Gavin, Assistant Division Commander of the 82nd Airborne Division, during a training exercise in England. U.S. ARMY SIGNAL CORPS, NATIONAL ARCHIVES.

It was not to be. From the invaders' standpoint, the little arched bridge at Chef du Pont and the nearby causeway over the Merderet marsh presented a tactical dilemma even worse than the one at La Fière. The Chef du Pont causeway extended on both sides of the river, not just on the west bank as at La Fière, so to approach the bridge from the east, Ostberg's men had no room for maneuver and were exposed to a galling enemy fire that made any paratrooper who advanced upright on the elevated roadway an easy target. The causeway was more than twice the length of the one at La Fière, so even if the GIs could seize the bridge, their problems would be far from over. Worst of all, about one-half mile from the bridge on the west bank, just south of the causeway, a magnificent old chateau named Isle Marie stood on slightly elevated ground, among ancient trees and gardens, on what amounted to an island fortress squarely in the middle of the marsh. The site was supposedly an ancient Viking stronghold, but in 1944, more than 1,000 years later, it was the Germans who took advantage of this nearly unassailable position to make life miserable for Gavin's men at Chef du Pont.

If the Germans retained control of the Isle Marie chateau, an 82nd Airborne attack westward along the Chef du Pont causeway appeared suicidal without massive artillery or air support, but to the paratroopers on D-Day, that kind of assistance was mere fantasy. Ostberg, a Brooklyn native and 1939 West Point graduate, nevertheless had to try to fulfill this nearly impossible mission. He and a group of 507th men rushed the bridge from the east, but the enemy fire was too hot. Ostberg himself made it onto the span but was promptly felled by several bullets, which tumbled him into the swamp. Captain Roy Creek, commander of the 507th's Company E, took over, and his first priority was to rescue Ostberg. Despite the enemy's ceaseless barrage of bullets and shells, seemingly all aimed at the little bridge, Creek's men managed to accomplish this object. Ostberg would recover and rejoin the 82nd, but he would be killed in Belgium in February 1945—news that must have devastated Ostberg's mother, who had also lost her husband in World War I.

Capt. Roy Creek
Commander, Company E, 507th Parachute Infantry, 1948
Speed seemed to be the answer. It was felt that the bridge must be taken before the Germans could organize their defense, so we made a semi-organized dash for it. We were too late. Two officers reached the bridge and were both shot, one toppling off the bridge into the water; the other falling on the eastern approach. The officer toppling into the river happened to be Colonel Ostberg. He was rescued shortly afterward by the heroic action of two 507th soldiers. The other officer was dead.

By the end of the day, Creek's men held the bridge, but the causeway on the Merderet's west bank remained a deadly no-man's-land. The turreted Isle Marie chateau on its forbidding island loomed over the roadway, and as long as the Germans held that place, Creek's men would not be going anywhere soon without substantial help. Sufficient help would not arrive for several days, and the Americans ultimately would not capture the Chef du Pont causeway until June 10, when the 90th Division's 358th Infantry came pouring across the Merderet just as the Germans defending the chateau were getting ready to pull out to avoid encirclement. Both the La Fière and Chef du Pont causeways had proved to be much tougher objectives than Generals Ridgway and Gavin had imagined.

While Ostberg and Creek endeavored to capture the Chef du Pont causeway, about four miles to the northwest the 507th's commander, Col. George "Zip" Millett, was fighting a battle more hopeless than that of Custer at the Little Big Horn. Millett and a large assemblage from his regiment had dropped into a particularly baffling area of the bocage west of the village of Amfreville, and a sizable body of the enemy stood between them and the Americans in and around La Fière. Should Millett try to join his comrades at La Fière — or should he wait for them to come to him? Whatever Millett's decision would be, the irritated enemy was making every effort to ensure that his men would end D-Day either dead or as prisoners of war, and so far that effort seemed to be working. Millett's nickname of "Zip" didn't seem very appropriate anymore.

RED DEVILS

No American airborne outfit on June 6 had a tougher job than the 508th Parachute Infantry. At eleven miles due west of Utah Beach, the area the top brass picked for the 508th's landing was by far the most isolated of the six D-Day drop zones. Furthermore, the "Red Devils," as the 508th paratroopers styled themselves, would have the misfortune of landing right in the middle of the German 91st *Luftlande* Division, a piece of bad luck that would not only make it impossible for the regiment to achieve its bold D-Day objectives, but also lead to extraordinary difficulties when the 508th's leaders attempted to gather their companies and battalions in any semblance of order.

Like the men of the 507th, the Red Devils came to the 82nd Airborne Division in early 1944, fresh from the United States. Col. Roy Lindquist, a former sergeant in the Maine National Guard and 1930 West Point graduate, had trained the 508th since its October 1942 inception, and now he would lead it into Normandy in its first combat mission. Gavin later noted somewhat sardonically that the bespectacled Lindquist was a top-notch administrator: "He knew how much he had of everything. He kept records like I've never seen before." But only D-Day would prove whether this skill had a positive impact on the 508th's performance in combat.

The abrupt descent of nearly 2,000 American paratroopers into the midst of the German 91st Division triggered chaos on both sides. The enemy's capacity to react aggressively to the airdrop was crippled from the start, when a 508th trooper, 1st Lt. Malcolm Brannen, killed the 91st's commander, General Falley, near Pont l'Abbé. But the 508th suffered an even more debilitating command paralysis than the enemy as a result of the death or capture of many key American leaders shortly after descending to the earth. Those lucky enough to survive this debacle were forced to wander the hedgerows stealthily, looking in vain for their men. At an August 1944 82nd Airborne debriefing back in England, the commander of the 508th's 3rd Battalion, Lt. Col. Louis Mendez, noted with amazement that even though he landed within a mile of the drop zone, "I didn't see my battalion for five days."

Maj. Shields Warren
Executive, 1st Battalion, 508th Parachute Infantry
I heard by word of mouth on D+3 or D+4 [June 9 or 10] that Lt. Col. Herbert Batcheller's [CO, 1st Battalion, 508th] body, and that of his radio operator, had been found together next to a hedgerow. Apparently he had absorbed a 30–40 round MG42 [machine gun] burst in the chest, which would have resulted in virtually instantaneous death. . . . To the best of my knowledge, no one in the 508th saw Herb Batcheller, or his radio operator, alive after the drop.

Capt. Jonathan Adams
Commander, Company A, 508th Parachute Infantry
Immediately behind me [in the C-47] was my runner, a young kid about 19 years old named [PFC Virgil] Gainer. I had picked him because he was so clean-cut, well bred, and just a damned nice kid. As we were standing in the door he remarked how beautiful the scenery was. . . . It really was one of the most beautiful sights I have ever seen—but I would not want to ever see again. It was a moonlit night, and the small hedgerowed fields contained more different shades of purple and green than I knew existed. Gainer then said, "It just doesn't seem right going to war in a country as peaceful as this." As far as I know, these were the last words he spoke, because about 45 minutes later he was the first American I came across. He was dead in his chute and apparently had been shot while still in the air and before he hit the ground.

Although a parachute drop is undeniably an offensive operation of the most dramatic kind, in that region of the Cotentin Peninsula west of the

Merderet River it was the Germans, not the Americans, who promptly seized the initiative when the 508th landed in their midst at about 2:15 A.M. on D-Day. Aggressive enemy patrols stalked small bands of paratroopers for hours in the hedgerow country near the village of Picauville, forcing the Red Devils on the defensive and obliging them to abandon any attempt to get near their key objectives.

All the 508th's D-Day goals were difficult, but unquestionably the most challenging of all belonged to Lt. Col. Thomas Shanley's 2nd Battalion. Shanley's mission was to seize two Douve River bridges at Beuzeville-la-Bastille and Étienville (sometimes called Pont l'Abbé) and to hold that river line against the enemy's anticipated counterattacks after D-Day. Even if the Germans had not been present in this vicinity in such large numbers, Shanley's task would have been arduous, for Beuzeville was three and a half miles from Shanley's drop zone, and the intervening ground lacked a road that could lead his men there directly. Finding one's way through the bocage at night on twisting country lanes was hard enough, but when the Germans were added to the equation, the plan that had appeared scarcely feasible on paper became almost impossible.

The twenty-six-year-old Shanley, a former lightweight boxer in the West Point class of 1939, was one of the youngest battalion commanders in the U.S. Army—and also one of its most brilliant. After the war, he proved that point by earning a doctorate in physics from Princeton. On D-Day, Shanley landed just north of Picauville amid heavy German fire, the first of many indicators that his route to the Douve River bridges would be crawling with the enemy. But if he could not fulfill that mission, he resolved to do something, anything at all, that would help his regiment hang on in its exposed position as the 508th's meticulously prepared invasion plan fell apart.

Lt. Col. Thomas Shanley
Commander, 2nd Battalion, 508th Parachute Infantry, August 13, 1944
I had only about 35 men with me at dawn. At that time I sent patrols out and started encountering fairly heavy resistance. At approximately noon we were very heavily engaged on three sides, and I pulled out. . . . [Later] I collected approximately 200 men and officers, lost members of the 508th from all battalions, and I set up 1,000 yards east of Picauville. With 200 men I had two machine guns, no mortars, and no other automatic weapons. By radio I got in touch with another group, which was commanded by Maj. [Shields] Warren. . . . Having almost no heavy weapons and with so many Germans between my group and the objective, I selected the one mission the regiment had that I felt I could accomplish: seizing a

crossing of the Merderet River. Major Warren's group joined mine, and we set up a defensive position on Hill 30, west of the Merderet. [This occurred about sunset, or 10:10 P.M.]

Like Shanley, Warren had led a little band of 508th paratroopers through the bocage, trying to bring order out of chaos and avoid the carnage that the Germans, with greater numbers and more lethal weapons, were actively trying to inflict upon any Americans they could find. Even so, thought Warren, there must be some way his group could inflict harm upon the enemy; but lacking men and firepower, he had to be patient.

Maj. Shields Warren
Executive, 1st Battalion, 508th Parachute Infantry, August 13, 1944
I landed about halfway between Picauville and the Douve. . . . I toured the area in ever-widening circles trying to collect as many men as I could. . . . I collected between 40 and 50 and headed for Gueutteville, just north of Hill 30. [The 1st Battalion's D-Day mission was to assemble near Hill 30 and remain in reserve. Upon Batcheller's death, Warren became the battalion commander.] I got up to Gueutteville and found part of [the 2nd Battalion's] D and E Companies and a platoon of the 505th under Lt. Medaugh. We were on the verge of attacking Gueutteville with 100 men, but we had no supporting weapons—just rifles and carbines. Since there was an estimated German battalion in Gueutteville, we just stayed on the hill and shot at them. About 15 truckloads of Germans went by in the direction of La Fière. After shooting at them all afternoon I got in contact with Colonel Shanley and joined forces [on Hill 30]. . . . [We] stayed there for five days.

Shanley and Warren were astonished when they arrived at Hill 30. Could this be the place the 508th had considered so important in its D-Day plans? U.S. Army maps had clearly displayed a commanding elevation at this site. It supposedly towered above the Merderet valley lowlands at a height of thirty meters, and if the maps were to be believed, the hill would be vital because of its dominance over both the La Fière and Chef du Pont causeways. But the maps were flagrantly in error. The highest point on "Hill 30" was in actuality about half that height, and from that location, the omnipresent hedgerows made it difficult to see even adjacent fields. After an examination of the misnamed hill, a U.S. Army historian later noted: "From the top of Hill 30, one had no sense of being on high ground. . . . With the trees in leaf, it commanded nothing." Now Shanley and Warren could see why, on the bottom of each U.S. Army map of Normandy, a stark warning appeared: "Elevations should be accepted with caution."

Hill 30 had hardly been worth the planners' time, but now the snafu was of no consequence. Shanley and Warren must remain there because there was no place else to go. They had too few men and not enough heavy weapons to attack, but until they ran out of ammunition, they could hold out in this location against almost anything the enemy could throw at them short of a panzer assault. So they would wait, hoping that Lindquist, Gavin, or Ridgway would eventually notice them. But with the flooded Merderet River at their backs, they were undeniably isolated, a 1944 version of the Great War's "Lost Battalion" in the Meuse-Argonne. Sooner or later they would need help; but in the meantime, they would keep the Germans busy.

The 508th's commander, Colonel Lindquist, could do nothing to ameliorate the deplorable situation his men were experiencing near Picauville and Hill 30 throughout June 6. Lindquist had been conveyed to Normandy in the same 314th Troop Carrier Group serial as Gavin, and most of those twenty-four C-47s had deposited their paratroopers about one mile northeast of the 508th's drop zone in the Merderet marshes north of La Fière. As the bulk of Lindquist's regiment had been dropped more than three miles south of that point, and the intervening countryside was swarming with Germans, he had not the slightest idea of the fate that had befallen his men when they descended to earth in Normandy. For all the good he was doing to control his outfit, he might as well have been on the moon.

But like so many other American paratroopers on D-Day, Lindquist concluded that it was better to do something rather than linger aimlessly and wait for someone to sort out the mess. Before dawn, he gathered as many GIs as he could find—mostly 508th regimental headquarters personnel—and led them southward down the Cherbourg railway toward La Fière. Colonel Ekman's 505th was battling there for the manor house and the bridge, and Lindquist's group would join in that fight, hoping to push across the Merderet later and locate his lost regiment.

508th Parachute Infantry, 82nd Airborne Division
U.S. Army Historical Division, Interview with Col. Roy Lindquist, July 1944

[At about 1:00 P.M.] Col. Ekman had conferred with Lindquist in the forward ground on the left, near the bridge, after [La Fière] had been cleaned out. . . . Ekman told Lindquist that inasmuch as the bridge was the 505th's mission, Maj. Kellam [CO, 1st Battalion, 505th] would come in during the afternoon and would take over the left flank with the remainder of the men from the 505th's 1st Battalion. Upon withdrawing from the river front, Lindquist's force was placed in reserve by Gen. Gavin right along the hedgerow short of the railway track.

CUTTING LOOSE

No one had ever said that the 82nd Airborne's D-Day mission would be easy. In all probability, General Ridgway was not surprised when he first learned of the stalemate at the La Fière and Chef du Pont bridges and the much more troubling predicaments west of the Merderet. To accomplish its tasks in the face of increasing German pressure, and indeed just to hold on to the positions it currently held, the 82nd must have more firepower, and soon.

The first of many sources of outside help had arrived shortly after 4:00 A.M., when the 437th Troop Carrier Group's C-47s approached the 505th's drop zone near Ste. Mère Église towing fifty-two Waco gliders. The Wacos carried a total of sixteen 57-millimeter antitank guns plus 220 troops, mostly gun crews, staff officers from division headquarters, and medical personnel. To reach their objective, the tow pilots had to fly over, above, or through the same clouds that had disordered several previous C-47 flights, and when they finally broke into clearer skies over the Cotentin Peninsula, they had only minutes to find the proper landing zone. Given the barrage of enemy fire sweeping through the night sky all around them, this was a difficult task. One C-47 tow ship was shot down, and more than one-fourth of the Wacos cut loose early or had their tow cables severed by enemy fire, leading to many glider landings west of the Merderet River in areas where German patrols were already actively hunting American paratroopers.

Glider pilots had harbored doubts about landing in the middle of enemy territory at night on fields that looked minuscule from several hundred feet up, and those doubts were confirmed when most of their Wacos were destroyed or severely damaged upon landing by crashing into hedgerows, trees, enemy obstacles, and even livestock. Happily for the glider pilots and their passengers, there were only a few fatalities, but many suffered severe injuries, such as compound fractures and concussions, and a great many more endured scrapes and contusions that in training would have excused them from duty for a day or two but on this historic day were hardly worthy of mention. As for the gliders' cargoes, of the sixteen guns and twenty-two jeeps conveyed into Normandy, only about half were in working condition after the landings.

84th Troop Carrier Squadron, 437th Group
Debriefing, 1st Lt. Andrew Forthmann and F/O Clayton Cederwall, June 9, 1944

We landed in a field at 329969 [a map coordinate, about one mile west of Ste. Mère Église] at 0406 hours. We were fired on while on tow and the glider was pierced in numerous places. Personnel were not hit while the pilot made a 360-degree turn and landed in a field uninjured. The glider hit a tree with its left wing, which in turn swung around and smashed the nose of the ship with the other wing. Paratroops came up and asked what the glider carried. When told it was a 57mm anti-tank gun, they were overjoyed and got a jeep to pull the glider away from the trees. We got the gun out and proceeded across a railroad track toward [the La Fière] bridge on the Merderet River. [In all probability this gun was one that helped repel the German attack with Hotchkiss H-39 tanks down the La Fière causeway that afternoon.]

Lt. Col. Raymond Singleton
Commander, 80th Airborne Antiaircraft Battalion,
82nd Airborne Division, August 13, 1944
We ran into a cloud bank, milky in texture, and we could see very little. There was a lot of flak, small arms fire, and machine guns. The glider pilots did a fine job. . . . We landed very smoothly. We took in sixteen guns, and the next day we had about five of those sixteen in the division area. [The 80th was officially designated an antiaircraft unit, but it had an antitank role as well.]

M/Sgt. Charles Mason
Headquarters Company, 82nd Airborne Division
The roar of the wind whipping the thin skins of the CG-4A glider made conversation almost impossible. Everyone remained quiet until someone up front spotted the beacon and yelled, "Cut loose!" We dove straight down. . . . Ack-ack was penetrating our glider. An artillery captain across from me had a big chunk ripped out of his groin. Colonel [Wolcott] Etienne, Division Surgeon, sitting alongside of me, had his hand smashed by a fragment, and I dressed it as best I could by light of tracers going through the glider. A fragment hit my shin but I did not discover it until two days later. . . . I was more concerned about seemingly sitting in a pool of blood without feeling any wound. Later I discovered that a fragment of ack-ack had hit my canteen and the water had mixed with blood from Colonel Etienne.

One of the 82nd's most eminent characters, Col. Ralph "Doc" Eaton, was conveyed to Normandy in the 437th Group's lead glider. The forty-five-year-old Eaton had been the 82nd's chief of staff and Ridgway's alter ego for eighteen months, and his affiliation with the 82nd dated to the division's founding in March 1942, eight months before it converted from infantry to airborne status. In World War I, Eaton had served in the trenches as a litter-bearer—hence his nickname—and then entered the U.S. Military Academy, graduating near the bottom of the 1924 class. As Eaton remembered his harrowing D-Day glider flight, "I landed in the 101st Division zone and was rather severely hurt in landing [three broken ribs, serious contusions on both legs] when my tow plane was shot down and the glider made—shall we say—a forced landing." In the ensuing days, Eaton tried to fulfill his role as chief of staff, but his obvious immobility forced Ridgway to have him evacuated to England for proper medical care.

For years, it had been the parachutists rather than the glider troops who made the headlines. But the evident hazards of glider operations in Normandy made an immediate impression on the U.S. Army's top generals. On June 25, Eisenhower cabled General Marshall in Washington, recommending that glider troops receive a wage increase to bring their pay in line with paratroopers. Marshall would agree—and so would Congress. It was long overdue.

CHAPTER 7

So This Is France

MISSION ACCOMPLISHED

The plan was undeniably impressive. General Collins's staff had covered every component of the Utah Beach invasion in meticulous detail, and the result was a plan book bursting with vital information, specifying down to the minute what every VII Corps unit must do on D-Day. The plans were genuine evidence that the U.S. Army had come of age, and the dismal days of 1940 and 1941, when the American government had provided its soldiers with neither the resources nor the incentive to fight a global war of colossal proportions, were now truly distant memories.

Although the 4th Infantry Division and many of its attached units had not yet seen combat, they were unquestionably ready. In contrast, the enemy was not: Had a copy of the Utah invasion plan fallen into German hands, even optimistic Nazi generals promptly would have been converted into pessimists, for the American scheme of attack plainly demonstrated that the Allies were now conducting the war on a higher plane than Hitler ever could have imagined. Their resources were seemingly limitless, their military expertise was evident, and above all, their resolve was apparently unshakable. Against a foe of this kind, Germany could no longer win the war.

Brig. Gen. Harold Blakely
Commander, 4th Division Artillery
The 4th Infantry Division at that time was, I think, as highly trained as any unit
could expect to be short of actual combat. . . . It was an extremely well-trained,
equipped, and conditioned division, and I think the general feeling of all the senior
officers was one of confidence—realizing that we might take a beating on the
beach.

General Collins, like most successful U.S. Army commanders in World
War II, was not a tyrant and believed that thorough and honest debate
among his staff would smooth the planning process and greatly improve
the chance that an ambitious military operation like the Normandy invasion
would succeed. Collins considered this practice critical for an operation as
significant as the Utah Beach assault, and it was during the last of these
staff debates in May 1944 that a special operation had been hatched, one
that would be launched in total darkness before dawn on D-Day, more than
two hours before the first 4th Division troops were scheduled to land in
Normandy.

Not much time remained before the men would be shut into their marshalling areas and training would virtually come to a stop. If the plan
needed modifications, now was the time to do it. At that staff meeting,
Collins asked, "Have we forgotten anything that any person here can
remember?" General Blakely responded, "Has anybody considered the Iles
St. Marcouf?" These two seemingly insignificant islands lying five miles
northeast of Utah Beach hardly seemed worthy of consideration, especially
as recent air photographs had shown them to be lacking enemy artillery
pieces. That the islands had been considered significant militarily at one
time in the past, however, was proved by the presence of a large and sturdy
Napoleonic-era fort on the Ile du Large, the larger of the two islands. This
fort lay less than two miles north of the boat lanes the navy would use to
bring 4th Division troops to Utah Beach, and even if it did not currently
appear to be an enemy bastion, it seemed that the German Army always
found a way to surprise its adversaries. The Americans had learned that lesson the hard way so far in this war, and they did not want to learn it again.

There was no way to avoid the issue: The Iles St. Marcouf would have
to be taken by direct assault before dawn. Normally this would be a job for
the U.S. Army's Rangers, but Collins lacked those celebrated commando-
style troops on his VII Corps troop list. Those Ranger outfits that were

Utah Beach and Iles St. Marcouf: H-Hour, June 6, 1944

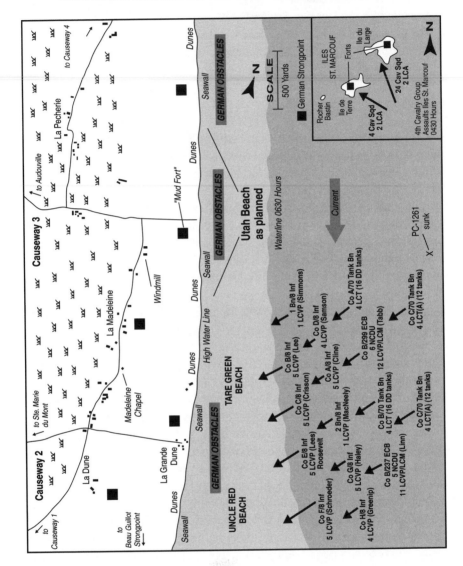

available were already committed to critical D-Day missions at Pointe du Hoc and Omaha Beach; so instead the job fell to the 4th Cavalry Group, a reconnaissance outfit that had been one of the last U.S. Army units to give up its cherished horses in the rush toward mechanization in 1941.

No one denied that the cavalrymen's task would be treacherous. Even if not a single German occupied the Iles St. Marcouf, the Royal Navy landing craft crews drawn from the British transport *Empire Gauntlet* would have to load the GIs into four LCAs, locate those two minuscule islets in darkness, sail through waters swarming with enemy mines that had not yet been swept, and land their passengers on a rocky shoreline that only expert coxswains could reach safely.

Lt. Col. Edward Dunn, the thirty-one-year-old task force commander and 1936 West Point graduate, devised a simple plan of attack. At 4:30 A.M., guided by a pair of two-man scout sections in rubber boats, two British landing craft, each loaded with about thirty troopers, would land on what the dubious planners had cautiously categorized as a "beach" on the Ile du Large. The other two landing craft would peel off and land their GIs on the smaller island, Ile de Terre. The islands were too small for any elaborate maneuvers, so in the event Germans were present, there would definitely be some intense close-in fighting.

Fortunately, the enemy was absent—but even so, the Iles St. Marcouf were an exceptionally dangerous place.

"Has anybody considered the Iles St. Marcouf?" Ile de Terre, the smaller of the two islands comprising the Iles St. Marcouf, as seen from a U.S. Navy warship on D-Day. U.S. NAVY, NATIONAL ARCHIVES.

4th Cavalry Group
After-action Report, June 1944

About 100 yards from their respective beaches, the scouts sank their rubber boats by puncturing them with knives and swam the rest of the way to their objectives. Armed only with knives, the scouts crawled ashore at approximately 0415 and marked the limits of the beaches with flashlights. Sgt. Harvey Olson and Pvt. Thomas Killoran, 4th Squadron, were the first Americans to land on Ile de Terre; Sgt. John Zanders and Cpl. Melvin Kinzie, 24th Squadron, the first to land on Ile du Large. [These four were the first Allied soldiers to land by sea on French soil on D-Day.] Immediately upon receiving signal from shore, the four LCAs headed for the beaches at full speed. . . . [Upon landing] both detachments swept inland in the dark at a dead run toward their objectives, in each case an old Napoleonic fort sited on the high ground in the center of each island. There were several loud explosions on each island as the troops ran over and detonated land mines. Sgt. John Onken, Troop A, 4th Squadron, was the first to fall, killed instantly by an "S"-mine. . . . Ile du Large [had] a wide moat that had to be crossed to reach the fort. This was done by use of grappling hooks, ropes, and a scaling ladder. . . . It was apparent that there were no Germans on either island. Therefore, the 4th Cavalry's first message to VII Corps was dispatched: "Mission accomplished."

1st Lt. Alfred Rubin
24th Cavalry Squadron, 4th Cavalry Group

Five of us were clearing an area of the deadly "S"-mines, which shoot buried canisters from the ground to a height of about five feet, explode, and shoot ball bearings in all directions. [GIs called these "Bouncing Betties."] After an initial pop, which warns one of the activation of the booby trap, he has about four seconds to hit the ground. . . . [Once] I was the only man to hear the pop of an S-mine. I shouted "Down!" to the men in my area. Most of us hit the ground in time. . . . I recall one man spitting up ball bearings.

Lt. Col. Edward Dunn
Commander, 4th Cavalry Squadron, 4th Cavalry Group

One member of our British Navy crew of this [LCA] sat calmly in the stern under his World War I-type tin hat, manning a hand pump that was taking water out of the boat at approximately half the rate it was coming in, With British phlegm, he even took time to relight a damp cigarette. As I watched my men unload, I thought I detected a slight look of relief on his face. But he kept pumping steadily and calmly as the craft withdrew from the beach, and I thought: "There'll always be an England." . . . I recall Lt. George Thomas, who led the first wave [to Ile de Terre], being evacuated, badly wounded, just as I came to shore. His words were: "Good luck, Colonel. I'll be back." He was back, to win the DSC and several more Purple Hearts. I also recall Capt. Wales Vaughn, in charge of my detachment on Ile du Large, fearlessly disarming a 500-kilogram bomb that the Germans had booby-trapped inside the old fort on the island.

Although not a single German soldier had been present on the Iles St. Marcouf, the enemy had managed to kill two GIs and wound seventeen more. True, the Americans had liberated a small part of France, but if the Germans managed to inflict casualties on the GIs at the rate they had on St. Marcouf, the road to Berlin would indeed be long.

OLD PRAIRIE BELLE

The general appeared much older than his fifty-six years. That impression was accentuated by his ever-present walking stick and his unsteady gait, the product of a World War I knee wound and severe arthritis. He had a rough face, with a nose that apparently had been broken too many times, but his grin was so broad and toothy that one could easily perceive, as one subordinate noted, that "he loved everybody." It was obvious that he had spent too much time outdoors: In a letter to his wife, he described his own skin as "leathery brown." A little after 1:00 A.M. on June 6, the general was just one of a throng of hundreds of American soldiers massed on the deck of the transport *Barnett,* preparing to board their landing craft in the dark for the twelve-mile journey to Utah Beach. When the young soldiers watched the elderly gentleman struggle to cross a plank from the *Barnett*'s deck to a landing craft slung in its davits, an awkward procedure even for much more youthful and agile men, they took pity on him and offered help, a proposal that the general always brusquely rejected with a sharp wave of his cane. He was accompanying the 4th Division's first assault troops to land in France, and boarding an LCVP was nothing compared to what he would endure once he stepped ashore. That would be the true test of his endurance.

War is a young man's pursuit, and the U.S. Army normally transferred fifty-six-year-old generals to desk jobs or quietly retired them from the service. For the 4th Division to put in the forefront of the invasion a man who look liked a semicripple, and who had recently recovered from a near-fatal case of pneumonia, seemed foolhardy in this, the momentous operation of World War II. Even worse, the general's name was Brig. Gen. Theodore Roosevelt Jr., and if this son of a former president—and distant cousin of

"I believe I can contribute." Brig. Gen. Ted Roosevelt Jr., of the
4th Infantry Division. U.S. ARMY SIGNAL CORPS, NATIONAL ARCHIVES.

the current one—was killed on Utah Beach, the home front would find that
news profoundly discouraging.

Like his father, Ted Junior was a man with an iron will, and he had
employed every persuasive power in his repertoire to accompany the assault

troops ashore on D-Day. General Bradley had only recently assigned Roosevelt to the 4th Division as a "supernumerary" general officer, a temporary and strictly unofficial position. But if Roosevelt's job within the division was hazy, he had to find a niche worthy of his renowned name. During the interminable wait for the invasion in the marshalling areas in England, he had openly expressed his desire to show his well-known face to the first-wave assault troops on Utah Beach and inspire them in what promised to be an exceptionally tense situation for troops in their first combat. At first the 4th Division's commander, General Barton, had denied Roosevelt's appeal to land with the first wave, appreciating that if Roosevelt was killed, critical eyes would be cast upon Barton and the entire 4th Division. Roosevelt, however, could not be suppressed. He had composed a short letter that changed Barton's mind, but Barton later confessed that he felt there was a good chance that Ted Junior would not survive D-Day.

Brig. Gen. Theodore Roosevelt Jr.
Supernumerary General Officer, 4th Division, Letter to Barton,
May 26, 1944
The force and skill with which the first elements hit the beach and proceed may determine the ultimate success of the operation. . . . With troops engaged for the first time, the behavior pattern of all is apt to be set by those first engaged. [It is] considered that accurate information of the existing situation should be available for each succeeding element as it lands. You should have when you get to shore an overall picture in which you can place confidence. I believe I can contribute materially on all of the above by going in with the assault companies. Furthermore I know personally both officers and men of these advance units and believe that it will steady them to know that I am with them. [Roosevelt landed with Company E, 8th Infantry.]

In a letter to his wife, Eleanor, Roosevelt prepared her for the worst by noting straightforwardly that he would be landing in the first wave at Utah Beach. Equally distressing to Eleanor was the news that their son Quentin would be going onto Omaha Beach with the 1st Division only an hour after the initial wave.

Brig. Gen. Theodore Roosevelt Jr.
Supernumerary General Officer, 4th Division, Letter to his wife, Eleanor,
June 3, 1944
I don't think I've written you, but I go in with the assault wave and hit the beach at H-Hour. I'm doing it because it's the way I can contribute most. It steadies the

young men to know I'm with them, to see me plodding along with my trench cane. . . . At first "Tubby" [Barton] did not want me to go, but eventually, after I'd written a formal letter stating my reasons, he agreed. . . . And so the old Prairie Belle [Roosevelt's nickname] will come humping along up the beach in the first wave. Quentin, I believe, goes in at H+60.

Roosevelt's soul was hardly that of a soldier. His genes had yielded to him a flair for politics and literature, and the rigors of army life hardly seemed compatible for such a *bon vivant*, a man who had routinely corresponded before the war with the likes of Pearl Buck, Edna Ferber, Robert Frost, Helen Hayes, and Rudyard Kipling, and who had himself authored such eclectic books as *Trailing the Giant Panda* and *Three Kingdoms of Indo-China*. Teddy Junior loved poetry, and when he walked onto Utah Beach on June 6, 1944, he carried in his pocket a small book of poems by Winthrop Praed, an eminent early nineteenth-century English humorist. This tome, along with Roosevelt's ubiquitous cane and a pistol he would not unholster throughout D-Day, would satisfy his simple needs on the beach throughout June 6. But Roosevelt also loved the U.S. Army, particularly the ordinary fighting man, and he considered it an honor to lead them into battle in Normandy.

Pvt. Hyman Edelman
Company E, 8th Infantry, 4th Division
We were all assembled on deck [on USS *Barnett*] when we heard speeches by our Brig. Gen. Teddy Roosevelt, Jr. and General Eisenhower. [Ike's speech was recorded.] I'll never forget General Roosevelt's closing words: "I'll see you tomorrow morning, 6:30, on the beach." He certainly was there.

Roosevelt was there; but as he noted in a letter to Eleanor five days later, "The moment I arrived on the beach I knew something was wrong." The 4th Division's entire first wave, consisting of more than 600 infantrymen in twenty landing craft, had come ashore considerably south of its intended landing point. Roosevelt was one of the first soldiers to discern this disturbing mistake, and his subsequent directive to the throng of GIs on the beach—"We're going to start the war from here!"—has become the defining moment of the Utah Beach invasion.

How could it have happened? Both Moon's sailors and Collins's soldiers had studied reconnaissance photos and terrain models of the coast for weeks, and they knew by heart every house and terrain feature on the two sectors that Utah Beach comprised: "Tare Green" on the north, "Uncle

Red" on the south. Admiral Moon had assigned three special patrol craft to each sector to guide the successive waves of landing craft to their proper objectives on shore. The expert sailors manning these six vessels operated highly accurate—and top secret—navigational gear and search radars, yielding near-perfect positional fixes and revealing coastal features with decent clarity, even through smoke and dust. A naval officer on one of those guide boats recalled that his sophisticated electronic equipment "was working perfectly" on D-Day, so the mislanding could not be attributed to equipment failure.

Historians took years to sort through the participants' confused and sometimes contradictory accounts, and even more than sixty years after the invasion, the reasons why the 4th Division landed appreciably astray from its proposed D-Day landing beaches are hardly clear. Above all, two factors—nature and the enemy—conspired to make the sailors' job of landing the assault force on time and on target exceptionally difficult, as tough as driving safely through a twisting tunnel with no headlights. The flat eastern coast of the Cotentin Peninsula has a uniformity that, when viewed from a mile or more offshore, reveals virtually no distinctive natural features. Those few coastal landmarks visible to Allied sailors on D-Day were man-made, mostly small beach houses and a single large windmill, but orders had specified that those structures would in all likelihood be destroyed by the terrific preinvasion air and naval bombardment.

That bombardment may have been valuable and uplifting to the soldiers who were about to set foot in France, but for the navy's coxswains steering their landing craft ashore, it suddenly made their jobs infinitely more challenging. The impact of the naval shells and aerial bombs on the beach had produced a vast cloud of dust, thicker than London's celebrated fog, which billowed seemingly in slow motion above the coastline. That frustrating haze would not dissipate anytime soon, and what little the sailors had been able to see of the beach earlier was now completely obscured. As the coxswains left their guide boats behind about one-third of a mile offshore, it was anybody's guess where they were headed.

Brig. Gen. Theodore Roosevelt Jr.
Supernumerary General Officer, 4th Division, Letter to his wife, Eleanor,
June 11, 1944
We passed a capsized craft [probably PC-1261, one of the six Force U guide vessels, which had hit a German mine en route to Utah Beach at about 5:45 A.M.], some men clinging to it, others bobbing in the waves. . . . As we peered over the gunwale the shore seemed nearer, but veiled as it was in the smoke and dust of the

bombardment it was hard to make it out. Suddenly the beach appeared before us—a long stretch of sand studded with wire and obstacles.

The destruction of PC-1261 was an obvious indicator that the enemy was fully capable of adding to the confusion. The little patrol boat had an importance far out of proportion to its size, for Force U had designated it a "primary control vessel," and it was supposed to guide landing craft from the transport area, twelve miles out to sea, to a point a few miles offshore where they would begin the final leg of their journey to the Uncle Red sector of Utah Beach. A second guide boat that could have substituted for PC-1261 was hours late because its propellers had fouled a buoy cable in the Channel.

That the invasion had not opened perfectly was obvious to those keen-eyed men who observed what was happening around them in the muted early-morning light. Eventually someone in authority reassigned one of the Tare Green guide boats to Uncle Red, but still some landing craft were behind schedule, and wave formations that had looked so neat on paper suddenly were not so neat anymore. The apparent problem was that seven LCTs conveying twenty-eight U.S. Army tanks were appreciably late arriving off the beach from the distant transport area. These tanks belonged to the veteran 70th Tank Battalion and were duplex drive (DD) amphibious models that, according to invasion orders, were an integral element of the first wave and must launch from their LCTs at sea and land at "H-Hour [6:30 A.M.] or as soon after as possible."

The top secret DDs were decidedly sensitive machines, and even a moderate swell generated by a vessel passing close by could swamp them with ruinous effect. It hardly seemed sensible to force coxswains of LCVPs, packed with assault troops and roaring toward the beach at top speed, to pass directly through lines of swimming tanks as they plodded ahead through the tossing sea at four miles per hour, but unless those coxswains dramatically altered course, that was exactly what they would have to do at a few minutes before H-Hour on June 6. To avoid the fragile tanks, many LCVP coxswains apparently did indeed swing their vessels to their left, or southward. Consequently, they headed for the swelling cloud of smoke and dust, somewhere behind which was the French coast, considerably to the south of their objectives.

Then there was the offshore current, that phenomenon of Normandy that could swiftly make even experienced sailors look like landlubbers. The U.S. Navy could hardly profess ignorance of the current's effects, as top secret Overlord orders had repeatedly warned landing craft crews what to expect. Off Utah Beach, the current was particularly powerful, flowing alternately north and south at nearly four miles per hour at its peak. Furthermore, at high- and low-tide peaks, its behavior was almost supernatural, as it abruptly reversed itself and eventually regained its astonishing momentum in the opposite direction, a process that occurred regularly three or four times per day.

Even the meticulously prepared Overlord invasion documents could not claim to understand exactly how the currents worked, and all their impressive tables of facts and figures were accompanied by the stark warning: "Use With Caution." To add to the confusion, there were several baffling secondary currents off the eastern Cotentin; one actually flowed in a circle, and another alternately pushed and pulled water into and out of the *Bancs du Grand Vey* estuary at the southeastern base of the peninsula, where the Douve and Vire Rivers flowed into the sea. It was, as many sailors commented, a hell of a place to fight a war.

On D-Day, the Americans commenced their landing at Utah Beach on a low but rising tide, at a time when the offshore current flowed southward, steadily building up momentum to a peak shortly after H-Hour. No matter how many times sailors had been warned about the current, it was not easy even for the skilled navigators aboard the guide ships to compensate for its subtle effects. As H-Hour approached and LCVP coxswains and DD tank drivers made their final runs onto the beach, the current shoved them inexorably southward, a process that sailors and soldiers may not even have noticed, as the billowing smoke and dust on the beach produced by the air force and navy obscured any useful reference points on the shoreline.

So much for the invasion plan. Before a single GI set foot on Utah Beach, a myriad of natural and human factors had combined to alter that plan profoundly. The Americans were considerably south of where they were supposed to be. But good soldiers adapt to circumstances, and if General Collins's men were indeed good soldiers, they must now prove it.

Rear Adm. Don Moon
Commander, Force U, D-Day Action Report, June 21, 1944

The Uncle Red secondary control vessel [LCC-80] was disabled by fouling a buoy before entering upon her duties, and the Uncle Red primary control vessel [PC-1261] was destroyed, probably by a mine, at H-35 [5:55 A.M.]. The consequences of these two casualties were potentially most serious. The initiative of officers on the Tare Green primary control vessel [PC-1176] in assigning the Tare

Green secondary control vessel [LCC-60] to take over control duties for Uncle Red Beach was most commendable. . . . In spite of careful briefing [and] use of reference vessels with special navigation equipment . . . the initial landings in the Utah area were approximately 1,000–1,500 yards to the left [south] of those originally intended. This error, which might have been most serious in many cases, actually proved to be advantageous in this instance because both obstacles and land defenses at the actual landing beaches were less advanced and more easily defeated than those at the beaches originally designated.

GIVE 'EM HELL

One of the enduring myths of Utah Beach is that the American success there on D-Day was gained with minimal effort and little bloodshed. When compared with the fierce struggle at Omaha Beach, in retrospect one senses that the assault troops on Utah merely mopped up a few feeble and unenthusiastic enemy troops on the beach and promptly pushed inland to relieve the beleaguered paratroopers.

Although those legends carry some measure of truth, no veteran of the Utah Beach invasion could ever declare that his accomplishments on June 6, 1944, were easy. How could they be when extremely accurate and heavy German artillery fire was plunging onto Utah Beach throughout D-Day? It was the randomness of this barrage that was so unnerving: One moment a GI would be standing next to some comrades, and the next an ear-splitting explosion would hurl shell fragments through the air, indiscriminately wounding or killing men, perhaps even tearing their bodies apart. The Germans' dominant weapon in the Cotentin certainly was their artillery, and with so many enemy batteries lining the high ground a mile or two behind the shoreline, some of which were enclosed in virtually impenetrable concrete casemates with nearly perfect observation of the coast, that artillery fire would continue to kill Americans on Utah Beach well after D-Day.

In the opening stage of the Utah invasion, the assault troops had to worry about much more than just German artillery. The enemy's resistance nests sited on the dunes beyond the beach were decidedly active when the 4th Division stormed ashore at 6:30 A.M., and almost every GI who was there in the first hour of the attack witnessed German machine gun and sniper fire. Col. James Van Fleet, the commander of the 4th Division's 8th Infantry—the first American unit to land on Utah Beach—corroborated that fact when he noted in a 1947 letter, "There was lots of small arms fire on Utah Beach—one of my first sergeants was killed by machine gun fire just as the leading waves of LCVPs touched down." Furthermore, to push inland, the Americans had to traverse the dunes behind the beach and maneuver around the enemy's resistance nests, a costly journey because those paths often took them straight into enemy minefields, densely packed with deadly Bouncing Betties and many other types of insidious killers.

True, nothing on Utah could compare to the maelstrom of Omaha Beach. But the facts are inescapable that the Utah invasion easily could have degenerated into chaos in its first two or three hours, as the Omaha invasion indeed did. That in actuality it did not could be directly attributed to how effectively the Utah invasion plan worked in comparison with the near-fatal complications at Omaha. Immediately prior to H-Hour, Ninth Air Force B-26 Marauders successfully dropped thousands of bombs on Utah with deadly effect—but on Omaha, not a single piece of ordnance from the Eighth Air Force fell anywhere near the beach. On Utah, demolition engineers and sailors efficiently cleared lanes through German beach obstacles—whereas on Omaha, only a marginal portion of this vital task was completed before high tide because of the enemy's hot fire. At Utah, DD amphibious tanks managed to swim to shore safely—but at Omaha, more than two dozen were swamped and lost at sea. Finally, German reserves in the Cotentin Peninsula could not rescue their beleaguered comrades in the coastal defenses because two American airborne divisions had landed in their midst; in contrast, German reinforcements from the interior could move to Omaha in comparative safety on June 6.

On both beaches, Germans survived the Allied preinvasion bombardment in sizable numbers, but that number was substantially greater on Omaha than it was on Utah. More important, on Omaha, those enemy troops occupied high ground that was nearly unassailable, and many of them fought from positions that provided them with near-perfect fields of fire directly into the flanks of the GIs as they stormed out of their landing craft, a circumstance that produced appalling casualties among the invaders. In contrast, at Utah, those Germans who had endured the shower of bombs from the Ninth Air Force prior to H-Hour had only to peer out of their pillboxes' apertures to appreciate that their task was impossible. They had no high ground and could shoot only at what they could see—which was not much. About the only thing the dazed defenders could indeed perceive was hundreds of obviously fervent American soldiers rushing across the beach and up the dunes, heading straight for the German resistance nests with deadly intent. Ultimately, the American success on Utah could be attributed in large measure to overwhelming numbers and terrain highly unfavorable to the defender.

Such an apparently effortless success on Utah Beach must have astonished the men who planned that invasion. During the planning process, the Utah assault had always seemed risky, because the Cotentin was so distant from the other four invasion sites, and the flooded terrain behind the coast made any movement inland highly problematic. No one knew what to expect, but General Collins had to prepare for the worst. Those staff officers who understood how German generals made war presumed that the enemy would do its best to make that worst-case scenario a reality on D-Day.

Maj. Gen. J. Lawton Collins
Commander, VII Corps, Field Order 1, May 28, 1944
The assault on Utah Beach will be pushed at all costs.

The GIs of the 4th Division had been lucky—this time. Later in the war, their luck would run out, and they would suffer nearly 23,000 battle casualties in the next eleven months in places like the Norman hedgerows near St. Lô; the Hürtgen Forest in Germany; and, during the Battle of the Bulge, in the Ardennes woods of Luxembourg. No Allied division in the European theater would lose more men, and not even the glorious memories of the 4th's liberation of Paris on August 25, 1944, could offset that somber distinction.

The infantrymen who shouldered the responsibility of leading the 4th Division ashore on Utah Beach were drawn from four companies of the venerable 8th Infantry Regiment, totaling about 620 troops. In total darkness, shortly after 3:00 A.M., these heavily burdened GIs clambered aboard twenty U.S. Navy and Coast Guard LCVPs from the decks of the transports *Barnett* and *Joseph T. Dickman*, and as soon as those landing craft were filled, the sailors adroitly lowered them from the davits into the sea, accompanied by the creaks and groans of countless cables strained to the limit by the cumbersome load.

Capt. John Moreno
Staff Officer, Force U, Western Naval Task Force
We were greatly impressed by how over-equipped the troops of the 4th Division in the assault wave were. They were issued so much equipment in their combat packs that they were unable to climb the accommodation ladders to embark. They actually had to be pushed up the ladders.

Capt. Leonard Schroeder
Commander, Company F, 8th Infantry, 4th Division
After mess [late on June 5] I along with the other company commanders were ordered to report to the 2nd Battalion commander [Lt. Col. Carlton MacNeely]. Brig. Gen. Theodore Roosevelt, Jr. was present for this meeting—in fact we assembled in his quarters. The general was reading western stories when we arrived. All commanders reported everything was ready. All we wanted was to get going. The hour being near midnight when the meeting was over, we wished each other well, shook hands and started to wander back to our bunks. . . . I remember [MacNeely] putting his arm around my shoulders and saying, "Well, Moose [Schroeder's nickname], this is it. Give 'em hell!" The colonel choked all up as I did, and the only words that seemed to come forth from me were, "Well, colonel, I'll see you on the beach!" . . . [Later] I spent about 30 minutes writing a letter to my wife. I told her where I was, what I was about to do, and how much I loved her.

Within minutes, the whipping wind soaked all occupants to the skin, and some boats took on so much water that it seemed unlikely they could reach shore before swamping. The troops were packed so tightly that the three or more hours they subsequently spent in those diminutive landing craft, tossed by the rolling sea as if they were mere bathtub toys, were among the most uncomfortable hours of the men's lives. As that agonizing experience unfolded, even enemy bullets on Utah Beach seemed trivial. The men desperately needed to get their feet on solid ground again.

U.S. Navy Task Force 125
D-Day Action Report, Transport Division Five, June 26, 1944
Wind was westerly, Force 5, causing considerable chop. [A Force 5 wind is from nineteen to twenty-four miles per hour, with waves greater than five feet. Other D-Day accounts report that the wind was Force 4, or thirteen to eighteen miles per hour.] This is bad weather for the operation of small craft; wind and chop caused the troops to be drenched and seasick. There can be no doubt that the fighting efficiency of troops is greatly reduced by spending three and one-half hours under cold, wet, seasick conditions.

Although the 8th Infantry had not seen a shot fired in World War II, the U.S. Army's top brass considered it a first-class outfit, a reputation earned in large measure by its extraordinary commander, Col. James Van Fleet. The fifty-two-year-old Van Fleet was a graduate of the same 1915 West Point class as Eisenhower and Bradley, but unlike his classmates, Van Fleet

"A fine unit that had all the elements a modern unit needs." Officers of the 8th Infantry. Seated, left to right: Maj. Oma Bates (S-3); Col. James Van Fleet (CO); Lt. Col. Fred Steiner (XO); Maj. Hugh McClary (Asst. S-3). Standing, left to right: Lt. Col. Conrad Simmons (CO, 1st Battalion); Lt. Col. Carlton MacNeely (CO, 2nd Battalion); Lt. Col. Erasmus Strickland (CO, 3rd Battalion).
COURTESY 8TH INFANTRY REGIMENT.

had gained valuable combat experience on the Western Front in World War I as a twenty-six-year-old battalion commander in the 6th Division. For Van Fleet, June 6, 1944, would initiate a seven-year period during which he experienced one of the most impressive career advances of any soldier in American history. His soldierly qualities demonstrated in combat starting on D-Day so impressed the army's leaders that by early 1945, they would promote him to major general in command of a corps; and by 1951, they would bestow upon him four-star rank and assign him command of the U.S. Eighth Army at a critical moment in the Korean War.

Col. James Van Fleet
Commander, 8th Infantry, 4th Division
The 8th Infantry was a southern regiment, made prior to the draft, mostly of country boys from Florida, Alabama, and Georgia. They were squirrel-shooters who weren't afraid of the dark, who could find their way forward in woods and feel at home. When the draft began, we were filled up with boys mostly from New York, and they brought to us the skills needed in a modern army—communications, motorization, mechanization. There was much conjecture as to whether the Yankees and Rebels would mix. Would there be fights? There were none at all. It was the most happy marriage you can imagine between the north and south into one fine unit that had all the elements a modern unit needs.

But for a soldier with such obvious combat skills, Van Fleet's career prior to D-Day was perhaps more astonishing than his subsequent meteoric rise. Throughout an interminable three-year period before the Normandy invasion, a time when U.S. Army officers with even marginal aptitude rose in rank faster than clerks could keep up with their promotions, the frustrated Colonel Van Fleet remained in command of the 8th Infantry, watching much younger men rise to superior rank and lead their outfits into combat. He must have wondered if he had been forgotten or, even worse, whether someone in Washington was blocking his promotion because of real or imagined leadership defects. Later, Gen. George Marshall, the wartime U.S. Army Chief of Staff, recalled that Van Fleet had been mixed up with another officer with a similar name who was an alcoholic. As a result of a case of mistaken identity, Van Fleet therefore had the extraordinary experience of holding command of the same regiment for nearly three years prior to introducing it to combat on D-Day. The men of the 8th Infantry were lucky to have him so long, and one officer remembered Van Fleet as "the best leader I have ever encountered—and I have encountered a lot of them." After a wait of such long duration, Utah Beach would be the place where Van Fleet would first demonstrate his great worth to his country in World War II.

The historic moment had arrived at last, an instant that the 8th Infantry's survivors would always remember as they aged. The sun was up now, low in the eastern sky, at the backs of the assault troops. The men were miserably seasick, crammed in their landing craft, racing toward an unseen shore veiled by a boiling fury of smoke and dust, the product of countless bombs and shells that had impacted there only moments before.

Just a few more minutes now. A few thousand yards offshore, the amazed GIs watched four special U.S. Navy vessels launch hundreds of whooshing rockets directly over their heads, a spectacle meant not only to boost the assault troops' morale, but also to pulverize any enemy soldiers unlucky enough to be on those weapons' receiving end. Unhappily for the spectators, no one could tell whether the rockets did any good. An action report of the rocket vessels' D-Day activities noted: "The majority of the craft did not see their target. . . . Low and varying degree of visibility [on the beach] made accurate calculation of their point of impact impossible."

About a quarter of a mile offshore, the coastline at last emerged through the smoke. The tide was out, and any GIs who cared to look over the sides of their LCVPs at the beach they were about to storm were astonished at its flatness and vast width. A distant seawall and low sand dunes were barely visible through the haze on the far side of the beach.

So this was France. . . . But there was not a sign of the enemy army that occupied it, except for a belt of peculiar beach obstacles between the surf and the seawall. At the moment, those obstacles seemed insignificant, a puny effort that could hardly stop an army as large as the one that would begin the liberation of Europe at this very point. It was 6:30 A.M., more than an hour after low water, and the tide was pushing ahead toward those obstacles at a rate matched only by a few places in the world. From their raised steering wells at the rear of the LCVPs, tense navy and coast guard coxswains could see the sea surging inexorably forward, ultimately to become rolling breakers that tumbled forward to smack hard on the beach. The coxswains could feel their craft caught by this relentless momentum as they neared the shore, and with one hand on the helm and the other on the throttle, they delicately steered their craft, searching for a place to touch down in that amorphous zone where water meets solid ground. They would know they were there when their LCVPs scraped bottom and jolted to a stop. Then the simple act of dropping their bow ramps, finally releasing their passengers for the coming fight, would usher in a new and decisive stage of World War II.

Brig. Gen. Theodore Roosevelt Jr.
Supernumerary General Officer, 4th Division, Letter to his wife, Eleanor, June 11, 1944

The little boats were now going full speed, slapping the waves with their blunt prows. . . . Then with a crunch we grounded, the ramp was lowered, and we jumped into water waist-deep and started for the shore. We splashed and floundered through some hundred yards of water while German salvos fell. Men dropped, some silent, some screaming. Up the 400 yards of beach we ran—Grandfather puffed a bit—then we reached the seawall. The company CO with whom I was, [Capt. Howard] Lees [of Company E], a great tower of a man, led his troops splendidly. He with his men started into the dunes to attack the German strongpoints.

Capt. M. C. Adair
Surgeon, 2nd Battalion, 8th Infantry, 4th Division, July 1944
I was in the assault wave at H-Hour. We came in on Utah, Uncle Red. Our LCVP was not hit, and there were not many other boats near us at the time we came in. We got off in hip-deep water. The shelling was heavy on the beach, but there were not many casualties.

S/Sgt. Harry Bailey
Company E, 8th Infantry, 4th Division
Artillery and small arms fire were all about the beach. My first scout [Pvt.] Douglas Mason from Michigan, was the first to reach the sand dunes, and I ran and dropped down beside him to look to see which way to go. He was immediately killed with a hit to the head by a sniper's bullet. I knew I had to move fast, or I would be next, so I ran forward as fast as I could go. The rest of the platoon followed.

Capt. Robert Crisson
Commander, Company C, 8th Infantry, 4th Division, July 1944
The spirit and morale of the men were fine. Even after passing what I took to be a naval patrol boat turned upside down [probably PC-1261], the men continued joking and kidding each other. They had to be reminded not to expose themselves. When we left the boats we had at least 100 yards of water to wade through. Many of the men yelled like Indians when we hit the water, and in fact several had their hair cut similar to the Mohawks [with] a tuft on top of the head.

LEFT AND RIGHT AND BACK AGAIN

They were so waterlogged and heavily burdened they could not run. The much anticipated arrival in France for the 4th Division invaders had turned into an interminable progression of graceless strides across a seemingly endless beach, an exhausting journey occasionally interrupted by enemy bullets and shells. The trip finally culminated in the lee of a low seawall that stood just above the high-water mark and separated the beach from a line of twenty-foot sand dunes, crowned by shaggy beach grass, just beyond. The wall ran as far as the eye could see up and down the coastline, and at its base, the troops could safely take a breather. But when the Germans deduced what was happening, they would positively launch a deadly mortar barrage that could cause scores of casualties among the clustered GIs. The troops would eventually have to move—but where?

As any soldier who ascended the dunes to get a better look at his surroundings had already perceived, something was amiss: The 8th Infantry was evidently in the wrong place. This stretch of the Normandy coast did not contain many prominent landmarks, so it was hard to tell; but the two most obvious features the GIs had studied back in England on their Utah Beach air photographs and terrain models—a large windmill and a curious rectangular earthen structure known as "The Mud Fort"—were nowhere in sight.

Brig. Gen. Theodore Roosevelt Jr.
Supernumerary General Officer, 4th Division, Letter to his wife, Eleanor, June 11, 1944

There was a house by the seawall where none should have been were we in the right place. It was imperative that I should find out where we were in order to set the maneuver. I scrambled up on the dunes and was lucky in finding a windmill which I recognized. We'd been put ashore a mile too far to the south. [Ironically, the mislanding brought the 8th Infantry ashore on the very spot that Colonel Van Fleet had once argued should be the focal point of the landing; the U.S. Navy had turned him down. In a 1973 interview, Van Fleet remembered that "the navy command said it would get into shallow water and our boats would ground."]

Capt. Robert Crisson
Commander, Company C, 8th Infantry, 4th Division, July 1944

The craft landed us and we began working our way down the sand dunes looking for the Mud Fort. An NCO reported to me, "Dammit, captain, there's no Mud Fort down there."

The bulky Utah Beach plan book had carefully choreographed the 8th Infantry's movements once its assault companies had hit the beach, but now that the troops were far off their marks, the immediate issue was whether to move north up the beach to the intended landing zone or start moving inland from where they were.

One of the hallmarks of the U.S. Army on D-Day was its adaptability, a trait that the 8th Infantry exhibited repeatedly on Utah Beach. In the invasion's first critical hour, those American officers who peered intently at their maps behind the seawall, from General Roosevelt and Colonel Van Fleet down to the youngest second lieutenant, all agreed that there was only one sensible course of action: move directly inland from their current locations;

eliminate the Germans wherever they were encountered; and somehow strike for the causeways leading off the beach. The 8th's junior leaders would have to take initiative, for this was not the way the plan was supposed to have been executed. But as long as those leaders could get their men off the beach, it was of no consequence how they did it. Paratroopers would be waiting on the other side of the causeways, and it was imperative that the 8th Infantry make contact with them as soon as possible.

Brig. Gen. Theodore Roosevelt Jr.
Supernumerary General Officer, 4th Division, Letter to his wife, Eleanor, June 11, 1944
I had to hot-foot it from left to right and back again, setting the various COs straight and changing the task. . . . Stevie [1st Lt. Marcus Stevenson, Roosevelt's aide] of course was with me, devoted and competent as always, his tommy gun ready to defend us if it became necessary. We set up a tiny CP with my radio behind the wall of a house.

Company E, 8th Infantry, 4th Division
U.S. Army Historical Division, Interview with 2nd Lt. John Rebarchek, July 2, 1944
Lieutenant Rebarchek said he was confused for a little while after landing because he didn't know that he had landed too far to the south. He kept looking for the Mud Fort, which was the first objective of his section. Then he looked for the old windmill. When he finally spotted it away off to the right, he knew that he had landed in a different place than planned. He decided to give up the original objective and go straight in.

The infantrymen's seemingly logical decision to move directly inland triggered a quandary from a logistical standpoint, for the U.S. Army engineers and U.S. Navy sailors whose job was to manage the beachhead needed to know immediately where they should set up their beach installations and guide follow-on waves of reinforcements ashore. A change of plans as significant as the one Roosevelt and his cohorts were about to initiate would be unsettling to the many engineer units that were about to land, for they had studied the meager Utah Beach road network for weeks. To suddenly relocate the landing beach a mile south of its intended site could promptly throw the sappers' meticulous designs into disarray.

The unit that would be most affected by the repositioning of the beachhead was the 1st Engineer Special Brigade, an outfit larger than an infantry division, which was responsible for ensuring the continuous movement of supplies and equipment across the beach on D-Day and afterward. Its deputy commander, Col. Eugene Caffey, came ashore in the first wave with the 8th Infantry's Company B, and a fortuitous meeting with Roosevelt on the beach led Caffey to the inevitable conclusion that his engineers, too, must swiftly revise their plans if they were to fulfill their critical mission.

Col. Eugene Caffey
Deputy Commander, 1st Engineer Special Brigade

I undertook to get word to the Navy that we were completely out of position and induce them to continue the landing at the place where we were instead of trying to conform to the original plan. This, as events proved, was a good decision because we were in the weakest part of the German lines and astraddle of the only road that led inland across the inundated areas just back of the dune lines. I think it was greatly to the credit of the 4th Division and the 1st Engineer Special Brigade that the officers and men immediately affected were not perturbed by this abrupt rearrangement of the planned battle, but went right ahead with the war as if this was the way they had always intended to do it.

So the 8th Infantry would go forward. For these men of the Ivy Division, the hop over the low seawall and ascent of the steep dunes would shortly bring them face-to-face, for the first time, with the renowned German Army. The 8th was a superbly trained and highly motivated military unit that had worked relentlessly for the past three years under Van Fleet's stern tutelage for this moment; but still the rumors from combat in North Africa, Sicily, and Italy hinted that the enemy was just as capable. The Germans had made the U.S. Army pay a high price in lives for every foot of ground gained in those campaigns, and they had fought with a toughness and resilience that American troops could not help but admire.

But on the morning of June 6, 1944, Van Fleet's men discovered an astonishing truth. If the first enemy soldiers encountered by the 8th Infantry in France were representative of the current state of the German Army, the Allies would surely be in Paris in a month—and Berlin soon after that. The enemy's coastal guardians, drawn from the 709th Division, had been pulverized by the naval and air bombardment, cut off from their comrades by the Americans' nighttime parachute drop, and utterly dejected by the absence of the Luftwaffe. And now resolute and heavily armed American infantrymen were streaming over the dunes by the hundreds, systematically blowing gaps through the barbed wire with bangalore torpedoes and firing bazooka rounds into pillbox apertures with deadly accuracy.

"We were completely out of position." VII Corps troops disembarking on Utah Beach on D-Day. The sand dunes at the high water line are visible in the background. U.S. ARMY SIGNAL CORPS, NATIONAL ARCHIVES.

The 8th Infantry's immediate task was to eradicate five enemy strong-points, constructed in a checkerboard pattern just beyond the beach. The Germans positioned three of those strongpoints directly on and immediately behind the dunes, separated from each other by intervals of about one mile. They sited the other two as backup positions about 700 yards inland, squarely in the intervals between the three strongpoints on the dunes. Each strongpoint had one or more concrete pillboxes housing automatic weapons and antitank guns, and was surrounded by minefields and barbed wire. Steady defenders might have held out for a considerable time in such formidable positions, but in truth, the enemy's resistance was anything but stiff. The 8th Infantry was easily able to maneuver in the wide gaps between the strongpoints, and when it commenced its attack, the few remaining Germans inside would be quickly dispatched or captured.

Led by Companies E and F at 6:30 A.M., more than 600 men from Lt. Col. Carlton MacNeely's 2nd Battalion had landed just south of a small cluster of buildings that hardly seemed worthy of the name it bore on U.S. Army maps: La Grande Dune. MacNeely's job was to wipe out the two southernmost strongpoints, and at about 7:00 A.M., his men pressed up and over the dunes to do exactly that.

Pvt. Robert Wolfram
Company E, 8th Infantry, 4th Division, September 14, 1944
I was the runner for the CO [Capt. Howard Lees], so I had to stay with him. As soon as the Germans saw us coming over the seawall, they started firing mortars and 88s at us. . . . We deployed out: Scouts were out ahead, and I was with the CO. Two houses just ahead of us had snipers in them, but we took these Germans with BARs. . . . The CO sent me back for a radio man. While I went back to find him I was hit [by artillery fire]. . . . As I was moving back, the third wave was coming in, and the first tanks as well—about 25 or 30 of them. I went on toward the seawall where they had an aid station, and I lay there three hours.

Company F advanced straight inland toward a German strongpoint centered on a small farm known as La Dune, about 700 yards beyond the shoreline. Happily for the Americans, an attack that could have been both costly and protracted turned out to be virtually effortless. Although the wary GIs had to watch their step continuously in case they had unknowingly entered a deadly German minefield, the enemy's resistance consisted only of scattered sniper fire. Indeed, most of the German troops here displayed an obvious desire to surrender rather than give their lives for their führer in this remote corner of France.

Capt. Leonard Schroeder
Commander, Company F, 8th Infantry, 4th Division
A group of the enemy surrendered, walking out with their hands up. These were the first we had ever seen. . . . They were armed to the hilt, so I pulled out my trench knife and proceeded to cut all their web equipment from their bodies. One German soldier hit the panic button and ran toward the beach. I suppose half of the company put bullets into him, thinking he was trying to get away.

The Utah Beach invasion plan was complex, but as far as MacNeely was concerned, his orders could be condensed into two words: move inland. The addition of Companies G and H had filled out the 2nd Battalion nearly to full strength, and it now turned 90 degrees to the south and headed for Causeway 1, beyond which MacNeely hoped to find the 101st Airborne. This movement was somewhat disorganized, but given the need for immediate action, there was no time to follow maneuver methods prescribed in field manuals. As they pressed forward, the GIs soon realized that their primary concern would be neither enemy bullets nor shells, but mines.

Capt. George Mabry
Operations Officer, 2nd Battalion, 8th Infantry, 1946

I saw seven men of Company G and was about to call to them when a terrific explosion occurred, killing three and wounding the others. It was apparent that one of these unfortunate individuals had stepped on a mine, which caused a number of additional mines to explode simultaneously. I began a circular movement and advanced about fifty yards when small arms fire from an enemy group pinned me. . . . Making a hasty survey of my position, I could see mines that had been uncovered by strong winds and shifting sand. I knew that I was in a minefield. A definite decision must be made—and quickly! . . . I elected to push through the mines and engage the enemy. [I leaped] for a shell hole, but my foot set off a mine. The explosion slammed me against the ground with a tremendous thud—no injuries from it—just shaken up a bit. . . . I saw a lieutenant of Company F [probably 1st Lt. Lawrence Hubbard] and called a warning to watch for mines, but it could not be heard above the noise of battle. The lieutenant crumpled under the explosion of a mine. I sprang up and rushed toward the dug-in Germans, stopping once to deliver a few rounds of fire before closing in. The last rush of twenty-five yards carried me to the enemy foxholes. The first German encountered was quickly exterminated and immediately the remaining six surrendered.

Somewhere at the far end of Causeway 1, 101st Airborne paratroopers were supposed to be waiting, so for MacNeely, speed was essential. Companies E and F turned left, following a lane that paralleled the coast about 700 yards inland. Companies G and H stayed near the shoreline and headed straight for a German strongpoint at a farm known as Beau Guillot, but the Germans manning this position demonstrated much greater resilience than had their comrades at La Dune.

Capt. James Haley
Commander, Company G, 8th Infantry, Distinguished Service Cross Citation, October 24, 1944

Captain James Haley landed at 0637 on Utah Beach. . . . Turning left at a gap in the seawall, he had advanced only 50 yards when leading elements of his unit became casualties in an enemy minefield. The rest of his men froze in position and hesitated to go forward. Haley, recklessly exposing himself to increasingly heavy hostile fire and the possibility of instant death from a mine, went into the minefield and

Utah Beach: Second Wave, 7:30 A.M., June 6, 1944

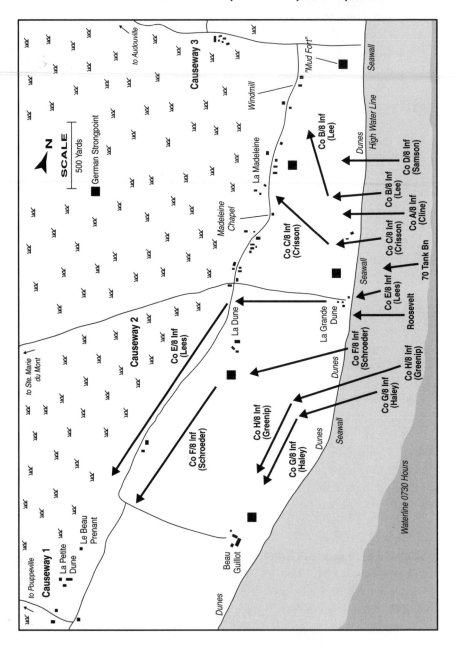

after having personally cleared a path through it, returned to his men and led them safely past this obstacle. . . . German snipers were delivering deadly fire upon the leading elements of Company G. . . . [Haley] personally led Company G in the assault of the [Beau Guillot] strongpoint, during which he was subjected to severe machine gun fire directed at him from pointblank range. . . . [Haley's] inspiring example and superb courage fired his men with sufficient determination to enable them to quickly destroy the strongpoint and clear this sector of the beach.

Van Fleet's 1st Battalion was led by Lt. Col. Conrad Simmons, a 1921 graduate of Columbia University. Simmons had the difficult task of dealing with the three remaining enemy strongpoints near La Grande Dune, and then moving north to force open a causeway over which his outfit had to advance inland toward the paratroopers with all possible speed. The Ninth Air Force B-26s and U.S. Navy warships had done particularly effective work in this vicinity, and those unfortunate German soldiers who had been the targets of the bombs and shells were either dead or utterly stunned, deaf to all sounds except the ringing in their ears produced by the thunderous deluge of weaponry. When Companies B and C dashed over the dunes toward the strongpoints, enemy resistance evaporated faster than a drop of rain on a sizzling sidewalk.

Capt. Robert Crisson
Commander, Company C, 8th Infantry, 4th Division, July 1944
We moved inland and began to knock out the houses along the road back of the dunes. Company B took Fort Madeleine [about 600 yards inland], assisted by a section of Company C. The left section of Company C took Fort U-5 [the coastal strongpoint at La Grande Dune]. There was almost no opposition at these forts. Some small arms fire was received from houses along the road, but the Germans gave up gladly when we closed in. A private ran up to me and said, "I've got two women over here." I asked him where he had them and he said, "In a ditch." I asked: "What the hell are you doing with two women in a ditch?" He said, "I don't want them to get shot." A sergeant chimed in with, "How old are they?" We immediately moved the two women and a male civilian into a safer spot. We established the company CP in the church at 444969 [a map coordinate, the site of the tiny Madeleine Chapel, which still stands].

PFC Robert Willard
Company B, 8th Infantry, 4th Division, September 14, 1944
We were told to push inland, and we went in as fast as we could. We were a whole assault team, 29 enlisted men and one officer. We went straight ahead toward a

house about 300 yards from the beach, and when we started over the seawall the Germans threw mortars and 88s. Some fellows got hit and these were our first casualties. We started crawling, and the lieutenant [1st Lt. Gail Lee, CO of Company B] told us to keep moving as it was the safest thing. The Germans were firing machine guns and small arms. . . . A road ran parallel to the beach and then turned sharply to the right and along here there was a small village of a few houses. We had to search each house, and each man had to take a room. We threw grenades and shot Germans in the houses, and they would come out after having enough of our small arms fire.

The 8th Infantry had shattered the enemy's coastal defenses in less than one hour, and the wide breach through which the rest of the 4th Division would shortly flow established beyond any doubt that the Atlantic Wall, once touted by Hitler as a symbol of Germany's military greatness, was a facade. But to the men of the Ivy Division, the easy conquest of the beach did not obscure the hard truth that much more challenging tasks still lay ahead on D-Day. More than 13,000 American paratroopers and gliderists were somewhere beyond the causeways leading off Utah Beach, and the lives of those men now depended on the rapidity with which the 4th Division could carry out its next mission. Those causeways, however, were tactical nightmares; and if the Germans had them covered, that mission would not be as easy to accomplish.

A LAST CUP OF HOT JAVA

Ike and Monty grasped the obvious requirement that the Normandy invasion must not fail, and that attitude pervaded every Allied outfit that would participate in the assault. If Operation Overlord could not gain a stable lodgment on the Continent, it would be a catastrophe for the Western Allies, whose planners would have to go back to their drawing boards for months to figure out another and better way to enter northwest Europe. Meanwhile, if Hitler continued to hold Field Marshal Rommel in high regard, the enemy would certainly continue to labor intensely on the Atlantic Wall, making it a much more formidable barrier than it had been in June 1944. In short, if the enemy could decisively defeat the Normandy invasion, the Anglo-American effort to end the war by crushing the German Army in western Europe would be momentarily paralyzed, a paralysis that would in all likelihood endure for a considerable period.

If the Normandy invasion was to succeed, the Western Allies had to master all aspects of amphibious operations—an overwhelming challenge, given the gloomy history of that type of warfare. One of the primary means by which American and British generals intended to enhance their chance of success on D-Day was to employ plentiful numbers of tanks in the invasion's initial waves. Tanks had unmistakably proved themselves as the paramount offensive ground weapon of World War II, but their role in amphibious warfare had seemingly been limited by several obvious factors, such as an effective means of getting them safely ashore in large numbers and then operating them efficiently in coastal terrain that would in all probability be inhospitable for tanks.

If Allied planners could figure out a way to employ tanks effectively in the invasion's opening stage, they assumed, they would gain an incalculable tactical advantage on D-Day. They deduced that the Germans would not expect large numbers of tanks to surge ashore with the assault troops. And as World War II combat had clearly established, tanks could have a decisive impact in battle if the enemy was inadequately prepared to counter them. By June 1944, the U.S. and Royal Navies possessed more than adequate numbers of landing craft capable of conveying tanks to the beach, but some Anglo-American generals resolved to find a better way of landing tanks on a coast that the enemy was prepared to defend vigorously at the waterline. Tank landing craft were slow, unarmored for the most part, and susceptible to sea mines and direct enemy fire. Just as infantrymen had been taught during training to avoid the potentially deadly practice of bunching up, tankers were especially uncomfortable and helpless when they and at least four of their tanks were packed onto the deck of an LCT heading for an enemy-occupied beach. The destruction of that LCT would lead to the loss of all tanks and dozens of crew members.

There had to be a better method, and a fifty-nine-year-old British general named Percy Hobart proposed an innovative way to do it. Hobart had been a professional soldier for a decade before the first tank was used in combat in 1916, but by 1944, the top brass recognized him as the Allies' chief proponent of specialized armored vehicles, such as mine-clearing tanks known as "Crabs" and flamethrower vehicles labeled "Crocodiles." The British Army had eagerly adopted these contraptions, and the men had promptly christened them "Funnies." By early 1943, Hobart had taken command of the 79th Armored Division, a unit equipped almost entirely with Funnies, and many of his regiments would play pivotal roles in Normandy and afterward.

Surely the most curious of all Hobart's Funnies was the duplex drive (DD) tank, a vehicle that had been conceived in 1940 in England by a Hungarian émigré named Nicholas Straussler. A DD tank could float and move through water under its own power at about four miles per hour, powered

by two propellers also acting as rudders. At sea, the DD tank rode very low
in the water and was completely concealed by a waterproof canvas screen,
giving the astonished enemy the impression that it was about to be invaded
by hordes of floating bathtubs with no evident military application whatsoever. Once a DD tank reached the beach, a crewman lowered the screen
and switched the transmission to power the wheels rather than the propellers, thereby allowing the tank to resume its conventional qualities and
advance inland on its tracks.

It seemed inconceivable that such a colossal steel vehicle could float,
but Straussler had come up with a way to do it.

Nicholas Straussler
Inventor, DD Tank

The design was commenced by putting a continuous rigid deck right around the
tank at approximately mud-guard level—just above the top of the tracks. A number of [metal] tubular frames were made, the contour of which generally corresponded to the outer rim of the decking. A very heavy rubberized canvas screen
was constructed to connect these tubular frames to the decking. The tubular
frames were spaced at suitable intervals so that when the canvas attachment was
made, the structure formed a hull, flexible in an up-and-down direction in a con-
certina manner. A number of compressed air tubes were placed on the deck and
attached to the screen. Inflation of these tubes raised the screen.

In spring 1944, DD tanks were still a closely guarded secret and had not
yet been tested in combat. That first test would come on D-Day: Four DD
tanks would be loaded aboard each LCT, and at about three miles offshore,
their crews would raise their canvas screens and drive the tanks down the
LCTs' ramps into the sea, where they would make their way to the beach
under their own power. If the DD tanks worked—and some prominent
Allied generals were doubtful, given Normandy's legendary offshore currents—the crews would lower the canvas screens upon reaching the beach,
suddenly exposing the Sherman tanks to the astonished enemy.

The enemy required powerful weapons to destroy a Sherman on land;
but at sea a Sherman was a fragile machine, highly vulnerable to nature's
whims. A DD tank was kept afloat on water by its raised canvas screen, but
the Sherman's thirty-two-ton weight forced the bulk of the tank underwater,
and consequently only two or three feet of the screen extended above the
waterline. The tankers therefore clearly grasped that even waves of moderate size could swamp their vehicle and send it to the bottom in an instant,

"Hobart's Funnies." A U.S. Army duplex drive tank with its canvas screen lowered for operations on land. U.S. ARMY SIGNAL CORPS, NATIONAL ARCHIVES.

like the gigantic piece of steel that it was. Sea conditions had to be just right if the tanks were to survive their launch and long journey to the beach, and on D-Day off Utah and Omaha Beaches, those conditions, although apparently satisfactory, were obviously rougher than DD tank crews were used to in training.

In the first fifteen minutes of the Utah Beach invasion, the Americans planned to land fifty-six Sherman tanks, thirty-two of which would be amphibious DDs. The remaining twenty-four, brought directly to the beach by LCTs mounting special armor, would be conventional tanks, eight of which were fitted with frontal bulldozer blades to assist engineers in clearing beach wreckage. Utah Beach was little more than a mile in length, and if those fifty-six tanks all made it ashore successfully and advanced across the beach evenly spaced, each tank would be separated from its neighbor by an interval of only about thirty-five yards. General Collins hoped that this awesome display of armored power would cause an enemy already demoralized by the air and naval bombardment to flee or surrender. The plan looked impressive and nearly foolproof on paper; but those GIs used to seemingly incessant army snafus noted with a tinge of cynicism that if you gave a staff planner a map and a pencil, he would tell you that he could win the war in a week.

On D-Day, the first tankers scheduled to drive their Shermans ashore on Utah Beach belonged to the 70th Tank Battalion, a unit that knew a great deal about amphibious warfare. This would be the third time in nineteen months that the 70th would storm an enemy-occupied coast, but one and all agreed that this invasion would make the others seem trivial in comparison. The Normandy invasion would be the first in which the 70th's tankers would operate DD tanks, and even hardened veterans could only guess at how their top secret machines would perform under real combat conditions. Only two of the 70th's tank companies, A and B, were trained to operate DDs, and D-Day orders stipulated that those two outfits must time the launch of their tanks at sea so that they would arrive on Utah Beach simultaneously with the first wave of assault infantry.

The 70th may already have tasted war, but nothing in its past could compare with the tragedy that unfolded shortly before dawn on D-Day as the eight U.S. Navy LCTs carrying the battalion's DD tanks plowed through the sea toward Utah Beach. As LCT-593, with four of Company A's DD tanks aboard, sailed over the shallow Cardonnet Bank about three miles south of the Iles St. Marcouf, it detonated an enormous German naval mine that instantly broke the vessel in two and with incredible force hurled its men, vehicles, and equipment into the air. The marked boat lane heading for Tare Green Beach through which LCT-593 had been sailing had already been carefully swept for enemy mines, so to those who witnessed this disaster, LCT-593's destruction was a profound shock. Even worse, there was nothing they could do about it other than to proceed with the mission as planned and hope that their landing craft would not meet a similar fate.

Sgt. Orris Johnson
Company A, 70th Tank Battalion

Sergeant Hill and I were standing and talking while our engines were warming up, the ramp was down, and it was a matter of minutes before we were to launch. We were on the first LCT in our line [probably LCT-595] and directly across from us on another LCT were another four tanks of our company. Both of us were looking that way when the LCT evidently hit a sea mine. I can still see a tank turning end-over-end what seemed to me at least 100 feet in the air. I think the only two words Hill and I said were "Gibson and Neil." [S/Sgt. Glen Gibson and Cpl. Don Neil, two friends of Johnson and Hill.] Two months later we learned that Gibson was the sole [army] survivor. [Sixteen Company A members, as well as several U.S. Navy sailors, were killed in the blast.]

70th Tank Battalion
Battalion History, 1950

When the LCT was still about 5,000 yards off Utah Beach, the craft struck a large mine. The four DD tanks and all personnel aboard were thrown into the sea. Sgt. Gibson landed about seventy-five yards from the wreckage of the LCT. The forward section of the craft had been sunk, but the stern half was still afloat. He swam to it and climbed aboard. He attempted to disentangle a navy enlisted man who was injured and caught in the door of the pilot's compartment. The LCT capsized, taking the navy man with it but throwing Gibson into the sea for a second time. He climbed upon a portion of the wreckage and was taken aboard an American LCM twenty minutes later. [Gibson was wounded in the head and legs and was eventually taken to a destroyer heading back to England. He rejoined the 70th Tank Battalion in July.]

The DD tank crews were proud of their anomalous vehicles, and now they intended to carry out their mission and finally divulge to the enemy the top secret weapon that allegedly would help throw the balance of amphibious warfare in the invader's favor. The tankers were trained to launch their DDs into the sea over the LCTs' bow ramps about three miles offshore, but on D-Day, the sailors brought their landing craft in about half that distance before swinging them into line, dropping their ramps, and giving the GIs the momentous signal to launch their tanks into the water. U.S. Army and Navy D-Day action reports do not agree on why the LCTs brought the DD tanks closer to shore than originally planned, nor do they specify who gave that order. But regardless of the order's origin, that decision proved eminently wise, for the seas were significantly calmer inshore than they were farther out to sea, and as all DD tankers knew, a choppy sea was an enemy to be feared more than the Germans. Of the 70th's twenty-eight surviving DD tanks, only one swamped at sea. The remaining twenty-seven rushed ashore on Utah Beach, and the drivers promptly readied their tanks for action by raising their propellers and lowering their canvas screens. What was behind those screens was a secret no longer.

General Hobart's assertion that DD tanks were practical weapons in an amphibious assault had been confirmed by the 70th Tank Battalion. That evidence, however, was far from conclusive, as the two tank battalions operating DD vehicles on Omaha Beach had achieved entirely different results on D-Day. Of the thirty-two DDs in the 743rd Tank Battalion scheduled to land on Omaha's western sector, not a single one launched at sea, because both army and navy officers had reckoned that the sea was too choppy to make the attempt. Consequently, all of the 743rd's DD tanks were brought directly to the beach on their LCTs. But the leaders of the 741st Tank Battalion, who held orders to land their thirty-two DDs on the opposite half of Omaha Beach, resolved to launch their tanks at sea as planned. They made the attempt about three miles offshore, as orders prescribed, but the effort was in vain. Twenty-seven of the 741st's DD tanks were swamped at sea, and only five made it to shore successfully—a result that was precisely the reverse of the 70th Tank Battalion's achievement on Utah Beach.

In retrospect, sailing the LCTs much closer inshore before launching the 70th's DD tanks off Utah had been a wise decision.

Maj. Gen. J. Lawton Collins
Commander, VII Corps, Autobiography, "Lightning Joe"

I put off in a small boat from our command ship *Bayfield* [during a DD tank training exercise off Slapton Sands] and went forward with the line of LCTs carrying the DDs of the 70th Tank Battalion. . . . Good-sized waves were pitching the LCTs about as we approached the shore and lowered the gangplanks to put off the DDs. From close alongside I watched the tanks drive off the ends of the gangplanks, their canvas collars barely avoiding gulps of water as they plunged overboard. Once the DDs settled down they rode very well. But I decided that I would insist that the Navy take the LCTs with our DDs as close to shore as possible on D-Day before dumping them off, a provision that proved both a lifesaver and a DD saver on D-Day.

Company B, 70th Tank Battalion
Unit Journal, June 6, 1944

Onboard the LCTs the men were up about 0300 watching the great show. About 0500 they gave us the word to make preparations for launching. While the engines were warming up and the DDs being made correct, the men were infiltrating into the ship's galley for a last cup of hot java before shoving off into the deep blue. At 0626 the Air Corps presented us with a very fine show and left the beaches we were to assault in a few minutes in great chaos, with heavy clouds of black and gray smoke hanging low over the well-fortified enemy pillboxes. We disembarked at 0630 despite a rough sea.

Just learning how to operate a DD tank back in England had been risky, as only a few feet of canvas stood between the tank and the sea. Should the sea overcome that barrier, the tank would promptly sink—and with it, possibly one or more of its crew members. The risk was worth it, however, if the tanks could swim ashore in some semblance of order, ready to open fire instantly with their big guns on enemy pillboxes that had so far resisted attempts by the infantry to destroy them.

But to the veteran crews of the 70th Tank Battalion, Utah Beach was something of an anticlimax. As their Shermans churned through the shallow surf up onto Utah's dry sand, the tense tank gunners, primed to open fire on any active enemy resistance nest, peered through their periscopes toward the seawall and discovered that there was virtually nothing to shoot at. The GIs of Colonel Van Fleet's 8th Infantry had come ashore about twenty minutes previously, and their presence in appreciable numbers on the dunes and behind the seawall hinted that they had for the most part already taken care of the German pillboxes that the tankers had practiced for so long to eliminate. To the men of the 70th, it was as if they had trained for months nonstop for a crucial football game, only to discover that the opponents did not show up.

1st Lt. John Casteel
Commander, Company B, 70th Tank Battalion, July 15, 1944
My company landed at 453965 [a map coordinate, about 400 yards south of La Grande Dune]. The tanks actually had little to do on the beach. They fired on some pillboxes, but in the main the pillboxes were already abandoned. However, the tanks stayed on the beach a half hour, mainly because the beaches were not yet cleared of obstacles, and because the engineers had not yet breached the seawall. When the wall was breached [by Companies A and C, 237th Engineer Battalion], the tanks moved through this defile in column, down U5 [the causeway leading to Ste. Marie du Mont], a narrow road leading partly through inundated fields.

Like the infantrymen they were supposed to support, the real war would begin for the tankers when they attempted to make contact with the 101st Airborne Division on the far side of the causeways.

General Board, U.S. Forces European Theater
Study No. 50, "Separate Tank Battalions—Employment of DD Tanks,"
Fall 1945
Colonel J. C. Welborn, Lt. Col. R. N. Skaggs, and Lt. Col. W. D. Duncan, who commanded the 70th, 741st, and 743rd Tank Battalions respectively on D-Day [Duncan was actually the 743rd's operations officer], stated that in their opinion, the DD device was not satisfactory for the purpose intended, and that medium tanks can be landed more effectively from LCTs directly onto the beaches than by swim-

ming in. Losses, in fact, were lower among the units that landed directly on the beach. . . . [However], British opinion from a 79th Armored Division report states that the DD tank was a great factor in the rapid and successful actions on D-Day.

HEROISM UNSURPASSED

War is an endeavor of supreme uncertainty, but on the morning of June 6, 1944, there was one fact upon which all military men would agree: By 10:30 A.M. Utah Beach, which only five hours previously had been a vast expanse of sand stretching more than 700 yards from the seawall to the surf, would be reduced to a narrow strip just a few yards wide, barely enough room for a GI to lie prone without getting his feet wet. American soldiers and sailors were intensely concerned about this natural phenomenon, because at high tide, the hundreds of beach obstacles the enemy had cleverly erected on the sands would be submerged in the surf and invisible to coxswains who held orders to bring their landing craft ashore according to Utah's strict invasion timetable. A sailor who was unfortunate enough to run his craft at high speed onto a seemingly innocuous log ramp or steel hedgehog could lose his vessel and all its passengers in an instant, especially if that obstacle was topped by a deadly mine.

On both Utah and Omaha Beaches, the invasion plan hinged on the immediate clearance of those beach obstacles by specially trained engineers and sailors. Failure to do so could bring the shoreward flow of troops, vehicles, and supplies to a halt as the Norman tide rose with astonishing rapidity. All senior army and navy officers agreed that success in the problematic venture known as amphibious warfare depended entirely on the application of overwhelming force in a timely manner, and if that effort was interrupted, even for a short while, the invasion in all probability would fail. Clearly the Allies must come up with some way to overcome Rommel's tactic of littering the beaches of Normandy with all sorts of crude but highly effective impediments.

American invasion planners had until recently considered the clearance of beach obstacles a naval responsibility. The U.S. Navy had assigned eleven Naval Combat Demolition Units (NCDU) to the Utah Beach mission, but their impending D-Day tasks were so formidable that the NCDU teams, each of which consisted of five enlisted sailors and one officer, would obviously have to be augmented to get the beach clearance job done punctually. The U.S. Army helped by contributing sixty-seven volunteers from various engineer outfits to the mission, effectively doubling the size of each NCDU. But even that was not enough. General Collins considered the beach clearance job so essential that he added twelve more twenty-six-man engineer demolition teams to the task, drawn from the U.S. Army's 237th and 299th Engineer Battalions.

If the engineers and sailors could manage to blow up the beach obstacles, someone was going to have to shove the wreckage out of the way before the rising tide covered it, thereby creating clear lanes for incoming landing craft to reach the beach. That task fell to eight Sherman tanks specially equipped with frontal dozer blades, scheduled to land fifteen minutes after the first wave from armored LCTs. If everything worked according to plan, in less than one hour the Americans would negate Rommel's prodigious effort to obstruct the Normandy beaches.

For a while, the U.S. Army had not been able to figure out what to do with the 237th Engineers. The battalion had received orders in the fall of 1943 to ship out to India, and it commenced the first leg of that long journey on November 14 from Hampton Roads, reaching North Africa twenty days later. When General Montgomery added the Utah Beach invasion to the Overlord plan in January 1944, top American commanders in England realized that the VII Corps would need much more engineer muscle to storm Normandy, and so the 237th, along with two other engineer units, suddenly found itself on a transport bound for Liverpool rather than Bombay. It was a big difference, as the surprised sappers from the 237th discovered when they were sent to the U.S. Army Assault Training Center on the north coast of Devon in April to learn how to demolish German beach obstacles. Although the engineers had not yet been officially notified of their role in Overlord, even the 237th's greenest privates could now figure out that their outfit would hold a vital and dangerous mission in the invasion, whenever it would come.

The second U.S. Army outfit that shared the mission of clearing Utah Beach of enemy obstacles, the 299th Engineers, also had experienced a recent and abrupt change in its destiny. The 299th had shipped out to England from New York on April 6, 1944, only two months before the invasion, so its members had to study and practice their D-Day duties in a hurry. Those duties were a definite challenge, for the 299th was the only ground unit among all those dozens that participated in Operation Overlord to have a major role in both the Utah and Omaha Beach invasions. According to invasion orders, Company B would join the 237th and the NCDUs in the beach clearance operation on Utah; the rest of the battalion would be committed to the corresponding mission on Omaha. For the 299th's members, who were in large measure natives of the Finger Lakes region of western New York, it would be an exceptionally harsh introduction to war. By the end of D-Day, one-quarter of the battalion's 650 men would be casualties, including 71 killed.

The beach clearance operation could not work unless demolition engineers and sailors worked in haste, for the tide on Utah Beach would rise so rapidly that the German obstacles would be nearly submerged little more than one hour after the invasion's commencement. Accordingly, to those who had to carry out the D-Day obstacle clearance mission, the job would be a challenge even in the unlikely event that the preinvasion bombardment killed or incapacitated every German in the coastal defenses. But those Americans assigned to this difficult task ultimately managed to fulfill it with a greater speed and efficiency than orders had dictated, a result that was achievable because Utah's obstacles turned out to be much less formidable than those on Omaha. Furthermore, enemy resistance on Utah was not as harsh as on Omaha, and in retrospect Utah's demolition men were extremely lucky to escape the fate of their brethren, who were slaughtered by enemy small-arms and artillery fire on Omaha Beach as they attempted to demolish beach obstacles in full view of German troops the navy and air force had failed to subdue.

The Utah Beach demolition plan called for the engineers and sailors to land from five to seventeen minutes after the 8th Infantry's first wave. They would then quickly jump to the task of blowing eight fifty-yard gaps through the German obstacles, through which landing craft as large as LCIs could safely pass at high tide. Coxswains steering later waves of landing craft ashore would be guided into the gaps by green flags mounted on buoys and by prominent signs placed on the beach squarely in the center of each gap. During training, the demolition men had carefully studied the most effective means of obliterating the various types of enemy obstacles, and in the end, they determined that the job could best be carried out with two-pound blocks of a plastic explosive known as C-2 and a TNT-like material called tetrytol. These materials were packed into satchels or simple sacks, which could be wrapped around the obstacles and detonated, thereby demolishing or at least breaking up the enemy obstructions that Rommel considered such a vital part of the Atlantic Wall.

The 237th's executive officer, Capt. Robert Tabb, would be in charge of demolition operations on Tare Green Beach, but he had slipped on the deck of his LCT and severely sprained his ankle, triggering anxiety that he would not be capable of executing control over his men. However, his first view of Utah Beach—along with the consumption of plenty of aspirin—

alleviated his concerns. He noted, "I was somewhat surprised that the beach obstacles were very light."

237th Engineer Combat Battalion
U.S. Army Historical Division, Interview with Capt. Robert Tabb, September 6, 1944
Operations didn't proceed quite according to plan. . . . One LCM with an engineer demolition team was hit by shell fire just as it lowered its ramp on [Tare] Green Beach. Six men were killed. Furthermore, the whole landing was shifted south about 1,000–1,200 yards. However, these mishaps and errors did not materially affect the success of the operations. . . . [Tabb] made for the beach, where he first sought cover and then met General Roosevelt walking the beach wall oblivious to the fire. Landing in France was as much of an anti-climax to Tabb as it was for many others. There was little of the expected excitement and not much confusion. The business of clearing the beach proceeded rapidly. There were fewer obstacles than expected, and the demolition parties therefore went ahead to clear the entire beach.

Col. Thomas Deforth Rogers
Commander, 1106th Engineer Combat Group, June 23, 1944
The beach obstacle demolition work southward of my landing point was concentrated (not according to plan) along a stretch about 200 yards wide. The executive, 237th Engineers [Captain Tabb], was exercising vigorous leadership and supervision over these operations. The only instructions I gave him were to widen the gap to the extent of his available explosives rather than to start new gaps. [Rogers, second in his 1934 West Point class, commanded all U.S. Army demolition units on Utah Beach.] All demolition parties were under artillery fire (and rocket fire, I believe) from the time they approached the beach from the sea until the task was finished. . . . I do not believe that the heroism of the men placing charges (connected from man-to-man with primacord [an explosive cord]) has ever been surpassed. I witnessed one party of six blown to bits—but the two adjacent parties continued their work without interruption.

2nd Lt. Herbert Cross
Company C, 70th Tank Battalion
Going in to the beach [in an armored U.S. Navy LCT, carrying two Sherman tanks and a tank dozer], Lt. [Benjamin] Riley kept talking about our engineers blowing up the underwater mines. It was actually the Germans shelling the beach, and I thought Riley was saying it was our engineers to keep the men from getting

scared. It was not until a shell landed very close to our landing craft that Riley realized we were being shelled. His expression was such that we all had to laugh, even at a time like that. [Riley was in charge of the tank dozers, which were supposed to clear the beach of wreckage.]

Like so many other components of the Utah invasion, the beach clearance plan actually worked, thanks in large measure to the speed and efficiency with which the demolition engineers and sailors carried out their work and the effectiveness of the preinvasion air and naval bombardment. In contrast, at Omaha Beach sailors steering their landing craft ashore during high-tide periods on D-Day faced extraordinary perils from submerged German beach obstacles, because intense enemy fire had made the engineers' task of clearing lanes through those obstructions nearly impossible.

Lt. Cmdr. Herbert Peterson
Commander, U.S. Navy Naval Combat Demolition Units, Utah Beach, June 29, 1944
Naval demolition units hit the beach at approximately 0635 [H+5 minutes], and started immediately to work on the obstacles, commencing from seaward. . . . Enemy shell fire, rockets, and some machine gun fire caused some casualties, but all hands worked rapidly, disregarding considerations of personal safety. . . . By 0800 it had been ascertained that all beach obstacles were removed [at a loss of] four killed and eleven wounded. . . . All hands are deserving of high praise. It was the first time under fire for practically all, but the work was carried on coolly, thoroughly, and quickly. This officer is proud to have commanded this group.

Field Marshal Rommel had spent countless hours haranguing his coastal defense troops that their hard labor spent erecting obstacles on the beaches of Normandy could save their lives later on. At least on Utah Beach, he was proved wrong. The German field marshal who had been christened "The Desert Fox" by his respectful opponents had himself been outfoxed by a few hundred U.S. Army engineers and U.S. Navy sailors, whose application of abundant explosives to Rommel's beach obstructions had negated all the enemy's backbreaking work. As the tide on Utah Beach rose, those obstructions were no longer a concern for American and British sailors who held orders to bring their landing craft ashore on Utah Beach after the first waves.

But Rommel was a wise enough soldier to know that he would need several defensive layers to foil an Allied invasion. His beach obstacles may not have worked, but he had devised other cunning techniques to stop

Allied landing craft from reaching shore—and U.S. Navy sailors were about to discover one of them.

THIS SHIP NEEDS HELP

By the time the first wave of American soldiers landed on Utah Beach at 6:30 A.M. on D-Day, the destroyer USS *Corry* had already been trading salvos with German coastal guns for almost an hour. As all of *Corry*'s sailors understood, this harrowing exchange of heavy shells could bring an end to their ship's existence in an instant, but *Corry*'s D-Day mission was significant, and that risk must be endured.

Launched four months before America's entry into World War II, *Corry* was a veteran ship that had conducted Atlantic patrols since the war's early days. She had participated in the November 1942 invasion of North Africa and later served with the Royal Navy's Home Fleet supporting convoys to Russia in frigid and treacherous arctic waters. On March 17, 1944, *Corry* had hunted down and helped destroy the German submarine U-801, an accomplishment that marked the pinnacle of *Corry*'s long war service so far. However, *Corry*'s renown would derive not from that event, but from her experience off Utah Beach on June 6, 1944—the last day of her existence.

As the hundreds of vessels constituting Adm. Don Moon's Force U slipped stealthily into position off the Cotentin's east coast several hours before dawn on D-Day, *Corry* had taken its prescribed station about one mile northwest of the Iles St. Marcouf in a narrow lane that supposedly had been swept clear of mines and marked with buoys by Allied minesweepers. *Corry*'s post was particularly dangerous: About fives miles to the west, the Germans had erected two heavy coastal batteries, and no Allied warship was closer to those menacing guns than *Corry*. One of those batteries, just north of the village of St. Marcouf, had four 210-millimeter guns, the largest pieces of enemy ordnance on the entire Normandy invasion front. These were bigger guns than those of a heavy cruiser and made *Corry*'s four 5-inchers seem puny in comparison.

Lt. Cmdr. George Hoffman
Captain, USS Corry

We were being fired upon by shore batteries [starting at 5:45 A.M.], so *Fitch* [another U.S. Navy destroyer two miles northward] and *Corry* were about the first ships to commence firing for the invasion—for purposes of self-preservation.

The German gunners' skill was impressive. Their shots produced foamy white geysers of seawater, noted by one crewman as "taller than *Corry*'s mast," and with each salvo, the Germans' aim got better. The enemy was firing slowly, deliberately, and it was only a matter of time before one of those shots smashed home on steel rather than water. That was a result that Hoffman wanted to avoid at all costs. To enhance his gunners' aim, Hoffman had at first anchored *Corry*, but now that the enemy had found his range, Hoffman knew that *Corry* must get under way at flank speed. To confuse the German artillerists, he ordered abrupt evasive maneuvers: full speed ahead; left full rudder; right full rudder. These were delicate movements, for Hoffman had to steer clear of the shallow reefs near the Iles St. Marcouf and at the same time attempt to stay in the supposedly safe lanes marked by minesweepers.

Corry's crew could not even see the enemy batteries that were shooting at them. All they could perceive, just for an instant, was a bright, almost ethereal flash of a German gun each time it fired. It would take several seconds for that shell to travel from its muzzle to the target, and many of *Corry*'s 250-man crew marked that interval praying that the shell would not strike home. *Corry* returned fire toward those flashes as rapidly as its gun crews could reload, so speedily that Hoffman recalled that empty brass shell casings "came pouring out of the turrets," and sailors had to hose down the 5-inch gun barrels to prevent them from overheating.

If any of *Corry*'s sailors had ever presumed D-Day would be easy, those thoughts quickly evaporated. *Corry* was now undeniably on the invasion's front line, a fact that was confirmed at 6:33 A.M., when several German shells slammed into the ship.

Lt. Cmdr. George Hoffman
Captain, USS **Corry,** *Action Report, June 9, 1944*
Corry was hit by a salvo of two or three 8-inch [actually 210-millimeter] projectiles that detonated in the engineering spaces and broke the keel, causing the immediate flooding of one engineroom, one fireroom, the subsequent flooding of the other fireroom, and the breaking in half of the vessel. An attempt was made to clear the area to estimate damage, but all electric power was lost, and the rudder was jammed, causing the ship to go in a circle until stopped. [At this point, Hoffman ordered the flag signal hoisted, "This ship needs help."] When the main deck was awash, word was given to prepare to abandon ship, and then followed a few minutes thereafter by the word to abandon ship. . . . The two-hour period of immersion was perhaps the most difficult of all for the survivors, as shells contin-

ued to fall, causing more dead and wounded. Currents made swimming away from the ship very difficult. . . . The water temperature was 54 degrees Fahrenheit, and as a result several men died of exposure. Survivors were rescued 0830–0900 by *Fitch, Hobson, Butler,* and PT-199. [Twenty-two of *Corry*'s crew died; thirty-three were wounded or injured.]

In the aftermath of the shell hits, many of *Corry*'s crew members were caught belowdecks, their escape routes blocked by crushed bulkheads and large pieces of debris. They were in a grave predicament and did not know whether anyone topside would recognize their plight amid the chaos of the moment, but fortunately a few of *Corry*'s sailors did, crawling down hatchways to the murky and rapidly flooding lower decks to drag their trapped companions clear of the compartments in which they shortly would have perished. For these acts, several of *Corry*'s sailors were decorated, including Lts. (jg) John Parrott and Howard Andersen and Ens. Paul Garay.

When *Corry*'s survivors gathered back in Britain shortly after the invasion, they were astonished to learn that Captain Hoffman had rewritten his June 9 action report after conferring with the captains of USS *Meredith* and *Glennon*, two U.S. Navy destroyers that had been lost off Utah Beach on June 8. Hoffman's original account had stated that German gunfire had sunk *Corry*; but his final and official June 19 report was entirely different. On the cover of that report, Hoffman declared firmly that on D-Day, *Corry* "struck a mine and sank." But *Corry*'s survivors could not be converted, and one ensign recalled, "We considered that the evidence of gunfire was overwhelming, and none of us had experienced anything that could be taken for the blast of a mine." The crew came up with many diverse theories as to why Hoffman had altered his report, but none were substantiated because the captain never publicly justified the change.

Corry sank in such shallow water that the upper parts of her superstructure and masts remained visible as she settled to the bottom, a stark reminder to all witnesses that the Germans were fully capable of inflicting the same punishment on any vessel off Utah Beach that they had just wreaked upon *Corry*. Twice before in his career, the commander of Force U, Admiral Moon, had seen how effectively the Germans could inflict such destruction: first, in July 1942, when the enemy had slaughtered the merchant vessels of Convoy PQ-17, which Moon's warships were supposed to protect; and again in April 1944, when German *Schnellboote* sank two ships and killed 750 men during the Utah Beach invasion rehearsal, Exercise Tiger. Much to Moon's dismay, on D-Day off Utah Beach, the Germans apparently were repeating their past performances. In the first thirty minutes of the invasion, two vital U.S. Navy warships and two LCTs had been destroyed with considerable loss of life, and back on his command ship, *Bayfield*, Moon had no idea how those disasters had unfolded.

Moon was most troubled by the potential destructive effect of German naval mines. Could it be that the enemy had deployed a new kind of weapon that the Allies could neither detect nor sweep? The waters off Utah Beach had been carefully swept for mines by expert Allied minesweeping crews, yet somehow Moon's ships were still blowing up. Even worse, over the next several hours, many more U.S. Navy landing craft were abruptly destroyed, heightening Moon's concern that if matters got any worse, the invasion fleet could be paralyzed.

Moon's misgivings concerning German naval mines were understandable, for those enemy weapons were indeed wreaking havoc on his armada. The enemy had planted hundreds of mines off Utah Beach, many of them cleverly deposited in waters that were exceptionally difficult for Allied minesweepers to clear. But despite fears that Hitler had deployed unsweepable new "wonder weapons," the mines planted between Force U and the beach were entirely conventional, and Allied sailors knew precisely how they worked. These mines were sophisticated pieces of ordnance that would detonate with devastating force when a ship passed overhead and the ship's magnetic signature or the sound of its propellers activated the mine's highly sensitive fuse. An Allied minesweeper could counter these mines in a number of ways, the most effective of which was by towing a device replicating a ship's magnetic or acoustic characteristics, thereby detonating the mine harmlessly. Why then were the Allied minesweepers' efforts on D-Day not wholly successful?

No one ever deduced a definitive answer, but in retrospect, some mine warfare experts speculated that the Germans may have fitted their mines with pulse delay mechanisms, ingenious gadgets that were capable of counting the number of Allied vessels passing overhead. Such a mechanism would detonate the mine to which it was attached only when the number of passing Allied vessels reached the numerical setting the Germans had applied to it. If, for example, the counter was set at "4," three Allied ships could pass overhead and activate the counter without detonating the mine, but when the fourth ship sailed by, it would explode. If the Germans had indeed implanted these devices on the mines lying off Utah Beach on D-Day, Allied minesweepers could have swept lanes from the transport area to the beach and given the gratifying "all clear" signal to the fleet, while the enemy's undetectable mines were still present and decidedly deadly. It was a devious way to fight, but all parties had long since agreed that gentlemen's wars were a thing of the past.

Furthermore, those German naval officers responsible for mining Normandy's coastal waters had taken advantage of the long, shallow Cardonnet Bank, which paralleled the Cotentin coast about five miles offshore on either side of the Iles St. Marcouf. These Germans knew their jobs, for the waters of the Cardonnet Bank were only about twenty-five feet deep and were perfect for "bottom" sea mining. The enemy could lay its mines there on the seafloor, where they would be exceptionally difficult to detect and sweep; and as all sea miners were aware, the shallower the water, the greater the blast effect of a bottom mine on a ship passing overhead. On D-Day, the Cardonnet Bank amounted to an undetectable barricade that killed far more Allied soldiers and sailors than the battalion of German infantry guarding Utah Beach—a detail that Admiral Moon did not fail to notice.

Rear Adm. Don Moon
Commander, Force U, Action Report, June 21, 1944
So far as is known, the Force U assault was the only one which had to be launched through a minefield. The boat lane lay squarely across the field on the Cardonnet Bank. Sweeping of all gunfire support areas and boat lanes was initially accomplished without cutting or detecting any mines in the assault area. Later, however, many mines came to life, a total of 124 [bottom] mines and 77 moored mines being detonated or cut. Most naval losses suffered were from mines.

When Moon learned of the violent end some of his vessels were meeting over the Cardonnet Bank, he realized that his minesweepers would have to reintensify their efforts to ensure that the vital boat lanes between the transport area and the beach were safe. As an official U.S. Navy report stated, "The rapid loss of these fine ships in swept waters distressed Admiral Moon considerably." The U.S. Navy was in charge of conveying General Collins's VII Corps troops from their transports to Utah Beach, and if the enemy's seemingly undetectable mines were posing such a severe danger to landing craft packed solidly with troops and equipment, Moon reckoned that the landing schedule might have to be delayed in the early evening of D-Day while the minesweepers tried again to make the boat lanes safe.

But to "Lightning Joe" Collins, this kind of decision displayed timidity, not prudence. In his memoirs, Collins noted that after his first few meetings with Moon in Plymouth in early 1944, "I detected a certain lack of firmness and a tendency to be overly cautious, which worried me." From

Collins's perspective, that caution was about to surface on D-Day, but he would use all of his plentiful persuasive powers to suppress it. Any delay in the Utah landing timetable would seriously disrupt Collins's plans, and as he was responsible to Bradley and Ike for succoring the paratroopers and initiating the drive to capture Cherbourg with all possible speed, Moon's holdup was out of the question. The German naval mines were undeniably a hindrance, but Collins considered that American soldiers were currently fighting for their lives in the hedgerows. The passage of U.S. Navy and Coast Guard landing craft over waters that obviously still teemed with deadly mines was just one of the risks that had to be accepted in an invasion that everyone knew would be hazardous.

Maj. Gen. J. Lawton Collins
Commander, VII Corps, May 16, 1946
I had decided not to go ashore on D-Day much as I would liked to have done so from a purely personal standpoint. Instead [at 4:00 P.M.] I sent ashore Maj. Gen. Eugene Landrum [deputy commander, VII Corps] and my G-2 [Col. Charles King] and G-3 [Col. Richard Partridge] to set up an advance headquarters in the vicinity of the 4th Division. Another reason for my remaining aboard *Bayfield* on D-Day was to insure that landing operations continued in spite of the rather rough water and adverse weather. While the Navy staff had cooperated wonderfully well with us, this was its first amphibious operation, and there was some indication on the early morning of D-Day that Admiral Moon and his staff were greatly concerned over the loss of vessels in the task force. My recollection is that one or two destroyers had been sunk and several landing craft had been hit by mines. This concern of mine was justified on the early evening of D-Day when Admiral Moon called me to his office and stated that he was giving consideration to a recommendation from his staff to suspend landing operations during the night. I urged that this not be done and after some discussion Admiral Moon decided to continue with the landing operations.

Moon's version of this affair will never be known, for by the time Collins provided this account to U.S. Army historians, Moon was dead from a pistol shot he had aimed at his own head.

THEY AIN'T SEASICK NO MORE
The invasion looked much smoother from the sands of Utah Beach than it did from *Bayfield*'s deck. True, intermittent German artillery fire was exploding on the beach, sometimes with appalling effect, but by 7:45 A.M. German resistance on the shoreline had been eliminated, reinforcements

were pouring ashore, and the assault troops were pushing inland toward the causeways to make contact with the 101st Airborne Division.

General Collins had anticipated a much more forceful enemy reaction on the coast, so to him the situation at midmorning on Utah Beach was categorically positive, even if plans had been momentarily thrown into disarray by the assault troops' mislanding a mile south of their intended spot. Ted Roosevelt Jr., the elderly general armed with nothing but a cane, a book of poems, and a pistol, had already addressed that predicament successfully, and the adaptable assault troops had responded to the hasty change of plans without difficulty. For a beach that many generals had considered the most hazardous of the Allies' five invasion sites, the assault was proceeding with remarkable efficiency.

Brig. Gen. Theodore Roosevelt Jr.
Supernumerary General Officer, 4th Division, Letter to his wife, Eleanor, June 11, 1944
Most of our work was done on foot. As the succeeding waves landed, I pushed them inland if they halted and redirected them when they started wrong. Shells continually burst around us, but all I got was a slight scratch on one hand. [According to Lt. Col. James Batte, CO, 87th Chemical Mortar Battalion, Roosevelt "proudly exhibited his hand, which had been slightly wounded by shell fire, as he greeted Col. Van Fleet and the rest of us."]

The beach was clear of the enemy, and the morning sun was still low in the eastern sky, but if the 4th Division was to attain its ambitious D-Day goals, there was no time to lose. For Colonel Van Fleet, the imperative task at 7:30 A.M. was to push his 8th Infantry across the inundated pasturelands behind Utah Beach to make contact with Maxwell Taylor's 101st Airborne. The simplest and fastest way for Van Fleet to achieve that goal would be to dispatch his men straight down the three causeways leading inland from the beach. An alert and determined enemy could easily thwart this movement, because the flooded fields adjacent to the narrow causeways would prevent the GIs from maneuvering around resistance, but the German defenders of Utah Beach had not been particularly impressive that morning, and if Van Fleet's luck held out, the guardians of the causeways, if any, would not be much better.

Van Fleet, Roosevelt, and others had to occasionally act as traffic cops, and with this sort of help, eventually the troops correctly figured out where they had to go and what they had to do once they cleared the beach. The two 8th Infantry battalions that had spearheaded the Utah invasion at

Utah Beach: Third Wave, 8:00 A.M., June 6, 1944

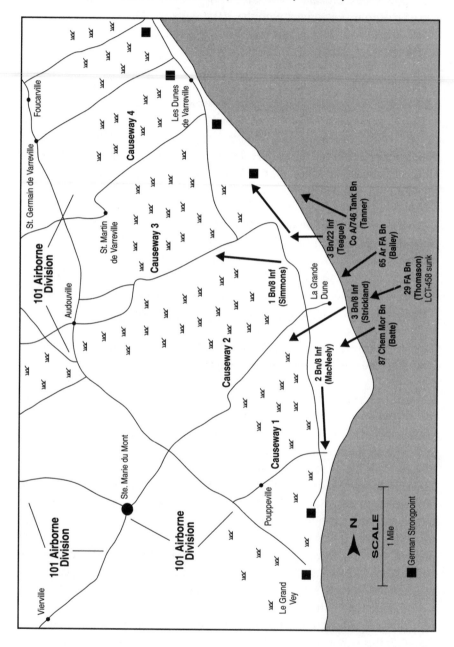

H-Hour were the first to start moving toward their objectives about an hour later: The 1st Battalion turned north, striking for Causeway 3; the 2nd Battalion marched south toward Causeway 1.

The Allies had always considered their success in Operation Overlord dependent on the rapidity with which they could pour troops into their five beachheads. The Germans were expected to counterattack those beachheads on D-Day or shortly thereafter, and the more troops and equipment the Allies had ashore when those counterattacks struck, the more easily they could defeat the enemy. Measured by that standard the Utah invasion was an astonishing success so far. By 8:30 A.M., two hours after the initial waves had landed, the only Germans remaining on Utah Beach were either dead or prisoners of war. Even better, thanks to the American paratroopers who had dropped into the Cotentin interior before dawn, no enemy reinforcements would come streaming down the causeways to drive the 4th Division back into the sea.

Meanwhile, Americans were swarming onto Utah Beach, right on schedule. The first reinforcements were the 3rd Battalion, 8th Infantry and the 3rd Battalion, 22nd Infantry, amounting to about 1,500 fresh troops. These outfits were followed in quick succession by several artillery, heavy mortar, armor, and engineer units. It was an ambitious timetable, and the enemy was doing nothing to slow it down. If that schedule held, the 4th Division's entire infantry contingent would be ashore before noon. The infantrymen had trained for months in amphibious operations, but that phase of their war had come to an unexpectedly hasty end, and it was time to think in terms of conventional land warfare again. When all the artillery and mortar units assigned to support the 4th Division were in place, the infantry could start fighting the war they had been trained to fight, and at their disposal would be the heavy firepower that was the hallmark of the American Army.

One of the first outfits to join Van Fleet on the beach was his own 3rd Battalion, which had crossed the Channel on June 5 onboard *Bayfield*, Admiral Moon's flagship. The eleven-mile journey to the beach in rolling and pitching LCVPs was not pleasant, but as the 3rd Battalion waded ashore on Utah Beach, its members noted happily that their predecessors had already neutralized the enemy's coastal strongpoints. Therefore, the 3rd Battalion's GIs were thankfully spared the task of knocking out concrete pillboxes on the dunes, a fight that many had imagined would be costly and slow. The enemy was still dropping plenty of artillery fire on the beach, but even so, when the 3rd Battalion trudged across the sand and assembled for the first time in its entirety in France opposite the smoldering beach cottages of La Grande Dune at about 8:30 A.M., it was in fairly good order. Old hands knew that the safest and wisest course of action was to get off the beach quickly and move inland, and led by its commander, Lt. Col. Erasmus Strickland, that is what the 3rd Battalion set out to do.

Strickland's mission was to take his battalion straight up the middle of the blossoming beachhead by following Causeway 2 across the inundated fields beyond the coast. As Causeway 2 came right down to the beach at La Grande Dune, Strickland's men did not have to look far to locate the point where they must begin their inland movement. The battalion's initial D-Day destination, the village of Ste. Marie du Mont, was obvious to all, for that village's beautiful domed church steeple beckoned over the coastal lowlands three miles to the southwest. No one could miss it, but the GIs reckoned that plenty of Germans would be situated between that village and the beach, and when the 3rd Battalion encountered them, its war would finally begin in earnest.

Maj. Frederick Collins
Executive, 3rd Battalion, 8th Infantry, 4th Division, June 29, 1944
The first waves of the 3rd Battalion landed at H+75 [7:45 A.M.] and proceeded down U-5 [Causeway 2, the road to Ste. Marie du Mont]. The battalion had an experience similar to others: nothing but artillery fire on the beach, and a few shells dropping on the water about 500 yards out. Some fire was received on our flanks as we proceeded inland. All boats got in without loss.

T/Sgt. Grady Vickery
Company I, 8th Infantry, 4th Division
We had trained for a long period of time. . . . All our leaders, including myself [Vickery was a platoon sergeant], were very cool and calm, and we felt we had done this all the time. Everything went off perfectly for my unit.

The 22nd Infantry's 3rd Battalion was commanded by Lt. Col. Arthur Teague, an engineer in civilian life who had been managing the renowned Mount Washington Cog Railway in New Hampshire when he was called into military service in 1941. Teague's outfit, which landed alongside Strickland's, had been the only 4th Division assault unit to be conveyed across the Channel on a British troopship, the SS *Empire Gauntlet*. Although this was a merchant navy vessel, the LCA landing craft slung on its davits were manned by experienced Royal Navy boat crews, who held responsibility for transporting the Yanks from *Empire Gauntlet* to Utah Beach, more than eleven miles away. British LCAs were vastly different from American

"Everything went off perfectly for my unit." Members of a heavy weapons
company of a 4th Division infantry unit move inland from Utah Beach on
D-Day. U.S. ARMY SIGNAL CORPS, NATIONAL ARCHIVES.

LCVPs, and in truth, many American infantrymen preferred the British
type, because its armor could stop rifle and machine-gun bullets, and it featured some measure of overhead protection from bursting shells.

Unlike Van Fleet's 8th Infantry, which had orders to push inland with
all possible speed, Teague's battalion would stay close to the sea throughout D-Day. As soon as it landed, the 3rd Battalion turned to its right, or
north, and proceeded straight up the shoreline, aiming to eliminate as many
German coastal strongpoints as possible. This would be a thankless and
costly task, for as soon as one enemy resistance nest was wiped out, there
would always be another to deal with less than a mile up the coast.

Lt. Col. Arthur Teague
Commander, 3rd Battalion, 22nd Infantry, 4th Division, July 3, 1944
The [enemy] positions were all mutually supported along narrow strips of land
between the high water mark and the inundation. At intervals there were mine-
fields. The method of attack followed in general the procedure taught at the
Assault Training Center [the U.S. Army amphibious warfare school in England].
The ATC taught that one could reconnoiter and get observation on a fortification,
which was impossible here because of the numerous hedges. [Instead] it was nec-

essary to approach within 75–100 yards with tanks and, combined with flamethrowers, assault the positions [directly], using demolitions and pole charges. We had naval fire and 4.2-inch mortars to replace our artillery, and the successive enemy positions were shelled by the navy before being assaulted. The tanks would be brought up for point-blank fire while the infantry maneuvered inland around the rear of the pillbox. As the battalion progressed up the coast, the maneuver of the infantry became more difficult since the neck of land between the beach and the inundation narrowed until the men had to wade waist-deep in order to get behind the fortifications. The enemy would let men wade up without firing a shot until they were right up to the pillbox, and then open up point-blank with machine gun fire and cut them down.

Assaulting a seemingly endless series of concrete pillboxes filled with German troops was not an easy assignment for GIs who had never seen combat, so Teague's battalion was specially reinforced for this mission by five Sherman tanks from Company A, 746th Tank Battalion. However, the tankers, who also were new to combat, quickly learned that the sandy, flat coastal terrain, which was littered with mines, was hardly suitable for their thirty-three-ton tanks. Even worse, the Germans had plenty of antitank weapons, and there were no spots for the Shermans to take cover. Accordingly, movement of any kind within view of a German pillbox immediately drew fire.

746th Tank Battalion
After-Action Report, June 1944
The 1st Platoon, Company A, under 2nd Lt. Clyde Tanner, with S/Sgt. Harold McNeeley as platoon sergeant, was detached from the battalion for the D-Day landing to the 3rd Battalion, 22nd Infantry. Landing at H+145 [8:55 A.M.], the platoon, after some initial difficulties in bogging on the beach, moved up [the coast road] and engaged in cleaning out house strongpoints. The platoon returned to the beach and proceeded northward on its original mission of clearing the beach area with the 22nd Infantry up to Quineville. This operation was not successful in that strong coastal defenses were encountered in the vicinity of Les Dunes de Varreville. The tank gun fire on concrete emplacements was only successful if placed in the embrasures. Assistance in the reduction of these pillboxes was obtained from naval vessels lying offshore. . . . During this operation one tank was lost to a mine and an anti-tank gun hit.

During training, American infantry leaders had been taught to call upon their supporting artillery to help them achieve their goals. Artillery was a hallmark of the U.S. Army, and skilled American gunners could drop howitzer shells right on top of a German resistance nest within minutes of being asked. Why risk a GI's life when a shell could do the same thing? Unfortunately, on the morning of D-Day, 4th Division GIs would have to carry on without this crutch, since it would take several hours for the U.S. Navy to bring the howitzers, their crews, and all their paraphernalia ashore. Naval guns would be a decent substitute for a while; and starting at about 7:30 A.M., there would also be another alternative: the 4.2-inch mortars of the 87th Chemical Mortar Battalion, which Collins had attached to the 4th Division for the Utah Beach invasion.

To the men of the 87th, who had arrived in England less than two months before D-Day, memories of training in the United States were still fresh. The 87th's mortars had originally been envisioned as quick and easy means of delivering gas shells over enemy lines, but as the U.S. Army in all likelihood would not employ chemical weapons in Europe, the mortar crews had learned to use their weapons as stand-in artillery. Their shells packed about as much power as a 105-millimeter howitzer shell, and the mortars themselves could be manhandled, a trait that would allow their operators to bring them ashore early on D-Day and quickly deploy on the beach, ready to fire. However, 330-pound mortars were not easy to move. The only way to do it was to break them down into three parts and fasten the components onto wheeled handcarts. According to the methods the mortarmen had practiced over and over again in training, the crews would dash off their landing craft when the 87th hit the beach and, like draft animals, drag their carts behind them. It was an unusual way to enter Europe, but if the mortars could be available to support 4th Division infantrymen within minutes of the landing, the effort would be worth it.

87th Chemical Mortar Battalion
Battalion History, 1945

Companies A and B landed at H+50 [7:20 A.M.] and set up on the beach ready to deliver fire on call from its forward observers who had landed with the leading infantry waves at H-Hour. Company A fired 20 rounds, and Company B fired 80 rounds. After approximately 40 minutes, both companies moved inland in order to keep up with the advance of the battalions they were supporting [1st and 2nd Battalion, 8th Infantry]. . . . This battalion was the sole "artillery" support for the 4th Division for approximately 6 hours. At all times the mortar companies kept pace with the advance of the supported infantry and were always in position, ready to fire, when called upon by forward observers. The infantry was amazed at the rapidity and accuracy with which our mortars replied.

"The infantry was amazed at the rapidity with which our mortars replied."
Troops from the 87th Chemical Mortar Battalion prepare to fire from positions
near Utah Beach on D-Day. U.S. ARMY SIGNAL CORPS, NATIONAL ARCHIVES.

Lt. Col. James Batte
Commander, 87th Chemical Mortar Battalion
I was on a British-made LCT that was open in the stern [known as an LCT-6 vari-
ant], hence the sea splashed in and washed about on the deck. We spent much time
sitting in our jeeps. This LCT carried the CO of the 8th Infantry, Col. James Van
Fleet, his staff, and COs of supporting troops. . . . We transferred to an LCVP for
the actual landing, and an LCVP next to us hit a mine and blew up. A soldier in
our craft stated, "The lucky bastards, they ain't seasick no more!"

If the U.S. Army planned to defeat the enemy in Normandy by the
application of overwhelming firepower, Colonel Van Fleet's 8th Infantry
would be among the first units to determine whether that principle actually
worked. As the primary executor of the Utah Beach assault, the 8th was the
lucky recipient of unprecedented levels of fire support. On D-Day, in addition to the navy and Batte's mortar outfit, Van Fleet would eventually have
two artillery battalions at his disposal, and given the potentially grueling
task of attacking straight over the causeways leading inland off Utah, that
extra firepower could well be the modifier that would tip the battle in favor
of the Americans.

One of those outfits heading to shore on LCTs to join Van Fleet was
the 65th Armored Field Artillery Battalion, a veteran unit that had partici-

pated in both the North African and Sicilian campaigns. Commanded by the twenty-nine-year old Lt. Col. Edward Bailey, a 1938 West Point graduate, the 65th had orders to move inland, make contact with the 101st Airborne, and offer its fire support to the paratroopers as soon as possible. Bailey did not yet know it, but only one of the twelve 75-millimeter howitzers that Troop Carrier C-47s had dropped into Normandy that morning for use by the paratroopers would be recovered, and the beleaguered parachutists would soon be in desperate need of artillery support. Bailey's eighteen self-propelled 105-millimeter howitzers, known as M-7 "Priests," would help remedy that situation. The Priests were tracked vehicles that were much more mobile than conventional towed howitzers, and if Bailey's orders demanded that he reach the 101st Airborne in a hurry, these were the right weapons for the job.

65th Armored Field Artillery Battalion
Battalion History for 1944, February 5, 1945
During disembarkation and the period on the beach, the battalion suffered from mines and artillery fire, two enlisted men killed; two officers and twenty enlisted men wounded. . . . One howitzer was put out of action by artillery fire. The track was blown from one howitzer by a mine. But for the heroic work under heavy fire of both officers and enlisted men of all batteries, the battalion would have been severely crippled. . . . Soon after the CP landed at 0931, battery minesweeping parties were called for and reconnaissance started in an effort to move the battalion inland. Mines, [enemy] fire, and our own tanks and engineer vehicles engaged in necessary movements made displacing exceedingly difficult. . . . Permission was obtained to use a temporary causeway bridge [on Causeway 2, the Ste. Marie du Mont road], which had been classified too weak to carry our vehicles.

Lt. Col. Edward Bailey
Commander, 65th Armored Field Artillery Battalion
I ran into General Roosevelt cracking the same corny jokes that he had in Africa. This was a reassuring sight, especially when he permitted me to use a bridge that was not supposed to carry my vehicles.

Another artillery unit that came ashore early on D-Day to support the 8th Infantry was the 4th Division's 29th Field Artillery Battalion, a unit that had worked closely with Van Fleet for years, and whose personnel were entirely familiar with their infantry brethren. For the invasion, the 29th's standard 105-millimeter howitzers, which had to be towed by trucks, were replaced by twelve M-7 Priests, the same self-propelled howitzers used by

Bailey's outfit. The Priests' celebrated mobility would allow the 29th to deploy for combat more quickly than a conventional artillery unit, a trait that could facilitate the 8th Infantry's job as it moved inland over the causeways.

The 29th was commanded by Lt. Col. Joel Thomason, a 1939 West Pointer who had taken command of the 509-man battalion in 1942 at the age of twenty-four. According to the invasion timetable, Thomason's outfit would land on Utah Beach at 9:30 A.M. from five LCTs, but that plan was thrown into disarray at 8:00 A.M. when LCT-458, carrying most of Battery B, was blown up by a German mine over the Cardonnet Bank. This was a catastrophe unmatched on Utah Beach on D-Day, as the blast killed thirty-nine gunners and injured nearly twenty more. More than two-thirds of all 29th Field Artillery Battalion soldiers killed in World War II died in this one terrible moment.

Capt. John Ausland
HQ Battery, 29th Field Artillery Battalion

My task once ashore was to guide our three artillery batteries to firing positions that we had selected in England from a detailed foam rubber relief map of the beach. After crossing the sand dunes that lay just beyond the seawall, I was unable to figure out where I was. When I asked an infantry officer to help me, he laughed and said the navy had landed the first wave several thousand yards south of where we were supposed to land. . . . When I went back to the beach, I told Colonel Thomason that I could find only two firing positions, not three, in the limited area between the sand dunes and the inundated area. As calmly as if we were on a practice landing he said, "It's all right. We'll only need two. Battery B hit a mine on the way in and the landing craft sank." Before I could think too long about the 60 men on the boat, Thomason told me to get moving and guide the other batteries to their firing positions.

29th Field Artillery Battalion, 4th Division
Interview with Lt. Col. Joel Thomason

After C Battery had gotten into position, Thomason went up to talk to the battery commander [Capt. Albert Head]. With him was his first sergeant [Sergeant Wood]. Thomason told Head, "Start firing as soon as you can, the moment you get a target. Fire away and use plenty of ammunition. It will help to keep up the morale of our troops." He told Head that he was going to walk down the road to find [the next firing position]. He walked down the road about 150 yards from the seawall. Then he remembered that he had left his radio behind. He walked back to Capt.

Head's battery and found that Head and Wood were both on stretchers. They had been hit by a shell burst, both badly wounded, and were being taken away.

After four years of training, a seemingly interminable cycle of route marches, field exercises, and drill, the men of the 4th Division could finally declare that they were no longer green. The Ivy Division had played its important part in the opening stage of the liberation of western Europe, and its performance had been as good as anyone could have expected. In contrast, the enemy's second-rate coastal defenders had obviously been caught by surprise on D-Day, and the 4th Division had overcome them far more easily than General Barton had anticipated. Luckily, the division had so far been spared the catastrophe suffered by the 1st and 29th Divisions on Omaha Beach. But how long that luck would hold was anybody's guess.

Lt. Col. Ulrich Gibbons
Headquarters, 4th Division Artillery
I had never been in combat, and any soldier, professional or "for the duration," wonders inside himself how he will measure up. I was a lieutenant colonel within a time span that [normally] would have advanced me only to 1st lieutenant. I was a West Pointer [class of 1939], upon whom rests a great imperative to set the military example, above all, in battle. I am not a prayerful man, but if I said any prayers on that interminable Channel crossing, one of the strongest was that I should prove able to do my part under combat stress.

CHAPTER 8

Get in There
and Take Chances

SEARCHING FOR AN ANSWER

One would assume that a major general in command of 20,000 troops who had just been hurled into Normandy in the most crucial military operation of World War II would be a man under almost unimaginable stress. But in truth, every soldier of the 4th Infantry Division was so familiar with the tasks expected of him on D-Day that virtually no guidance was required from the man who held the lofty job of division commander, Maj. Gen. Raymond Barton. If the invasion was flowing smoothly, as Barton sensed it was when he first set foot on Utah Beach at 9:05 A.M., there would be little for him to do. But as long as the 4th Division maintained its momentum and fulfilled its D-Day mission by dusk, he would gladly submit to the role of an exalted bystander.

Nevertheless, the supreme significance of the day made it clear to Barton that he must let his men see him, no matter what. Even if he stooped to the role of a mere traffic cop, a job he indeed performed for a considerable period that afternoon, the effect on the GIs would be invigorating. As he approached the beach, Barton could hear small-arms fire and large-caliber shells exploding in the distance, and initially he assumed that the cacophony was produced by his own division. But when a round exploded on the beach nearby, he immediately appreciated that the enemy was still active and the struggle ahead would not be easy. Like his men, Barton was new to combat, and it would take some time to get used to real war.

Maj. Gen. Raymond Barton
Commander, 4th Infantry Division
I, [1st Lt.] Bill York [Barton's aide], and [S/Sgt.] James Richards [Barton's driver] landed, dry-footed, by "snowbuggy" [an M-29 Weasel tracked vehicle] from an LCT. . . . The hostile artillery on my beach was thickening up by now. I had learned to recognize incoming fire. I had no contact nor communications with anyone but those present, [and I was] wondering where the temporary command post was I had sent Brig. Gen. [Henry] Barber [assistant commander, 4th Division] ahead to establish. . . . I had no more influence on the battle in the beginning than any platoon sergeant, [and] I felt more or less like a "2nd louie" [lieutenant]. Fortunately the operation on Utah Beach was going on well as planned, and no real command decisions were needed. My real contribution was just being there for my staff to rally on.

Within the invasion's first three hours, the 4th Division's top four leaders, all general officers, were ashore, one of whom was the inimitable Ted Roosevelt. Thanks to Roosevelt and the others, the initial confusion triggered by the mislanding nearly a mile south of the intended target had evaporated. But if later developments necessitated modifications to the battle plan, the 4th Division's generals were ready to exert personal control.

Maj. Gen. Raymond Barton
Commander, 4th Infantry Division
While I was mentally framing [orders], Ted Roosevelt came up. He had landed with the first wave, had put my troops across the beach, and had a perfect picture of the entire situation. I loved Ted. When I finally agreed to his landing with the first wave of the assault, I felt sure he would be killed. When I bade him goodbye in England, I never expected to see him again alive. You can imagine then the emotion with which I greeted him when he came out to meet me [near La Grande Dune]. I embraced him and he me. He was bursting with information.

Events on Utah Beach were transpiring with remarkable rapidity, far beyond the capability of Barton's harried staff in its spartan CP near La Grande Dune to keep up. By about 12:30 P.M., all three 4th Division infantry regiments were ashore and proceeding with their missions, an impressive fighting force that amounted to more than 8,000 highly moti-

Utah Beach: Later Waves, 9:05 A.M., June 6, 1944

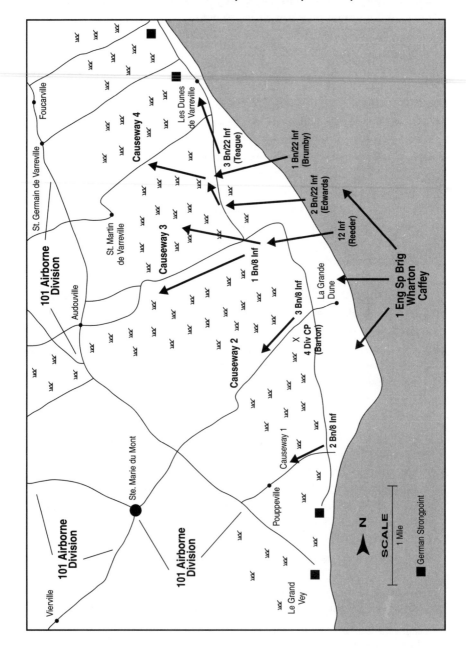

vated foot soldiers. The situation, as best Barton could figure it out, was this: Colonel Van Fleet was leading his 8th Infantry inland astride the three southernmost causeways, while the 22nd Infantry's 3rd Battalion attacked northward straight up the shoreline. The two remaining battalions of the 22nd had come ashore by 10:30 A.M. and were moving northwest straight across the inundated area to seek out the 101st Airborne somewhere beyond Causeway 4. Meanwhile, all three battalions of the 12th Infantry, amounting to about 3,000 men under the command of Col. Russell Reeder, had landed and were just starting to push inland over the sand dunes.

The thoroughness of the invasion plan had impressed all who had learned it, but now the reason for that attention to detail was immediately evident. Once they hit Utah Beach, all soldiers knew exactly what they had to do, and they did not need to be told to do it. For the 4th Division, four years of training was yielding highly positive returns.

22nd Infantry, 4th Division
D-Day Action Report, July 1945
The 1st Battalion, commanded by Lt. Col. Sewell Brumby, and the 2nd Battalion, commanded by Maj. Earl Edwards, landed at H+210 [10:00 A.M.] in LCIs. Their mission was to cross the beach and inundated area [on Causeway 4], attack to the northwest, reduce the [batteries] at Azeville and Crisbecq [the same battery that had sunk *Corry*], and then secure the high ground west and southwest of Quineville. . . . The 1st Battalion was unable to cross the inundation by road due to congestion of troops resulting from the change in landing beaches. The battalion got across the inundation [followed by the 2nd Battalion] wading waist-deep, frequently stepping into ditches where the water was over their heads. It was slow going, and fortifications farther north along the beach were firing machine guns across the swamps. The men frequently had to duck completely under water when a burst splashed near them. They traveled approximately two miles through the swamps to Road S-9 [the north-south route passing through St. Germain de Varreville]. Company A took 113 prisoners without losing a man.

1st Lt. Thomas Harrison
Commander, Company H, 22nd Infantry, 4th Division
I remember how our ship's captain [of a U.S. Navy LCI] let Major Edwards and myself on the bridge with him. The closer we got to shore, the more frightened the captain became. He had been in Italy and had a right to be. . . . As soon as we landed we heard artillery shells coming in on us. I hollered to my men to hit the dirt. The shells landed about 200 yards away. Everybody laughed, including

myself. [I recall] seeing our first German prisoner and how mean and tough he looked and how all my men acted. They hated him and cussed him.

Combat is a notoriously unpredictable pursuit; but when it was the 12th Infantry's turn to land on Utah Beach at about noon, the men of the regiment had the satisfaction of knowing that the invasion plan they had studied for so long apparently was working. True, the beach was a mile south of its intended site, but the enemy's coastal resistance nests had already been cleaned out, and the 12th would not have to fight its way off the beach, as many unfortunate follow-up infantry units from the 1st and 29th Divisions on Omaha Beach would be forced to do that day. There was still much work for the 12th Infantry to carry out before sunset, but that work would be inland, and now the regiment must get there with all possible speed. Paratroopers were waiting for the 12th, and their lives could depend on the efficiency with which Colonel Reeder's men carried out their mission.

When "Red" Reeder arrived in England to take command of the 12th Infantry on April 1, 1944, Ted Roosevelt Jr., had characterized the regiment to him as "the stepchild of the 4th Division." But if a military unit's spirit is defined in large part by its commanding officer, Reeder would soon correct the 12th Infantry's supposed lack of confidence. Five months before D-Day, Ike had described the forty-two-year-old Reeder as a "damned good man," and even before his arrival in England, he had been recognized throughout the U.S. Army as a master infantry tactician, a brilliant writer, and an exceptionally brave soldier. In late 1942, on direct orders from George Marshall, Reeder had journeyed to the Pacific to study American combat techniques as practiced on Guadalcanal and New Guinea. He produced an eighty-page pamphlet entitled *Fighting on Guadalcanal*, which so impressed Marshall that in 1943, he ordered 1 million copies printed and distributed among all American troops preparing for combat in all theaters. Reeder had learned how American soldiers were fighting this war by observing from the front, and by doing so, he had a Silver Star for gallantry pinned on his uniform by Gen. Douglas MacArthur and a Legion of Merit by General Marshall.

Col. Russell Reeder
"Fighting on Guadalcanal," 1943
The prowess of the enemy must NOT be over-emphasized. . . . Men should receive training in patience. Our national character is foreign to this idea. We are an impetuous people. Training in patience is needed as sometimes the men will be required to remain motionless and quiet for hours at a time.

A member of the West Point class of 1926, Reeder had so excelled at baseball as a cadet that New York Giants manager John McGraw, the legendary "Little Napoleon," had tried to make a professional ballplayer out of him. But Reeder's passion above all else was for soldiering, and he turned McGraw down, a rejection that the astonished McGraw probably had experienced only rarely before. Instead of roaming the basepaths at the Polo Grounds, Reeder was destined to participate materially in an event that would change the world. His participation in that event would be short, however: On June 11, he was struck by a German shell fragment, which, Reeder recalled, "almost cut off my [left] leg above the knee."

But that was five days in the future. On D-Day, Reeder's immediate problem was to push his regiment inland on causeways that were choked with troops, all of whom were heading in the same direction as Reeder's men. There was only one way to get moving, and that was to avoid the causeways and march straight across the flooded pasturelands beyond the beach. In his book, Reeder had extolled the value of patience, but in this

"The dreaded flooded area." Troops from the 4th Infantry Division moving through the inundated areas behind Utah Beach on D-Day. U.S. ARMY SIGNAL CORPS, NATIONAL ARCHIVES.

instance, he exhibited behavior that was unambiguously impatient. With a dramatic arm signal and the bellow "We are going through the flooded area!" Reeder led the way into the mire.

Maj. Gerden Johnson
Executive, 1st Battalion, 12th Infantry, 4th Division
The dreaded flooded area lapped at the toes of my shoes. . . . I said, "Let's go" and stepped off into the water. Every man followed, the first sergeant directly behind querying in a low voice, "What about mines?" Every field was surrounded by fences on which were hung white signs with red letters: "Achtung! Minen!" And for no reason at all except my own fear I said, "There aren't any mines here." . . . I met Brig. Gen. Theodore Roosevelt stomping up and down a dusty road, leaning on his cane and smoking his pipe as unperturbed as though he were in the middle of Times Square. He struck me as really enjoying himself. "Hi, Johnny!" he yelled, "It's a great day for hunting. Glad you made it!"

Col. Russell Reeder
Commander, 12th Infantry, 4th Division
The Germans had flooded the surrounding lowlands and meadows by damming streams, making a lake a mile wide. We had to cross the lake. We knew from spies and loyal Frenchmen that before the Germans made the lake they had bulldozed furrows so that every now and then the water, instead of being chest high, was about ten feet deep. Back in England our general had told us we might have to ford it. He equipped us with inflatable life preservers and we had paired men who could not swim with swimmers. I gave an arm signal and 3,000 heavily burdened infantrymen walked into the manmade lake. . . . When I saw non-swimmers near me in the lake struggling to go forward, hanging on to their weapons and equipment, I knew that we would win the war.

As his men labored to traverse the inundated fields, a dreadful contemplation played in the back of Reeder's mind. Later, Reeder recalled that moment: "Just before we departed England, the division commander said to me, 'Spies have informed us that the Germans have a way to put inflammable material on the flooded areas. Tell the men what to do if this happens.'" In a 1958 letter to Cornelius Ryan, Reeder remarked—"I'm still searching for an answer."

FUGITIVES FROM THE LAW OF AVERAGES
Many people did not want to admit it, but Monty was right. The way to make the Normandy invasion work, he had asserted, was to gather in

England every troopship, landing craft, transport plane, and glider that the United States and Britain could muster, pack them with assault troops, and hurl them on a broad front against the enemy. If on D-Day the Allies could pour men and equipment into Normandy by sea and air at the levels Monty recommended and maintain that flow for weeks thereafter, the grandiose scale of the assault would promise success, for the Germans would be stunned by the initial blow and would lack sufficient mobile reserves to counterattack all five of the Allied beachheads simultaneously. The Allies would be in Normandy to stay, and at that point, the battle would in truth hinge on a simple question of numbers. Given the Allies' control of the air and immense advantages in manpower and resources, they could not lose.

The Utah Beach invasion was a product of this type of strategic thinking, added to the Overlord assault plan at Montgomery's insistence only four months before D-Day. Anyone who stood on the Cotentin coastline about noon on June 6, 1944, and observed the flood of men and vehicles coming ashore on Utah Beach could not fail to be impressed at the Allies' obvious attainment of that basic principle of war known by military pundits as "concentration of force." As relentlessly as the rolling breakers, wave after wave of countless landing craft were surging ashore to disgorge their passengers and payloads onto the beach, and the enemy could do little to stop it. In the days ahead, that flow would increase to a torrent, a logistical achievement that the tired German Army could not hope to match.

But D-Day was only a start. If the Allies aimed to overwhelm the enemy in Normandy with a deluge of men and matériel, they must still prove that they could gain the upper hand on the battlefield, and all the lessons learned so far in World War II had confirmed that the German Army would not give up unless it was decisively beaten. The Germans were down—but not out.

For the GIs in the Cotentin Peninsula who must carry on that fight, the seemingly limitless supplies that were flowing ashore on Utah Beach must somehow be organized and transported to the front. This featureless expanse of coastline that under no stretch of the imagination could be called a harbor must swiftly be converted into a major point of entry for supplies that would sustain Collins's VII Corps as it expanded its beachhead and pushed on to Cherbourg. Only a highly trained and efficient unit could manage a depot of this magnitude, and happily for Collins, his 1st Engineer Special Brigade (ESB), commanded by Brig. Gen. James Wharton, was precisely that kind of outfit. The Utah invasion plan decreed that several 1st ESB units land on Utah within the first ninety minutes of the assault, offering irrefutable evidence to the participants that their vital tasks of mine clearing, bulldozing, and demolition work probably would have to be performed under enemy fire. But Wharton's core unit, the 2,500-man 531st Engineer Shore Regiment, was used to that sort of thing, as it had already managed invasions on beaches at Arzew, Algeria; Gela, Sicily; and Salerno, Italy. When the 531st received orders for its fourth amphibious invasion in nineteen months, one officer noted ruefully, "We all felt like fugitives from the law of averages."

4th Infantry Division
Field Order 1, Engineer Annex, 1st ESB D-Day Mission, May 15, 1944
The mission of the 1st ESB is to support the landings of the VII Corps in the Utah area beginning on D-Day by organizing and operating all shore installations necessary for debarkation, supply, evacuation [of wounded], and local security in order to insure expeditious movement across the beaches.

General Wharton's men would begin their work in earnest once the 4th Division cleared the Germans out of their coastal strongpoints. But in truth, working behind the front lines was hardly reassuring, because there was no place within the Utah beachhead that was safe on D-Day. Members of the 1st ESB had to fulfill dozens of vital tasks on June 6 in a timely manner by laboring in the open on and immediately beyond the beach, a stretch of coastline that not only was subject to a severe German bombardment, but also was crammed with thousands of invisible German mines that ultimately must be cleared by Wharton's engineers. Indeed, on D-Day, the 1st ESB's duties were just as dangerous as being on the front line, and by nightfall on June 6, it had more than 100 casualties, including 21 dead, to prove it.

Col. Eugene Caffey
Deputy Commander, 1st Engineer Special Brigade
One thing that had my attention all of D-Day while Utah Beach was under double enfilade artillery fire, which kept the air fairly full of scrap iron, was the way in which the bulldozer drivers went about their work with complete nonchalance. . . . All during that long day they drove back and forth along the beach assisting in dragging out drowned artillery and vehicles, in shoving off landing craft, and in grading out rough roads and trails. They were remarkable people.

1st Battalion, 531st Engineer Shore Regiment
D-Day Action Report, July 24, 1944
The 3rd Platoon of C Company, led by Lt. [Elmer] Garrett, advanced up U-5 [Causeway 2, the road to Ste. Marie du Mont] and cleared the roadway of mines under constant artillery and mortar fire. . . . The 1st Platoon of C Company, under

Lt. James Philbrick built a lateral beach road. Three men of this platoon, PFC Michael Prokopovich, Pvt. George Callendrella, and Pvt. William Gatt were killed by shellfire while working on the lateral road. The 1st Platoon of A Company, under 1st Lt. Marchant Cottingham, was scheduled to land at H+105 [8:15 A.M.]. It was aboard an LCT that also carried all of A Company's bulldozers, trailers, and road material. Their craft sank and all the equipment aboard was lost.

1st Engineer Special Brigade
D-Day Action Report, July 1944
The area back of the beach was mined extensively. Almost all types of mines were found. Anti-tank and "S" mines ["Bouncing Betties"] were found in greatest numbers. . . . Generally, the extent of mining was such that all fields were suspect, necessitating sweeping before use. Approximately 45,000 mines were lifted during the development of the beach and dump areas. All units of the brigade were trained in mine detection and clearance. This training proved to be invaluable, as each dump unit could search the area it intended to use and make it ready for use without waiting for help from engineers busily engaged on other necessary tasks.

Lt. Col. Elzie Moore
1st Engineer Special Brigade
I have never seen a higher morale in any body of men, civilian or military, than was in the 1st Engineer Special Brigade. We all felt we were men of destiny, engaged in the greatest military operation of all time, and we expected to succeed.

UNCORKING THE BOTTLE
If the invasion was working, there had to be hordes of paratroopers somewhere to the west of Utah Beach, and now it was the job of Colonel Van Fleet's 8th Infantry to find them. Van Fleet speculated that they would probably be located about two miles inland, beyond the point where the flat coastal marshlands rose up and abruptly changed into the bocage, the ancient land of twisting sunken lanes and massive earthen hedgerows enclosing countless tiny pastures. The bocage was perfect country for concealment, so if the paratroopers were indeed present somewhere beyond the high ground, the men of the 8th Infantry, who currently were moving cautiously westward on the three causeways coursing inland from Utah Beach, would have difficulty detecting them.

On Causeway 1, the southernmost of those three exit roads, Lt. Col. Carlton MacNeely's 2nd Battalion was probing inland, strung out in a long, disjointed column that stretched all the way back to the beach. MacNeely's

Utah Beach: Inland Penetrations, 10:00 A.M., June 6, 1944

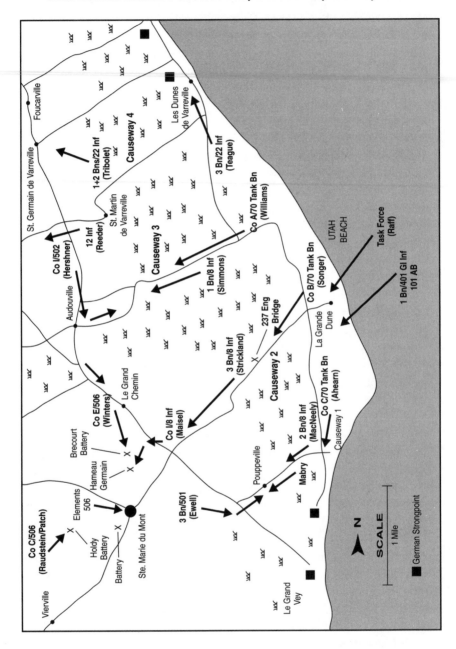

point squads had already seen enough German artillery fire on Utah Beach to know that bunching up could be fatal, but there was little room to spread out, since the meadows on either side of the roadway were mostly inundated. Furthermore, the wary GIs suspected that those rare pastures that were comparatively dry were filled with mines.

MacNeely's men headed straight for the high ground, about 500 yards ahead. Immediately beyond the ridge lay the village of Pouppeville, Mac-Neely's fundamental D-Day objective. But was Pouppeville occupied by friend or foe? No one had the slightest idea, but MacNeely must find out.

The 2nd Battalion was cheered by the presence of several Sherman tanks belonging to 1st Lt. John Ahearn's Company C, 70th Tank Battalion. If the enemy was in Pouppeville, those tanks would make a difference. But the Germans had foreseen that their enemies might use armor in this area and had laid antitank minefields athwart the obvious routes that the Shermans must use to move inland. The tankers had little choice in the matter, as the soggy meadows prevented them from driving their Shermans any substantial distance off the roads.

T/4 Anthony Zampiello
Company C, 70th Tank Battalion, June 25, 1944
About one and one-half miles southeast of Pouppeville, our tank struck a mine and was disabled. [Zampiello, a native of Pasadena, had named his tank "California Bomb."] Lt. Ahearn dismounted under fire to make a foot reconnaissance to observe the enemy who were close to our front. While so engaged he heard the cries of distress of a friendly infantryman who had stepped on a mine about 40 yards inside a known minefield. . . . Although Lt. Ahearn knew that this area was heavily mined, he ran back to our tank to obtain our first-aid kit and then ran to the wounded infantryman's assistance. By so doing he himself was seriously wounded by mines to the extent of losing one of his feet and possibly the other. When we saw what had happened, we ran to Lt. Ahearn's assistance, but he ordered us not to venture near him, asking instead for a rope with which to pull him to safety. When he was rescued, he encouraged us by saying, "We must get in there and take chances, otherwise we'll never get anywhere." [The U.S. Army awarded Ahearn the Distinguished Service Cross; Zampiello and gunner Pvt. Felix Beard were awarded Silver Stars. It was Beard's second Silver Star.]

As Colonel MacNeely's S-3 (operations officer), Capt. George Mabry was hardly expected to be at the forefront of the 2nd Battalion's thrust toward Pouppeville, but at about 11:00 A.M. on June 6, that was where he wanted to be. The twenty-six-year-old Mabry had dedicated four years of

"I pulled out my square of orange cloth and hoisted it on a stick."
Capt. George Mabry, operations officer for the 8th Infantry's
2nd Battalion, who was awarded the Distinguished Service Cross
for his D-Day actions. Later, in the Hürtgen Forest, the U.S. Army
would award Mabry the Medal of Honor.

service to the 8th Infantry, and now he was acting as his regiment's point, accompanied by a small band of infantrymen and a few of Ahearn's tanks. Mabry's group progressed warily over the causeway toward Pouppeville, trying to discern whether that distant village was occupied by the enemy. He and Sgt. Malvin Pike approached a tiny bridge over a brook and noticed with satisfaction that although the span was wired for demolition, the Germans had not blown it. Now they never would—and the Shermans eventually would roll over it toward Pouppeville. But as Mabry and Pike neared the bridge, they heard loud reports of gunfire, and soon thereafter, Mabry observed a dozen or so men dressed in the enemy's distinctive *feldgrau* (field gray) uniforms rushing toward them from the direction of the village. At least some of the cacophony of gunfire was generated by the unmistakable pop of American M1 rifles. Evidently, somewhere behind the hedgerows there were American soldiers driving the Germans out of Pouppeville toward Mabry.

The unfortunate enemy was trapped between the resolute paratroopers of Julian Ewell's 3rd Battalion, 501st Parachute Infantry, and the equally determined members of Mabry's 8th Infantry. Mabry and Pike commenced fire and hit several of the unsuspecting Germans as they rushed toward the bridge. The remaining enemy troops had no means of escape and threw their arms up in surrender.

Back in England, invasion planners had grasped that in circumstances such as this, 101st Airborne paratroopers and 4th Division infantrymen could mistake each other for the enemy and open fire, an error that would be easy to make in the inscrutable bocage and could cause considerable casualties. To avoid friendly fire accidents of this sort, the VII Corps issued both airborne and seaborne assault troops little orange flags, which the GIs were to wave if they held any doubts about who lay beyond the next hedgerow.

Capt. George Mabry
Operations Officer, 2nd Battalion, 8th Infantry

I pulled out my square of orange cloth and hoisted it on a stick over my head. I spotted a reply: an orange flag waved back and forth from a spot on the other side of the bridge. It had to be the paratroopers. . . . [Later,] I heard a noise in front of me and looked up. An airborne soldier jumped over a hedgerow with his rifle at the ready. The soldier was a member of the 101st Airborne. [It was 2nd Lt. Eugene Brierre, a 101st Airborne MP.] We shook hands and he told me that Gen. Maxwell Taylor, commanding general of the 101st, was [nearby] and would surely be glad to see me. [Later,] General Taylor, preceded by two men, crawled over the hedgerow into the road. I saluted and we shook hands. [The U.S. Army awarded Mabry the Distinguished Service Cross for his D-Day actions. He soon was promoted to the command of the 2nd Battalion and was awarded the Medal of Honor for his bold leadership of that outfit during the bitter fighting in the Hürtgen Forest in November 1944. Mabry thus became one of those rare soldiers who held the U.S. Army's two highest decorations for valor.]

The critical first stage of the airborne mission that General Bradley had considered indispensable to the fulfillment of the Utah Beach invasion had been accomplished. Some had been convinced that it would fail, and indeed, the chaos triggered by the nocturnal airdrop had thrown carefully laid plans into disarray. But somehow, on the causeways behind Utah Beach, that novel ingredient of warfare that American generals called "vertical envelopment" was working.

Maj. Gen. Maxwell Taylor
Commander, 101st Airborne Division
Shortly after the occupation of Pouppeville, we could hear the firing of the troops of the 4th Division approaching from the beach. To avoid the possibility of a collision of the two forces, I sent a patrol to meet them [under Brierre] and inform them of the situation around Pouppeville. Very soon the advance guard of the 8th Infantry appeared to the cheers of our parachutists. It was an historic moment, the long-planned junction of the air and seaborne assaults on Hitler's Fortress Europe.

2nd Lt. Eugene Brierre
Military Police Platoon, 101st Airborne Division
General Taylor ordered me to go down the road toward the beach and bring the highest ranking American officer back to him. This I did, and it was a captain, but I do not remember his name. [It was Mabry.]

That afternoon, several 70th Tank Battalion Shermans under the command of Lt. Thomas Tighe churned up Causeway 1 into Pouppeville, triggering a celebration.

T/5 George Koskimaki
General Taylor's Radio Operator, 101st Airborne Division
I remember how elated I felt when the first tanks poked their way through the streets. One paratrooper rushed forth and planted a kiss on the first tank.

Col. Gerald Higgins
Chief of Staff, 101st Airborne Division, 1945
I talked to the commander of the lead company of the 8th Infantry and also to several tankers who had come from the exit. They told me that the landing was going much better than had been expected and this of course was the most encouraging news that we had received up until that time. After the taking of Pouppeville, however, Taylor had still heard nothing from the other elements of the division.

While this notable meeting of 101st Airborne and 4th Division troops was taking place on Causeway 1, a similar scene was unfolding about three miles to the northwest at the hamlet of Audouville-la Hubert, near the western terminus of Causeway 3. Audouville lay in the low ground of an east-west valley that cut straight through the ridge paralleling the coast about two miles inland. It was an even lesser place than Pouppeville, consisting only of a few scattered farmhouses and buildings straddling the exit road.

The 8th Infantry's 1st Battalion, commanded by Lt. Col. Conrad Simmons, had landed at H-Hour, shattered the enemy's coastal defenses, and was moving cautiously westward along Causeway 3, a road just fifteen feet wide, surfaced with stones and elevated just a few feet over the inundated fields. Several DD tanks of the 70th Tank Battalion's Company A rolled forward between the columns of troops marching on both sides of the road. With their canvas flotation screens now lowered, the DDs looked like real Sherman tanks again, and they boosted the infantrymen's spirits considerably. Dozens of German soldiers had fled Simmons's advance, but like their comrades on Causeway 1, they could not escape the trap that the 101st Airborne had set a few hours earlier. On the west side of the exit road, paratroopers from Company I, 502nd Parachute Infantry, led by Capt. Ivan Hershner, were waiting; and when the unwary enemy troops approached Audouville, Hershner's men opened fire and could hardly miss. Sometime before noon, Hershner shook Simmons's hand in Audouville. Causeway 3 was secure.

8th Infantry, 4th Division
S-3 Journal, June 6, 1944
The 1st Battalion got onto Causeway 3 about 1100 and moved steadily across the causeway, which had not been mined, but air-bombed [by the Ninth Air Force], causing craters. Two tanks and one tank dozer got stuck, causing vehicular congestion until about 1500. The inundated area was from ankle- to neck-deep. . . .

German resistance was determined, but undertaken by small parties. [Prisoners] were evacuated to beach. They include Poles, Czechs, and Georgians.

Aboard his command ship *Bayfield*, General Collins was elated when at noon he received the news that Causeways 1 and 3 were open. Collins had never doubted that Barton's 4th Division could successfully storm Utah Beach. Rather, he had harbored some misgivings about the 4th's ability to advance across the inundated area beyond the beach, terrain that was entirely favorable to the defender. To Collins, Utah Beach was a corked bottle, and if the combined efforts of Taylor's 101st Airborne and Van Fleet's 8th Infantry could not swiftly pop that cork by opening up the beach exit roads, the Utah bottle would burst with potentially disastrous consequences for both the thousands of VII Corps troops piled on the beach and the roughly equal number of paratroopers stranded in the interior. But by early afternoon on June 6, that dilemma had been solved.

Maj. Gen. J. Lawton Collins
Commander, VII Corps, May 16, 1946
[Question posed by Col. S. L. A. Marshall, Chief Historian, ETO:] Did you feel you had to have two or more exits to insure success of the operation? [Collins's reply:] Yes, we did; but the reports we had from shore indicated that everything was going very well and that we were able to get across the inundated area at several points. That was something we were terribly concerned about. . . . We had feared that the Germans would have machine guns on the far side of the inundated area and that they would have all the causeways mined on the west side. I got reports in substance that assured me that the far side was not being held in strength. This was the thing we were primarily concerned with.

GO, SERGEANT, GO

General Collins may have been pleased with the early seizure of Causeways 1 and 3, but his VII Corps could never win a decisive victory on D-Day unless Causeway 2 was under American control by dusk. This thoroughfare was the central exit road on the 4th Division's invasion front and led to the vital crossroads village of Ste. Marie du Mont, about three miles from the coast. Barton had to move his division inland promptly to relieve the 101st Airborne—and beyond it the 82nd—and this roadway provided the quickest and most direct means of doing so. But if the enemy could deny Causeway 2 to the Americans and hold on to Ste. Marie du Mont throughout D-Day, or even longer, the 101st Airborne's link with the beachhead would be tenuous at best; and even worse, General Taylor's goal of swiftly capturing Carentan and linking up with the 29th Division coming west out of the Omaha beachhead could be foiled.

The enemy had hundreds of troops in the environs of Ste. Marie du Mont on the morning of D-Day, mostly artillerymen, support troops, and headquarters personnel. Had it not been for the startling descent of hordes of American paratroopers directly in their midst shortly after midnight on June 6, the Germans would have been capable of establishing a coherent defensive position, thereby blocking the 4th Division's entry into the village. But when the Utah Beach invasion commenced at 6:30 A.M., the scattered enemy troops in and around Ste. Marie du Mont were too busy fighting for their own survival against the energetic paratroopers to worry about the new and more severe threat posed by the American forces pushing inland from the coast.

For the Germans, all was chaos: communications were out; no one seemed to be in charge; even rear-area fighting positions were under attack; and any attempt to move into the bocage beyond the limited domain of the few established German strongpoints was made almost impossible by roving bands of American parachutists. The enemy could not even retain control of Ste. Marie du Mont itself, although the American parachute battalion assigned to capture it had landed off-target several miles away. Paratroopers from other 101st Airborne outfits who had landed near the village managed to keep the enemy's garrison busy most of the morning, engaging the Germans in confused close-range fighting on streets and alleys, inside buildings—and even within the church in the town square. Battling one's fellow man inside a twelfth-century house of God hardly seemed a virtuous thing to do, but warfare in June 1944 was a pitiless pursuit, and those men who had been trained for years to kill Nazis did not allow this irony to keep them from their tasks. When the first Americans rushed through the doors of the Église Notre-Dame into the gloomy interior, they swiftly discovered that the enemy was inside too. A close-range firefight promptly erupted, filled with blasts of rifles and submachine guns and the metallic clanging of empty shell casings on the ancient stone floor, sounds of battle that the narrow confines of the transept and nave amplified to a deafening degree. Evidently neither side would find sanctuary in this church on D-Day.

If the enemy wished to hold Ste. Marie du Mont and its causeway leading to the sea, they would need reinforcements at once. Although the Germans had positioned several reserve units in the interior of Normandy for just such a purpose, the unexpected Allied invasion had triggered crises in so many different and widely spaced locales that the quantity of German reserves was entirely inadequate to deal with all those threats simultaneously. The best that could be expected was to order the reserves forward to plug the largest of the holes the Allies had blasted in the German lines, but in the Cotentin Peninsula, even that limited goal was next to impossible, because German reinforcements would have to fight their way through scattered bands of American paratroopers to reach their objectives. On the morning of June 6, no one in the German high command seemed to know precisely where those paratroopers were located.

At 6:00 A.M. in his command post in faraway St. Lô, the senior German commander in Normandy, Gen. Erich Marcks, ordered one of those reserve units, the 6th *Fallschirmjäger* Regiment, to move into the Cotentin to help stabilize a situation that seemed to be deteriorating by the minute. The 6th was an elite outfit of 3,500 paratroopers, many of whom surely noted with a twinge of envy their opponents' remarkable ability to carry out that form of warfare the Germans themselves had practically invented, but which they themselves would not carry out again in the current war. Now, in one of war's inevitable ironies, the 6th *Fallschirmjäger* Regiment's first combat action of World War II would be to hunt down and kill as many of their American counterparts as possible. But the 6th was stationed too far away from Ste. Marie du Mont to make much difference in that critical sector on D-Day, and it lacked sufficient trucks to move with a speed worthy of the army that had invented blitzkrieg. It would be evening by the time the German paratroopers made solid contact with the Americans, and by that time, the German positions on the causeways behind Utah Beach had long since collapsed.

On the morning of June 6, the unfortunate enemy defenders of Ste. Marie du Mont and its environs had not yet realized that their commanders would let them down and provide no help whatsoever in the imminent struggle for the most critical of the Utah Beach causeways. Those defenders would have to wage a hopeless fight against overwhelming odds, and not many of them had an inclination to risk their lives in a battle that could have only one outcome.

Before the multitude of Anglo-American troops swarmed into Normandy on June 6, 1944, German soldiers feared Allied warplanes more than any other component of their adversary's war machine. That spring, the occupiers of Normandy continually wondered: Where is the Luftwaffe? Allied fighters and bombers roamed the skies over Normandy with such impunity that German soldiers swiftly learned that their units' survival depended entirely on concealing their locations from the probing eyes of Allied pilots. It was impossible to hide obvious defensive positions, such as coastal strongpoints or heavy guns protected by concrete casemates, but for rear-area sites that were less distinct, the enemy could easily conceal sizable combat units if their soldiers were skilled in the art of camouflage, especially in the patchwork of tiny pastures and leafy hedges that made up the bocage country.

The Germans had achieved that goal admirably in and around Ste. Marie du Mont. In May 1944, they had managed to install an entire artillery battalion of more than 400 men from the 91st *Luftlande* Division within a mile of that town. The ubiquitous hedgerows provided such good cover that the first time the Americans figured out that the artillerymen were there was when some unlucky paratroopers either dropped or stumbled directly into fields that in the dark seemed empty but actually were occupied by a substantial number of German troops. The enemy gunners had deployed the three batteries that formed their outfit in a semicircle north, west, and south of town, each in its own independent fighting position. Each battery consisted of four 105-millimeter howitzers, and under the watchful eyes of German spotters on the high ground beyond the coast, who could observe and adjust artillery fire directed at the beach, those twelve guns' unrelenting salvos were having a frightful effect among the GIs who were piling onto Utah Beach in the invasion's first few hours.

The job of eliminating that enemy battalion fell to Col. Robert Sink's 506th Parachute Infantry. But before he considered exactly how he would do it, Sink would have to unravel the mystery of his own regiment's whereabouts. By midmorning, Sink could account only for portions of Lt. Col. William Turner's 1st Battalion. Sink's 3rd Battalion was miles to the south on an independent mission aimed at capturing the two bridges over the lower Douve River. As for Lt. Col. Robert Strayer's 2nd Battalion, which held orders to seize Ste. Marie du Mont and Causeways 1 and 2, no one on Sink's staff had the slightest idea of its location.

What currently passed for Turner's 1st Battalion would have to do. This outfit had been designated Sink's "regimental reserve" on D-Day, to be held back for any unanticipated emergency — and now that emergency had come. A few dozen parachutists from the 502nd and 506th had already run into one of the three German howitzer batteries near Ste. Marie du Mont, about 500 yards west of town, next to a tiny hamlet named Holdy. Rumors were already spreading among the paratrooper grapevine that some of the unfortunate GIs who had landed near Holdy during the night had been taken prisoner and had not been treated by their captors according to the laws of the Geneva Convention.

To dispose of the Holdy battery, Sink dispatched seventy-five men under the command of Capt. Lloyd Patch, commander of the 1st Battalion's

Headquarters Company, and Capt. Knut Raudstein, commander of Company C. The arrival of these reinforcements left the Germans with almost no hope of escape, but they continued to fight tenaciously, just as they had been trained to do. Thanks to an unidentified paratrooper who proved himself an expert in the use of the U.S. Army's 2.36-inch rocket launcher, popularly known as the "bazooka," the Americans would speedily overcome the enemy.

Capt. Knut Raudstein
Commander, Company C, 506th Parachute Infantry, 1948
We left the buildings at Holdy and moved to a stone farmhouse about twenty yards from the battery. Our machine gun was set up in the road and one belt fired at the position. . . . The fire caused the [German] gun crews to leave their pieces and take cover in the surrounding ditches, and the howitzers were thereafter not fired by the enemy. . . . Just as we were moving out [to attack], our battalion anti-tank officer, with one bazooka and two men from the anti-tank platoon, arrived from Holdy. They were sent around a lateral hedgerow to get into position where they could fire into, or preferably enter, the ditch. The two flanking elements moved forward while the machine gun fired short bursts. Both flanking units crossed the road at the same time and advanced toward the entrances to the ditch, throwing grenades. The enemy threw grenades back. . . . The defenders gave little resistance once the trench was entered because the blast of the rockets from one flank and the continual concussion of grenades from the other took most of the fight out of the artillerymen. [Later] we found the bodies of several parachutists who had landed within the enemy position [before dawn].

1st Battalion, 506th Parachute Infantry, 101st Airborne Division
U.S. Army Historical Division, Interview with Capt. Lloyd Patch, July 1944
It was a confused action. . . . By the time the Patch-Raudstein force came up, the 50 or 60 Germans defending the area had all pulled back to within the gun position. The force started a double envelopment, Patch moving around one flank with half the men while Raudstein and the remaining men started a sweep around the hedgerows on the other. But while they were busy in this turning movement, a man with a bazooka opened up on the battery, firing from a hedgerow directly in front of the guns. The rockets hit among the men and ammunition with terrible effect; all fight died in the survivors. . . . [Patch recalled that the bazooka man yelled, "Come on! All you got to do is kill the rest of them!"] The two groups under Patch and Raudstein were able to close in and destroy them with rifle fire. A ditch behind the guns was choked with enemy dead when the ground was overwhelmed.

The Holdy battery was no more.

Ste. Marie du Mont's renowned church steeple loomed a few hundred yards to the east, but Patch suspected that the Germans were using it to observe and adjust mortar fire on his men. He summarily organized an ad hoc gun crew, loaded a shell into one of the captured howitzers, and aimed a point-blank shot at the steeple. The first try missed, but the second put a hole in the base of the steeple's dome and immediately drove whoever was in the tower out of it. According to 101st Airborne D-Day lore, however, it was not Germans, but members of Patch's own company who occupied the steeple when Patch shelled it.

The Germans had positioned another battery about 1,000 yards north of Ste. Marie du Mont just across a narrow dirt road from an old manor house called Brécourt. It was a strong and well-camouflaged site, but the enemy failed to deploy adequate numbers of scouts in outpost positions in the surrounding bocage. Consequently, as stealthy American paratroopers arrived in that area after sunrise, they were able to achieve a decisive tactical advantage by detecting the enemy without being detected themselves.

Most of those paratroopers belonged to Strayer's 2nd Battalion of the 506th, which had gradually congregated several miles north of its drop zone and was slowly making its way south toward its D-Day objectives near Ste. Marie du Mont. It was a long journey through countryside that could mystify even the best map readers, and there were occasional accidental encounters with wandering enemy bands. But shortly after dawn, scouts at the point of Strayer's column made their way down into the marshy valley south of Audouville and cautiously ascended the high ground on the opposite side. According to the paratroopers' maps, if they followed a north-south road through a hamlet called Le Grand Chemin, they would reach their objectives at Causeways 1 and 2.

But just beyond Le Grand Chemin, the point men detected the German battery near Brécourt. The presence of an enemy strongpoint at that location was a surprise to all, but Strayer's staff immediately resolved to destroy it. The 2nd Battalion's operations officer, Capt. Clarence Hester, called for 1st Lt. Richard Winters of Company E and ordered him to attack the battery. What normally would have been a job for 150 men, Winters would have to execute with only about a dozen, for at this point on June 6, that number of GIs was the limit of Company E's manpower. But the careless Germans had yielded to Winters the advantage of surprise, and he was able to maneuver his little group around the enemy's flanks before commencing the assault.

1st Lt. Richard Winters
Executive, Company E, 506th Parachute Infantry, June 22, 1944
First thing I did was have everybody drop all equipment except ammunition and grenades, for that's all we'd need, if things went good or bad. Then I placed one of my two machine guns in a position where he could give us a little covering fire as we went more or less into position. Next I divided the group into two units. One went with Lt. [Lynn] Compton, the other with myself. He took one hedge, I another.

It worked. Covered by the machine guns and a Company E member armed with a carbine who had climbed a nearby tree, Winters and his redoubtable followers methodically worked their way down the zigzag trench connecting the enemy's four howitzers, grenading and blasting with close-range small-arms fire any Germans who dared to offer resistance. The Americans captured each howitzer in turn and ultimately destroyed them all with explosives. Winters, who was later awarded the Distinguished Service Cross for this exploit, recalled that his group suffered ten casualties in the attack, four of whom died. But his audacious onslaught had eliminated four of the enemy's key pieces of ordnance that had been hurling deadly shells onto Utah Beach all morning.

Colonel Sink's 506th Parachute Infantry held many essential D-Day missions, but the most imperative was to ease the 4th Division's inland passage across the soggy ground behind Utah Beach via Causeway 2 to Ste. Marie du Mont. Despite Sink's difficulty in assembling his regiment on the morning of June 6, undersize groups of his men had somehow accomplished that goal. The 506th's ongoing battle for Ste. Marie du Mont and its obliteration of the German batteries at Holdy and Brécourt had prevented the enemy from establishing an ordered defense of Causeway 2, so when Colonel Van Fleet's 3rd Battalion, 8th Infantry, led by Lt. Col. Erasmus Strickland, started to move west off the beach down that vital roadway, the enemy's feeble resistance was hardly adequate to stop the American juggernaut.

T/Sgt. Grady Vickery
Company I, 8th Infantry, 4th Division
My platoon was advance guard after we got inland, and I remember Col. James Van Fleet waving his .45, saying, "Go, sergeant, go!" At the time I was forward with my two scouts, and we were really moving out down this road.

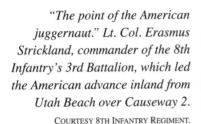

"The point of the American juggernaut." Lt. Col. Erasmus Strickland, commander of the 8th Infantry's 3rd Battalion, which led the American advance inland from Utah Beach over Causeway 2.
COURTESY 8TH INFANTRY REGIMENT.

PFC Rudolph Mozgo
Company I, 8th Infantry, 4th Division
We had moved in from the beach and came across an American tank [from Company B, 70th Tank Battalion] that had taken a direct hit from an anti-tank gun. An American soldier was half in and half out of the tank, dead. [This was probably T/4 James Partin, the only Company B tanker killed on D-Day.] Later, I was to see many more dead, but this sight I think I'll remember forever. [Another Company B tank, commanded by Sgt. Carl Rambo, was lost as a result of engine failure at a blown bridge over a small culvert a mile in from the beach and was pushed off the road by a bulldozer—a sight that almost every GI who passed inland on Causeway 2 would remember.]

In truth, rather than challenging the American advance from Utah Beach to Ste. Marie du Mont, the enemy troops in that locale displayed a categorical inclination to pack up and escape the trap that was about to be snapped shut by the 4th and 101st Divisions. Strickland's battalion, led by Capt. Frederick Maisel's Company I, observed obvious evidence of this fact when it reached the high ground at the western side of Causeway 2 and approached an old farmhouse named Hameau Germain, about one-half mile due north of Ste. Marie du Mont. The Germain farmstead was situated only a few hundred yards from Brécourt, and Winters's recent destruction of the German battery there had obviously infused all nearby enemy troops with a fervent desire to depart the area.

Captain Maisel's troops were astonished by their first sight of a sizable body of enemy troops. The German Army had conquered much of Europe by means of a masterful execution of mechanized warfare, but instead of panzers, half-tracks, and trucks, Company I's incredulous scouts perceived dozens of horses hauling a column of guns and wagons down the long driveway leading from the farmhouse to the main road. It looked more like a Napoleonic army than one that had invented modern warfare. Hameau Germain had obviously been an enemy command post of some sort, protected by a battery of 88-millimeter antiaircraft guns. The Germans were attempting to redeploy inland with all their equipment, including the 88s, their ammunition, and wagonloads of supplies.

Led by Maisel, parts of Company I moved into the fields north of the road. They would make a cross-country approach to Germain, almost totally shielded by the formidable hedgerows bordering the pastures. Like Winters's stealthy approach to Brécourt, this tactic succeeded, and the enemy did not detect Company I's presence until the GIs had advanced to almost point-blank range. Even so, when the Germans realized that the Americans were about to strike, they attempted to make a hasty escape. Their horse drivers lashed their teams forward, and suddenly the tempo of the horses' hoofbeats and the rattling of the equipment heaped high on the wagons picked up considerably. It was a vain hope; and what was about to happen to that unfortunate group of enemy soldiers would epitomize the current state of Nazi Germany's fortunes in World War II.

Sgt. Samuel Norris
Company I, 8th Infantry, 4th Division

We encountered an artillery unit that was moving. They were on a small road with hedgerows on each side. The 88s were being pulled by horses. After we killed the lead units, the road was blocked. We encircled them, and after they found out there was no way out, they began to surrender. [Three weeks after the ambush, the 3rd Battalion's second-in-command, Maj. Fred Collins, noted, "The Germans started to run, and we mowed them down—fifty of them."]

Capt. Frederick Maisel
Commander, Company I, 8th Infantry, Silver Star Citation, June 28, 1944

Organizing supporting fire and an assault group, Captain Maisel personally led the attack, capturing fifty Germans and three 88mm guns. Captain Maisel displayed great courage and calm, effective leadership with utter disregard for his own life. His example inspired his men to substantially greater effort.

Maisel himself was an equestrian who carried a photograph of his own horse in his wallet. In their assault against the enemy's horse-drawn column in the Germain farmhouse lane, the Americans had by necessity shot and killed several horses, and Maisel's subordinates later recalled that the death of so many animals in the attack distressed their captain greatly.

The road to Ste. Marie du Mont, coveted by the 4th Infantry Division since Barton had devised his first plans for the Utah Beach invasion in February 1944, was open. Aided by the 237th Engineers' hasty construction of a ten-yard steel treadway bridge over a culvert a mile inland—the first of thousands of bridges the U.S. Army would construct in northwest Europe over the next year—the 4th Division and all its associated vehicles could now flow freely inland.

On the evening of D-Day, the 4th Division's legendary old doughboy, Brig. Gen. Ted Roosevelt Jr., stumbled into the classic American paratrooper, Col. Robert Sink, near Ste. Marie du Mont. After exchanging salutes and shaking hands, Roosevelt removed his helmet. "The removal of

"A soaring Renaissance monument to the glory of God." American troops in front of the church in Ste. Marie du Mont on D-Day. U.S. ARMY SIGNAL CORPS, NATIONAL ARCHIVES.

my helmet is symbolic," Roosevelt declared to Sink. "I would like to take off my hat to every member of the 101st Airborne Division."

BETWEEN THE DEVIL AND THE SEA

Four miles away, in that desolate marsh where the Douve River and countless canals and tributaries twist and turn on their way down to the sea, the roles of hunter and hunted were reversed. The 101st Airborne's 501st Parachute Infantry had come to earth here, and its commander, Col. Howard Johnson, did not take long to discern that his regiment had landed in a hornet's nest in which the enemy held the upper hand tactically from the start. Like Colonel Sink of the 506th, Johnson was initially astonished by the fact that the nocturnal airdrop had seemingly caused his regiment to evaporate. Battalions that held orders to seize objectives with hundreds of men were forced to make the attempt with only a few. The rest, including several key commanders, had disappeared into the bocage or had been promptly shot or captured upon landing in the midst of an entire German battalion from the 91st Division that had been posted in and near the village of St. Côme du Mont. But paratroopers had been trained to carry on despite the inevitable chaos of a nighttime drop, and that is precisely what Johnson intended to do.

The German corps commander, General Marcks, was particularly worried about this locale. The road running north from Carentan through St. Côme du Mont and on to Ste. Mère Église was the main artery by which Marcks could sustain and replenish his units in the eastern Cotentin Peninsula. It was the 501st's mission to sever that artery, and if it did, the Utah beachhead would be almost entirely secure, because any German counterattack aiming to drive the invaders back into the sea would be effectively blocked far short of its ultimate objective.

On the morning of D-Day, Johnson had managed to accomplish at least one of his goals: the seizure of the La Barquette dam, spanning the Douve River two miles north of Carentan. Meanwhile, a small group of paratroopers from Sink's 3rd Battalion under Capt. Charles Shettle had captured two minor bridges farther downstream, preventing any German movement across the lower Douve. Those successes were indeed impressive, but Johnson would not be satisfied unless by nightfall his men were sitting on the Carentan–Ste. Mère Église road and occupying St. Côme du Mont.

An essential military principle asserts that the side holding the high ground gains a considerable military advantage on any battlefield. But at sunrise, many of Johnson's men found themselves in the low, marshy land of the Cotentin's vast *marais*, with little useful cover and enveloped on three sides by noses of high ground little more than a mile distant. That the Germans held this lofty terrain in strength became obvious to the Americans as the severity and lethality of German artillery and mortar fire on Johnson's positions increased markedly as D-Day wore on. Looking down on the Americans from a height advantage of seventy-five feet or more, the Germans could adjust their salvos with uncanny accuracy; and in the marshland around La Barquette and farther downstream, there was no decent place for the paratroopers to take cover. In the early afternoon, Johnson was moving a column of reinforcements down to the dam when enemy observers spotted them. What followed convinced Johnson's men that high ground was indeed decisive on this battlefield—and currently it was the Germans who held it.

501st Parachute Infantry, 101st Airborne Division
U.S. Army Historical Division, Interview with Col. Howard Johnson,
July 1944

"All hell broke loose," [Johnson said]. The Germans had apparently observed the column's progress but had reserved their fire. Their weapons were zeroed-in on the point where the lane met the canal road. Machine gun, rifle, mortar, and 88 [actually 105-millimeter howitzer] fire all enveloped Johnson's group in a twinkling. The men in the point went flat. The main body tried to find cover alongside the lane. Johnson worked his way forward, crawling up to the men at the point. He felt sudden alarm. The fire had broken around him so quickly and with such intensity that he was afraid he had led his men into a deadfall and that the whole force might be wiped out before he could extricate it. . . . [Johnson] found himself between the devil and the sea. He had no counter for [the enemy's fire], and if he stayed there he would certainly be destroyed. Too, he felt that the enemy observation was good enough that any attempt to move would not be less fatal.

One method that Johnson's paratroopers could try to escape their current predicament was to seize the high ground from the Germans, who were using it to turn the La Barquette area into an inferno. To achieve its main D-Day objectives, the 501st must eventually capture St. Côme du Mont, which stood on the highest ground in this locality, and the prevailing thought in the minds of American officers who had been fortunate enough to survive the airdrop and gather a sizable body of men was to launch an attack toward that place immediately, before the enemy had time to entrench and enhance his positions. Johnson dispatched patrols to reconnoiter the ground, but they returned with pessimistic news. The soggy ter-

501st Parachute Infantry: Afternoon, June 6, 1944

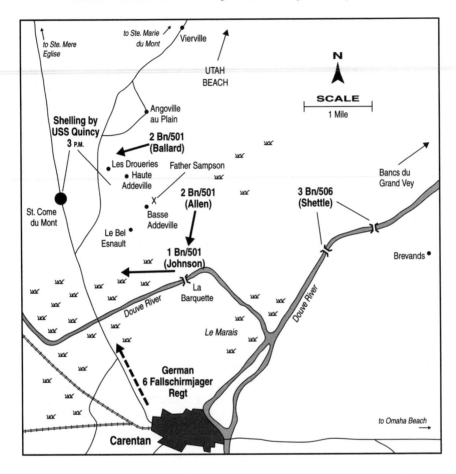

to Ste. Mere Eglise

to Ste. Marie du Mont

Vierville

UTAH BEACH

N

SCALE
1 Mile

Angoville au Plain

Shelling by USS Quincy
3 P.M.

2 Bn/501 (Ballard)

Les Droueries

Haute Addeville

Father Sampson

Bancs du Grand Vey

St. Come du Mont

X

Basse Addeville

2 Bn/501 (Allen)

3 Bn/506 (Shettle)

Brevands

Le Bel Esnault

1 Bn/501 (Johnson)

La Barquette

Douve River

Douve River

Le Marais

German 6 Fallschirmjager Regt

to Omaha Beach

Carentan

rain between La Barquette and the Carentan–St. Côme du Mont road was as flat as a board, devoid of cover, and dominated by the nearby elevated ground. Any attack across that land would have less chance of success than Pickett's Charge, and Johnson could not spare the men for such a futile endeavor. Instead, he would hold tight at La Barquette, slowly expanding his enclave as more men made their way into his lines.

Two other notable groups of 501st paratroopers lay little more than a mile north of La Barquette, one under Lt. Col. Robert Ballard at Haute Addeville, and the other under Maj. Richard Allen at Basse Addeville. Ballard and Allen had resolved to attack westward toward St. Côme du Mont; but like Johnson, they learned that attacking superior numbers of Germans who occupied commanding terrain did not offer much chance of success. Johnson reflected on his regiment's situation and concluded that his only recourse was to gather as many of his men as possible at La Barquette and take offensive action from there, so periodically during the day, he contacted Ballard and Allen by radio or courier and ordered them to move down to the Douve.

But both men found it difficult to comply. At one point, according to a 2nd Battalion radio operator, Ballard responded to his commander's directive by declaring: "I'm in no position to move right now. I've got my hands full with a good-sized enemy force right in front of me." Ballard's group never was able to make it to La Barquette by nightfall, and according to the U.S. Army historian who investigated the 501st's role on D-Day, "Johnson felt strongly that Ballard had let him down [and] there developed a rift between the two men, which caused some bitterness and much misunderstanding." The feud did not endure for long, for Johnson was killed four months later in Holland.

Colonel Johnson had one weapon at his disposal that the Germans could not answer, and starting at 3:00 P.M., he began to use it. One of the men who had jumped into Normandy with the 501st was a U.S. Navy lieutenant by the name of Farrell, who led a nine-man team that had been trained to communicate with offshore warships by means of a heavy but entirely man-portable SCR-609 radio. In midafternoon, Farrell and part of his team journeyed down to La Barquette from Basse Addeville and were promptly subjected to the fury of the enemy's nearly continuous barrage of that locale. Every GI who survived that frightful fire yearned for retribution, and with Farrell's arrival, his SCR-609 was just the item they needed to obtain that revenge. The radio was tuned to a frequency that was monitored by the crew of the heavy cruiser USS *Quincy,* which was currently anchored several miles offshore, engaging German batteries north of Utah Beach with its nine 8-inch guns.

The church steeple at St. Côme du Mont towered over these flatlands, and Johnson reasoned that the Germans were using it as an observation post to direct their deadly artillery barrage. Farrell contacted *Quincy* at 3:00 P.M. and shortly thereafter, the cruiser opened fire on the village. On and off for the next seven hours, *Quincy*'s main battery fired on enemy positions in and around that town, expending more than 200 rounds of 8-inch shells. To the GIs who could observe *Quincy*'s work, revenge was indeed sweet.

USS *Quincy*
Heavy Cruiser CA-71, Bombardment Group, Force U, War Diary,
June 6, 1944
1500: Fired main battery at Target 377882 [a map coordinate, the precise location of the St. Côme du Mont church]; 15 rounds. . . . 1530: Opened fire on infantry strongpoint 378882 [just to the east of the church]; 42 rounds—mission accomplished.

501st Parachute Infantry
U.S. Army Historical Division, Interview with Col. Howard Johnson,
July 1944
The work of the *Quincy*'s batteries was uncannily accurate. The shells played right along the ridge at St. Côme du Mont. It impressed Johnson that the German mortar fire fell off almost immediately. Major Allen, watching the results from his position at Basse Addeville, said to Johnson, "That fire would help Ballard. How about getting some over to him?" It was arranged, but in a roundabout fashion. Ballard gave his sensing to Allen by radio, and in turn Allen relayed them to Farrell—who in turn relayed them to *Quincy*.

As evening set in, Major Allen's force at Basse Addeville finally managed to disengage and move down into the low ground near the Douve to join Johnson's main group at La Barquette. But Allen's band had been fighting the enemy at close range all day, and more than a dozen paratroopers, currently lying in an old farmhouse that medics had converted into a makeshift aid station, had suffered wounds severe enough to prevent them from accompanying their comrades down to the river. They would have to be left behind, and Capt. Francis Sampson, the 501st's Catholic chaplain and a Notre Dame graduate, known as "Father Sam," volunteered to remain with them, accompanied by a medic who had been selected by chance according to the old-fashioned practice of drawing straws.

Capt. Francis Sampson
Chaplain, 501st Parachute Infantry, Autobiography, "Paratrooper Padre"
I told the regimental surgeon [Maj. Francis Carrel] that I was staying with the wounded. The Germans had perpetrated so many atrocities that I thought I might be able to keep the men from getting panicky and possibly keep the Germans from adding another crime to their list. As soon as the last of our forces had left, I made a white flag from a sheet and hung it out the door. . . . [The next morning,] I looked out and saw Germans setting up a machine gun in the front yard. I grabbed the white flag and went out. A German jumped at me and stuck a gun in my stomach. A couple of [German] paratroopers marched me up the road about a quarter of a mile. One of them pushed me against a hedgerow and the two stepped back about ten feet and pulled back the bolts of their weapons. . . . Then there were some shots fired just a few feet over our heads. It was a German noncom firing to attract the attention of the men I was with. . . . He was a fine-looking tough soldier about twenty-five. He spoke to my two captors and told me in broken English to come with him. I told him I was a Catholic priest and showed him my credentials. And to my real amazement he snapped to attention, saluted, made a slight bow, and showed me a medal pinned inside his uniform.

Sometime during that difficult afternoon, Colonel Johnson must have drawn the disheartening conclusion that the Cotentin *marais* into which his regiment had dropped was an area that the enemy could reinforce much more easily than the Americans could. Consequently, the 501st must fight on alone against increasingly poor odds for the rest of D-Day—and for an ensuing period the length of which the paratroopers could only estimate. By early evening, the Germans had moved more than 3,000 men of the 6th *Fallschirmjäger* Regiment into the St. Côme du Mont area, and with their arrival, Johnson's men at La Barquette would worry more about survival than carrying out the rest of their D-Day missions. The Americans soon conferred a nickname upon that dreary and coverless low ground, one that summed up their predicament in only two words: "Hell's Corners."

AN OBJECTIVE CALLED XYZ

Meanwhile, on the opposite extremity of the 101st Airborne's front, seven miles to the north, the 502nd Parachute Infantry had achieved most of its D-Day missions at comparatively slender cost. The 502nd controlled two of the four roads leading inland off Utah Beach, Causeways 3 and 4; and even better, the Germans' heavy battery at St. Martin de Varreville, which VII Corps commander Collins defined as "one of his greatest concerns," had turned out to be an empty threat, for when Lt. Col. Steve Chappuis's

2nd Battalion seized that site before dawn, the surprised Americans discovered that the Germans had transported the guns to another location.

Allied intelligence reports indicated that the German members of that battery had appropriated the dozen or so houses and farm buildings that constituted the tiny hamlet of Mézières, about a mile west of St. Martin, for barracks and storehouses. A German battery had 135 men on its rolls, and given the enemy's reputation for fighting tenacity, even those troops stationed at Mézières, well back of the forward gun positions, could not be expected to stay passive while only a short distance away the 502nd strove to accomplish its missions of eliminating the battery and opening up the causeways.

The 502nd's 1st Battalion, commanded by Lt. Col. Patrick Cassidy, would make sure that the Germans at Mézières did not get in the way, a job that was considered straightforward enough that only Company A would be needed to fulfill it. That outfit's D-Day orders were simple: "Company A will on initial phase move to and wipe out any enemy located in or near buildings in areas X, Y, and Z" (the 101st's code letters for the Mézières area). But as so often happens in war, what was supposed to be simple turned out to be anything but.

A Seattle native and a 1937 graduate of Oregon State College, Cassidy had joined the Regular army at a time when a military career was an unpopular choice among graduates of civilian colleges. In 1940, Cassidy had served as a lieutenant at Fort Lewis, Washington, with the old 15th Infantry, whose executive officer was Lt. Col. Dwight D. Eisenhower. Later, Cassidy undertook airborne training, and when he assumed command of the 502nd's 1st Battalion, his men immediately nicknamed him "Hopalong," after the legendary cowboy character Hopalong Cassidy, played by Hollywood actor William Boyd in the hugely popular westerns of the 1930s.

On D-Day, Troop Carrier pilots had given Cassidy a good drop, only a few hundred yards north of Mézières. In the predawn darkness, he had gathered about seventy men from his battalion and other outfits, and he promptly marched them south toward that objective. As the sun came up, Cassidy's group reached a key road junction located squarely between the German battery at St. Martin and the barracks-storehouse complex at Mézières. If an enemy counterattack developed later that would aim to push the invaders back into the sea, this would be a critical position to hold—and Cassidy thereupon resolved to hold it. In his new command post, a sturdy old Norman farmhouse adjacent to the intersection, he deployed his meager force in an all-around defense. Then, drawing about a dozen men from

502nd Parachute Infantry: Objective XYZ

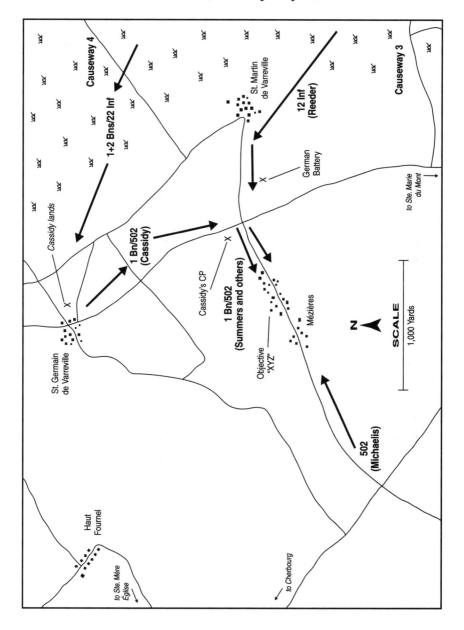

several different 1st Battalion companies, Cassidy dispatched that group down the road to the west to see if the enemy occupied the nearby buildings known by the "X-Y-Z" code letters in the invasion orders. If so, the men were to secure those structures immediately.

There were indeed plenty of Germans in the Mézières farm buildings, far more than the meager force Cassidy had sent to subdue them. Nevertheless, S/Sgt. Harrison Summers, accompanied by Lt. Elmer Brandenberger and Privates John Camien and William Burt, immediately set out to depopulate that hamlet of the enemy. It was a protracted and tough fight, in which the GIs methodically progressed from building to building, killing or capturing any enemy troops who resisted. It took heavy fighting, but ultimately Summers and his comrades overcame the demoralized enemy and gained Cassidy's objective, a classic example of the old military adage that audacity can achieve decisive success in battle even against overwhelming odds.

1st Battalion, 502nd Parachute Infantry, 101st Airborne Division
U.S. Army Historical Division, Interview with S/Sgt. Harrison Summers, July 1944

Sergeant Summers did not know one other man on his detail. He walked right up to the first house and kicked the door in. The Germans inside were firing through the slots, and he burst on them before they could turn. He shot four of them with a tommy gun. . . . [Moving on to another farmhouse,] Summers went on by himself and smashed the door in, firing as he did so. There were six Germans inside: He tommy-gunned them before they could move. They were firing at the road and were still stooping when he got them. . . . Summers went through the next five houses in the same manner, one man aiding him: Pvt. John Comin [actually Camien], armed only with a carbine. They switched weapons from house to house, one covering with the carbine while the other rushed the door with the tommy gun. The houses were thick and stone-walled, and the walls were slotted with fire ports. The Germans kept firing on the road. The machine gunner [Burt] kept plastering the embrasures. Summers and [Camien] went on from building to building . . . fighting and firing and saying nothing to one another.

Pvt. John Camien
Company B, 502nd Parachute Infantry, 101st Airborne Division, November 14, 1945

A French girl told us there were five Germans hiding in the closet [in a large farmhouse situated north of the road]. I put a burst of tommy-gun fire into the door, heard a scream, the door flew open and one German soldier fell dead onto the floor. Another attempted to run up the stairs. Sergeant Summers shot him and killed him. There were three more men in the closet who I kept covered with my tommy gun. I turned them over to Lt. Brandenberger. From there on Sgt. Summers and myself cleaned out the next four or five houses, taking about seven or eight prisoners, and killed about ten Germans. . . . The last remaining building appeared to be a German barracks because we encountered heavy small arms fire. [It was a two-story stone barn.] At this time Lt. Brandenberger deployed all of his men around the building. A heavy firefight ensued between the Germans and us. This continued for about an hour. . . . None of the Germans [in the barn] were left alive. [According to Camien, Brandenberger was severely wounded in the fight for the barn, nearly losing an arm. Summers, however, recalled that Brandenberger was wounded much earlier in the battle. When Brandenberger was brought back to the road junction for medical treatment, he blurted to Cassidy: "Sir, I'm terribly sorry I got hit. I didn't do my job very good."]

A mission that had almost been an afterthought had ended up being much more difficult to fulfill than the 502nd's main D-Day objectives in and around St. Martin de Varreville. But with the help of reinforcements sent forward by Cassidy and the unexpected arrival from the opposite direction of a sizable group of paratroopers under the command of the 502nd's executive, Lt. Col. John Michaelis, Mézières was in American hands by midafternoon.

It was just in time. After clearing Utah Beach, nearly 3,000 GIs of the 4th Division's 12th Infantry under Col. Red Reeder needed to use the Mézières road to reach their D-Day objectives north of Ste. Mère Église, and if they were held up, the Utah beachhead would be much smaller than General Collins wished by nightfall on D-Day. But thanks to Summers and his redoubtable band, Reeder's men would not be delayed.

S/Sgt. Harrison Summers
Company B, 502nd Parachute Infantry, 101st Airborne Division, July 1944
[U.S. Army historical officer Lt. Col. S. L. A. Marshall asked Summers to explain the factors that drove him to perform so heroically at Mézières:] I have no idea why. I now know that it was a crazy thing to do, and I wouldn't do it again in the same circumstances. But once started, I felt I had to finish. The other men were hanging back. They didn't seem to want to fight. [The U.S. Army awarded Summers a Distinguished Service Cross for this action. Later he gained a battlefield commission as a 2nd lieutenant.]

The simple arrangement of the last three letters of the alphabet in consecutive order scarcely seemed an appropriate method to evoke Summers's remarkable D-Day exploit at Mézières, now celebrated as one of the most notable moments in 101st Airborne history. But for all members of the Screaming Eagles on D-Day and afterward, the appellation "XYZ" was perfectly adequate.

CHAPTER 9

Something to Behold

THEY SHALL NOT PASS

U.S. Army generals understood that in the new form of warfare called vertical envelopment, paratroopers must get used to a sense of isolation. After an airdrop behind enemy lines, it could be days before conventional ground forces fought their way through to the drop zones, and during that period, the paratroopers would be on their own.

The generals professed confidence that their highly motivated and well-equipped airborne units could hang on, but still, aboard his VII Corps command ship *Bayfield* on the evening of D-Day, Maj. Gen. J. Lawton Collins was deeply concerned over the fate of the 82nd Airborne Division. At 6:15 A.M., just minutes before the first waves of the 4th Division would land on Utah Beach, Collins had sent a simple radio message to the 82nd's commander, Maj. Gen. Matthew Ridgway: "Report progress of attack; report location of command post." Throughout June 6, neither Ridgway nor anyone else in the 82nd had replied. For all Collins knew at sunset on D-Day, the bulk of the 82nd Airborne's paratroopers could be dead or prisoners of war. Until he found out what had happened to them, Collins would have to stick with the prearranged invasion plan and hope that Barton's 4th Division could push off Utah Beach and reach Ste. Mère Église as swiftly as possible. That would be the surest method of determining the 82nd Airborne's fate.

Maj. Gen. J. Lawton Collins
Commander, VII Corps, May 16, 1946
I felt that things ashore were going very well [on the evening of D-Day] but was still concerned about the position and condition of the 82nd Airborne Division. We kept calling the 82nd from *Bayfield* as originally planned, but we could not raise them in any way on D-Day. Lt. Col. [Orlando] Troxel [4th Division operations officer] stated that a message was received in the early evening of D-Day to the effect that the enemy was attacking elements of the 82nd from the northeast and south. However, this message was not clearly identified as having come from the 82nd. Two-way communication between the 82nd and 4th Divisions was not established.

What Collins did not know was that only parts of the 82nd's audacious airdrop from eight to eleven miles inland from Utah Beach had succeeded, and that by the afternoon of June 6, the operation that had started so dramatically as an airborne offensive had by necessity evolved into an almost strictly defensive mission. The 82nd thereupon would strive to hold the important ground that it had gained on D-Day and must wait until at least June 7 to do more. The German high command had swiftly roused its reserves on the morning of June 6 to counterattack Ridgway's men, but the 82nd's three D-Day drop zones were so distant from the coast that his paratroopers and gliderists had to bear the brunt of those enemy assaults completely alone. In truth, as D-Day wore on, the Germans applied such mounting pressure against three sides of the 82nd's enclave that even the confident Ridgway at times must have harbored doubts that his division could hang on.

In the 82nd's two drop zones west of the Merderet River, the situation was particularly critical. The enemy had reacted so vigorously to the invasion in that locale that scattered bands of American paratroopers quickly discerned that their primary object must now be to avoid destruction rather than attempt to achieve their now unattainable D-Day objectives. The Germans had forced small parties of Americans into isolated pockets on the far side of the Merderet, and as the battle developed, those glum GIs perceived that in all likelihood they would be stranded for some time in the lonely hedgerows like cornered animals.

East of the river, the 82nd Airborne was in much better shape, although its status was still imperfect. By the afternoon of June 6, Ridgway's troops had established solid bastions at the critical Merderet bridges at La Fière and Chef du Pont, and even though for the moment any offensive movement to relieve their beleaguered comrades west of the Merderet seemed

82nd Airborne Division: Afternoon, June 6, 1944

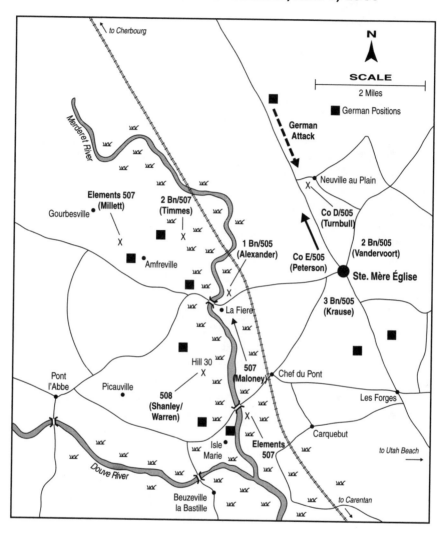

"The Chief." 1st Lt. Turner Turnbull of Company D, 505th Parachute Infantry, an Oklahoma native and son of a full-blooded Choctaw father and Scottish mother. Turnbull's stand at Neuville saved the 82nd Airborne's northern flank on D-Day. He was killed on June 7. COURTESY FRANKIE R. JAMES.

problematic, the men had the satisfaction of knowing that if the Germans tried to launch a counterattack across those two bridges aimed at driving Collins's seaborne invaders back into the Channel, the 82nd Airborne would be standing squarely in their way. Like Marshal Pétain at Verdun in 1916, General Ridgway had resolved: the enemy shall not pass.

The 82nd Airborne had also succeeded in establishing a stronghold in and around Ste. Mère Église. That critical crossroads town was one that the Germans must recapture if they wished to counterattack the Utah beach-head, and starting a few hours after dawn, they endeavored to do just that. The enemy's first attack came from the south, and although the Americans held firm, Ste. Mère Église was of such acute significance to Ridgway that the commander of the 505th Parachute Infantry, Lt. Col. William Ekman, decided to assign both his 2nd and 3rd Battalions to its defense rather than just the 3rd as the regiment's D-Day orders had originally specified. Those same orders had charged Lt. Col. Benjamin Vandervoort's 2nd Battalion to deploy in a defensive position about one and a half miles north of Ste. Mère Église on a ridge near the village of Neuville au Plain, but Ekman's hasty modification to the plan signified that Vandervoort could dispatch only a single platoon of forty-three men from Company D, led by 1st Lt. Turner Turnbull, to defend the northern front, rather than the entire 2nd Battalion of nearly 600 men.

In those days, any GI with American Indian ancestry was invariably labeled "Chief" by his comrades, and within the ranks of the 505th Parachute Infantry, that was the nickname by which Turnbull, who was half

Choctaw, was known. A prewar member of the Oklahoma National Guard, Turnbull was an experienced soldier and a hardened combat veteran of the Sicilian campaign, during which he had been badly wounded. Shortly after sunrise, Turnbull's little group marched up to Neuville and deployed behind some typical Norman hedgerows on either side of the main road coursing northward from Ste. Mère Église to Cherbourg. For a few hours, the bocage was quiet—not a German in sight. But the enemy was bound to come down this road in force soon, for every 82nd Airborne trooper knew from his D-Day briefings that plenty of German units were scattered over the northern half of the Cotentin Peninsula, and when they finally stirred into action, only Turnbull's platoon would stand between them and Ste. Mère Église.

At about 1:00 P.M. Vandervoort called on his isolated platoon at Neuville. Vandervoort had broken his left shinbone in the airdrop and could hardly walk, but a gentle French woman in Ste. Mère Église had donated an ancient pair of crutches to him, which helped a little. Even better, the 82nd Airborne's predawn glider landings had deposited a few jeeps outside of town, and Vandervoort promptly commandeered one of them, along with a driver and two radio operators, to take him up to Turnbull's position. A second jeep followed in Vandervoort's wake, towing a 57-millimeter antitank gun that would prove useful to the Chief if he would be attacked by enemy armor.

When Vandervoort met Turnbull, the Neuville front was still quiet, but that state of affairs was about to change. A Frenchman bicycling past the American lines had just informed the GIs that several American paratroopers escorting a horde of German prisoners were coming down the road from the north and would come into view momentarily as they crested a ridge less than a mile away. That could be good news—but Vandervoort and Turnbull sensed that something was amiss.

Lt. Col. Benjamin Vandervoort
Commander, 2nd Battalion, 505th Parachute Infantry,
82nd Airborne Division

As Turnbull and I walked over to his position and talked, we kept watching the highway from the north. Shortly, a long column of troops appeared in the distance with vehicles scattered at intervals through their ranks. If these were prisoners, there were more than a battalion of them. We could make out the field gray of the German uniform. On their flanks were individuals in [American] paratrooper uniform waving orange panels [the Allied recognition signal]. Somehow it looked just too good to be true. I told our 57mm anti-tank gun crew to go into position on the right of the road where a house offered some concealment. When the advanc-

"Somehow it looked just too good to be true." Two American paratroopers behind a hedgerow. The one on the left is hoisting a piece of colored cloth on the muzzle of his weapon as a recognition signal to nearby U.S. troops.
U.S. ARMY SIGNAL CORPS, NATIONAL ARCHIVES.

ing column had closed to within 1,000 yards, I told Turnbull to have his machine gun that was covering the road fire a burst into the field on the left of the column. That did it. The alleged German "prisoners" deployed instantly on both sides of the road, and the leading vehicle, a self-propelled gun, opened fire on our position. Our anti-tank gun crew returned the fire and set fire to the leading vehicle and one more that moved up behind it. . . . The German infantry began to move forward on both sides of the road. . . . I told Turnbull to delay the Germans as long as he could, then withdraw to Ste. Mère Église.

Vandervoort returned to Ste. Mère Église in his jeep to warn the paratroopers defending the town's northern fringes that the enemy might soon be approaching. Meanwhile, Turnbull's determined band fought on against a German force that historians later speculated was the vanguard of a 91st *Luftlande* Division column amounting to several thousand men. Precisely how many men this vanguard actually contained, no one could tell, but it certainly was far more than Turnbull's forty-three. In truth, the Americans were so outnumbered that holding on for any longer than a few minutes seemed impossible. But the paratroopers were entrenched in good cover on commanding ground, and to reach the American position, the enemy had to traverse a low valley with no cover, under direct and withering fire from Turnbull's force. Nevertheless, the enemy pressed home the attack, and the battle grew in intensity by the minute. The loud crack of the Americans' M1 rifles and the hammering of their machine guns and Thompsons were interspersed with the ripping blast of the Germans' machine pistols, the sharp bang of their potato masher grenades, and the whooshing gust of their mortars. If sound levels can define a battle's intensity, then the deafening resonance of this fight, concentrated in such a small area, plainly indicated both sides' resolve to fight.

Turnbull's platoon held on for more than two hours, but ultimately the Germans correctly figured out that their superior numbers would enable them to get around the Americans' Neuville position with little difficulty. There was nothing Turnbull could do to stop such a tactic, and when the enemy started to maneuver around his flanks, he realized that he had done enough and it was time to follow Vandervoort's directive and withdraw. But pulling out would not be simple, as dozens of German soldiers were separated from Turnbull's men by only a hedgerow or two, and they could observe every movement the Americans made. Even worse, many GIs had suffered such severe wounds that they could neither move by themselves nor be carried away by their comrades.

Back in Ste. Mère Église, Vandervoort had prepared for such an eventuality when he ordered Capt. Clyde Russell, the commander of Company E, to send a platoon north to Neuville to support Turnbull's beleaguered paratroopers and to cover their inevitable withdrawal. These fresh reinforcements, led by 1st Lt. Theodore Peterson, arrived at an opportune time.

1st Lt. Theodore Peterson
Company E, 505th Parachute Infantry, 82nd Airborne Division
We moved quickly and cautiously on the west side of the road to Neuville. Turnbull had a guard posted at the position we entered, who seemed to be expecting us. Turnbull was very calm and he had the situation well in hand for the rough position he was in. . . . [We] set up a line of fire on Turnbull's left. . . . [Later,] all hell broke loose. The enemy moving west down the road near a farmhouse to our immediate front walked right into our hidden left flank, which was stretched out along our hedgerow. Cpl. [Thomas] Burke, who had already won a Silver Star [in Sicily], and three or four riflemen, held their fire until the enemy was within a few feet of them. Then they opened fire. The surprised enemy took off in every direction, losing a good number of men. With that the whole platoon opened fire with

everything it had. This included Sgt. [Otis] Sampson, the greatest and most accurate mortar sergeant in the business. [Sampson was an old horse cavalryman from
the interwar Regular army who had joined the paratroopers at the advanced age of
thirty.] During all this havoc, a runner from Turnbull reported to me that they had
successfully withdrawn their platoon. . . . Having accomplished our mission, we
made a tactical withdrawal, firing as we left. . . . [At one point], peeking through
a hedgerow, I saw our battalion commander [Vandervoort] sitting on the back of a
jeep, legs hanging over the back, one of which was in a cast, crutches beside him,
just as calm as can be, talking on his radio.

Sgt. Otis Sampson
Company E, 505th Parachute Infantry, 82nd Airborne Division,
June 25, 1944
We moved the mortar continuously so as to not give Jerry a target. The rifle
squads were doing a good job—Jerry's fire was falling off. A mortar round landed
in the tree over our CP, but there was no damage. A lane ran from the dirt road up
over the low hill. A paratrooper lay as he had fallen exposed on its crest. The Jerries were trying to move some men from the left of the lane to the right. One man
at a time would cross at timed intervals. I judged when another would cross and
put a round in the tube. The timing was perfect. . . . I could hear the Jerries yelling
as we were leaving. It reminded me of an unfinished ballgame. They were yelling
for us to come back and finish it.

Of Turnbull's forty-three men, twenty-seven were either dead or so
seriously wounded that they could not participate in Turnbull's withdrawal
to Ste. Mère Église. But a Company D medic, Cpl. James Kelly, offered to
remain with the injured GIs. When the pullout commenced, the Germans
swiftly moved in and captured them all. (The survivors were later freed
when VII Corps captured Cherbourg on June 26.) Only about a dozen of
Turnbull's men, some of whom were wounded but could still walk, made it
back to Ste. Mère Église.

Turner Turnbull's stand at Neuville had disordered the enemy's column
moving south toward Ste. Mère Église, buying Ridgway precious time to
solidify the defense of that town. But Turnbull had only a few hours to
appreciate his crucial accomplishment; the next day, he was killed by a German mortar shell. The significance of his fight at Neuville on the afternoon
of D-Day, however, was established by the irrefutable details that the strong
German force moving southward against the 82nd Airborne's enclave would
fail to recapture Ste. Mère Église on June 6 and would have no impact whatsoever on the American troops pushing inland from Utah Beach. This was
just the sort of feat that American invasion planners had hoped their air-

borne forces could accomplish on D-Day, and Turnbull's diminutive group had proved that those hopes were realistic.

That evening, Vandervoort's paratroopers received some help from an unexpected source. A U.S. Navy spotter who had jumped into Normandy with the 82nd Airborne managed to contact the USS *Nevada* by radio, and that ancient veteran of Pearl Harbor contributed several 14-inch shells at a range of more than eleven miles to disrupt the enemy's alarming buildup near Neuville just before sunset. Vandervoort's executive, Capt. James Maness, remarked that the impact of *Nevada*'s rounds reminded him of a "West Texas dust storm."

Ste. Mère Église was in American hands for good.

The 505th's remaining battalion, the 1st, had fought a hard battle on the afternoon of D-Day at the La Fière bridge, that essential crossing site over the Merderet River two miles west of Ste. Mère Église. By evening, the situation at La Fière had developed into a stalemate: The Germans did not dare to try another attack over the coverless causeway leading to the bridge, but the Americans, too, would certainly be decimated if they used that roadway over the marshlands to move west of the river and rescue the many bands of isolated paratroopers who were struggling to hang on against increasing enemy pressure. This impasse greatly favored the Germans, for they had a substantial amount of supporting artillery, whereas the paratroopers had scarcely any. Consequently, the Germans were satisfied to allow their artillerymen to demonstrate their skills, and they mercilessly bombarded the eastern bank of the Merderet for hours, causing American casualties to mount. The GIs could do nothing in response except dig deeper foxholes and pray that the Germans' ammunition supply would soon run out.

In the early evening, the 82nd's second-in-command, Brig. Gen. James Gavin, who had become de facto commander of all American troops on the Merderet front, reported on the situation at La Fière to General Ridgway at the division's command post near Ste. Mère Église. The two men agreed that if the 82nd could make no further offensive movements for the remainder of D-Day, they must concentrate their efforts on defeating any German attempt to cross the Merderet at La Fière.

Brig. Gen. James Gavin
Assistant Division Commander, 82nd Airborne Division, August 16, 1944
I went back to the La Fière bridge, arriving there well into the latter part of the afternoon. [It was actually evening.] The fighting had greatly increased in intensity. German mortar and high velocity artillery fire were coming down on the nose overlooking the bridge. The battalion executive, Maj. [James] McGinity, had been killed. [As had the CO, Maj. Frederick Kellam, and when Gavin arrived at the

bridge, he appointed Lt. Col. Mark Alexander, the 505th's XO, as commander of the 1st Battalion.] The situation rapidly developed to a very serious stage. I sent an officer to Lt. Col. [Arthur] Maloney [XO, 507th Parachute Infantry, then at Chef du Pont], instructing him to bring all of his force, less about a platoon, [to La Fière]. . . . Maloney arrived with about 200 men. He was directed to deploy his force on both sides of the main road leading to the causeway. . . . By darkness the situation appeared to be well in hand, except for a few German snipers who were apparently still alive in our position.

But by shutting the door in the enemy's face along the Merderet, Ridgway and Gavin had to acknowledge the unfortunate truth that the several groups of 82nd Airborne paratroopers surrounded on the far side of that river would have to hold out against superior numbers of the enemy for a time period that the two generals could only hope would be short. That an attempt must soon be made to rescue those unlucky men was paramount in every paratrooper's mind. But the prevailing question was whether they could hang on long enough to be rescued.

By sunset on D-Day, three sizable groups and countless smaller bands of 82nd men were trapped west of the Merderet. The northernmost of these consisted of nearly 200 men under the command of the 507th's Lt. Col. Charles Timmes, all of whom were holed up in an apple orchard a mile northwest of the La Fière bridge on the fringe of the Merderet swamp. Timmes did not have a functional radio, and he therefore could only wonder whether Ridgway and Gavin were aware of his plight. But the Germans knew precisely where he was, and they bombarded the orchard relentlessly with mortars and artillery, inflicting heavy casualties. Timmes's men did not have any heavy weapons with which to respond, and with their backs against the swamp, their leader did not think a retreat was advisable.

Enveloped on three sides by the enemy, the resolute but battered paratroopers could not budge from the orchard for three days. On June 9, they were finally relieved by an attack across the Merderet by the 325th Glider Infantry, and the following day, Ridgway informed a grateful Timmes that trucks would come to get him and his survivors, who would be pulled back for a short rest.

Lt. Col. Charles Timmes
Commander, 2nd Battalion, 507th Parachute Infantry,
82nd Airborne Division
While awaiting the arrival of the trucks, contrary to all rules of the 82nd Division, I sprawled out on the ground in the open field without my helmet—and unshaved.

I woke up to have none other than General Ridgway gaze into my face. He greeted me with a smile and congratulations and told me to keep up the good work. Needless to say I was most embarrassed and expected the worst. He showed genuine consideration and compassion for our exhausted men.

Two miles to the south, a group of isolated parachutists even larger than Timmes's had occupied the utterly misnamed Hill 30 on the evening of D-Day, only to discover that this position, marked so prominently on U.S. Army maps, possessed virtually no military value. This congregation of more than 300 men, led by Lt. Col. Thomas Shanley and Maj. Shields Warren of the 508th Parachute Infantry, faced precisely the same predicament as Timmes's group. Backed up against the formidable Merderet swamp, with swarms of the enemy on three sides, Shanley's and Warren's only realistic military option was to dig in and wait for American forces on the opposite side of the Merderet to mount a relief operation.

In the meantime, the paratroopers on Hill 30 had to endure sometimes severe enemy pressure, mostly in the form of intermittent mortar and artillery barrages, as their rations, ammunition, and medical supplies fell to critical levels. But even in this tight spot, Shanley and Warren must have been encouraged by the close proximity of friendly forces. Perched in a tree with a pair of binoculars, a paratrooper could easily perceive friendly troops less than a mile eastward at Chef du Pont, currently under firm American control. Furthermore, Shanley had something Timmes did not: a working radio. When he used it during the night of June 6, he could communicate with his superiors and at least inform them of his group's existence, location, and condition. But Shanley soon grasped the hard truth that a radio link to higher headquarters, although reassuring, by no means guaranteed his men's survival. Until the situation east of the Merderet stabilized, Shanley's flock would simply have to wait. That wait endured for nearly four days, not coming to an end until the 90th Division's 358th Infantry attacked across the Merderet on June 10 and finally relieved Shanley's worn-out paratroopers.

Of all the unfortunate groups of 82nd Airborne soldiers trapped on the west side of the Merderet on D-Day, none faced a greater dilemma than the one led by the 507th's commander, Col. George "Zip" Millett. This substantial aggregation of paratroopers was pocketed in the bocage near the village of Amfreville, four miles west of Ste. Mère Église, squarely in the middle of a body of German troops as angry as bees in an overturned hive. Those enemy soldiers knew the exact fields where Millett's band had sought refuge, and they responded wrathfully to any American attempt to escape. Millett's situation was virtually hopeless. However long it took General Ridgway to relieve Timmes and Shanley, it would take him longer to reach Millett's much more distant pocket. Furthermore, whereas the 82nd's other isolated groups could at least secure their positions by anchoring their flanks on the Merderet marshlands, Millett's outnumbered men were boxed in on all sides, completely lacking any piece of favorable terrain that could enhance their perimeter.

For almost three days, Millett's men hung on in this remote enclave, waiting for a rescue that did not come. Early on June 9, they tried to break out to the east, but many of the paratroopers, including Millett, stumbled into the German lines in the dark and were captured. Ridgway would have to find a new commanding officer for the 507th soon.

RIDGWAY'S CROAKER

The man Ridgway would designate on June 15, 1944, to take over the 507th, Col. Edson Raff, was one of the U.S. Army's most celebrated parachutists. A native New Yorker and 1933 West Point graduate, the thirty-six-year-old Raff had led the first American parachute mission of World War II in the opening moments of Operation Torch, the November 1942 invasion of North Africa. By June 1944, the American public already knew him as the author of the popular book *We Jumped to Fight*, which detailed his North African experiences in ways that some senior U.S. Army officers viewed as egotistical.

Raff was the kind of soldier that Robert E. Lee used to describe as a "croaker." Although his peers admired his soldierly skills, they also readily perceived that he was perpetually disgruntled and did not hesitate to air views that were distinctly contrary to the common principles and attitudes professed by most paratroopers. His nickname of "Little Caesar" confirmed his formidable reputation as a disciplinarian and fanatical trainer of troops, a standing that led some to despise him, others to appreciate his dedication to the warfighting profession.

Raff was one of those rare members of the U.S. Army who did not think highly of Matthew Ridgway. He described Ridgway's staff officers as "sycophants" and added: "My personal opinion of Ridgway was that he was a conceited, self-centered, narcissistic man. I thought—God help us when we get into combat under him."

Raff's startling attitude no doubt explained why he did not play a major role on D-Day with the 82nd Airborne, despite his exalted airborne experience and high rank. Ridgway had plans for Raff on D-Day, but they did not involve landing behind enemy lines by parachute. Rather, Raff

"Ridgway's Croaker." Col. Edson Raff (on right), commander of a special 82nd Airborne Division task force on D-Day, points out objectives on a map to some of his officers. U.S. ARMY SIGNAL CORPS, NATIONAL ARCHIVES.

would command a small mechanized task force that was ordered to land on Utah Beach in U.S. Navy landing craft, an invasion method Raff considered pedestrian and highly vexing to his airborne soul. He later noted, "To a paratrooper that was enough to condemn a man forever."

"Task Force Raff" may have been a demeaning command for a man of Raff's ambition, but in truth, VII Corps commander Collins considered its D-Day role vital. At about 1:00 P.M., Raff would land on Utah Beach with seventeen Sherman tanks from Company C, 746th Tank Battalion, and four six-wheeled "Greyhound" armored scout cars from Troop B, 4th Cavalry Squadron, and swiftly move inland toward Ste. Mère Église to join up with those elements of the 82nd Airborne that had parachuted into that vicinity before dawn. Forty-one foot soldiers from Company F, 401st Glider Infantry, who had also landed on Utah Beach courtesy of the U.S. Navy, would accompany Raff's task force by the somewhat uncomfortable and dangerous method of riding on the tanks. Later, as Raff's column rolled inland, it would pick up twenty-one stray paratroopers who had been wandering the bocage looking for some action. In truth, such an assemblage of troops and vehicles would normally be the responsibility of a captain or major, but thanks to Ridgway, Colonel Raff got the job on D-Day. The proud Raff, who yearned for greater glory, in later years passed over his experiences with this small command when relating war stories.

Nevertheless, Task Force Raff did a good job on June 6, penetrating farther inland than any American force that landed by sea on D-Day, a particularly impressive achievement, as Raff's vehicles did not get moving off Utah Beach until after 2:00 P.M. By that time, General Collins's frequent radio messages to Ridgway from the VII Corps command ship *Bayfield* had failed to trigger any response, so Raff's men would have to accomplish what radios could not. If Ridgway was still alive, he in all likelihood would be somewhere near Ste. Mère Église, so that was where the armored column must head—and where Raff aimed to find the man he openly detested.

With the members of the 401st Glider Infantry perched awkwardly on the Shermans' steel hulls, the tanks and armored cars rolled forward over Causeway 2 to Ste. Marie du Mont. Raff and his executive officer, Maj. Ralph Ingersoll, stayed near the head of the column in a jeep specially fitted with an armored windshield and a .50-caliber machine gun mounted in the rear. Before the war, Ingersoll had been a noted editor and founder of an unusual New York City daily newspaper called *PM*, a journal that accepted no advertising and featured writing by such notables as Ernest Hemingway, Dorothy Parker, and James Thurber. Ingersoll's newspaper career came to a halt when he entered the U.S. Army, and now he was on the frontline of the Normandy invasion, an experience he would recall two years later in his memoir *Top Secret*.

Maj. Ralph Ingersoll
Executive, Task Force Raff, Top Secret, *1946*

By the time we reached the steeple [of the Ste. Marie du Mont church] I had seen from our landing craft, something had blown the top off it. It stood in a little village square in which the sight that fascinated me most was a corpse of a German soldier in a roadway near the corner. It had been run over by so many tracked vehicles that it was ironed flat like a figure in a comic strip: really, absolutely flat, the arms of its gray uniform at right angles to its pressed and flattened coat. Its black boots and the legs that were in them were just as flat and thin as if they had been cut from a sheet of dirty cardboard. There was an MP [from the 4th Division] ahead of us, standing in the square and, without being asked, he simply pointed us a way through what looked like an alley. Beyond, there was an open road and again we rocked and roared on into France.

Task Force Raff and Evening Glider Missions, June 6, 1944

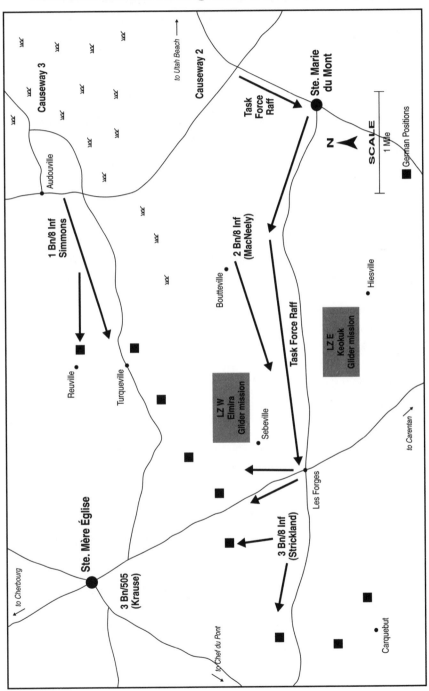

So far, so good. Three miles ahead was a road junction called Les Forges, and when Task Force Raff reached that spot late in the afternoon of D-Day, all it had to do was turn right and drive north two miles on the road that coursed straight as an arrow to Ste. Mère Église. Still no Germans—and if Raff's luck held out, he could be shaking hands with Ridgway in the town square within ten minutes. When the drivers swung their vehicles to the right at the intersection, however, they suspected trouble, and they were right. One-half mile north of Les Forges, the Ste. Mère Église road dropped into a low valley, a few hundred yards beyond which loomed a sharp ridge perpendicular to the road. If the Germans were resolved to make a stand, that ridge was the place to do it.

Raff's long column of tanks and armored cars came to a halt as the officers scanned the far side of the valley with binoculars. Some 4th Division troops who had made it this far a few hours earlier advised the tankers that the enemy lay somewhere ahead, where exactly they did not know. If Task Force Raff still intended to get to Ste. Mère Église, it must learn the enemy's whereabouts on its own. When its first tanks and armored cars drove warily down into the valley, the enemy's immediate and violent reaction provided the Americans with obvious evidence that they would now have to fight their way through to Ridgway.

Company C, 746th Tank Battalion
D-Day Action Report, July 1944

With the [4th Cavalry] reconnaissance elements leading, the company moved northwest along the road to Ste. Mère Église, but was forced to hastily deploy before reaching the creek at 354943 [a map coordinate, in the valley north of Les Forges] because of heavy anti-tank fire coming from the high ground across the creek. Lt. [Joe] Mercer and his 1st Platoon [of five tanks] deployed to the left of the road, engaging the anti-tank guns on the enemy's right flank. In this action three tanks were lost and Lt. Mercer mortally wounded. The 3rd Platoon under Lt. [Harold] Plagge deployed to the right of the road and approached the creek in an effort to flank the enemy positions on his left. The platoon was unable to cross the creek and one tank bogged down. . . . Lt. [James] Shields of the 2nd Platoon deployed along a narrow front adjacent to the main road and engaged the guns from those positions. S/Sgt. Buza moved his tank forward, succeeded in crossing the creek, and reached the high ground. . . . He radioed Capt. [James] Crawford [CO, Company C] for instructions, stating that he could not proceed to Ste. Mère Église because he was unable to secure support from other tanks. Capt. Crawford ordered Sgt. Buza to return to the platoon.

"We rocked and roared on into France." A U.S. Army Sherman tank moves inland from Utah Beach on D-Day. The cart at left is filled with German prisoners. U.S. ARMY SIGNAL CORPS, NATIONAL ARCHIVES.

The alert Germans had correctly deduced that the American troops pushing inland from Utah Beach would head straight for Ste. Mère Église by this route, and consequently, by the time Task Force Raff arrived in late afternoon, the enemy had already deployed abundant troops and antitank guns on the ridge south of town that the Americans had to traverse to reach their objective. The determined German troops were dug in, superbly camouflaged in the bocage, and had every foot of the valley north of Les Forges covered with lethal firepower. By evening, Raff had reached the inevitable conclusion that his tanks and armored cars could never crack this position by direct assault. He'd need plentiful reinforcements from the 4th Division, but General Barton's GIs had come a long way since H-Hour and already had achieved about as much as they expected on June 6. They were beginning to dig in for the night, well satisfied with their D-Day performance.

Raff could attempt to maneuver around the enemy's flanks, but that would involve turning his entire column around and heading west for more than a mile to an alternative road. There was not enough time for that—

darkness was near. He could try to push his armored vehicles off the roads deep into the pastureland, but in this unfathomable bocage country, the tanks would be boxed in by the massive, impenetrable hedgerows and would never get anywhere. It was too late to do anything more. Raff had to acknowledge that his troops would not reach the 82nd Airborne Division on D-Day as his orders had prescribed. Rather, they must settle in for the night and try again the next day.

At 9:00 P.M. on D-Day, an entirely different problem was demanding Raff's attention. Starting shortly after that hour, IX Troop Carrier Command was scheduled to tow a sizable group of Waco and Horsa gliders, packed with 82nd Airborne troops and artillery, to a landing zone in the farm fields around Les Forges. With the unmovable Germans entrenched on the ridge north of the Les Forges crossroads, those gliders and their tow planes could be blasted to bits in the sky if that mission was carried through as planned.

It was too late to call it off, however. The C-47s and their gliders were already nearing the landing zone in what Major Ingersoll described as "a beautiful formation . . . two or three hundred feet high, not far above the tree tops." The men of Task Force Raff could only sit back and watch what was about to unfold.

DON'T KNOCK A GLIDER MAN

If glider operations were a feasible component of the 82nd Airborne's repertoire, the D-Day mission known as "Elmira" must prove it. It was more than three times as large as any other American glider mission on June 6, involving four different Troop Carrier groups with a total of 176 C-47s towing in an equal number of gliders. Elmira involved so many C-47s and gliders that to lessen the chance of midair collisions in the crowded sky over Landing Zone W, Troop Carrier planners had divided the mission into two echelons. The first would land just before sunset; the second, immediately after. If the plan worked, the gliders would deposit on the ground near Les Forges a total of twenty-four 75-millimeter and 105-millimeter howitzers, thirteen 57-millimeter antitank guns, fifty-nine jeeps, and 437 passengers, mostly medical personnel and gun crews. General Ridgway had foreseen that the 82nd Airborne would have an acute need for heavy weapons by the evening of June 6; but now, his immediate difficulty was to avert the calamity that could occur if the gliders attempted to fly in right on top of the German positions south of Ste. Mère Église.

Nearly four-fifths of Elmira's gliders were British-made Horsas. Constructed almost entirely of wood, a Horsa could carry nearly a four-ton load—double the capacity of a Waco. American pilots, however, considered the heavier Horsa more difficult to tow than a Waco, and even worse, it had a much shorter glide time, thereby increasing a glider pilot's already high stress level. Landing such a difficult and unfamiliar machine in the gloomy shadows of twilight in close proximity to a vigilant enemy would not be easy.

If Ridgway could not contact Collins aboard *Bayfield* to inform him of his current predicament, the general probably would have no better luck trying to alert Troop Carrier Command of the potential dangers awaiting the gliders near Les Forges. Nevertheless, he tried to divert Elmira to a safer landing spot by ordering his paratroopers to mark the same drop zone northwest of Ste. Mère Église on which the 505th Parachute Infantry had landed that morning, which was now securely under American control. Ridgway's effort, however, was in vain. The C-47 and glider pilots had received no intelligence back in England that the situation on the ground demanded remedial action. Furthermore, according to Elmira orders, pilots would be searching for their landing zone on the far side of Ste. Mère Église, more than three miles to the southeast of Ridgway's location, and chances were that they would never perceive the signals the paratroopers were displaying on the alternative zone.

They came streaming into Normandy from the east, directly over Utah Beach, at such low altitude and in formations of such impressive dimensions that any American soldier or sailor who witnessed the sight from below could not fail to gain supreme confidence that the Allies were now in Normandy to stay. For a while, Elmira seemed as though it might be a milk run: no enemy fire, nothing but friendly ships and troops below. But as they neared the landing zone near Les Forges, the alarmed pilots could discern that the enemy was full of life.

1st Lt. Tony Raibl
Communications Officer, HQ Battery, 82nd Airborne Division Artillery, 1948
In crossing the Channel in the waning light of D-Day, the sight below was truly something to behold! There were sky trains and ships of all types below, as far as the eye could see, not to mention fighter planes darting everywhere. . . . The first indication that maybe all was not well came when we were within sight of LZ "W." The lead planes of our serial were now well within the range of the enemy weapons [and] the Germans seemed to be concentrating their fire on the tug ships rather than the gliders. One must admire these C-47 pilots. Flying at less than 150 miles per hour at an altitude of 1,500 feet or less, with no armor protection and no self-sealing gas tanks, must be a trying experience that takes great courage.

When the gliders were cut loose from the tow ships, their pilots had only a few minutes to circle around, losing altitude with frightening rapidity, before picking a field on which to execute a landing. With luck, the passengers would emerge from the controlled crashes unscathed and proceed to carry out the jobs for which they had practiced for so long.

In an attempt to divert the gliders from the deadly ridge, Raff and others tossed orange smoke grenades in the pastures behind the frontline. It did little good.

Col. Edson Raff
Commander, Task Force Raff
To my horror, at 2100 the glider lift came in low over the valley. Every enemy weapon opened fire on the train of C-47 and gliders. Like watching a movie in which the full plot was known, I realized that the smoking, knocked-out tanks [from the 746th Tank Battalion] were appearing as landing markers in the evening light to the pilots, so unerringly did they release the gliders over that valley. Some Troop Carrier aircraft then circled slowly around, flying over the enemy across the valley on the way back to England. At least two were hit by fire and exploded over the enemy-held hill. Gliders were crashing into hedgerows all around the valley. Some even landed in the enemy's woods. The British gliders, made of wood, completely disintegrated in the crashes. Men tumbled out, completely stunned.

All around Task Force Raff, dozens of Horsas and Wacos floated down like swooping seagulls, generating not a sound except the rush of air over wings and along fuselages. The disciplined enemy waited until they were within range and then shattered the silence with a tempest of fire. The gliders ran the enemy's gauntlet, and when they finally touched down on earth, they bumped and skidded forward crazily as their pilots applied the brakes with all their strength to avoid crack-ups with hedgerows, trees, livestock — and even other gliders. In one pasture little bigger than the size of a football field north of an ancient chateau named Sébeville, eight gliders landed in quick succession, three of which crashed into the surrounding hedgerows. Those men lucky enough to survive the landings then faced the even greater peril of enemy fire the moment they emerged from the gliders to take their first steps in Normandy.

83rd Troop Carrier Squadron, 437th Group
D-Day Mission Report, Horsa No. 1, Serial 30, June 10, 1944
We landed at 2110 hours. We were fired on by machine guns, some bullets piercing the glider. We made a 90-degree turn to keep away from the fire. We crashed

through some trees and hit a four-foot ditch which washed out the nose wheel and smashed in the front of the glider. Lt. [Robert] Frank [the pilot] was injured, having a fractured left leg and deep gash on the left leg above the knee. We were sniped at on the ground and hit the ditch to avoid the fire. [Later] we had to chop the glider in half to get the jeep out, but the entire load and personnel were all right. Lt. Frank was removed in a milk cart to the hospital by a corporal, a French woman, and a French boy.

In retrospect, the Elmira mission was costly. According to an official air force study, 10 glider pilots died in the operation, 7 were unaccounted for, and 29 suffered wounds or injuries. As for the gliderists, 28 were killed and 106 injured or wounded, a loss rate of nearly one-third. Before D-Day, the paratroopers commonly used to speak of their glider comrades with contempt. But according to one paratrooper who witnessed the Elmira landings, "After Normandy I never heard an experienced paratrooper knock a glider man."

1st Lt. James Coyle
Company E, 505th Parachute Infantry, 82nd Airborne Division
I was standing in a ditch along the edge of a road when I heard a terrific crash behind me. As I turned I saw a glider crashing through some large trees across the road. I just had time to drop in the ditch. . . . The glider slid across the road, stopping with the wing right on top of me and extending along the ditch. By some miracle I didn't get a scratch, but when I crawled from under the wing I saw that the glider had struck a large tree, which split it the entire length of one side. The men seated on the other side were just crawling out of the wreckage. Of approximately thirty-five men and two officers in the glider, about half got out under their own power, including a lieutenant. From him I learned that they were from one of our divisional artillery battalions [the 320th]. He wanted to remain to aid his injured men, but he had an artillery piece in another glider that landed nearby, and we needed artillery support badly. By promising to take care of his injured men as best we could, I persuaded him to take his men who were not injured and get the gun in action. All of the men we dug out of the wreckage were unconscious or semi-conscious, and they were all badly injured.

1st Lt. Claibourne Cooperider
Headquarters Company, 2nd Battalion, 505th Parachute Infantry,
July 1944
While talking to my platoon leader, some gliders began to cut loose from C-47s. Knowing that I was in an open field and that any of these gliders might land on me,

I jumped into a foxhole with another man. No sooner had I gotten into this hole when a glider landed directly on top of the mortar platoon leader's hole into which he had ducked. The glider slid on and smashed into trees immediately in front of me, throwing the contents everywhere. I went off to see what help I could be and noticed one chap lying on his back trying to pull out his pistol. We reassured him as I ran over to him and asked him how many men were in the plane. He told me: nine. He did not seem too badly hurt and hearing other men calling for medics, I started looking for others who were in various stages of approaching death.

Every 82nd Airborne staff officer had grasped that the Elmira glider mission would be a risky endeavor, but the division's drop zones were a long way from Utah Beach, and given the distinct possibility that the 82nd would be isolated for several days, Ridgway presumed that help in the form of heavy weapons flown in by gliders on the evening of D-Day would be a critical necessity. However, the cost of the operation in men and equipment, as well as the fact that most of the Horsa and Waco glider loads had landed in the neighborhood of the 8th Infantry and Task Force Raff rather than within the 82nd's perimeter at Ste. Mère Église, established that it would have been wiser to hold off on such an immense glider operation until the situation on the ground became more clear to the Troop Carrier pilots who had to execute it.

In contrast, Maxwell Taylor had foreseen that if his 101st Airborne Division managed to achieve most of its D-Day missions, it in all likelihood would be firmly linked with the 4th Division by the evening of D-Day, with a secure and direct lifeline to Utah Beach. Most of the reinforcements and heavy weapons that Taylor would desperately need starting on June 7 to initiate his attack on Carentan could therefore be brought to Normandy not by glider, but by the much safer and more reliable method of U.S. Navy landing craft. According to the 101st's D-Day plan, virtually all of Taylor's glider-trained infantrymen and artillerymen would be brought to Normandy by sea starting at about 1:00 P.M. on June 6 and continuing through the following day. In fact, on D-Day, little more than 300 101st Airborne gliderists would land in Normandy by the method they had trained so long and hard to master.

Even so, Taylor had made plans for a limited glider mission on the evening of D-Day, code-named "Keokuk." Consisting of thirty-two Horsa gliders from the 434th Troop Carrier Group, based at Aldermaston airfield in England, Keokuk was scheduled to arrive at 9:00 P.M. on a landing zone two miles west of Ste. Marie du Mont, the same zone on which Brig. Gen. Donald Pratt, Taylor's second-in-command, had been killed in a glider crash early that morning. In total, the Horsas would convey to Normandy six antitank guns, several jeeps, and 157 men, mostly staff officers, signalmen, military policemen, and gun crews. Like all of the June 6 glider missions in the Cotentin Peninsula, however, the execution of the Keokuk mission was anything but smooth.

Headquarters, 101st Airborne Division
Summary, Keokuk Glider Mission, July 19, 1944
It had been felt that with the benefit of daylight [sunset on June 6 was not until 10:10 P.M.] it would be possible to use the Horsa glider in spite of the small number of fields of suitable size. The landing was executed with considerable loss as gliders crashed in trees and hedges, some landing south of our lines in the presence of the enemy. Out of this serial, fourteen were killed, thirty were injured or wounded, and ten were missing or captured. In spite of crash landings, the equipment suffered little damage.

M/Sgt. John McCarthy
Divisional HQ Company, G-1 Section, 101st Airborne Division
Our glider contained a jeep and attached trailer filled with equipment. The jeep was for Col. Gerald Higgins, the division chief of staff. . . . Our pilot did a superb job as he dropped onto the soft field. The tricycle landing gear prevented it from nosing over, and the glider came to rest twenty yards from a hedgerow. . . . Glider 3, which was just in front of ours, slammed into an earthen bank and collapsed in a pile of splinters. The co-pilot was killed, as were several MPs and headquarters people. I raced over to give aid and was immediately fired upon from a hedgerow corner. I assumed a prone position quickly. . . . I managed to snake forward to the wrecked glider, where I located an old friend, Sgt. John Paris. [Paris was an MP who, along with others, had orders to guard Taylor's command post.] He was one of the badly injured who had been pulled from within the wrecked glider. We had entered service together from Chicago, and both of us had been with the 101st Division since it was activated at Camp Claiborne, Louisiana in 1942. Unfortunately, Paris died a few minutes later from his injuries.

CHAPTER 10

Proud of You

FRICTION OF WAR

For the soldiers of General Barton's 4th Infantry Division, trudging over the causeways to Ste. Marie du Mont or slogging through the flooded pasturelands beyond the beach to St. Martin de Varreville, one thought prevailed over all others: The invasion is working. On the evening of D-Day, there could no longer be any doubt that the crucial assault for which the Ivy Division had practiced for years would turn out well. The GIs had been taught that the Germans would be exceptionally tough fighters, but at least during the first day of battle in Normandy, they had turned out to be nothing of the sort, and 4th Division casualties had been lighter than expected. The 4th Division's first combat of World War II had begun surprisingly well.

Brig. Gen. Theodore Roosevelt Jr.
Supernumerary General Officer, 4th Division, Letter to his wife, Eleanor, June 11, 1944
I must have walked twenty miles up and down that beach and over the causeways. Toward afternoon I went inland myself. Everything was in wild confusion still. It always is on a landing. Soldiers were everywhere. Occasionally groups of prisoners would pass, disheveled, dirty, unshaven. There was the continuous rattle of rifles and machine guns. I managed to see the three regimental COs [Van Fleet of

the 8th; Reeder of the 12th; Tribolet of the 22nd]. All were well set and confident. My sole food was a cake of D-ration chocolate, but I did not feel hungry. By this time the "Rough Rider" [Roosevelt's jeep] was ashore and Stevie [1st Lt. Marcus Stevenson, Roosevelt's aide] and I were set.

Ted Roosevelt clearly believed in that old army adage that generals must lead from the front. Roosevelt had been with the 4th Division for only a few months, but he was already a bona fide hero to those fighting men whose highest praise for a leader with stars on his helmet could be summed up by the simple phrase "a soldier's soldier." Roosevelt was indeed such a man, and the memory of him armed with nothing but a walking stick, limping up and down Utah Beach and the causeways beyond, was one that hundreds of 4th Division veterans would evoke in old age when they recalled D-Day. Such a remembrance was particularly poignant, because a month after the invasion, Roosevelt was dead.

Brig. Gen. Theodore Roosevelt Jr.
Supernumerary General Officer, 4th Division, Letter to his wife, Eleanor, June 14, 1944
The battalion CO with whom I landed [Lieutenant Colonel MacNeely, 2nd Battalion, 8th Infantry] told me that at first the men said, "That old man can't come in on the first wave." [I] may be old, but I can hold the ranks steady under losses and disaster and drive them forward. . . . By the way, Tubby Barton has recommended me for the Medal of Honor, but don't put in any hopes for that. The corps CO [Collins] does not like me, although he admits I'm a "very gallant officer." Of course I'd value the decoration if it came through—far more than promotion, but we, you and I, are not in this war for personal honor or notoriety. It's far too grave a matter for that. [The U.S. Army awarded Roosevelt the Medal of Honor posthumously on September 28, 1944. He had died of a heart attack on July 11.]

The Utah Beach assault obviously had succeeded, but Barton and Roosevelt still had much work to do. One of the most imperative goals in General Montgomery's Overlord plan was a speedy capture of the port of Cherbourg on the northern tip of the Cotentin Peninsula. Back in England, Collins's May 28 orders to his corps were a classic example of military simplicity: "VII Corps assaults Utah Beach on D-Day at H-Hour and captures Cherbourg with minimum delay." Collins's concept of how this goal must be achieved had been entirely clear. He had insisted that once the 4th Division had conquered the beach and moved inland over the causeways, Barton must focus his energy on Cherbourg, for the entire Allied military effort in Normandy could depend on a speedy opening of its vital harbor. According to Overlord plans, Cherbourg must be liberated by June 21, but if the Germans did not manage to stiffen their defenses to a much higher level than they had displayed on Utah Beach, optimistic Allied staff officers speculated that the Americans could be in Cherbourg much sooner than that.

Still, there were many problems. Cherbourg was thirty miles from Utah Beach, and the intervening ground was among the most favorable defensive terrain in France. Furthermore, given the enemy's resiliency in previous campaigns, it was entirely likely that the Germans would recover their balance after the shock of D-Day and make those thirty miles appear a lot longer to the American soldiers who must fight their way over that interval. To Collins, speed was essential: If the VII Corps could execute a blitzkrieg as crushing as the one the enemy had achieved in 1940, the Germans probably would never recover their balance after D-Day, and Barton's men could march into Cherbourg with little effort and, even better, few casualties.

But June 6, 1944, was just the beginning of a long war for the 4th Division, and its infantrymen had not yet learned to be cynical about objectives drawn on maps by staff officers armed with pencils, sitting in the relative comfort of rear-area headquarters. To anyone who carefully scrutinized the phase lines sketched by VII Corps planners on their top secret D-Day maps, those lines were categorically ambitious. By nightfall, the VII Corps expected the 4th Division's 12th Infantry to have penetrated thirteen miles inland, and for the 22nd Infantry, that figure was about ten miles. Those would be hefty marches even under the simplest of circumstances, and they were greatly complicated by the fact that they must be undertaken after an uncomfortable cross-Channel passage from England, a long journey from the troopships to Utah Beach in congested landing craft, and a disorderly assembly on a beach that was under intermittent and highly accurate enemy artillery fire.

Even worse, the narrow causeways leading off Utah Beach, although in theory adequate to carry the vast amount of traffic that must head inland on D-Day, turned out to be remarkably fragile. A demolished span over a tiny drainage ditch, a broken-down tank, or an unexpected enemy barrage could bring the lengthy columns of men and vehicles to a halt and trigger traffic jams worse than those on Broadway at rush hour. Experienced soldiers described such unforeseen disruptions in military operations as the "friction of war," but when that friction occurred on D-Day, it threw the VII Corps plan more and more behind schedule.

12th and 22nd Infantry: Afternoon, June 6, 1944

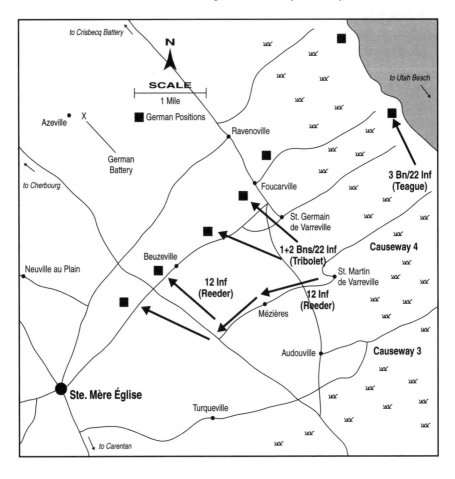

to Crisbecq Battery

N

SCALE
1 Mile

■ German Positions

to Utah Beach

Azeville X

German
Battery

to Cherbourg

Ravenoville

Foucarville

St. Germain
de Varreville

3 Bn/22 Inf
(Teague)

1+2 Bns/22 Inf
(Tribolet)

Causeway 4

Beuzeville

Neuville au Plain

St. Martin
de Varreville

12 Inf
(Reeder)

12 Inf
(Reeder)

Mézières

Audouville

Causeway 3

Ste. Mère Église

Turqueville

to Carentan

746th Tank Battalion
D-Day Action Report, July 1944
Along the route over the inundated area there was considerable congestion due to knocked-out vehicles blocking the narrow exit roads. At one point the entire battalion as well as many elements behind it were stopped by a bogged halftrack in the center of the road. Maj. [Lynn] Yeatts [XO, 746th Tank Battalion] on going forward found the personnel of the vehicle waiting for wreckers that could not have possibly gotten to it. Enemy fire was increasing in intensity, and it was imperative that the battalion clear the inundated area. The halftrack was pushed off the road into the bog and had already half-disappeared from view before the column was well under way.

Col. Red Reeder's 12th Infantry and Col. Hervey Tribolet's 22nd Infantry had avoided the congestion by shunning the roads and pushing their regiments directly across the flooded meadows beyond Utah Beach, but the movement of more than 4,000 heavily armed men through the mire was unavoidably slow. Moreover, the regiments' jeeps and trucks, as well as supporting tanks and artillery, could not follow. By the time the 12th and 22nd reached the far side of the marsh, it was already midafternoon, and they still had traveled only about half the distance their objective lines dictated they must reach by sunset.

Reeder's 12th Infantry came out of the swamp near St. Martin de Varreville, where the 502nd Parachute Infantry had already achieved the most important of its D-Day missions, among them the seizure of a nearby strongpoint supposedly occupied by a fearsome German battery—which turned out to have no functional guns. Reeder's men had orders to establish contact with the paratroopers, immediately pass through their positions, and head into the bocage to their objectives several miles north of Ste. Mère Église. If their preinvasion briefings were accurate, they would eventually run into Ridgway's 82nd Airborne Division en route to their D-Day phase lines.

Col. Russell Reeder
Commander, 12th Infantry, 4th Division
We walked out of the German-made lake at the village of St. Martin de Varreville, where ducks, angry at the intrusion, quacked along its cobblestone street. Everyone threw away his life preserver, and I ordered gas masks dropped to lighten the heavy load. I figured Germans would not use poison gas here. The masks were valuable, so they were piled up and a soldier was detailed to guard each pile. These three sol-

diers did not like being left behind. In a few minutes we began fighting German infantrymen in the rough hedgerows. . . . It was hard to see into a hedgerow field, or out of one. We were fighting Germans at ranges of 15 to 200 yards.

The 12th plodded westward out of St. Martin, past the hamlet of Mézières, where Sergeant Summers and his comrades of the 101st Airborne had only recently concluded their astonishingly bold attack on the farm buildings known as "XYZ." Plenty of German corpses were strewn around Mézières, obvious evidence that the deeper Reeder's men wandered into hedgerow country, the tougher their D-Day job was going to get. The 12th Infantry column soon reached an intersection, and scouts guided it to the right, or northwest, along a narrow road lined with lofty hedgerows, which were still new enough to the men to evoke wonderment. All the while, a troubled Reeder considered: Where is the 82nd?

Maj. Gerden Johnson
Executive, 1st Battalion, 12th Infantry, 4th Division
In his eagerness to press the attack forward, [Col. Reeder] was up with our assault companies, picking out points of advantage for the riflemen, urging and in some cases leading squads forward. . . . One of the reasons for the urgency was that part of our mission was to reach and relieve elements of the 82nd Airborne Division. . . . Col. [Charles] Jackson [CO, 1st Battalion] came up to inquire about the 82nd Airborne. I could see that lack of information about them was beginning to worry him too. Up ahead the assault companies had changed direction and again the Germans were contesting every field with machine gun and rifle fire as they fell slowly back. . . . We had not gone far up the road when at about 4 PM we came upon a lieutenant and three paratroopers from the 82nd Airborne. Their faces were blackened, their helmets camouflaged, and their clothing torn. They were the meanest looking men I have ever seen. "Don't ever give one of them sons-of-bitches a break. Kill them. The only good Germans are dead ones," [one paratrooper said]. I was still harboring the delusion that we were lucky to be fighting civilized Germans instead of barbaric Japs.

Colonel Tribolet of the 22nd Infantry had the exceptionally tough job of penetrating several miles into hedgerow country on Reeder's right flank with two-thirds of his regiment, while the remainder—the 3rd Battalion— attacked north up the shoreline from Utah Beach, striving to eliminate each enemy coastal strongpoint in succession for a distance of eight miles. As his men deployed and commenced their advance northward, Tribolet immediately grasped that he could not achieve his D-Day goals by sunset. The regiment's front extended for more than three miles, much of which was flooded grassland behind the coast, and as a result, Tribolet would have trouble communicating with and issuing orders to his men. Despite the help of U.S. Navy warships, the enemy's coastal strongpoints held out for longer than expected, and instead of the eight-mile advance stipulated in orders, the 3rd Battalion advanced less than four.

Meanwhile, Tribolet's other two battalions discovered a truth that every American outfit in Normandy would learn on D-Day and afterward. In this peculiar hedgerow country, military operations seemed to occur in slow motion. When an infantryman advanced across a meadow and took cover behind one of the bocage's ubiquitous earthen embankments topped with leafy shrubs, he never knew for sure whether a single German soldier or an entire enemy company of 150 men—or perhaps no one at all—lay beyond the next hedgerow. As all GIs agreed after only a single day of combat in the Cotentin, this was not the way they had been trained to fight a war.

U.S. Army VII Corps
"Lessons Learned While in France," July 26, 1944
Hedgerow fighting as done by the Germans in Normandy was very confusing to our troops initially. It was difficult to figure out just how to attack an enemy who was able to change positions so rapidly without being observed. As we gained in experience we realized that by working in small teams with automatic weapons supporting these teams, we could move down the sides of the hedgerows with a minimum of casualties and drive the enemy from his positions.

Meanwhile, the regiment that had borne the brunt of the amphibious assault on Utah Beach, Colonel Van Fleet's 8th Infantry, had moved inland across the causeways as planned, but as soon as the troops penetrated into the hedgerows, they quickly learned the same hard lesson as their 12th and 22nd Infantry brethren. This bocage would take some time to get used to, and there certainly would be no blitzkriegs here. The only sensible course of action would be to probe steadily but cautiously forward, but by the time the 8th Infantry stumbled upon solid enemy opposition on the prominent ridge south of Ste. Mère Église—the same pocket of resistance that would stymie Task Force Raff—it was too late for Van Fleet to do anything more than order his men to dig in for the night and plan for an attack on the morrow. Somewhere beyond that ridge lay Ridgway's 82nd Airborne, but the much coveted linkup with the paratroopers would have to be delayed.

Lt. Col. William Gayle
Historical Officer, 4th Division, "The 8th Infantry on D-Day," June 1944

The 3rd Battalion moved west of Ste. Marie du Mont for almost three miles, meeting little or no resistance. The battalion reduced a pocket of resistance upon crossing the north-south highway [at Les Forges] and was ordered to swing north along this all-important road. Late in the evening, as the battalion approached the high ground one mile south of Ste. Mère Église, the Germans gave surefire indication of the bitter battle to come. When it became apparent that the Germans, holding the commanding ground, were going to force a fight, Lt. Col. Strickland [CO, 3rd Battalion] decided to withdraw some 200 yards and dig in for the night. . . . The 2nd Battalion began picking up some loose ends as it moved from Pouppeville to Ste. Marie du Mont and then to Boutteville, protecting the regiment's left-rear. . . . During this time the 1st Battalion had been moving west without contact with the rest of the regiment. At Reuville, the 1st Battalion met the same type of opposition that the 3rd Battalion was encountering. Late in the evening the resistance at Reuville was finally overcome, but when the battalion attempted to push into Turqueville that night, it was repulsed with several casualties. Thus ended D-Day for the 8th Infantry. In this short period of time, the regiment had broken the beach defenses along a two-mile front and shoved the enemy back seven miles. Considering the accomplishments and the pre-invasion estimates, the number of casualties was extremely low: 29 killed and 110 wounded.

TOUGH 'OMBRES

The Utah Beach invasion was undeniably a 4th Infantry Division show. With the exception of some 82nd and 101st Airborne gliderists who came ashore from U.S. Navy landing craft rather than their customary Wacos and Horsas, virtually every infantryman who waded through the surf onto Utah Beach up until late afternoon on D-Day wore the 4th Division's green-and-brown ivy-leaf patch on his left shoulder. But even a division as skilled as the 4th could not sweep through the Cotentin and capture Cherbourg by the target date of June 21 without substantive help. Accordingly, in expectation of the tough fights that would mark the route northward to Cherbourg, VII Corps commander Collins resolved to land as many infantrymen as possible on Utah Beach on D-Day. When the last of the 4th Division's nine infantry battalions had made it ashore shortly after noon on June 6 and commenced its inland trek, Collins turned to a follow-up division, the 90th, to sustain the steady flow of American riflemen into Normandy. The beach would be secure by the time the men of the 90th Division took their first steps in France, but there certainly would be a need for plentiful fighting men in the near future . . . and then the 90th's turn would come.

The 4th and 90th Divisions were almost opposites. The 4th had been raised eighteen months before America entered World War II and was composed of historic units with venerable traditions from the old Regular army; the 90th was a wartime creation, activated in March 1942 in Texas and populated overwhelmingly by conscripts fresh out of basic training who were still learning the fundamentals of soldiering from Field Manual 21-100, the timeless *Soldier's Handbook*. But despite their fundamental differences, the 4th and 90th shared several traits. Both had spent a considerable period in the States as experimental motorized divisions, an idea that the top brass eventually abandoned, much to the chagrin of GIs who enjoyed riding in trucks more than marching. Both divisions also were latecomers to the European theater: The 4th was not shipped to Britain until late January 1944; the 90th arrived in early April. Above all, virtually no one in either division had experienced combat before D-Day. For both divisions, the Cotentin Peninsula would be the grueling setting in which the men would learn how actual war differed so fundamentally from training.

The 90th's shoulder patch featured the letters "T" and "O" in red, superimposed on a square piece of brown cloth. The "T" stood for Texas, the "O" for Oklahoma, the two states from which most of the 90th's recruits had been drawn in 1917. In 1942, the 90th hauled in draftees to its Texas base camp from all over the United States—although reportedly 20 percent of its men were Texans—and the division's leaders needed a hard-hitting new slogan to build up their troops' morale. From that moment forward, the men of the 90th affirmed that the "T" and "O" signified that the division was populated entirely by "Tough 'Ombres." More than two years of rigorous training had instilled in the troops an attitude that the 90th truly was tough, altogether set for its pivotal role in Normandy.

On D-Day, General Barton exerted temporary control over two battalions of the 90th's 359th Infantry, commanded by Col. Clarke Fales, a fifty-year-old West Point classmate of Collins and Ridgway. Loaded up in nine U.S. Navy LCIs, Fales and his force of close to 2,000 men would take their first steps into the continent of Europe at 4:00 P.M. The test for which the 90th had prepared for so long back in Texas was at hand. The division's personnel may have regarded themselves as tough, but the Germans were undeniably tough too. Who would turn out to be tougher?

1st Lt. J. Q. Lynd
Company A, 359th Infantry, 90th Division
The morning of June 6 was wet and chilly for us, and the metal deck was slippery. The sea was choppy and rough as forty-two of us climbed over the side and

loaded into the small prow-ramped LCVP [probably a larger LCM, as LCVPs typically carried only thirty-one men]. Almost immediately as our group started the run toward the beach, the [LCM] to our right blew: a brilliant flash, thunderous crack explosion. We ducked, our craft lurched, seemed to lift in a quick bucking motion, then dropped, slapping the ocean surface with a terrific impact. What happened? A mine? Artillery hit? We'll never know. . . . Utah Beach was a confused array of metal obstacles, scrambled barbed wire, columns of thick black smoke, the pungent odor of burning rubber, crumpled bodies of dead and wounded soldiers. . . . Our orders were to keep moving, attack, do not stop, move to the high ground as rapidly as possible. The units that followed would care for the wounded. Our soldiers obeyed as they had been trained.

90th Infantry Division
"A History of the 90th Division in World War II," 1946

As the boats approached the shore, the troops leaped into the hip-deep water with weapons held high overhead, raced across the artillery-churned sands of Utah Beach, past the burning vehicles caught in previous barrages, and found momentary protection at a seawall 400 yards distant. The beach was constantly shelled, and inevitable casualties were suffered. PFC David Atcuson was the first to fall, the first among many in the 90th to give his life. [The 90th lost 2,963 men killed in action in World War II.] At four in the afternoon the disembarking of [the 1st and 3rd Battalions, 359th Infantry, commanded by Maj. Clyde Benbrook and Lt. Col. James Casey] was completed. Still attached to the 4th Division, the two battalions moved immediately to an assembly area near St. Martin de Varreville, approximately two kilometers west of the beach. That same evening, PFC Samuel Maples, outposting the assembly area, detected elements of an enemy patrol and fired his BAR. Two Germans were killed, one wounded, and one taken prisoner. And so the 90th Division for the first time drew blood.

The 90th Division was ashore in its entirety by June 8. The original Overlord plan called for it to join with Barton's 4th Division in a concerted offensive to the north aimed at the speedy capture of Cherbourg. In actuality, however, the 90th never got near Cherbourg. General Collins fundamentally changed the 90th's role after D-Day when the 82nd Airborne's situation along the Merderet River finally crystallized. Several pockets of paratroopers were cut off west of the Merderet, and Collins ordered the 90th to join with the 82nd in an offensive across that river to succor those isolated troops. Collins then directed the 90th to initiate a vigorous attack to the west, straight across the neck of the Cotentin, an offensive that, if successful, would cut the peninsula in two, isolate Cherbourg, and lead to the eventual demise of its German garrison.

It would therefore be along the Merderet River, and not in the Cherbourg hills, that the 90th Division would get its first real taste of battle. To attack across the flat and featureless Merderet marshlands and then push westward into the bocage would have challenged even a veteran division; for the green 90th Division, it turned out to be an exceptionally harsh introduction to war. A dissatisfied General Collins later noted that the 90th Division's personnel, the so-called "Tough 'Ombres," displayed "inadequate training and lack of leadership" in their first few days of combat, and he and others subsequently initiated extensive command changes to correct those deficiencies. Apparently it worked. Four months later, the man who had led the 8th Infantry ashore on Utah Beach, James Van Fleet, took over the 90th Division, and his army commander, George Patton, observed in 1945 that the 90th ultimately became "one of the greatest divisions that ever fought."

THE RIGHT PLACE AT THE RIGHT TIME

The Americans would soon learn that June nights in Normandy were astonishingly short. "We have these long days with only a few hours of night," Ted Roosevelt wrote to his wife on June 12. "We have too little time for rest and sleep." On D-Day, full darkness did not set in until such a late hour that a GI, lacking any artificial light, could easily read outdoors until after 10:00 P.M. By that time, the sun was just about to dip below the western horizon, heralding a sharp fall in temperature that would make the night uncomfortable for those many soldiers whose uniforms were still saturated from their passage to the beach or their treks across the inundated marshlands. Elongated shadows of the bocage's omnipresent hedgerows and apple trees cast by the last moments of muted sunshine reminded General Barton that he must now retire to his makeshift command post near the beach and evaluate his 4th Division's performance on the day that all agreed would be remembered for generations.

When Barton peered at his situation map, running his finger along the latest known positions of his frontline units, he realized that the Utah Beach invasion would go down in history as one of those rare military operations that in large measure had gone according to plan. True, there had been problems: The initial landing south of the intended target beaches could have thrown the invasion into disarray, but thanks to General Roosevelt and Colonels Van Fleet and Caffey, it did nothing of the sort. Furthermore, the situation within the beachhead at nightfall was far from perfect, and Barton had to deal with some exasperating and troubling information gaps, notably the whereabouts and status of Ridgway's 82nd Airborne Division. But that was war, and Barton was sufficiently familiar with its proverbial fog to know that whatever intelligence difficulties he faced, the enemy certainly was in much worse shape. Even the pessimists had to agree that the invasion had succeeded, and Barton resolved that that success must continue the following day.

Maj. Gen. Raymond Barton
Commander, 4th Infantry Division

June 6 ended with vast satisfaction to me. Neither myself nor my division had ever been under fire. We were well trained and had top ésprit de corps. By nightfall of D-Day we were ashore, well inland, an intact, operating division—and now proven veterans. From then on the 4th never had any doubts about doing its job, whatever it might be. The division commander realized that he knew how to put his troops at the right place at the right time and that they would do the right things. They did.

D-Day now belonged to the ages: Politicians had conceived it; generals had planned it; thousands of anonymous fighting men had executed it; and historians would define and interpret it. On first consideration, any historical dissection of the Utah Beach portion of the D-Day assault could not fail to draw a fundamental conclusion: Unmistakably, the invasion had worked. By sunset on June 6, 4th Division GIs had linked up with 101st Airborne paratroopers at Ste. Marie du Mont and Pouppeville and St. Martin de Varreville, and with those convergences, the amphibious war for which the Ivy Division had trained for so long came to an abrupt end and a new and vastly different war began. It was the beginning of the struggle that Americans had been told would eventually lead to Hitler's downfall, and now the first resolute steps on the road to Berlin had been taken.

Lt. Col. Ulrich Gibbons
Headquarters, 4th Division Artillery

As we pulled into an apple orchard around sunset, there were paratroopers of the 101st Airborne riding Normandy farm horses around. One of them, who had found some Calvados [an intoxicating Norman apple brandy], said: "Colonel, do you want to see some of these damn German potato-masher grenades go off?" It was in the mood and temper of that day that I said, "Why not?" So we walked a

*"D-Day now belonged to the ages." Members of the U.S. Navy's 2nd Beach
Battalion on Utah Beach examine German "Goliath" miniature tracked
vehicles, which were packed with explosives and could be maneuvered and
detonated by remote control.* U.S. NAVY, NATIONAL ARCHIVES.

few yards off the road and spent ten minutes throwing German grenades into the
mare cage behind a farmer's barn. . . . However, by midnight Operations, 4th Division Artillery was in full swing: communications established to our artillery battalions, firing charts set up, operations reports and fire plans for the next day's
combat prepared. The 4th Division was operational on the continent of Europe—
headed toward Cherbourg.

The 4th Division's war had undeniably changed in a hurry, but for the
4th's D-Day invasion partner, the 101st Airborne Division, that change was
even more acute. Thousands of 101st paratroopers had descended in the
dark twenty hours earlier into the swamplands and bocage of the Cotentin
Peninsula, and those twenty hours had changed forever the way generals
would think about warfare.

For most of June 6, the 101st's commander, Maj. Gen. Maxwell Taylor, could scarcely fathom the whereabouts of his division. The majority of

his paratroopers seemed to have vanished into the hedgerows, and for Taylor to discern with certainty the key events that were occurring around him was nearly impossible. However, no one—least of all paratroopers—had expected this new form of warfare to be neat and comprehensible, with orderly arrows drawn on maps by staff officers delineating the advances of military units with all the certainty of chess moves. At least for the first few hours in Normandy, those parachute units existed only in staff officers' imaginations, and during that period, the 101st by necessity had fought an unfathomable war in which leaders, including Taylor himself, guided countless small groups of men over unfamiliar terrain to seize key objectives before the stunned Germans could recover their senses. Taylor later summarized this untidy stage of the 101st's first combat operation with these memorable words: "Never were so few led by so many."

Maj. Gen. Maxwell Taylor
Commander, 101st Airborne Division, February 1946
While I had a reasonably clear idea of what the local situation around Pouppeville was, I knew nothing at all about the other elements of the division. All commanders had, however, the prearranged plans which were ample to meet any developments of the situation. I felt no concern about the need of redirecting the efforts of the local commanders during the first twenty-four hours.

Only as the D-Day situation gradually crystallized could Taylor head for his crude command post at Hiesville and leave the patrols to more junior officers. When 4th Division troops emerged from the causeways and marshlands beyond the beach to link up with the 101st, Taylor could finally conclude that his division's airdrop for the most part had been successful; and when at sunset on June 6 he scrutinized his situation map, he could note with profound satisfaction that in the last twenty hours, the 101st Airborne, with the help of the 4th Division, had executed a thorough reversal upon the enemy. As both sides dug in for the night, Taylor's men for the most part held the initiative; and rather than launching their customary counterattacks the following day, anxious enemy commanders worried more about how to extricate the many pockets of German troops that had been cut off by the Americans' coordinated sea and air assault. If this was what a massive airborne operation could do to the enemy, then perhaps the proponents of vertical envelopment had been right all along: This type of military operation would change the way wars were fought.

But General Taylor's attitude on the night of June 6 was by no means entirely positive. Much of Col. Howard Johnson's 501st Parachute Infantry

Utah Beachhead: Close of Day, June 6, 1944

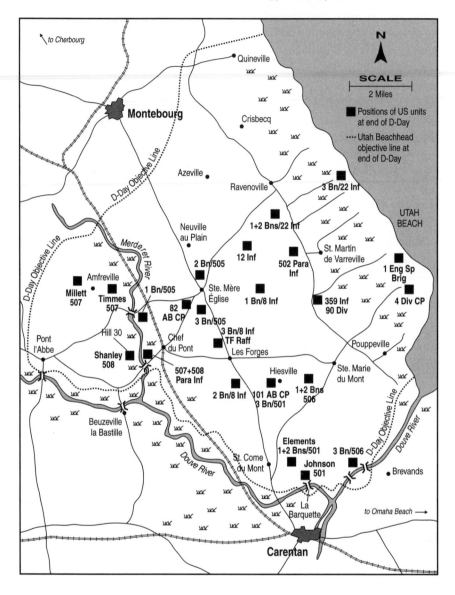

and a single battalion of the 506th, which had landed on the southernmost of the D-Day drop zones six miles from Utah Beach, were unaccounted for. One of Johnson's key objectives was the village of St. Côme du Mont, but the enemy's unexpectedly tenacious defense of that area on D-Day had prevented the Americans from seizing it. With St. Côme du Mont and its critical road in enemy hands, the Germans held a particularly favorable counterattack route against the southern flank of the Utah beachhead, and if they could rush mobile reinforcements to that sector, such a counterattack could be devastating to Taylor's scattered troops.

During the Overlord planning process, the Allied top brass had always been troubled by the lengthy separation of Utah Beach from the other four D-Day landing sites. The generals' tension would not lessen until the Utah beachhead was securely linked with the others, but the enemy's firm retention on D-Day of the road connecting St. Côme du Mont with Carentan yielded obvious evidence to the Allies that such a linkage would not be easy to achieve. Even worse, the 101st Airborne could expect no immediate assistance from American forces pushing westward from Omaha Beach, for that invasion had experienced unforeseen troubles and nearly turned out to be a disaster. Although General Gerow's V Corps had eventually established a slender foothold ashore on D-Day, the 29th Division's mission of linking up with the 101st Airborne somewhere near Carentan would now be delayed—for how long, no one could tell.

Taylor was satisfied with his division's D-Day performance, but such hard work lay ahead that his satisfaction must have been merely momentary. The 101st did well on June 6, but its achievements could be significantly diminished if the enemy could prevent the linkup of the Utah and Omaha beachheads and launch an effective counterattack against this vulnerable seam of Collins's VII Corps front. Taylor therefore grasped that the 101st must capture St. Côme du Mont and Carentan without delay, a job that promised to be just as difficult as the division's D-Day mission.

To prepare for that strenuous fight on the morrow, Taylor and his chief aides would first need a good rest.

Maj. Gen. Maxwell Taylor
Commander, 101st Airborne Division
We were all dead tired: We got to Hiesville [the 101st's command post], verified that we had the place well defended, and then Brig. Gen Tony McAuliffe [the 101st's artillery commander] and I decided to get some sleep. We got upstairs in this farmhouse, where there were two lumpy beds. Tony undressed, and I said, "Tony, you'd better keep your pants on because this thing isn't in the bag by any

means." But against my advice he undressed. We had just gotten to sleep when the Krauts came in and bombed the hell out of the place; and the question was who could get down the stairs first. I had my pants on, and I had a definite advantage, so I got downstairs before Tony could—but it almost wrecked my feet. [Taylor had suffered a leg injury playing squash on June 4, and he later noted that "it was torture to walk for the first week in France."]

WE FIGHT ALONE

They had failed to establish radio contact with anyone beyond their lines, and the units outside those lines had failed to reach them. Had the invasion plan worked as intended, General Ridgway would have been in regular communication throughout D-Day with Collins aboard the VII Corps command ship *Bayfield*, and the 4th Division and Task Force Raff would have made it all the way through to the 82nd Airborne Division's stronghold at Ste. Mère Église by sunset. But like so many complex military operations in World War II, the execution of the 82nd's June 6 airdrop clearly demonstrated that theory does not always coincide with reality. Accordingly the 82nd's paratroopers and gliderists must fight on alone until at least June 7— and perhaps long after that.

Those 82nd men who had learned the hard lessons of airborne warfare in Sicily and Italy in 1943, including Generals Gavin and Ridgway, had come to expect this kind of uncertainty in the Normandy invasion, and in retrospect, they would profess that the division's seemingly fragile status on the night of June 6 had not unduly alarmed them.

Maj. Gen. Matthew Ridgway
Commander, 82nd Airborne Division

We couldn't get in touch with anybody—neither the troops that were supposed to be coming in over the beaches by now, nor with anybody back in England, nor with anybody afloat. In short, we were in the typical situation for which you must be prepared when an airborne division goes into battle. . . . For thirty-six hours we had no means of knowing how well or badly we were faring.

Despite the considerable percentage of 82nd Airborne paratroopers who were unaccounted for on the night of D-Day, when Ridgway contemplated his division's fortunes in his austere command post just southwest of Ste. Mère Église, he at least had the satisfaction of knowing that his men had accomplished the most important objectives specified by Collins's May 28 invasion orders. The 505th Parachute Infantry had seized Ste. Mère

Église at dawn, and despite the enemy's determined efforts to take it back, at nightfall the Americans were in firm control of that town and the important roadways that passed through it. True, the 505th was almost surrounded, but that unfortunate situation was expected to change on June 7 with the arrival of the 4th Division and Raff's tanks and armored cars.

Lt. Col. Benjamin Vandervoort
Commander, 2nd Battalion, 505th Parachute Infantry
[In late afternoon of June 6,] Col. Bill Ekman [CO, 505th] stressed the importance of stopping the Germans at Ste. Mère Église so that they could not continue south to attack the amphibious landing areas. . . . As the sun sank, firing was going on along the entire northern edge of Ste. Mère Église. German patrols were edging in to force us to expose our camouflaged positions by firing so they could be brought under artillery and mortar fire later. The airborne evening resupply serial came in over our original drop zone to the northwest, releasing bundles and gliders. [This was at about 9:00 P.M.] The [Troop Carrier] pilots had guts. They took no evasive action. The C-47s flew low and fast in a tight double column straight and level through a curtain of flak and small arms fire that was thrown up by the Germans attacking from Neuville au Plain. From time to time an airplane would be hit: trailing smoke and losing what little altitude it had, it would fall out of column and disappear to the east toward the invasion beaches.

Farther to the west, the 82nd Airborne controlled the vital Merderet River bridges at La Fière and Chef du Pont, and with those two sites in American hands at the end of D-Day, the enemy would not be capable of launching a counterattack against the 4th and 101st Divisions from the west anytime soon. The status of those 82nd Airborne paratroopers who had dropped west of the Merderet on June 6 was downright bleak, however. Both the 507th and 508th Regiments had failed to accomplish their D-Day goals; an even greater source of concern was the enemy's forceful response to the sudden arrival of the Americans in their midst. The Germans had swiftly pushed the paratroopers into several isolated pockets, and their ability to hang on until Ridgway could organize an attack across the Merderet was doubtful. But a crisis of this kind, which might have distressed a more conventional general, did not distress Ridgway. According to Ridgway, such a predicament would always be the normal consequence of a massive airdrop behind enemy lines, and any airborne commander who could not deal with that sort of pressure should transfer to a conventional infantry division before it was too late.

Maj. Gen. Matthew Ridgway
Commander, 82nd Airborne Division, November 12, 1948
I am not aware that any unit in the Normandy assault accomplished its mission completely by June 7. The 82nd Division had by this time accomplished the major part of its several missions. It had strong forces on the west bank of the Merderet opposite the La Fière causeway. It had intermittent patrol contact with these forces. It had yet to make solid contact with all of its units west of that river, and in the case of Lt. Col. [Thomas] Shanley's battalion [2nd, 508th], didn't do so until the forenoon of June 9. It did, however, have all the terrain that the VII Corps was then in any position to exploit.

For the most part, the 82nd Airborne Division was populated by soldiers who adhered to Ridgway's way of thinking. If the rigorous methods by which Ridgway had trained his troops were supposed to yield not only skilled fighters, but confident ones, D-Day proved that those methods had succeeded.

Lt. Col. Robert Wienecke
Operations Officer, 82nd Airborne Division, G-3 Report, Evening,
June 6, 1944
Short 60 percent infantry; 90 percent artillery. Combat efficiency: excellent.

Maj. Gen. Matthew Ridgway
Commander, 82nd Airborne Division, Message to All 82nd Soldiers,
9:51 A.M., June 7, 1944
To all regiments: Proud of you—Inform all ranks. [Signed], Maj. Gen. Ridgway.

CHAPTER 11

The First Day
of a Long Struggle

THE COURAGE OF TWO O'CLOCK IN THE MORNING
And so it was done. The Allies had their coveted foothold in northwest
Europe, and suddenly the light at the end of the proverbial tunnel appeared
much brighter. Back on the home front, there had always been supreme
confidence that Hitler and his hated Nazis would eventually be brought to
a violent end, but how long would it take? True, there had already been
important victories, but the road to Berlin still might take years to travel,
and the Germans had given no signals that they were ready to quit. After
June 6, 1944, however, that road seemed considerably shorter than it had
been twenty-four hours earlier. D-Day had done what it was supposed to
do; and perhaps the clear and immediate signal it offered the Des Moines
housewife, the Welsh coal miner, the Brooklyn teenager, and the fighting
man overseas was the heartening realization that their confidence in final
victory had not been misplaced.

If the Nazis were not ready to quit, then the Allies must make them. It
would take 335 more days of hard fighting to do it, and it would cost too
many good men, but the invasion of Normandy imparted incontrovertible
evidence to the Nazis that the Western Allies were willing to pay a high
price to bring the war to an end as they had always said they would: with the
unconditional surrender of Germany. If the Allies continued to display the

skill and resolve they had exhibited on June 6, 1944, that surrender could not be far off.

On D-Day, the Allies struck the enemy in Normandy a devastating blow from which it would take the surprised Germans days to recover. Across a front of fifty miles, the Allies surged ashore on five invasion beaches. Despite the energetic efforts on the part of Field Marshal Rommel to fiercely contest the Allies' amphibious assault directly on the shoreline, the German coastal defenders were overwhelmed, in most cases in just an hour or two, and could do virtually nothing on June 6 to stop the onslaught. Meanwhile, Allied air forces had dropped three airborne divisions behind enemy lines, obvious proof to the Germans that they were not the only ones to have mastered the innovative techniques of modern warfare. In truth, on June 6, 1944, the creators of blitzkrieg had themselves become one of its victims.

Still, when the dust triggered by the D-Day invasion finally settled, Ike and Monty and Bradley perceived that their plans for the Normandy assault had perhaps been a little too ambitious. By nightfall on June 6, none of the five beachheads had achieved the sizable dimensions that staff officers had drawn onto the plan books' overlays with bold arrows and phase lines. At one beach—Omaha—the invaders were so far short of their terrain goals that Overlord's planners wondered whether that invasion's timetable was irretrievably broken.

Although the Utah Beach invasion had come closer to accomplishing its D-Day objectives than any of the other four assaults, the VII Corps commander, General Collins, recalled that he was "not altogether satisfied with the corps progress" at the close of June 6. He decided to depart his command ship *Bayfield* early on June 7 and head ashore to solve what he considered his two most pressing problems. First, Ridgway's isolated 82nd Airborne Division must be promptly located and succored; second, the 4th Division had to set out immediately on the long road to Cherbourg before the Germans had time to recover from the shock of the invasion.

These were hardly crises on the scale faced by Collins's counterpart on Omaha Beach, General Gerow, whose troops clung to a beachhead less than a mile deep by sunset on D-Day. In contrast, the 4th Division had penetrated more than six miles inland, and once the inevitable linkup with the 82nd was achieved, the beachhead would expand by a considerable degree. If the Allies' object was to pour as many fighting men as possible into the Cotentin Peninsula on D-Day, Collins had succeeded admirably. According to figures computed by the VII Corps staff, a total of 21,328 men, 1,742 vehicles, and 1,695 tons of supplies were conveyed ashore across Utah

Beach on June 6. Furthermore, more than 14,000 American paratroopers and gliderists descended into Normandy on D-Day, and when that figure was added to the computation, the total number of soldiers who entered the Cotentin Peninsula on June 6 swelled to more than 35,000 men.

Lt. Gen. Omar Bradley
Commander, First U.S. Army, Autobiography, **A Soldier's Story,** *1951*

In contrast to Omaha, where the shadow of catastrophe had hung over our heads all day, the landing on Utah had gone more smoothly than during rehearsal [Exercise Tiger] five weeks before. As G-2 [Col. Benjamin Dickson, First Army's intelligence officer] had predicted, the beach was held by second-rate static troops. Except for casemated artillery north of Utah, the resistance quickly collapsed. In tallying up G-1 [Col. Joseph O'Hare, First Army's personnel officer] reports almost a week later, I found that Collins had cracked the wall on Utah Beach at a cost of fewer than 350 casualties in his assault force. [Actually, VII Corps casualties were much higher than Bradley's figure.]

If, as Monty insisted, the addition of Utah Beach to the Overlord assault plan would substantially enhance the Allies' chance of overall success in the Normandy invasion, Collins had to ensure that his VII Corps assault on D-Day would work. That the Utah invasion was in fact a brilliant military triumph was attributable to several factors, the most significant of which was that the American assault troops, both seaborne and airborne, were superlatively prepared for the task. In sharp contrast, the German defenders were not. The Utah invasion was also marked by an exceptionally high level of teamwork between American ground, air, and naval forces, an accomplishment that up until that time in the war had been lacking in Allied combined operations.

Had the enemy been better prepared to receive the invasion, and had the Americans failed to prepare their assault so meticulously and execute it with such consummate skill, the Utah landing certainly would not have been the smashing success it was. In that event, the capture of Cherbourg and the linkup with the Omaha beachhead would have been substantially delayed, a result that easily could have turned Utah Beach into another Anzio—a stagnant beachhead firmly sealed off from the main battlefront by vigilant and unmovable Germans. But in reality, the outcome of the Utah Beach operation was entirely different from the flawed result at Anzio, a fundamental dissimilarity that could be ascribed to a level of dynamism exhibited by American assault troops and their leaders at all command levels on D-Day that was not displayed at Anzio.

The major unit tasked by Collins to execute the Utah Beach invasion, the 4th Infantry Division, was unquestionably one of the most highly trained outfits in the U.S. Army in the spring of 1944. Only rarely in military history has a unit endured such a lengthy and vigorous wartime training period in preparation for its first combat as the Ivy Division did in World War II. Upon America's entry into the war in December 1941, the 4th was one of those rare U.S. Army units that were operational and nearly ready for combat, although at that time its expertise was noticeably below the high levels it would achieve by 1944. For two years prior to D-Day, the 4th trained continuously for modern warfare under one commander, the redoubtable Maj. Gen. Raymond Barton, who guided his unit with an iron hand through rigorous amphibious warfare exercises at Camp Gordon Johnston, Florida, and on the beaches of Devon, England, at the U.S. Army Assault Training Center. In June 1944, no unit in the U.S. Army deployed to the European theater could claim to be better trained in amphibious warfare techniques than the 4th Division.

The regiment that was in the 4th Division's vanguard in the Utah invasion, the 8th Infantry, had the good fortune to enhance its military skills for three years under the leadership of one of the U.S. Army's most outstanding soldiers, Col. James Van Fleet, who only a few years later would rise to four-star rank in command of the Eighth Army during the Korean War. When the 8th first entered combat on Utah Beach, it was unquestionably ready, and it struck the German coastal defenders such a concentrated blow, accompanied by an impressive display of resolute leadership at all levels from squad leaders to regimental commander, that the unfortunate enemy did not stand a chance.

The contrast between the 4th Division and the German unit deployed along the Cotentin's east coast on D-Day, the 709th Division, was acute. The 709th was a mediocre outfit with questionable morale and limited mobility, spread so thinly over a coastal sector more than thirty miles in length that only a portion of a single battalion received the brunt of the Americans' ferocious assault on the morning of June 6. The unquenchable demands of the Russian front had caused the German high command to transfer the 709th's best troops out of the division long before D-Day, in some cases to be replaced by unenthusiastic Soviet prisoners of war convinced to pick up arms against the Allies.

Furthermore, Utah's low sand dunes were hardly dominating defensive terrain, and the 709th's entirely unimpressive coastal fortifications did not make this naturally mediocre line of resistance much better. If there were not enough German troops to make the coast impregnable, Field Marshal

Rommel's notion of coastal defense would rely on millions of mines and thousands of beach obstacles strewn over potential landing sites as a means of frustrating an Allied assault. By D-Day, however, the 709th Division had neither the resources nor the manpower to plant those impediments on the east coast of the Cotentin Peninsula in the numbers Rommel had envisioned. Ultimately, on Utah Beach, Rommel's mines and beach obstacles amounted to nothing more than a minor nuisance to the American invaders.

Even with all its handicaps and shortcomings, the 709th could have offered much more stubborn resistance on Utah Beach and the critical exit roads behind the coast had it received a definite indication from the German high command on June 5 or earlier that an Allied invasion was imminent. On D-Day, however, the American assault undeniably caught the Germans by surprise, and that detail alone reduced the effectiveness of their defenses all across the Normandy front by a substantial factor.

In the aftermath of the invasion, those enemy coastal defenders lucky enough to have survived the fury of the American assault on Utah Beach reflected indignantly on the almost complete lack of support proffered by the German high command on D-Day. The illustrious Luftwaffe was nowhere in sight. Even worse, German reserves deployed in the Cotentin interior, including the first-rate 91st *Luftlande* Division, never showed up. According to the downhearted defenders, with such abysmal levels of support, the defenders' nearly immediate submission to the invaders' application of overwhelming force on Utah Beach was inevitable.

The principal explanation for the 709th Division's isolation on June 6 was that Allied air forces had gained air supremacy over northern France well before D-Day. As a result, the Luftwaffe could not thwart any Allied air operation, be it a bomber attack, fighter patrol, reconnaissance mission, or an airborne drop, nor could German bombers interfere even marginally with the massive Allied invasion fleet during its cross-Channel passage. This was a decisive factor in the Allies' success, for the 709th's defenders could not hide from Allied air detection, nor could they prevent Allied bombers from attacking coastal fortifications with impunity. When the Americans struck at 6:30 A.M. on June 6, even junior leaders had a remarkably clear picture of the Germans' shoreline defenses gained from relentless air reconnaissance. Furthermore, immediately before H-Hour, the enemy was subject to a concentrated and highly effective aerial attack by nearly 300 Ninth Air Force B-26 Marauder bombers, a bombardment that the Germans could not stop, and that left most of the surviving defenders stunned.

The most alarming contemplation in the minds of 709th Division soldiers before dawn on D-Day was that thousands of American parachutists and glider troops had suddenly been deposited somewhere behind the shoreline, for what intent the German coastal defenders had not yet discerned. That purpose would shortly be revealed, and when it was, the effect on the enemy's defenders would be intensely demoralizing, for they would be forced to carry out their soldierly duties with hostile and highly determined American troops in both their front and rear. Soon the Germans realized that this was a vise from which they could not possibly escape.

The science of vertical envelopment was so new in June 1944 that effective procedures and techniques were still being learned and developed even as D-Day was about to take place. Nevertheless, despite the chaos of the assault, the massive American airborne operation on D-Day was unquestionably a success, particularly when viewed from the perspectives of Generals Montgomery and Bradley, the two men who had been the most vociferous proponents during the Overlord planning process of a substantive airborne envelopment of the German coastal defenses on D-Day. Monty and Bradley, along with Collins of the VII Corps, had consistently avowed that the broad gap between Utah and the other invasion beaches made the VII Corps' seaborne assault of Utah Beach a highly risky endeavor without a collaborative airborne mission. Those Allied generals supposed that the Germans' effort to restrict the invaders' inland movement from the coast by flooding the meadowlands behind the shoreline necessitated the seizure of the western exits of Utah's four narrow causeways. It was a job that could be carried out only by skilled paratroopers and gliderists in a surprise airborne attack.

Senior Allied commanders therefore perceived the American airborne operation as an essential part of the Utah landing by facilitating the 4th Division's amphibious invasion and, even more important, smoothing the inland passage of the seaborne troops. For the most part, that perception was valid: By the time the 4th Division was ready to start moving off the beach over Utah's four precious causeways a few hours after the initial landings, the 101st Airborne already controlled those causeways' western exits. The 101st also managed to subdue several lethal enemy artillery batteries within easy range of Utah Beach, and as a result, the 4th Division was spared countless casualties as it pushed inland.

A consideration equally important to Allied planners was the security of the Utah beachhead in the invasion's aftermath. General Bradley had demanded that Collins's VII Corps capture the port of Cherbourg with all possible speed, and the attainment of this objective must not be delayed by German counterattacks like the ones the enemy had carried out so effectively at Salerno and Anzio. Therefore, several elements of the American

D-Day airborne plan were structured to secure the flanks of the beachhead and block obvious enemy counterattack routes by seizing and holding vital crossroads towns, such as Ste. Mère Église and St. Côme du Mont, and the key bridges and dams over the Merderet and Douve Rivers.

These goals were certainly ambitious, especially as this was the first time in history that an airborne operation of such immense size would be attempted at night directly over territory occupied by thousands of enemy troops. Those combat veterans who had experienced the Sicily drop expected the Normandy operation to result in chaos—and they were right. Neither the 82nd nor the 101st managed to achieve all their vital objectives on D-Day, particularly in the two drop zones west of the Merderet River, but even so, the overall effect of the airborne mission was to ensure that the American foothold in the Cotentin would be utterly secure. On June 6 and afterward, the enclaves occupied by the 82nd and 101st Divisions on the fringes of the lodgment area barred German counterattacks from penetrating into the delicate beachhead, just as a breakwater sheltering a great harbor checks the sea from surging into its protected waters. Thanks to the airborne troops, the Americans never lost the initiative in the Cotentin after D-Day, a feat they had failed to achieve at Salerno and Anzio.

Starting at 6:30 A.M. on D-Day, the Americans gained the tactical ascendancy in the Cotentin Peninsula, and they resolved to retain it until they captured their paramount initial objective in Normandy—Cherbourg. General Collins never lost sight of the fact that the Utah invasion was only a first step on the road to this great port, and consequently, he resolved to expand the Utah beachhead in the invasion's aftermath as aggressively and swiftly as possible. The many successes achieved by both airborne and seaborne forces on D-Day enabled the 4th Division to begin its northward push toward Cherbourg immediately, unconstrained by enemy counterattacks. As fresh VII Corps outfits poured ashore in the next several days, Collins would strive to expand the beachhead both to the west and south. Ultimately the 101st Airborne would capture Carentan, thereby forging a vital link between the Utah and Omaha beachheads. Simultaneously, the 82nd and 90th Divisions would attack west of the Merderet River, the first step in a major American effort to cut the Cotentin Peninsula in two and isolate the enemy's Cherbourg garrison.

Those men who planned the American airborne operation on D-Day had focused so intently on its execution and terrain objectives that they did not foresee one of its most beneficial consequences. When hordes of American airborne troops descended into the Cotentin Peninsula without warning early on June 6, the startled enemy simply could not fathom what was going on. General Bradley recognized this truth when he noted in his auto-biography, "The sudden presence of [Allied] paratroopers behind the Atlantic Wall in Normandy created immense confusion and fear among the German defenders, and that alone justified their employment."

The enemy occupiers of Normandy had gotten used to the comparative comforts of garrison life in a prosperous agricultural land, but before dawn on June 6, 1944, those troops unexpectedly heard the distressing sound of nearly 1,000 American transport aircraft roaring over their heads at incredibly low altitudes, disgorging countless paratroopers into the night sky, all of whom floated gracefully down to earth only to disappear into the impenetrable bocage. Where had they gone—and what was their intent? The enemy failed to answer those questions throughout June 6, but every German soldier from private to division commander understood that plentiful Americans were out there somewhere, and there was not a road in the eastern Cotentin that was safe to travel that day. The German high command learned that lesson when Maj. Gen. Wilhelm Falley, commander of the 91st Division, ran into 82nd Airborne paratroopers near his headquarters and was promptly shot dead. As the result of dozens of chance encounters of this kind between American GIs and the hated enemy they had vowed to kill with no mercy, the Germans were momentarily paralyzed. In truth, any confusion triggered among American parachute units as a result of their sometimes scattered nighttime airdrops generated infinitely more confusion on the German side, from which the enemy needed plenty of time to recover.

The Anglo-American proponents of vertical envelopment were henceforth taken much more seriously when Allied military chiefs debated the future conduct of the war, for instead of mere theory, airborne commanders now had actual experience of large-scale combat operations they could draw on to demonstrate the usefulness of this new form of warfare. True, the execution of the D-Day airborne mission had been far from perfect, and obviously there was still much to learn, but at least in the Cotentin Peninsula on D-Day the historical evidence was overwhelming that American airborne troops had thoroughly confounded the enemy and helped ensure the success of the Utah Beach invasion by seriously degrading the German reaction to the landing.

An examination of the American D-Day airborne mission points to three main reasons for its success. First, the operation was executed on a massive scale, larger by far than anything the Allies had attempted before in World War II; second, IX Troop Carrier Command crews had undergone flight training that had prepared them to carry out a nocturnal mission of unprecedented size and danger confidently and successfully; third, the rigorous combat training undergone by American airborne troops had thoroughly primed them for the irregular methods of warfare they faced when fighting behind enemy lines in their first day in Normandy.

The size and density of the 82nd and 101st D-Day airdrops were their greatest strengths. In the July 1943 Sicily invasion, the Americans had managed to deposit only four parachute infantry battalions on the ground in the attack's opening phase; in contrast, the June 6, 1944, air assault, in which Troop Carrier C-47s managed to drop nineteen parachute battalions into Normandy in a period of just a few hours, was almost five times as large. Furthermore, D-Day planners had sited the six American drop zones so compactly that they all fit into a hypothetical box little more than eight miles in length and four miles in width, a drop area that amounted to only about thirty-six square miles. Depositing so many paratroopers into such a comparatively small space greatly alleviated the negative effects of scattered drops, since the chances were high that even if a stick missed its drop zone by a wide margin, it would still land within the battle zone in a locale where its members could attack the enemy and help in some way, large or small, to achieve the airborne divisions' overall objectives. It may not have been tidy—but it worked.

The immense size of the American airborne mission on June 6 was a daunting challenge for Troop Carrier aviators, most of whom had not experienced combat before D-Day. Still, most of the airmen, sailors, and soldiers—including paratroopers—who participated in the Normandy invasion were equally new to warfare; and like all those others, when viewed from the standpoint of their actual D-Day performance, Troop Carrier crews on the whole carried out their missions with notable skill and remarkable bravery. Only thoroughly trained pilots could fly incredibly tight C-47 formations at night, at comparatively low altitudes, adhering to the harsh dictates of a rigid timetable. When blinding cloud banks and intense enemy antiaircraft fire were added to the equation, the pilots' job of finding their proper drop zones in the inky blackness suddenly became considerably more difficult and infinitely more perilous. Nevertheless, when historians later examined Troop Carrier's June 6 airdrop in detail, they concluded that nearly 60 percent of its pilots dropped their paratroopers within two miles of their drop zones. The aviators unquestionably went into harm's way to fulfill this mission, and 155 Troop Carrier casualties and the destruction or damage of nearly one-third of the participating C-47s proved it. True, the airdrop was not perfect. Nonetheless, in retrospect, the fact that the majority of 82nd

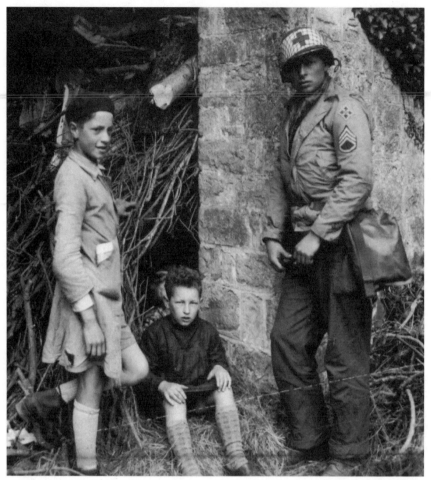

"You must really stay when you figure you are losing." A 4th Infantry Division
medic and two Norman children on D-Day. U.S. ARMY SIGNAL CORPS, NATIONAL ARCHIVES.

and 101st Airborne missions on D-Day were accomplished successfully in
a timely manner yields the irrefutable conclusion that Troop Carrier's contribution to the overall success of the invasion was substantial.

The voluminous plan books spelling out Operation Overlord were
comforting to the troops who bore the heavy responsibility of carrying out
the invasion, but in large measure, those plans fell apart the moment the
enemy opened fire. One of the most prominent themes of the U.S. Army's
D-Day experience, however, was the ability of a few key leaders to adapt
effectively to the shock and chaos of battle and repeatedly demonstrate the

necessary initiative to rectify calamitous situations that could have caused the American share of the D-Day invasion to fall apart. The June 6 experiences of the 82nd and 101st Divisions clearly corroborated this point. Objectives that were supposed to be seized by battalions 600 strong were captured instead by a handful of men, sometimes with a mere lieutenant at the forefront.

Brig. Gen. James Gavin
Assistant Division Commander, 82nd Airborne Division

Moral courage is by far the most difficult kind of courage. Even at two o'clock at night in the face of a heavy enemy attack, you must make decisions—and make the right decisions. Napoleon used to remark on "the courage of two o'clock in the morning." [Napoleon's actual quote: "The most important qualification of a soldier is fortitude under fatigue and privation. Courage is only second; hardship, poverty, and want are the best school for a soldier."] Physical courage is easy. Moral courage is a tough one, I'll tell you. You must really stay when you figure you are losing; and get up off your face and make a counterattack when things seem to be all going against you. . . . Looking back I have no doubt that the participation of the 101st and 82nd Airborne Divisions together made possible the success of the amphibious landing [on Utah Beach] and the overall success of the Normandy operation.

Meanwhile, in the chaos of the D-Day airdrop, those senior airborne officers who were supposed to manage the operation found themselves nearly alone, lacking any precise knowledge of the whereabouts of their regiments or divisions. Nonetheless, many of them took firm and immediate control of the situation and gathered as many stragglers as possible. Despite the obvious and seemingly crippling problem that the number of men currently under their sway hardly amounted to a full-strength company, they searched for ways to retain the initiative and contribute somehow to the fulfillment of their missions.

In training, 82nd and 101st Airborne troops had been taught repeatedly that their new form of warfare was unconventional. Those rare and resourceful leaders who had heeded those lessons grasped that in the early stages of an airborne assault, initiative was essential. Under circumstances as alarming and perplexing as those on D-Day, however, the possibility of sorting out the disordered drop at first appeared remote. No one seemed to know what was going on, and most were not in any position to find out. Out of this chaos emerged a determination on the part of a comparatively small number of resilient souls to bring the war to the enemy as forcefully as possible. Accomplishments that seemed impossible to achieve were indeed attainable simply because the airdrop had generated more alarm and disorder among the Germans than the Americans. Before the enemy could recuperate from the bewilderment of the airborne assault, a small number of American paratroopers had already accomplished most of their important objectives and, by doing so, had contributed decisively to the success of the Utah invasion.

Col. Bruce Bidwell
Observer, War Department Operations Division, Letter to General Marshall, July 1, 1944

Airborne units were badly scattered and intermingled on landing. The majority of the men had no opportunity to secure their heavy arms and equipment. In spite of all this, the operation was a success. It succeeded, however, only because the airborne troops slugged it out with the defenders and had no thought other than to achieve eventual victory.

LOST SOULS

When U.S. Army historians began their massive task of documenting the Normandy campaign, somehow a perception took hold among observers of this epic event that the American victory on Utah Beach on D-Day was achieved easily and at very slight physical cost. In his 1983 memoir *A General's Life*, General Bradley helped perpetuate this assessment when he made the entirely inappropriate and inaccurate statement that "Utah Beach was a piece of cake." Such a historical viewpoint has been sustained into the twenty-first century, but it is entirely false, as any soldier or sailor who participated in the Utah planning process or moved across Utah Beach and beyond its sand dunes throughout D-Day would readily confirm.

To some degree, this false impression was generated by the enemy's inability to mount more than a token defense of the coastline against the 4th Division's initial assault wave at 6:30 A.M. on D-Day. What German bullets could not do, however, more subtle and indirect killing methods, such as mines and artillery, could. Both on land and at sea throughout June 6, unsuspecting American soldiers and sailors set off invisible German mines with alarming frequency and deadly consequences. One battery of the 4th Division's 29th Field Artillery Battalion lost all four of its howitzers and nearly sixty men in an instant, when a mine blew its LCT out of the water during the run-in to the beach, a fate suffered by several other landing craft on D-Day. When 124 troopers from the 4th Cavalry landed on the

Iles St. Marcouf prior to H-Hour, they stumbled into Bouncing Betty mines sown by the enemy in such profusion that the Americans suffered nineteen casualties in just a few minutes—though not a single German soldier occupied the islands.

On D-Day, the enemy's most potent weapon in the Cotentin Peninsula was neither mines nor machine guns, but artillery. When VII Corps staff officers examined intelligence reports before the invasion on the enemy's defensive posture in the Cotentin, even a military novice could discern that the copious German artillery within range of Utah Beach would submit the invaders to a relentless barrage throughout June 6, and unless the Americans could manage to neutralize those lethal weapons swiftly, such a barrage could endure for days. The Americans could not escape the fact that to sustain their push inland on D-Day and prepare for a vigorous offensive to take Cherbourg, they must pour men, equipment, and supplies ashore at a prodigious rate. Compared with Omaha, Utah Beach was a small place, little more than a mile in length, and at any given time on D-Day, that confined space would be so crowded with troops, vehicles, and ammunition that enemy artillerymen would never see such a lucrative target again in their lives.

On the high ground a mile or more behind the coastline, the Germans had emplaced at least eighteen heavy guns of 150-millimeter size or larger, plus many more howitzers of lesser calibers. All were within easy range of the shoreline, and some even had a clear line of sight to it. For the skilled enemy artillerymen and their forward observers, firing steady salvos at a beach swarming with American troops was a comparatively simple task, and the result, particularly on the morning of D-Day, was lethal. These salvos may not have had as powerful a psychological impact on the invaders as machine-gun fire, but they were just as deadly; and for much of June 6 on Utah Beach, it was simply a matter of luck whether one would survive the abrupt and ear-splitting arrival of a German heavy artillery shell. For a substantial number of American troops on D-Day, their luck ran out.

Lt. Col. Ulrich Gibbons
Headquarters, 4th Division Artillery
It was pure relief to find that under the shelling of my first twenty minutes in combat [on Utah Beach]—the worst I have ever been under in two years, World War II or Korea—I retained my ability to think, act, plan. My reaction under this first shelling, therefore approached exhilaration. With time and increasing sophistication I came to a considerably more rational view.

In the afternoon, German artillery fire subsided by a significant degree as 101st Airborne paratroopers worked steadily to eliminate the enemy's field batteries around Ste. Marie du Mont. Also, the surviving German guns had only limited quantities of shells and could not maintain continuous fire without quickly running out of ammunition. Even so, German artillery remained a genuine hazard to the Americans on Utah Beach throughout D-Day. Most of the enemy's heavy batteries were positioned north of the invasion area and therefore could be neutralized only by Allied air attack, naval fire, or direct ground assault. Those batteries, however, were protected by such solid concrete casemates that they were virtually invulnerable to aerial bombs and naval shells, and it would take at least a day for the 4th Division to progress sufficiently northward to capture them by direct assault. Even then, success would not be guaranteed, as the German batteries were formidable strongpoints, guarded by large garrisons and thoroughly prepared for all-around defense with small concrete blockhouses, minefields, and barbed wire. In truth, securing these positions promised to be just as arduous as the 4th Division's task on D-Day.

If the Utah Beach invasion is still perceived as a victory obtained at comparatively trivial cost, probably the most significant factor perpetuating that illusion is the U.S. Army's official casualty count. *Cross-Channel Attack*, the U.S. Army's 1951 history of the D-Day invasion, states that 4th Division casualties on June 6 "were less than 200." In actuality, this figure was certainly over 300; but of much greater significance than a simple miscount was the volume's failure to specify casualty figures from the multitude of VII Corps units specially attached to the 4th Division for the invasion, such as engineer, armor, chemical mortar, and cavalry outfits. Many of these units suffered significant casualties: The 1st Engineer Special Brigade, for example, lost twenty-one men killed and ninety-six wounded; the 237th Engineer Combat Battalion, six killed and thirty-three wounded; the 70th Tank Battalion, nineteen killed and ten wounded. When these casualty figures are added to the 4th Division's total for the D-Day invasion, the yield is nearly triple the "less than 200" casualties proclaimed in *Cross-Channel Attack*.

Another essential indicator of the unappreciated perils of the Utah invasion is the personnel loss endured by the U.S. Navy, U.S. Coast Guard, and Royal Navy in the landings. From the naval perspective, the Utah assault was the most hazardous of the five D-Day invasions. In the somewhat understated words of the official U.S. Navy history of D-Day: "Force U's part in the invasion was characterized by considerable trouble with minefields." On D-Day off Utah Beach, boat lanes for hundreds of gunfire support ships and landing craft had to traverse very shallow banks that were perfect places for the Germans to sow large numbers of sophisticated and powerful naval mines resting on the seafloor. These mines were exceptionally difficult to detect and sweep, and the shallower the water, the more devastating their effect. In some cases, that effect was stunning, such as the obliteration of an LCT conveying part of the 29th Field Artillery Battalion to the beach, and the loss of another LCT carrying DD tanks of the 70th Tank Battalion in a blast so violent that witnesses reported tanks hurled dozens of feet into the air.

Total naval casualties in the Utah invasion cannot be established by the modern researcher with precision, but they must have been considerable, given the destruction as a result of mines and gunfire of at least nine warships and large landing vessels, plus greater numbers of smaller LCVP and LCM landing craft. The loss of the destroyer *Corry* in the fire support lane near the Iles St. Marcouf resulted in twenty-two deaths and thirty-three injuries, and the destruction of the minesweeper USS *Osprey* by a mine killed six sailors and wounded twenty-nine more. U.S. Navy combat demolition units suffered fifteen casualties, including four deaths, while clearing Utah Beach of German antilanding obstacles with U.S. Army engineers in the invasion's first minutes.

Although the Utah Beach invasion was a conventional amphibious operation, it is misleading to view that venture strictly through such a narrow historical lens. When one reads General Collins's VII Corps D-Day invasion directive, known as Field Order 1, it is entirely clear that the Utah assault was just part of a large-scale offensive against the German occupiers of the Cotentin Peninsula, an operation that involved not only an amphibious attack, but also the largest airborne operation in the history of warfare up to that time. Although the 82nd and 101st Airborne Divisions were directly subordinated to Bradley's First Army, not VII Corps, Collins's orders meticulously spelled out the goals of both airborne and seaborne forces, a clear indicator that the 4th, 82nd, and 101st Divisions depended on one another for success in the upcoming invasion.

Lt. Gen. Omar Bradley
Commander, First U.S. Army, July 25, 1945
In my opinion the primary role of airborne troops in the operations which have just been completed has been to assist in an attack on a strongly held enemy position, especially one which is behind an obstacle. . . . The airborne operations back of Utah Beach, where there was a water hazard behind the beach, were essential for the success of the attack.

This broad perspective of the Cotentin invasion articulated by Generals Bradley and Collins must be echoed by twenty-first century D-Day historians, but in large measure it has not. When one views that invasion from the standpoint of its principal leaders, it is striking how challenging and costly it was for the Americans to achieve ultimate victory in the Cotentin Peninsula on June 6, 1944. In the amphibious portion of the invasion, VII Corps and Force U suffered the casualty total of about 800 men, low in comparison to nearly 5,000 on Omaha. One of the primary reasons for this vast disparity in losses was that 82nd and 101st Division troops absorbed a large number of casualties that certainly would have been suffered by the seaborne forces had the invasion plan not included a major airborne ingredient.

The 14,000 airborne soldiers who landed in Normandy on D-Day played an instrumental role in tying down, and in many cases routing, sizable bodies of enemy troops who otherwise would have focused their undivided attention on the American troops coming ashore on Utah Beach. In achieving this important goal, both the 82nd and 101st Airborne Divisions suffered heavy casualties. According to August 1944 analyses undertaken by both divisions after their return to England from Normandy, on D-Day the two divisions suffered a total of about 2,500 casualties, shared almost equally between the 82nd and the 101st. Nearly 60 percent of these victims purportedly were either killed in action or captured, an astonishingly high percentage of men permanently lost to their units, proving beyond doubt that the U.S. Army's concept of vertical envelopment was indeed a decidedly perilous brand of warfare.

Parachute and glider units were not the only ones to endure significant casualties in the D-Day airborne mission. The IX Troop Carrier Command, whose C-47 transports and Waco and Horsa gliders conveyed the 82nd and 101st to Normandy, lost 155 crewmen on June 6, 128 of whom were killed or missing in action. More than 40 percent of those Troop Carrier personnel who were killed or captured on D-Day were glider pilots. Of the 1,134 C-47s that participated in the June 6 parachute and glider missions, nearly one-third were destroyed or suffered significant flak damage.

When one views the joint seaborne and airborne invasion of the Cotentin Peninsula on June 6, 1944, in its entirety and sums up the personnel losses noted by after-action reports of the participating units, a total of about 3,450 American soldiers, sailors, and airmen became casualties during that invasion's execution. Reportedly more than half of these men were permanently lost to their units as a result of death or capture.

The Omaha Beach invasion was a much more grandiose operation than the one on Utah Beach, but if the 14,000 paratroopers and gliderists who landed in Normandy in support of the 4th Division are added to Utah's troop total, both invasions ultimately deposited about the same number of men in France on June 6—approximately 35,000 each. In the Omaha invasion, which is now commonly perceived as a model of carnage almost unmatched in American military history, at least 4,700 souls suffered death, wounds, or capture on D-Day. In an invasion of nearly equal size, the dual seaborne-airborne assault of the Cotentin Peninsula resulted in the surprisingly high casualty sum of 3,450 men—roughly three-quarters of the Omaha figure. This number signifies a loss rate only slightly smaller than the Omaha invasion, yet to the modern observer, it is Omaha Beach rather than the more complex and innovative invasion of the Cotentin Peninsula that has come to symbolize America's grueling D-Day experience.

That the invasion of Normandy was a profoundly perilous enterprise from the American perspective is proved conclusively by the extraordinary figure of more than 8,000 casualties suffered by U.S. servicemen regardless of how or where they entered France on D-Day. Some methods of entry were undeniably more risky than others—but none were easy. And in the weeks ahead, combat in the Norman hedgerows would not get any easier. June 6, 1944, was merely the first day of a long struggle whose end no one could foresee.

WHAT A PLAN!

Monty's and Ike's first glimpses of the Overlord invasion plan in late 1943 had convinced them that in this, the most decisive military operation of World War II from the Anglo-American standpoint, the Western Allies must focus their considerable industrial and military might to achieve success. In retrospect, they were right. From their experience of amphibious warfare and their familiarity with the enemy's cunning fighting methods in the Mediterranean, they drew the simple conclusions that for the invasion of Normandy to work, the frontage of the initial D-Day assault must be as broad as the Allies could make it, and that assault must be applied at an unprecedented level of fury, simultaneously, all across that front. As General Montgomery frequently noted in his addresses to Allied assault troops before D-Day, "The violence, speed, and power of our initial assault must carry everything before it."

Many sensible and experienced Allied soldiers had already drawn identical conclusions, but those with lesser status than Montgomery and Eisenhower could not succeed in swaying the highest reaches of their nations' military and political circles in time to obtain the resources necessary for such a vast undertaking. The D-Day invasion was scheduled for early May 1944, but Ike and Monty had arrived in Britain to take charge only in January. Their jobs would hardly be business as usual: If the Normandy invasion was to be as large as those two generals envisioned, there was virtually no time for discussion. American and British military service chiefs, with the blessings of Roosevelt and Churchill, were going to have to issue orders with uncommon speed for ships and planes to be transferred to Britain in the vast numbers that Ike and Monty demanded.

With additional sea and air resources, Ike and Monty could add two new invasion beaches to COSSAC's original three as well as expand the D-Day airborne assault plan by a considerable factor. The enhanced Overlord invasion plan called for more than 160,000 troops to land in Normandy on D-Day across a front more than twice the length of the assault area initially conceived by COSSAC. In contrast, had COSSAC's Overlord scheme been adhered to without modification, in all probability less than 100,000 men would have landed in Normandy by sea and air on D-Day.

One of the two new beaches Monty added to the Overlord plan in January 1944 was Utah. Launching an amphibious invasion against the southeastern corner of the Cotentin Peninsula posed several risks, the most severe of which was the glaring and substantial geographic gap that would separate Utah from the other four landing sites, an interval that the aggressive Germans were sure to exploit in the aftermath of the invasion. Monty provided an innovative remedy to that dilemma: the employment of unprecedented numbers of American airborne troops in direct support of the Utah invasion, who would drop beyond enemy lines before dawn on D-Day and seize key objectives immediately behind the coast and deep in the interior. Such an operation was undeniably risky, but to the men who had to execute the Utah landing from the sea, that risk would be worth it if the airborne troops could keep the Germans at bay as the seaborne invaders secured the beach, pushed inland, and later strove to link up with American troops thrusting westward out of the Omaha beachhead. Lacking a strong airborne component, many experienced military men could not view the Utah Beach invasion as a sensible operation of war.

Reality proved that when paratroopers and gliderists were added to the mix, the Utah invasion indeed made sense. For a plan that did not even exist four months before D-Day, the Americans' combined seaborne and airborne assault of the Cotentin Peninsula on June 6, 1944, turned out remarkably well, and from the Allies' standpoint, it had the positive impact on the subsequent campaign in Normandy that Ike, Monty, and Bradley had foreseen.

The speedy capture of the port of Cherbourg was among the Allies' highest priorities in Normandy, and the success of the Utah invasion and its associated airborne operations enabled General Collins to set his mind on that goal as soon as the 4th Division had cleared Utah Beach. That Collins's VII Corps could liberate Cherbourg by June 26 could be directly ascribed to the successful American lodgment in the Cotentin on D-Day.

By landing on the Cotentin's east coast on June 6, the Americans in effect outflanked the Douve and Vire Rivers, both of which were formidable defensive positions separating the Cotentin Peninsula from the Allies' main invasion front in Calvados. Had Utah Beach and the American airborne missions not been included in the Overlord invasion plan—and they were notably excluded until Monty and Ike arrived on the scene in January—those river lines would have provided the enemy with an exceptionally strong position that would have substantially delayed and possibly blocked the inevitable American offensive toward Cherbourg launched from the Omaha beachhead. In that event, it would have taken the Allies much more time and cost a far greater number of casualties to capture Cherbourg than it did, and any delay in capturing Cherbourg in turn would have negatively affected the massive logistical buildup the Allies required to support the armies they hoped would soon carry the war beyond Normandy to Paris, the Rhine, and ultimately Berlin.

In his postwar memoirs, Field Marshal Montgomery noted that his attitude toward the Normandy invasion was shaped by "lessons learnt in the stern school of active battle fighting," one of the most important of which was this: "If your flanks and rear are secure, you are well placed for battle." In early 1944, when Monty added Utah and Sword Beaches and their linked airborne operations to the western and eastern flanks of the proposed Overlord invasion front, he strove to achieve that aim; and when the proverbial dust triggered by the D-Day invasion settled at dark on June 6, it was indeed clear that his simple theory had merit. With secure American and British lodgments on the extremities of the invasion front in the Cotentin Peninsula and astride the Orne River, starting on June 7 the Allies could build up and expand their three central invasion sites, including the still unsettled beachhead at Omaha, almost totally unhindered by enemy action on their flanks.

Ike and Monty had based their modified SHAEF invasion plan of January 1944 on entirely simple and sensible—yet commonly overlooked—military principles. By opening up five doors into the Continent on D-Day instead of COSSAC's three, the initial D-Day invasion would tie down more German units, diffuse more enemy counterattacks, and greatly intensify the confusion triggered by the invasion among the German high command. In truth, had the three-division COSSAC plan been carried out rather than SHAEF's five-division assault, all of the German reserve units in and near the Cotentin Peninsula, including the first-rate 91st Division and 6th Parachute Regiment, would not have been pinned down by the Allied invasion. Consequently, they would have been free to maneuver on D-Day and in all likelihood would have begun to deploy into position to counterattack the vulnerable western flank of the Omaha beachhead, about twenty miles away, on June 7 or 8. In that event, as at Salerno, the Germans could have seized the initiative in the days following the invasion, and the severe tribulations experienced by the Omaha assault troops on D-Day actually could have worsened in the ensuing forty-eight hours. That the shaken Omaha invasion force was quickly able to recover its balance after D-Day, unimpeded by any significant enemy action, offers obvious proof that the Utah Beach invasion materially alleviated a potentially disastrous military situation by tying down sizable German military units that could have been profitably employed elsewhere.

In retrospect, the near disaster and shocking casualties on Omaha Beach have tended to dominate historical accounts of the American D-Day experience, but in truth, it was the Utah invasion that provided the Americans with the initial impetus they needed to start carrying out their strategic design in Normandy. The Utah assault not only was much more successful than the one at Omaha, but also gave the Americans the extensive lodgment they needed in the Cotentin Peninsula to set out on the road to Cherbourg as quickly as possible. No one could deny that the American invasion of the Cotentin Peninsula had accomplished what it was supposed to, an achievement that contributed strikingly to the overall success of the invasion of Europe on June 6, 1944.

That invasion would change the world—a truth that was acclaimed even before the clock struck midnight on that day of days.

Winston Churchill
Prime Minister of Great Britain, Speech to Parliament, June 6, 1944

I have to announce to the House that during the night and the early hours of this morning the first of the series of landings in force upon the European Continent has taken place. [Loud cheers interrupted Churchill at this point.] The liberating assault fell upon the coast of France. An immense armada of upwards of 4,000 ships, together with several thousand smaller craft, crossed the Channel. Massed airborne landings have been successfully effected behind enemy lines [more loud cheers], and landings on the beaches are proceeding at various points. . . . So far the commanders who are engaged report that everything is proceeding according to plan. And what a plan! This vast operation is undoubtedly the most complicated and difficult that has ever occurred. It involves tide, wind, waves, visibility, both from the air and the sea standpoint, and the combined employment of air, land, and sea forces in the highest degree of intimacy and in contact with conditions which could not and cannot be fully foreseen. [Mr. Greenwood, a Labor MP, responded:] The House, by its applause, has shown its gratitude to all those who have bled and fought. We are living through momentous hours now. [We must] pledge ourselves and our physical and spiritual resources to the unstinted aid of the men and women who are serving overseas, to let them know the pride we shall feel in their victories and the sadness we shall feel about their losses.

Allied Casualties on Utah Beach and in Cotentin Peninsula, June 6, 1944

Unit	Killed	Wounded	Missing	Total
4TH INFANTRY DIVISION				
8th Infantry Regiment	29	110	0	139
22nd Infantry Regiment	13	34	4	51
12th Infantry Regiment	c. 10	c. 30	0	c. 40[a]
29th Field Artillery Battalion	39	22	0	61
Other 4th Division units				c. 20[a]
Total 4th Infantry Division				311
90TH INFANTRY DIVISION				
359th Infantry Regiment	1	1	0	2
Total 90th Infantry Division	1	1	0	2
VII CORPS/FIRST ARMY UNITS				
4th Cavalry Group	2	18	0	20
237th Engineer Combat Battalion	6	33	0	39
299th Engineer Combat Battalion	4	19	0	23
297th Engineer Combat Battalion	1	0	0	1
298th Engineer Combat Battalion	0	2	0	2
1st Engineer Special Brigade	21	96	0	117[b]

Unit	Killed	Wounded	Missing	Total
87th Chemical Mortar Battalion	2	3	0	5
70th Tank Battalion	19	10	0	29
746th Tank Battalion	4	4	0	8
65th Armored Field Artillery Battalion	2	22	0	24
Other VII Corps/First Army units				c. 10[a]
Total VII Corps/First Army				278
U.S. NAVY/COAST GUARD AND ROYAL NAVY				
Naval combat demolition units	4	11	0	15
USS *Osprey*	6	29	0	35[c]
USS *Corry*	22	33	0	55
USS PC-1261				c. 15[a]
USN/USCG/RN landing craft crews				c. 100[d]
Naval shore fire control parties				c. 15[e]
Total U.S. Navy/Coast Guard				235
AIRBORNE DIVISIONS				
82nd Airborne Division				1,259[f]
101st Airborne Division				1,240[g]
Total Airborne Divisions				2,499
NINTH AIR FORCE				
IX Bomber Command	30	0	0	30
IX Troop Carrier Command	27	128	0	155
Total Ninth Air Force	57	128	0	185
Grand Total				3,510
Exercise Tiger, April 1944	750	300		1,050
Grand Total w/ Tiger				4,560

[a] Indicated figure is casualty approximation based on official unit records that do not specify number of killed, wounded, and missing.

[b] Includes 531st Engineer Shore Regiment and U.S. Navy's 2nd Naval Beach Battalion.

[c] Minesweeper, lost night of June 5.

[d] Landing craft losses on D-Day included four LCT, two LCI, plus many more smaller LCMs, LCVPs, and LCAs.

[e] Includes NSFCP with 82nd and 101st Airborne Divisions.

[f] See Harrison, *Cross-Channel Attack,* 300.

[g] Ibid., 284.

Medal of Honor and Distinguished Service Cross Awards for Valor on Utah Beach and in Cotentin Peninsula, June 6, 1944

The Medal of Honor is the highest military decoration that may be awarded to members of the armed forces of the United States. The U.S. Army's version of the medal was established in 1862 by congressional resolution, later approved by President Abraham Lincoln, to recognize soldiers who "shall most distinguish themselves by their gallantry in action, and other soldierlike qualities."

In World War II, any unit that considered one of its members worthy of the Medal of Honor was required to file paperwork to higher headquarters on behalf of that soldier, including supporting eyewitness accounts by at least two unit members. A three-member evaluation board would then consider whether that soldier had exhibited the medal's requirement for "conspicuous gallantry and intrepidity at risk of life above and beyond the call of duty."

Only a single soldier was granted a Medal of Honor among those 35,000 members of the VII Corps and 82nd and 101st Airborne Divisions who participated in the invasion of the Cotentin Peninsula on D-Day, June 6, 1944. This award was conferred posthumously to Brig. Gen. Theodore Roosevelt Jr. in September 1944, as Roosevelt had died of a heart attack in July. Roosevelt is often incorrectly termed the second-in-command of the 4th Infantry Division on D-Day. That job was held by Brig. Gen. Henry Barber, a classmate of Collins and Ridgway in the West Point 1917 class, a

highly decorated World War I officer, and a veteran o.   Islands
campaign in World War II. Roosevelt was actually a su,   general
officer provided to the 4th Division by General Brad.   1944.

Brig. Gen. Theodore Roosevelt Jr.
Supernumerary General Officer, 4th Division, General Ora
September 28, 1944

For gallantry and intrepidity at the risk of his life above and bey
duty on 6 June 1944, in France. After two verbal requests to accon
ing assault elements in the Normandy invasion had been denied, Br
sevelt's written request for this mission was approved, and he landed
wave of the forces assaulting the enemy-held beaches. He repeatedly
from the beach, over the seawall, and established them inland. His valc
and presence in the very front of the attack and his complete unconcer
under heavy fire inspired the troops to heights of enthusiasm and self-
Although the enemy had the beach under constant direct fire, Brig. Gen. R
moved from one locality to another, rallying men around him, directed a
sonally led them against the enemy. Under his seasoned, precise, calm, and
tering leadership, assault troops reduced beach strongpoints and rapidly n
inland with minimum casualties. He thus contributed substantially to the suc
ful establishment of the beachhead in France.

In the U.S. Army, the Distinguished Service Cross (DSC) is secon
precedence to the Medal of Honor. It was established in January 1918
President Woodrow Wilson upon the recommendation of Gen. John Pers
ing, commander of the American Expeditionary Force in World War I.

The U.S. Army awarded 61 DSCs to airborne and seaborne troops who
participated in the invasion of the Cotentin Peninsula on June 6, 1944.
These men are listed alphabetically below, along with the units to which
they belonged.

> Ahearn, 1st Lt. John, 70th Tank Battalion
> Amerman, 2nd Lt. Walter, 101st Airborne Pathfinder
> Barba, Cpl. James, 502nd Parachute Infantry
> Bolderson, Pfc. John, 505th Parachute Infantry
> Brooks, 1st Lt. Elton, 506th Parachute Infantry
> Caffey, Col. Eugene, 1st Engineer Special Brigade
> Ceffalo, Pfc. John, 505th Parachute Infantry
> Danforth, Cpl. Virgil, 501st Parachute Infantry
> Ditullio, Pfc. Dominick, 505th Parachute Infantry

Doerfler, 2nd Lt. Eugene, 505th Parachute Infantry
Dolan, Capt. John, 505th Parachute Infantry
Dunagan, 1st Lt. Sidney, 50th Troop Carrier Squadron
Eberle, 1st Lt. George, 502nd Parachute Infantry
Haley, Capt. James, 8th Infantry
Harbaugh, Pvt. Francis, 101st Airborne Division
Harris, 1st Lt. Ernest, 502nd Parachute Infantry
Harrison, Sgt. Bailey, 101st Airborne Division
Heim, Pvt. Marcus, 505th Parachute Infantry
Henshaw, 1st Lt. Robert, 237th Engineer Combat Battalion
Johnson, Col. Howard, 501st Parachute Infantry
Krause, Lt. Col. Edward, 505th Parachute Infantry
Lillyman, Capt. Frank, 101st Airborne Pathfinder
Lockwood, Pvt. John, 508th Parachute Infantry
Mabry, Capt. George, 8th Infantry
MacNeely, Lt. Col. Carlton, 8th Infantry
McGee, Capt. (Chaplain) Tildon, 101st Airborne Division
Mendez, Lt. Col. Louis, 508th Parachute Infantry
Millener, Lt. Col. Raymond, 101st Airborne Division
Montilio, Pfc. George, 506th Parachute Infantry
Muir, 2nd Lt. Marvin, 439th Troop Carrier Group
Murrin, S/Sgt. Richard, 70th Tank Battalion
Nothel, Sgt. Henry, 70th Tank Battalion
Ostberg, Lt. Col. Edwin, 507th Parachute Infantry
Patch, Capt. Lloyd, 506th Parachute Infantry
Peterson, Pfc. Lenold, 505th Parachute Infantry
Pryne, Pfc. Gordon, 505th Parachute Infantry
Purvis, S/Sgt. Darvin, 70th Tank Battalion
Raudstein, Capt. Knut, 506th Parachute Infantry
Reeder, Lt. Col. Russell, 12th Infantry
Ridgway, Maj. Gen. Matthew, 82nd Airborne Division
Roberts, Cpl. Ernest, 508th Parachute Infantry
Sampson, Capt. (Chaplain) Francis, 101st Airborne Division
Santarsiero, 2nd Lt. Charles, 506th Parachute Infantry
Schmidt, 2nd Lt. George, 501st Parachute Infantry
Songer, 1st Lt. Francis, 70th Tank Battalion
Sosnack, Pvt. Andrew, 101st Airborne Division
Stach, Maj. Paul, IX Bomber Command
Steiner, Lt. Col. Fred, 8th Infantry
Summers, S/Sgt. Harrison, 502nd Parachute Infantry

Taylor, Maj. Gen. Maxwell, 101st Airborne Division
Townsend, 2nd Lt. John, 70th Tank Battalion
Tubbs, 1st Sgt. Herbert, 501st Parachute Infantry
Vandervoort, Lt. Col. Benjamin, 505th Parachute Infantry
Van Fleet, Col. James, 8th Infantry
Van Valkenburg, Pvt. John, 507th Parachute Infantry
Weir, Sgt. William, 501st Parachute Infantry
Welborn, Lt. Col. John, 70th Tank Battalion
Winters, 1st Lt. Richard, 506th Parachute Infantry
Zahn, Sgt. Donald, 506th Parachute Infantry
Zeigler, 1st Lt. Harvey, 505th Parachute Infantry
Zwingman, Pvt. Otto, 508th Parachute Infantry

The 61 DSCs awarded for valor in the invasion of the Cotentin Peninsula amounted to little more than one-quarter of the 214 total DSCs awarded by the U.S. Army on D-Day. Of those 214 DSCs, nearly three-quarters were granted to participants in the Omaha Beach invasion, even though the number of men who landed in the Cotentin by sea or air on D-Day was roughly equal to the number who came ashore on Omaha.

First-Wave Units on Utah Beach

The following U.S. Army and Navy units constituted the initial assault waves on Utah Beach on June 6, 1944, starting at H-Hour, or 6:30 A.M.

8TH INFANTRY REGIMENT, 4TH INFANTRY DIVISION
Col. James Van Fleet
Regimental Staff
   Executive Officer: Lt. Col. Fred Steiner
   S-1 (Personnel): Capt. John Galvin
   S-2 (Intelligence): Maj. Walter Todd
   S-3 (Operations): Maj. Oma Bates
   S-4 (Supply): Capt. Robert Bare
   Surgeon: Maj. George Armbrecht

1st Battalion (Transport: USS Joseph T. Dickman, USCG)
Lt. Col. Conrad Simmons
   Company A: Capt. Carl Cline
   Company B: 1st Lt. Gail Lee
   Company C: Capt. Robert Crisson
   Company D: 1st Lt. Joseph Samson

2nd Battalion (Transport: USS Barnett)
Lt. Col. Carlton MacNeely
Company E: Capt. Howard Lees
Company F: Capt. Leonard Schroeder
Company G: Capt. James Haley
Company H: Capt. John Greenip

3rd Battalion (Transport: USS Bayfield, USCG)
Lt. Col. Erasmus Strickland
Company I: Capt. Frederick Maisel Jr.
Company K: Capt. John Spangler
Company L: Capt. John Reckord
Company M: Capt. Robert Rappleye

3rd Battalion, 22nd Infantry (Transport: SS Empire Gauntlet [British])
Lt. Col. Arthur Teague
Company I: Capt. Joseph Samuels
Company K: Capt. Charles Earnest
Company L: Capt. Edward Gatto
Company M: Unknown

70TH TANK BATTALION
Lt. Col. John Welborn
Company A (16 tanks, 8 dozers on 8 LCT-A): Capt. Stewart Williams
Company B (16 DD tanks on 4 LCT): Capt. Francis Songer
Company C (16 DD tanks on 4 LCT): 1st Lt. John Ahearn

BEACH OBSTACLE CLEARANCE TEAMS
Lt. Col. Hershel Linn, 237th Engineer Combat Battalion
Executive Officer: Capt. Robert Tabb
Company B, 237th ECB: Capt. Victor Calvisino
Company B, 299th ECB: Capt. Ambrose Manion
U.S. Navy Demolition Units: Lt. Cmdr. Herbert Peterson

4th Cavalry Group (Transport: SS Empire Gauntlet [British])
Col. Joseph Tully
4th Cavalry Squadron: Lt. Col. Edward Dunn
24th Cavalry Squadron: Lt. Col. F. Gaston

Initial Parachute and Glider Assault, Cotentin Peninsula, 12:20–4:15 A.M., June 6, 1944

The following parachute and glider units from the 82nd and 101st Airborne Divisions, dropped or towed into Normandy by the Ninth Air Force's IX Troop Carrier Command, participated in the initial predawn airborne assault on Normandy, June 6, 1944.

The following abbreviations are used: AA Bn: antiaircraft battalion; A/B: Companies A and B (both equipped with 57-millimeter antitank guns); A/C: aircraft; ACG: assistant commanding general; ARTY CO: artillery commander; CG: commanding general; CO: commanding officer; COS: chief of staff; FA Bn: field artillery battalion; IX TCC PF: Ninth Troop Carrier Command Pathfinder Force; TC: Troop Carrier; XO: executive officer.

101ST AIRBORNE DIVISION
CG: Maj. Gen. Maxwell Taylor
ACG: Brig. Gen. Donald Pratt
ARTY CO: Brig. Gen. Anthony McAuliffe
COS: Col. Gerald Higgins

Pathfinders

Unit	Commander	TC Group	UK Airfield	No. A/C
Pathfinders	Capt. Frank Lillyman	IX TCC PF	North Witham	11

502nd Parachute Infantry (Drop Zone A)
CO: Col. George Van Horn Moseley
XO: Lt. Col. John Michaelis

Unit	Commander	TC Group	UK Airfield	No. A/C
1st Battalion	Lt. Col. Patrick Cassidy	436	Membury	36
2nd Battalion	Lt. Col. Steve Chappuis	438	Greenham Common	36
3rd Battalion	Lt. Col. Robert Cole	438	Greenham Common	45
377th FA Bn	Lt. Col. Benjamin Weisberg	436	Membury	54

506th Parachute Infantry (Drop Zones C and D)
CO: Col. Robert Sink
XO: Lt. Col. Charles Chase

Unit	Commander	TC Group	UK Airfield	No. A/C
1st Battalion	Lt. Col. William Turner	439	Upottery	45
2nd Battalion	Lt. Col. Robert Strayer	439	Upottery	36
3rd Battalion	Lt. Col. Robert Wolverton	440	Exeter	45

501st Parachute Infantry (Drop Zones C and D)
CO: Col. Howard Johnson
XO: Lt. Col. Harry Kinnard

Unit	Commander	TC Group	UK Airfield	No. A/C
1st Battalion	Lt. Col. Robert Carroll	441	Merryfield	45
2nd Battalion	Lt. Col. Robert Ballard	441	Merryfield	45
3rd Battalion	Lt. Col. Julian Ewell	435	Welford	45

"Chicago" Glider Mission (Landing Zone E)

Unit	Commander	TC Group	UK Airfield	No. A/C
A/B 81st AA Bn Lt. Col. X.B. Cox		434	Aldermaston	52*

82ND AIRBORNE DIVISION
CG: Maj. Gen. Matthew Ridgway
ACG: Brig. Gen. James Gavin
ARTY CO: Col. Francis March
COS: Col. Ralph Eaton

Pathfinders

Unit	Commander	TC Group	UK Airfield	No. A/C
Pathfinders	Capt. Neal McRoberts	IX TCC PF	North Witham	9

505th Parachute Infantry (Drop Zone O)
CO: Lt. Col. William Ekman
XO: Lt. Col. Mark Alexander

Unit	Commander	TC Group	UK Airfield	No. A/C
1st Battalion	Lt. Col. Frederick Kellam	315	Spanhoe	47
2nd Battalion	Lt. Col. Benjamin Vandervoort	316	Cottesmore	36
3rd Battalion	Lt. Col. Edward Krause	316	Cottesmore	36

507th Parachute Infantry (Drop Zone T)
CO: Col. George Millett
XO: Lt. Col. Arthur Maloney

Unit	Commander	TC Group	UK Airfield	No. A/C
1st Battalion	Lt. Col. Edwin Ostberg	61	Barkston Heath	36
2nd Battalion	Lt. Col. Charles Timmes	61	Barkston Heath	36
3rd Battalion	Lt. Col. William Kuhn	442	Fulbeck	45

508th Parachute Infantry (Drop Zone N)
CO: Col. Roy Lindquist
XO: Lt. Col. Harry Harrison

Unit	Commander	TC Group	UK Airfield	No. A/C
1st Battalion	Lt. Col. Herbert Batcheller	331	Folkingham	36
2nd Battalion	Lt. Col. Thomas Shanley	314	Saltby	36
3rd Battalion	Lt. Col. Louis Mendez	313	Saltby	36

"Detroit" Glider Mission (Landing Zone O)

Unit	Commander	TC Group	UK Airfield	No. A/C
A/B 80th AA Bn	Lt. Col. Raymond Singleton	437	Ramsbury	52*

*Fifty-two C-47s towing fifty-two CG-4A Waco gliders. Glider loads included sixteen
57-millimeter antitank guns.

Ninth Air Force, IX Troop Carrier Command, June 6, 1944

The following U.S. Army Air Force Troop Carrier units participated in the airborne assault on Normandy, June 6, 1944.

The following abbreviations are used: CG: commanding general; CO: commanding officer; TC: Troop Carrier.

IX TROOP CARRIER COMMAND
CG: Maj. Gen. Paul Williams

50th Wing
CO: Brig. Gen. Julian Chappell

Unit	Commander	TC Squadrons
439th Group	Lt. Col. Charles Young	91, 92, 93, 94
440th Group	Lt. Col. Frank Krebs	95, 96, 97, 98
441st Group	Col. Theodore Kershaw	99, 100, 301, 302
442nd Group	Col. Charles Smith	303, 304, 305, 306

52nd Wing
CO: Brig. Gen. Harold Clark

Unit	Commander	TC Squadrons
61st Group	Col. Willis Mitchell	14, 15, 53, 59
313th Group	Col. James Roberts	29, 47, 48, 49
314th Group	Lt. Col. Clayton Stiles	32, 50, 61, 62
315th Group	Col. Hamish McLelland	34, 43, 309, 310
316th Group	Col. Harvey Berger	36, 37, 44, 45

53rd Wing
CO: Brig. Gen. Maurice Beach

Unit	Commander	TC Squadrons
434th Group*	Col. William Whitacre	71, 72, 73, 74
435th Group	Col. Frank MacNees	75, 76, 77, 78
436th Group	Col. Adriel Williams	79, 80, 81, 82
437th Group*	Col. Cedric Hudgens	83, 84, 85, 86
438th Group	Lt. Col. John Donaldson	87, 88, 89, 90

*Conducted glider missions "Chicago" and "Detroit" on morning of D-Day.

Ninth Air Force, IX Bomber Command, Utah Beach Bombing Mission, 6:09–6:27 A.M., June 6, 1944

The following U.S. Army Air Force B-26 Marauder medium bomber groups participated in the air bombardment of Utah Beach, June 6, 1944. All attacks were made at altitudes ranging from 4,000 to 6,000 feet.

The following abbreviations are used: A/C TO–A/C ATK: aircraft taking off–aircraft attacking; DF: delayed fuse; IF: instantaneous fuse.

IX BOMBER COMMAND
Brig. Gen. Samuel Anderson

Unit	A/C TO–A/C ATK	Time	Total Bomb Load
344th Group	56–50 B-26	0609	797 250-lb. IF
387th Group	54–43 B-26	0614	688 250-lb. IF
323rd Group	54–49 B-26	0617	781 250-lb. IF
394th Group	54–31 B-26	0618	490 250-lb. IF
397th Group	53–51 B-26	0622	810 250-lb. IF
386th Group	54–53 B-26	0624	848 250-lb. IF
322nd Group	16–16 B-26	0627	30 2,000-lb. DF
Total	341–293 B-26		4,414 250-lb. IF; 30 2,000-lb. DF

U.S. Navy Force U
Bombardment Group

The following Allied warships participated in the naval bombardment of Utah Beach starting at 5:36 A.M., June 6, 1944.

FORCE U BOMBARDMENT GROUP
CO: Rear Adm. Morton Deyo

Name	Type	Nationality	Captain
Nevada	Battleship	U.S. Navy	Capt. P. M. Rhea
Erebus	Monitor	Royal Navy	Capt. J. S. Colquhoun
Tuscaloosa*	Heavy cruiser	U.S. Navy	Capt. J. B. Waller
Hawkins	Heavy cruiser	Royal Navy	Capt. J. W. Josselyn
Enterprise	Light cruiser	Royal Navy	Capt. H. T. Grant
Black Prince	Light cruiser	Royal Navy	Capt. D. M. Lees
Soemba	Gunboat	Netherlands	Lt. Cmdr. H. H. Propper
Hobson	Destroyer	U.S. Navy	Lt. K. Loveland
Fitch	Destroyer	U.S. Navy	Cmdr. K. Walpole
Forrest	Destroyer	U.S. Navy	Commander Letts
Corry	Destroyer	U.S. Navy	Lt. Cmdr. G. Hoffman
Herndon	Destroyer	U.S. Navy	Cmdr. G. Moore
Shubrick	Destroyer	U.S. Navy	Lt. Cmdr. W. Blenman

Name	Type	Nationality	Captain
Butler	Destroyer	U.S. Navy	Cmdr. M. Matthews
Gherardi	Destroyer	U.S. Navy	Cmdr. M. Curtin
Rich	Destroyer escort	U.S. Navy	Lt. Cmdr. E. Michel
Bates	Destroyer escort	U.S. Navy	Lt. Cmdr. H. Wilmerding
Hotham	Frigate	Royal Navy	unknown
Tyler	Frigate	Royal Navy	unknown

*Admiral Deyo's flagship

Capt. Frank Lillyman's Pathfinder Stick, June 6, 1944

The following eighteen pathfinders from the 502nd Parachute Infantry, 101st Airborne Division, were the first U.S. Army soldiers to land in Normandy on D-Day. They landed by parachute at about 12:15 A.M., June 6, 1944, near St. Germain de Varreville. Their C-47 was piloted by Lt. Col. Joel Crouch; the copilot was Capt. Vito Pedone; and the navigator was Capt. William Culp.

> Capt. Frank Lillyman, CO
> 1st Lt. Robert Dixon
> 1st Lt. Samuel McCarter
> S/Sgt. Thomas Walton
> Cpl. Owen Council
> Pfc. Delbert Jones
> Pfc. Phillip Sangenario
> Pfc. Frederick Wilhelm
> Pvt. Jarris Clark
> Pvt. Paul Davis
> Pvt. John Funk
> Pvt. John MacFarlane
> Pvt. August Mangoni

Pvt. John Ott
Pvt. Francis Rocca
Pvt. Raymond Smith
Pvt. Buford Williams
Pvt. John Zamanakos

Uniform and Equipment of U.S. Army Paratroopers, 82nd and 101st Airborne Divisions, June 6, 1944

Paratroopers in the 82nd and 101st Airborne Divisions were typically outfitted with the following uniform items and equipment on D-Day. These items varied depending on the soldier's rank and specialty, and even according to personal preferences:

UNIFORM

Wool drawers, long	Parachute boots
Wool undershirt	Parachute suspenders
Wool socks	Web belt
Olive drab trousers	Dog tags
Olive drab shirt	Cartridge belt
Jump jacket	Arm brassard
Jump pants	(for chemical detection)
Helmet, with netting and liner	Gloves
Anti-gas cape	Raincoat

Uniform items were treated with a protective chemical to prevent enemy chemical agents from penetrating through the fabric to the skin.

EQUIPMENT

M-1 rifle, disassembled, in gun case
Bayonet
Entrenching tool
M-1911 .45 pistol, with holster
Hand grenades
Gammon (antitank) grenades
Smoke grenades
Orange recognition flag
Rifle ammunition
Pistol ammunition
Blocks of TNT
Musette bag
Three K rations
Two D rations
Towel
Blanket
Handkerchiefs

Parachute
Reserve chute
Life vest ("Mae West")
Trench knife
Hunting knife
Machete
Canteen
Canteen cover
Canteen cup
Antitank mine
First-aid kit
Gas mask, with case
Utensils
Extra socks
Extra underwear
Compass
Cigarettes

Notes

As in my previous book, *Omaha Beach*, the historical information in this work is drawn overwhelmingly from primary sources written by D-Day participants in the immediate aftermath of the invasion. This material includes unit journals, after-action reports, war diaries, postcombat interviews, correspondence, medal citations, and official unit histories. Thirty years of experience in historical research has convinced me beyond doubt that information collected as close as possible in time after a momentous military event is the most reliable factual source available to the historian. I still hold firmly to the general rule I submitted in *Omaha Beach*: The closer in time to June 6, 1944, an account originated, the more I trusted it.

Nevertheless, primary sources, particularly those pertaining to the massive American airborne operation on D-Day, can exasperate even the most dedicated of World War II researchers because of their many glaring gaps and inconsistencies. By necessity, therefore, I frequently relied on secondary source data, such as veterans' recollections or unit histories originating years after D-Day. I tried to limit my use of such information, however, striving as much as possible to corroborate it with primary sources. Still, it is inevitable that historians reconstructing an event as complex and chaotic as the Normandy invasion will be forced to make educated guesses about the precise details of a battle, and in several instances during the course of this book, I had to do exactly that.

Luckily, I am working in an age when it is still possible to consult the participants themselves when thorny research issues arise, and I took advantage of this on dozens of occasions, both in person and through correspondence. Indeed, I have the extreme good fortune of living just a few hundred yards away from a 101st Airborne Division D-Day veteran, Ray Geddes, who gracefully tolerated my probing questions and became a good friend as I wrote this book.

One vital collection of D-Day information that I used extensively was the Cornelius Ryan Memorial Collection of World War Two Papers at the Ohio University Library in Athens, Ohio. Ryan collected this material in the 1950s for his D-Day classic, *The Longest Day*, and the papers are maintained in such an orderly fashion by the librarians that it is a pleasure for the researcher to work with them. Most of the D-Day veterans who responded to Ryan's questionnaires were still young men, and their memories preserved in this collection are invariably sharp and poignant. One of the most valuable parts of Ryan's papers, from my perspective, was his extensive correspondence with Raymond Barton, the 4th Infantry Division commander on Utah Beach. Solid information on this key D-Day figure in other archival repositories is difficult to find; consequently, Ryan's files on Barton are exceptionally helpful. D-Day historians must be grateful to Cornelius Ryan, for without his work, our knowledge of the invasion would be much less distinct today.

In the following section, I provide the sources from which I obtained all of the book's firsthand accounts, quotations, and various historical details. Each citation lists the originator or military unit providing the account, the first few words of that account (in italics), and a reference specifying as closely as possible the location from which that material was drawn. The following abbreviations are used to denote archival repositories, military unit types, and an assortment of other names, words, and phrases:

AC:	author's collection
ACM:	author's collection, veteran's unpublished manuscript
AD:	airborne division
AF:	air force
AFB:	air force base
AG:	army group
AIOC:	Advanced Infantry Officers Course
AOR:	Army Operational Records, (part of NARA Record Group 407)

BM:	Bernard Montgomery Papers, Imperial War Museum, London
CI:	Combat Interview files (part of NARA Record Group 407)
CMB:	chemical mortar battalion
CMH:	Center of Military History, Historical Manuscripts Collection, Fort McNair, Washington, DC
CP:	corps
CR:	Cornelius Ryan Collection, Mahn Center for Archives–Special Collections, Alden Library, Ohio University, Athens, OH (locations identified by box [B] and folder [F])
DE:	Dwight Eisenhower Library, Abilene, KS
DEP:	Dwight Eisenhower Papers, Johns Hopkins University Press
DSC:	Distinguished Service Cross
E:	entry (NARA location indicator)
ECB:	engineer combat battalion
ESB:	engineer special brigade
ESR:	engineer shore regiment
FAB:	field artillery battalion
FB:	Fort Benning Infantry School Library, Fort Benning, GA
FM:	field manual
FRUS:	Foreign Relations of the United States
IA:	interview by author
ID:	infantry division
IR:	infantry regiment
LC:	Library of Congress
MHI:	Military History Institute, Carlisle Barracks, PA
ML:	Miscellaneous List files (part of NARA Record Group 407)
MS:	National Archives manuscript
NA or NARA:	National Archives and Records Administration, College Park, MD
NHC:	Naval Historical Center, Washington Navy Yard, Washington, DC
PIR:	parachute infantry regiment

PRO: Public Record Office, UK
RG: NARA Record Group
TB: tank battalion
TCG: Troop Carrier Group
TCS: Troop Carrier Squadron
TF: task force
USAF: U.S. Air Force
USFET: U.S. Forces European Theater
USN: U.S. Navy
USNA: U.S. Naval Administration in WWII: *The*
            Invasion of Normandy (vol. 5)

CHAPTER 1: AN UNSOUND OPERATION OF WAR
First Impressions (pages 1–4)

Marrakech, *most lovely place*, quoted from Celia Sandys, Churchill's granddaughter, on "Publication and Resources," International Churchill Society website, www.winstonchurchill.org. **Montgomery,** *100 percent fit*, Montgomery, *Memoirs*, p. 60. **Dinner,** details, Montgomery, *Memoirs*, p. 191. **Churchill,** *Auld Lang Syne*, Gilbert, *Winston Churchill: Road to Victory*, pp. 631–32. **Montgomery,** *The initial landing*, Montgomery, *Memoirs*, p. 192. **Churchill,** *Pirates of Penzance*, Gilbert, *Churchill: Road to Victory*, pp. 631–32. **Churchill,** *I was encouraged*, Gilbert, *Churchill: Road to Victory*, pp. 632–33.

Like a God from Olympus (pages 4–13)

Montgomery, *The more I examined*, BM, quoted in Hamilton, *Master of the Battlefield*, p. 490. **Barker,** *Monty took the floor*, MHI, Interview with Forrest Pogue 10/16/46, CMH Collection, Pogue Interviews. **Montgomery,** *Urgent*, DE, SHAEF, Barker Papers, Box 1. **McLean,** *Monty's action*, MHI, Interview with Pogue 3/13/47, CMH Collection, Pogue Interviews. **Montgomery,** *One of the lessons*, Montgomery, *Memoirs*, p. 193. **Montgomery,** *he did not consider*, DE, SHAEF, Barker Papers, Box 1. **Montgomery,** *early capture of a port*, DE, SHAEF minutes 1/21/44, Barker Papers, Box 1. **Montgomery,** *It is desirable*, DE, SHAEF minutes 1/21/44, Barker Papers, Box 1.

Not Enough Wallop (pages 13–19)

Montgomery, *Here in England*, BM, quoted in Hamilton, *Master of the Battlefield*, p. 527. **de Guingand,** *any other trained soldier*, de Guingand, *Operation Victory*, p. 341. **Quebec,** *The Prime Minister said*, FRUS, *Washington and Quebec* volume, p. 896. **Butcher,** *not enough wallop*, Butcher, *My Three Years with Eisenhower*, p. 434. **Eisenhower,** *I examined*, DEP, War Years, vol. III, p. 1653. **Bradley,** *When Bradley arrived*,

MHI, Interview with Pogue 10/14/46, CMH Collection, Pogue Interviews. **Montgomery,** *displaced strategists*, Montgomery, *Memoirs*, p. 232. **Hughes-Hallett,** *Monty gives*, MHI, Interview with Pogue 2/12/47, CMH Collection, Pogue Interviews. **Coningham,** *He wouldn't fight*, MHI, Interview with Pogue 2/14/47, CMH Collection, Pogue Interviews. **Smith,** *Bradley last night*, MHI, Interview with Pogue 5/13/47, CMH Collection, Pogue Interviews. **COSSAC,** *An attack with*, FRUS, *Washington and Quebec*, p. 489. **U.S. Army,** *especially obstructive*, NA, RG 407, AOR 4 ID.

Stakes Incalculable (pages 19–25)

Churchill, *In conversation*, Kimball, *Churchill and Roosevelt Correspondence*, vol. II, pp. 653–54. **Roosevelt,** *my understanding*, Kimball, *Churchill and Roosevelt Correspondence*, vol. II, p. 662. **Eisenhower,** *very deep conviction*, DEP, War Years, vol. III, p. 1672. **de Guingand,** *bang the table*, de Guingand, *Operation Victory*, p. 342. **Nelson,** *25,000 or more lives*, Mowry, *Landing Craft and the War Production Board*, p. 29. **SHAEF Conference,** *two airborne divisions*, DE, SHAEF minutes 1/24/44, Barker Papers, Box 1. **Bradley,** *discussion of airborne*, Brereton, *Brereton Diaries*, p. 236. **Portal,** *highly organized system*, quoted in Harrison, *Cross-Channel Attack*, pp. 184–85. **Troop Carrier,** April 1944 data, Warren, *Airborne Operations in WWII*, p. 8.

CHAPTER 2: STEADFAST AND LOYAL
Lightning Joe (pages 26–29)

Eisenhower, *a bit uneasy*, DEP, War Years, vol. III, pp. 1715–16. **West Point 1917 class,** details, *U.S. Military Academy Register of Graduates*. **Bradley,** *talks our language*, Collins, *Lightning Joe*, p. 179. **Taylor,** *General Collins*, MHI, S. L. A. Marshall Papers, 2/25/46 letter Taylor to Marshall. **Collins,** *just lucky*, Collins, *Lightning Joe*, p. 179. **Collins,** *From the point*, NA, RG 319, CMH working papers, *Utah Beach to Cherbourg* correspondence, 10/1/48 letter Collins to Colonel Reeder.

Ivy Men (pages 29–36)

22/4, *The officers*, MHI, Microfilm records, 22 IR/4 ID. **Barton,** *strict disciplinarian*, MHI, 3/73 Van Fleet interview by B. Williams. **Barton,** *firm and brisk* and *I am your leader*, Rothbart, *Soldier's Journal*, pp. 55, 99.

Valor without Arms (pages 36–40)

Parsons, *Every pilot*, IA, 9/19/03. **FM 100-5,** *Troop Carrier forces*, MHI. **Brereton,** *no illusions*, Brereton, *Brereton Diaries*, p. 267. **Gavin,** *C-47 crews*, MHI, Gavin Papers, 7/7/82 letter to W. Breuer.

Rendezvous with Destiny (pages 40–49)

Eisenhower, *lick the Hun,* DEP, War Years, vol. III, p. 1739. **Gavin,** *Until we devise,* MHI, Gavin Papers, 2/14/44 diary entry. **Eisenhower,** *I do not believe,* DEP, War Years, vol. III, p. 1440. **Lee,** *corps d'élite,* Autry, *General William C. Lee,* p. 104. **Parachute officer,** *cooperate with 82nd,* Blair, *Ridgway's Paratroopers,* p. 52. **Gavin,** *I don't think Bill,* MHI, Gavin Papers, 1/4/83 interview; also, Blair, *Ridgway's Paratroopers,* p. 31. **Lee,** *rendezvous with destiny,* Autry, *General William C. Lee,* p. 130. **Warren,** *My first contact,* MHI, Clay Blair Papers, 10/24/83 letter to Blair. **Ewell,** *I was watching,* MHI, Blair Papers, 4/28/83 letter to Blair. **Eisenhower,** *The risks Taylor ran,* Eisenhower, *Crusade in Europe,* pp. 183–84. **Ridgway,** *Gavin possesses,* MHI, Gavin Papers. **Gavin,** *There is a feeling,* MHI, Gavin Papers, 2/19/44 diary entry. **Gavin,** *Leigh-Mallory said,* MHI, Gavin Papers, 1975 oral history. **Montgomery,** *gutless bugger,* PRO, 21 AG Papers; also quoted in D'Este, *Decision in Normandy,* p. 166. **Gavin,** *My future,* MHI, Gavin Papers, 2/19/44 diary entry. **Johnson,** *I'm proud,* Critchell, *Four Stars of Hell,* p. 36. There are many versions of Johnson's speech; see also Bando, *Vanguard of the Crusade,* p. 28; and McLaughlin, *D-Day + 60 Years,* p. 59.

CHAPTER 3: OVERTURE TO OVERLORD
Soldiers of the Reich (pages 50–53)

von Schlieben, *career,* Chandler, *The D-Day Encyclopedia,* pp. 482–83. **Dollmann,** *In view of,* NA, RG 338, MS B-839. **von Schlieben,** *If one had called* (and following quotes), NA, RG 338, MS B-845.

A Poor Place to Fight (pages 53–58)

Utah Beach, *9655 yards,* NA, RG 407, AOR VII CP.

Dress Rehearsals (pages 58–64)

Rabe, *Shortly before 0200,* Greene, "What Happened off Devon," *American Heritage,* February 1987. **LST-511,** *First heard,* NA, RG 38, TF 125, Box 319. **Geddes,** *At approximately 0210,* NA, RG 38, TF 125, Box 319. **U.S. Air Force,** *The effect of Eagle,* Warren, *Airborne Operations in WWII,* p. 26. **Johnson,** *Major Farris,* Johnson, "Operation Eagle and the Hand of God," *Airborne Quarterly,* Spring 2003, pp. 23–24.

A Man Called Moon (pages 64–73)

Moreno, *We went in,* Stillwell, *Assault on Normandy,* p. 226. **Collins,** *He is certainly pleasant,* Collins, *Lightning Joe,* p. 186. **22/4,** *On May 18,* MHI, Microfilm records, 22 IR/4 ID. **Roosevelt,** *Well Bunny Dear,* LC, Theodore Roosevelt Jr. Papers, Box 61. **Bradley,** *Hard to believe,* MHI, Chester Hansen Diary, June 6, 1944. **U.S. Navy,** *Had this not been done,* NHC, USNA, pp. 498–99. **U.S. Navy,** *somehow achieved,* NHC,

USNA, p. 500. **Moon,** *close to a miracle*, NA, RG 38, TF 125, Moon's Operation Report. **U.S. Navy,** *On the night*, NHC, USNA. **Brereton,** *The stupidity*, Brereton, *Brereton Diaries*, p. 274.

Silent Killers (pages 73–77)

Ruge, *comparatively few mines*, NA, RG 338, MS A-982. **Mine Squadron 7,** *USS Osprey*, NA, RG 38, Stack 370, Box 279. **Brown,** *Lady Godiva*, NHC, S. E. Morison Papers, article by Captain McEathron on U.S. minecraft in Operation Neptune used by Morison in preparation for *The Invasion of France and Germany*.

In Harm's Way (pages 77–83)

Quincy, *At 0452*, NA, RG 38, USS *Quincy*, Box 1360. **Johnson,** *We were running*, CR, B13–F44. **Farquharson-Roberts,** *The fire bell*, Oakley, *Royal Marines and D-Day*, p. 9. **Force U,** *All hands*, NA, RG 38, Box 317.

Marauder Men (pages 83–91)

USAAF, *air superiority*, Davis, *Carl A. Spaatz and the Air War in Europe*, p. 214. **Anderson,** *Enthusiasm was always*, Francis, *Flak Bait*, p. xii. **Wood,** *This is the day*, Moench, *Marauder Men*, pp. 193–95. **Intelligence,** *Weak to moderately heavy*, MHI, *Operations by IX Bomber Command, Ninth AF*, AAF Historical Study No. 36, 10/45, pp. 71–74. **Beaty,** *How we ever managed*, Francis, *Flak Bait*, p. 256. **9AF,** *The attacking planes*, NA, RG 407, E 427, ML, Box 24147. **Moench,** *It was the first time*, B-26 website, www.b-26marauderarchive.org. **Roosevelt,** *Suddenly we heard*, LC, Roosevelt Papers, Box 61. **Snow,** *It is difficult*, NA, RG 407, ML, Box 24147.

CHAPTER 4: NIGHT OF NIGHTS
Another Little Big Horn? (pages 92–98)

Gavin, *Neptune has been*, MHI, Gavin Papers, 5/26/44 diary entry. **Collins,** *On May 26*, NA, RG 407 AOR VII CP. **Leigh-Mallory,** *I hesitate*, DE, Pre-Presidential Papers, Leigh-Mallory folder, Box 71. **Eisenhower,** *You are quite right*, DEP, War Years, vol. III, pp. 1894–95. **Gavin,** *Either this 82nd Division*, MHI, Gavin Papers, 5/25–27/44 diary entries.

Lighting the Way (pages 98–106)

Williams, *Pilots of aircraft*, F.O. 1 copy at USAF Air Mobility Command Museum, Dover AFB, DE. **Pathfinders,** *details*, article by Crouch in Young, *Into the Valley*, pp. 96–99. **SHAEF,** *The standard night marking*, NA, RG 407, AOR 82 AD, "SHAEF Op Memo No. 12." **Sperber,** *We flew at a very*, Johnston, *Troop Carrier D-Day Flights*, article by Sperber, "D-Day Pathfinders," pp. 120–21. **Joseph,** *As the men left*, FB,

Joseph, AIOC, 1947–48, *Operations of a Regimental Pathfinder Unit, 507th PIR, in Normandy.* **Wilhelm,** *Coming into the jump,* CR, B10–F12.

Flying like a Gosling with a Mother Goose (pages 106–14)
Sink, *night of nights,* Sink's 6/5/44 message is reproduced in Bando, *Vanguard of the Crusade,* p. 26. **Ingram,** *Suddenly Corgill's C-47,* article by Ingram in Young, *Into the Valley,* pp. 123–25. **Young,** *On approaching,* Interrogation Check List, 6/6/44, 439 TCG, reproduced in Young, *Into the Valley,* p. 577. **Hitztaler,** *Coming in low,* NA, RG 18, E 7, Box 3947. **Field Order 1,** *Pilots will be held,* F.O. 1 copy at USAF Air Mobility Command Museum, Dover AFB, DE. **506 PIR,** *Tracer bullets,* NA, RG 407, E 427, Boxes 14437–39. **93 TCS/439 TCG,** *Intense anti-aircraft,* postmission interrogation, 6/6/44, 439 TCG, quoted in Young, *Into the Valley,* p. 126. **Muir,** *get above the formation,* Muir DSC citation, General Orders 58, U.S. Strategic Air Forces Europe. **Santarsiero,** *One of our planes,* CR, B10–F2. **Orcutt,** *I remember,* IA, 2/12/04. **Shanley,** *A lot of jumpmasters,* MHI, 8/13/44 82 AD debriefing, Roy Lindquist Papers. **U.S. Air Force,** *Although the pilots,* Warren, *Airborne Operations in WWII,* p. 59. **14 TCS/61 TCG,** *At 0226,* NA, RG 18, E 7, Box 3947.

CHAPTER 5: HITTING THE SILK
Fog of War (pages 115–19)
Hayn, *At 1:11 AM,* CR, B26–F18. **Gavin,** *Standard German,* Gavin, *Airborne Warfare,* p. 65. **Falley,** *Don't kill!,* Lord, *History of the 508th Parachute Infantry,* p. 26; also, Ryan, *The Longest Day,* pp. 269–70. **Ridgway,** *killing division commanders,* Ridgway, *Soldier,* p. 8. **325/82,** *General Falley,* NA, RG 407, AOR 82 AD, Box 12358. Previous accounts of Falley's death avowed that Falley had been the one thrown from the car and killed when he drew his pistol. But Baumann's account establishes that Falley was killed while seated in the car.

The Heinies Were Chagrined (pages 119–25)
502 PIR, *You could write a book,* CR, B10–F3; the writer was 2nd Lt. Earl Schmid. **Moseley,** *strike terror,* quoted from Mark Bando's 101 AD website, www.101airborneww2.com. The source of the quote was Lt. Col. John Michaelis, Moseley's executive, who also noted Moseley's erratic behavior on D-Day. **502/101,** *At 0048,* NA, RG 407, E 427, Boxes 14429–31. **Stopka,** *The lead scout,* NA, RG 338, Stack 290, Box 13, First Army awards, Harris DSC file. **Chappuis,** *pretty well spread,* Chappuis 11/30/95 oral history transcript, LSU. **Johnson,** *I had about 30,* Koskimaki, *D-Day with the Screaming Eagles,* p. 184. **Eisenhower,** *top-notch officer,* DEP, War Years, vol. IV, p. 2261.

Just a Kid (pages 125–33)

Young, *At our pilot briefing,* Young, 6/6/44 diary entry, quoted in Young, *Into the Valley,* p. 148. **Gavin,** *Bourbon Bob,* MHI, Gavin Papers, 1/4/83 interview. **Taylor,** *exceptional skill,* MHI, Blair Papers, quoted from Taylor's 1944 official evaluation of Sink. **Sink,** *head examined,* CR, B10–F5. **Matheson,** *It had been an old,* FB, Matheson, AIOC, 1949–50, *Operations of the 506th PIR in the Normandy Invasion.* **Sink,** *At our first command post,* CR, B10–F5. **Strayer,** *We were glad,* CR, B10–F8. **Taylor,** *I landed alone,* MHI, S. L. A. Marshall Papers, 2/15/46 letter Taylor to Marshall. **Ewell,** *finest officer,* T/4 Ray Geddes, IA, 5/15/04. **Morin,** *Our plane was hit,* McLaughlin, *D-Day + 60 Years,* p. 10; from Morin statement 8/44. **Taylor,** *It was apparent,* MHI, S. L. A. Marshall Papers, 2/15/46 letter Taylor to Marshall. **Danforth,** *Captain Kraeger,* Koskimaki, *D-Day with the Screaming Eagles,* p. 135. **Legere,** *I was shot,* CR, B9–F30. **Geddes,** *Legere was yelling,* McLaughlin, *D-Day + 60 Years,* p. 105.

Dying as Men Would Die (pages 133–41)

Wolverton, *not a religious man,* Crookenden, *Dropzone Normandy,* p. 101. **Smith,** *I shall never forget,* Smith, "I Saw Them Jump to Destiny," *Airborne Quarterly,* Summer 2003, pp. 93–95; submitted by Randy Hils. **McKnight,** *Apparently the Germans,* FB, McKnight, AIOC, 1947–48, *Plans and Operations of the 506th PIR on D-Day.* **3/506/101,** *Captain Shettle,* NA, RG 407, E 427, Box 14438. **Johnson,** *I heard a scream,* CMH, "The Fight at the Lock," File 8-3.1 BB2, p. 6. **Doss,** *About 0630,* CR, B9–F22. **Basse Addeville,** *scarcely even a village,* Critchell, *Four Stars of Hell,* p. 48. **2/501/101,** *Dawn was cracking,* CMH, "The Fight at the Lock," File 8-3.1 BB2, p. 22.

A Recipe for Disaster (pages 141–44)

Glider pilot, *recipe for disaster,* FO George Buckley, "A Glider Pilot's Story," *Airborne Quarterly,* Fall 2003, p. 54; submitted by G. Timmins. **Taylor,** *very superstitious,* CR, B10–F9. **Buckley,** *As soon as the rope,* Buckley, "A Glider Pilot's Story," *Airborne Quarterly,* Fall 2003, p. 55. **Natalle,** *One of the five,* CR, B9–F37.

CHAPTER 6: ALL-AMERICANS
From the Frying Pan to La Fière (pages 145–54)

Renaud, *one or two more tomorrow,* CR, B25–F53. **Gavin,** *unforceful supervision,* MHI, Gavin Papers, 2/11/44 diary entry. Batcheller reportedly carried on an affair with a local Irish woman and neglected the 505th's training; see Blair, *Ridgway's Paratroopers,* p. 193. **Ingrisano,** *milk run,* IA, 9/26/03. **Krause,** *abrasive personality* and *psycho,* MHI, Blair Papers, Allen Langdon, 5/1/84 letter to Blair; and Blair, 6/27/83 letter to Vandervoort. **Krause,** *close to 200,* MHI, 8/13/44 82 AD debriefing, Lindquist Papers. **Krause,** *secured Ste. Mère Église,* Marshall, *Night Drop,* p. 25. **Gavin,** *best* *battalion commander*, MHI, Gavin Papers, 9/1/82 letter to W. Breuer. **Ridgway,** *one of the bravest*, Ridgway, *Soldier*, p. 7. **Vandervoort,** career, CR, B9–F1. **Putnam,** *Luckily it was a simple*, CR, B8–F31. **Ridgway,** *Please express*, MHI, Blair Papers. **Vandervoort,** *I was sitting*, MHI, Blair Papers, 9/5/83 letter to Blair. **Ridgway,** *nucleus of my headquarters*, MHI, Ridgway Papers, 11/12/48 letter to Chief, Historical Division U.S. Army regarding inaccuracies in *Utah Beach to Cherbourg*. **Vandervoort,** *about 0410*, MHI, 8/13/44 82 AD debriefing, Lindquist Papers. **Wood,** *Lt. Col. Vandervoort*, CR, B9–F5. **Dolan,** *About 700–800 yards*, CR, 3/23/59 letter to Gavin, B7–F52. **Coxon,** *was a blow*, CR, 3/23/59 Gavin letter to Ryan, B8–F27.

Sacred Ground (pages 154–64)

Gavin, *I wish that someone*, MHI, Gavin Papers, 2/26/44 diary entry. **Gavin,** *Millett was awful*, MHI, Gavin Papers, 1/4/83 interview. **Gavin,** *Quiet as a mouse*, MHI, Gavin Papers, 1/4/83 interview. **Timmes,** *lot of difficulty*, MHI, 8/13/44 82 AD debriefing, Lindquist Papers. **D/507/82,** *The tanks*, NA, RG 407 AOR 507 PIR. **Owens,** *anti-tank mines*, CR, Owens account attached to 3/23/59 Gavin letter to Ryan, B8–F27. **Heim,** *bazooka gunner*, NA, RG 338, Stack 290, Box 13, First Army awards, Heim DSC file. **Dolan,** *heaviest small arms*, CR, 3/23/59 letter to Gavin, B7–F52. **Gavin,** *At about 0430*, NA, RG 407, AOR 82 AD. **Maloney,** *As I reached*, CR, B8–F18; also, *Not so good*, FB, Creek, AIOC, 1948–49, *Operations of a Mixed Group of the 507 PIR in the Invasion of France*. **Gavin,** *Lt. Col. Ostberg*, NA, RG 407, AOR 82 AD. **Creek,** *Speed seemed to be*, FB, Creek, AIOC, 1948–49, *Operations of a Mixed Group of the 507 PIR*.

Red Devils (pages 164–68)

Gavin, *He knew how much*, MHI, Gavin Papers, 1/4/83 interview. **Mendez,** *I didn't see*, MHI, 8/13/44 82 AD debriefing, Lindquist Papers. **Warren,** *word of mouth*, MHI, Blair Papers, 12/3/83 letter to Blair. **Adams,** *Immediately behind*, CR, B7–F33. **Shanley,** *about 35 men*, MHI, 8/13/44 82 AD debriefing, Lindquist Papers. **Warren,** *I landed*, MHI, 8/13/44 82 AD debriefing, Lindquist Papers. **Historian,** *top of Hill 30*, Marshall, *Night Drop*, p. 47. **508/82,** *Col. Ekman had conferred*, NA, RG 407 AOR 508 PIR; interview by S. L. A. Marshall.

Cutting Loose (pages 169–71)

84 TCS/437 TCG, *We landed*, NA, RG 18, E 7, Boxes 433–34. **Singleton,** *We ran into*, MHI, 8/13/44 82 AD debriefing, Lindquist Papers. **Mason,** *The roar of the wind*, CR, B8–F19. **Eaton,** *I landed*, CR, B7–F55; also, Blair, *Ridgway's Paratroopers*, p. 235. **Eisenhower,** gliderist wage increase, DEP, War Years, vol. III, pp. 1948–49.

CHAPTER 7: SO THIS IS FRANCE
Mission Accomplished (pages 172–77)

Blakely, *The 4th ID*, CR, B13–F9. **Collins,** *Have we forgotten*, CR, B17–F27. **4th Cavalry Group,** *About 100 yards*, CR, B17–F50; also NA, RG 407, E 427, Box 18118. **Rubin,** *Five of us*, CR, B18–F54. **Dunn,** *British Navy crew*, CR, B17–F50.

Old Prairie Belle (pages 177–84)

Roosevelt, *he loved everybody*, Reeder, *Born at Reveille*, p. 227; also see Jeffers, *In the Rough Rider's Shadow*. **Roosevelt,** *force and skill*, LC, Roosevelt Papers, Box 61. **Roosevelt,** *I don't think*, LC, Roosevelt Papers, Box 61. **Edelman,** *We were all assembled*, CR, B13–F25. **Roosevelt,** *start the war from here*, Ryan, *The Longest Day*, p. 233. **Naval officer,** *working perfectly*, AC, taped interview by Jon Gawne with Sims Gauthier of LCC-60. **Roosevelt,** *We passed a capsized*, LC, Roosevelt Papers, Box 61. **Moon,** *The Uncle Red*, NA, RG 38, TF 125, Box 319.

Give 'Em Hell (pages 184–91)

Van Fleet, *lots of small arms*, NA, RG 407, AOR 8 IR. **Collins,** *pushed at all costs*, NA, F.O. 1, RG 407, AOR VII CP. **Moreno,** *greatly impressed*, CR, B15–F51. **Schroeder,** *After mess*, CR, B14–F17. **USN TF 125,** *Wind was westerly*, NA, RG 38, TF 125, Box 319. **Van Fleet,** *The 8th Infantry*, MHI, 3/73 oral history interview by B. Williams, pp. 46–7. **Van Fleet,** mistaken identity, Braim, *The Will to Win*, p. 93. **Van Fleet,** *best leader*, MHI, Robert Rowe Papers, interview with George Mabry, p. 14. **Rockets,** *The majority of the craft*, NA, RG 38, Box 262. **Roosevelt,** *The little boats*, LC, Roosevelt Papers, Box 61. **Adair,** *I was in the assault*, NA, RG 407, CI, 4 ID. **Bailey,** *Artillery and small arms*, Babcock, *War Stories*, pp. 44–45. **Crisson,** *The spirit and morale*, NA, RG 407, CI, 4 ID.

Left and Right and Back Again (pages 191–200)

Roosevelt, *There was a house*, LC, Roosevelt Papers, Box 61. **Van Fleet,** *our boats would ground*, MHI, 3/73 oral history interview by B. Williams. **Crisson,** *The craft landed*, NA, RG 407, CI, 4 ID. **Roosevelt,** *hot-foot it*, LC, Roosevelt Papers, Box 61. **E/8/4,** *Lt. Rebarchek*, NA, RG 407, CI, 4 ID. **Caffey,** *I undertook*, CR, B17–F41. **Wolfram,** *I was the runner*, NA, RG 407, E 427, ML, Boxes 24240–42. **Schroeder,** *A group of the enemy*, CR, B14–F17. **Mabry,** *I saw seven men*, FB, Mabry, AIOC, 1946–47, *Operations of the 2/8 IR in the Landing at Utah Beach*. **Haley,** *Capt. James Haley*, NA, RG 338, Stack 290, Box 12, First Army awards, eyewitness statement by Mabry in Haley DSC file. **Crisson,** *We moved inland*, NA, RG 407, CI, 4 ID. **Willard,** *We were told*, NA, RG 407, E 427, ML, Boxes 24240–42.

A Last Cup of Hot Java (pages 200–208)

Straussler, *The design,* UK Tank Museum at Bovington website, www.d-daytanks.org.uk. **Johnson,** *Sgt. Hill and I,* CR, B18–F16. In his naval history of the Utah landing, *The Invasion of France and Germany,* Samuel Eliot Morison says that it was LCT-597, not LCT-593, that blew up. However, LCT-597 carried Company B DD tanks, and that outfit did not lose any DDs at sea on D-Day. LCT-597 was sunk later in the day, but without its tanks onboard. **70 TB,** *When the LCT,* 70 TB History, *History of the 70th Tank Battalion,* p. 61. **Collins,** *I put off,* Collins, *Lightning Joe,* p. 187. **B/70 TB,** *Onboard the LCTs,* NA, RG 407, E 427, Box 16635. **Casteel,** *My company landed,* NA, RG 407, AOR 70 TB. **General Board,** *Col. J. C. Welborn,* MHI, USFET Study No. 50, "Separate Tank Battalions."

Heroism Unsurpassed (pages 208–13)

Tabb, *somewhat surprised,* Military.com website, Tabb D-Day memoirs, www.military.com/Content/. **237 ECB,** *Operations didn't proceed,* NA, RG 407, E 427, Box 24204. **Rogers,** *The beach obstacle,* NA, RG 407, E 427, Box 18762. **Cross,** *Going in to the beach,* CR, B13–F21. **Peterson,** *Naval demolition units,* NA, RG 38, TF 125, Box 319.

This Ship Needs Help (pages 213–18)

Hoffman, *being fired upon,* CR, B14–F47. **Corry,** *taller than* Corry*'s masts,* Lt. (jg) Francis McKernon, 2/25/82 letter to shipmate. **Hoffman,** *came pouring,* 6/9/44 Hoffman radio interview with Edward R. Murrow, USS *Corry* website, www.uss-corry-dd463.com. **Hoffman,** *Corry was hit,* AC (courtesy Kevin McKernon), Hoffman's 6/9/44 letter to Admiral Stark, Commander U.S. Naval Forces Europe; the second half of Hoffman's account is from his 6/19/44 report, CR, B13–F35. **Decorations,** Roscoe, *U.S. Destroyer Operations in WWII,* p. 350; also, correspondence with Garay's son, 6/9/04. **Ensign,** *We considered that,* ACM, Robert Beeman, *The Sinking of USS* Corry: *A Personal Account,* p. 13. **Moon,** *So far as is known,* NA, RG 38, TF 125, Moon's Action Report. **Navy,** *distressed Adm. Moon,* NHC, USNA, p. 505. **Collins,** *I detected,* Collins, *Lightning Joe,* p. 193. **Collins,** *I had decided,* MHI, S. L. A. Marshall Papers, 5/16/46 conference, VII Corps D-Day operations. Collins's G-2, Colonel King (West Point, 1928), was killed on 6/22/44.

They Ain't Seasick No More (pages 218–29)

Roosevelt, *Most of our work,* LC, Roosevelt Papers, Box 61. **Batte,** *proudly exhibited,* CR, B17–F35. **Collins,** *The first waves,* NA, RG 407, AOR 8 IR. **Vickery,** *We had trained,* CR, B14–F30. **Teague,** *The enemy positions,* NA, RG 407, CI, 4 ID. **746 TB,** *The 1st Platoon,* NA, RG 407, E 427, Box 16712. **87 CMB,** *Companies A and B,* NA,

RG 407, E 427, Boxes 18506–08. **Batte,** *I was on a British*, CR, B17–F35. **65 FAB,** *During disembarkation*, NA, RG 407, E 427, Boxes 19756–57. **Bailey,** *I ran into*, CR, B17–F32. **Ausland,** *My task once ashore*, Ausland, 6/6/84 article, *International Herald Tribune*. **29 FAB,** *After C Battery*, CR, B14–F25. **Gibbons,** *I had never been*, CR, B13–F33.

CHAPTER 8: GET IN THERE AND TAKE CHANCES
Searching for an Answer (pages 230–36)

Barton, *I, 1st Lt. Bill York* and *While I was mentally*, CR, B13–F7. **22/4,** *The 1st Battalion*, MHI, Microfilm records, 22 IR/4 ID; also NA, RG 407, CI, 4 ID, 7/2/44. **Harrison,** *I remember*, CR, B13–F39. **Roosevelt,** *stepchild of the 4th Division*, Reeder, *Born at Reveille*, p. 228. **Eisenhower,** *damned good man*, DEP, War Years, vol. III, p. 1685. **Reeder,** *The prowess*, Reeder, *Fighting on Guadalcanal*, pp. 67–68. **Reeder,** *almost cut off* and *The Germans had flooded*, Reeder, 6/6/84 article, *New York Times*. **Reeder,** *We are going through*, Reeder, *Born at Reveille*, p. 248. **Johnson,** *The dreaded*, CR, B13–F44. **Reeder,** *searching for an answer*, CR, B14–F12.

Fugitives from the Laws of Averages (pages 236–39)

531 ESR, *all felt like fugitives*, CR, B19–F7. **4 ID,** *The mission*, NA, RG 407, AOR 4 ID, Field Order 1. **Caffey,** *One thing*, CR, B17–F41. Wharton was subsequently assigned as assistant commander, 9th Infantry Division; and then, on August 11, 1944, as commander, 28th Infantry Division. However, he was killed in action on August 12. **1/531 ESR,** *The 3rd Platoon*, NA, RG 407, E 427, Box 19626. **1 ESB,** *The area back*, NA, RG 407, E 427, Box 19039. **Moore,** *I have never*, CR, B18–F34.

Uncorking the Bottle (pages 239–46)

Zampiello, *About one and one-half*, NA, RG 338, Stack 290, Box 1, First Army awards, Ahearn DSC file; also Jensen, *Strike Swiftly*, p. 142. **Mabry,** *I pulled out*, Babcock, *War Stories*, p. 103; also MHI, Rowe Papers, interview with Mabry. **Taylor,** *Shortly after*, Taylor, *Swords and Plowshares*, p. 81. **Brierre,** *Gen. Taylor ordered me*, Koskimaki, *D-Day with the Screaming Eagles*, p. 140. **Koskimaki,** *I remember*, Koskimaki, *D-Day with the Screaming Eagles*, p. 141. **Higgins,** *I talked*, ACM, *Interview with Gerald Higgins on Normandy Operation*. **8/4,** *The 1st Battalion*, MHI, Microfilm records, 8 IR/4 ID. **Collins,** *Did you feel*, MHI, S. L. A. Marshall Papers, 5/16/46 conference, VII Corps D-Day operations.

Go, Sergeant, Go (pages 246–56)

German artillery, Harrison, *Cross-Channel Attack*, p. 283; the battalion was 2/191st Artillery. Reportedly the 91st Division used 105-millimeter mountain howitzers, a lighter version of standard German field howitzers. **Raudstein,** *We left the buildings*,

FB, Raudstein, AIOC, 1948–49, *Operations of 1/506 PIR in the Vicinity of Carentan.* **1/506/101,** *It was a confused,* CMH, "The 506 PIR in the Normandy Drop," File 8-3.1 BB3. **Winters,** *First thing I did,* Koskimaki, *D-Day with the Screaming Eagles,* p. 231; Mr. Koskimaki informed the author that this statement was drawn from Winters's 6/22/44 diary entry. A few members of Company F also participated in Winters's assault. **Vickery,** *My platoon,* CR, B14–F30. **Mozgo,** *We had moved,* CR, B14–F6; also Jensen, *Strike Swiftly,* p. 140; and *History of the 70th Tank Battalion,* p. 62. **Norris,** *We encountered,* AC, provided courtesy of Frederick Maisel Jr. **Collins,** *The Germans started,* NA, RG 407, CI, 4 ID. **Maisel,** *Organizing supporting fire,* AC, provided courtesy of F. Maisel Jr. **Roosevelt,** *removal of my helmet,* CR, B10–F5.

Between the Devil and the Sea (pages 256–61)

501/101, *All hell broke loose,* CMH, "The Fight at the Lock," File 8-3.1 BB2. **Ballard,** *no position to move,* Koskimaki, *D-Day with the Screaming Eagles,* p. 127. **Johnson,** *felt strongly,* and *work of Quincy's batteries,* CMH, "The Fight at the Lock," File 8-3.1 BB2. **Quincy,** *fired main battery,* NA, RG 38, USS *Quincy,* Box 1360. **Sampson,** *I told the regimental surgeon,* Sampson, *Paratrooper Padre,* pp. 47–48.

An Objective Called XYZ (pages 261–66)

Collins, *greatest concerns,* MHI, S. L. A. Marshall Papers, 5/16/46 conference, VII Corps D-Day operations. **A/502,** *Company A,* NA, F.O. 1, RG 407, AOR 101 AD. **1/502/101,** *Sgt. Summers,* NA, RG 407, E 427, Boxes 14429–31, "Action of 502-1 on D-Day"; this paragraph is drawn from the original account by S. L. A. Marshall, written in July 1944 shortly after his interview with Summers. It differs in some significant ways from Marshall's later book *Night Drop* and his account of the XYZ fight, "Cassidy's Battalion" (CMH, File 8-3.1 BA9). **Camien,** *A French girl,* Bando, *101st Airborne, Screaming Eagles at Normandy,* pp. 70–71. **Brandenberger,** *terribly sorry,* NA, RG 407, E 427, Boxes 14429–31, "Action of 502-1 on D-Day." **Summers,** *no idea why,* CMH, "Cassidy's Battalion," File 8-3.1 BA9.

CHAPTER 9: SOMETHING TO BEHOLD
They Shall Not Pass (pages 267–77)

Collins, *Report progress,* MHI, Microfilm records, 82 AD. **Collins,** *I felt that things,* MHI, S. L. A. Marshall Papers, 5/16/46 conference, VII Corps D-Day operations. **Vandervoort,** *Turnbull and I,* MHI, Blair Papers, correspondence with Blair. **Peterson,** *We moved quickly,* CR, B8–F29. **Sampson,** *We moved the mortar,* account from Airborne Museum in Ste. Mère Église, Normandy. **Turnbull,** casualties, Langdon, *Ready,* pp. 55–57. **Maness,** *West Texas dust storm,* Langdon, *Ready,* p. 57. **Gavin,** *I went back,* NA, RG 407, AOR 82 AD. **Timmes,** *While awaiting,* MHI, Blair Papers, 8/16/83 letter to Blair.

Ridgway's Croaker (pages 278–84)

Raff, *My personal opinion* and *condemn a man*, MHI, Blair Papers, Edson Raff Memoirs. **Ingersoll,** *By the time*, Ingersoll, *Top Secret*, pp. 125–26. **C/746 TB,** *reconnaissance elements*, NA, RG 407, E 427, Box 16712. **Ingersoll,** *beautiful formation*, Ingersoll, *Top Secret*, pp. 130–31.

Don't Knock a Glider Man (pages 284–89)

Raibl, *crossing the Channel*, FB, Raibl, AIOC, 1948–49, *Operations of the 82nd AD Artillery in Normandy*. **Raff,** *To my horror*, CR, B8–F32. **83 TCS/437 TCG,** *We landed at 2110*, NA, RG 18, E 7, Boxes 433–34. **Elmira,** casualties, Warren, *Airborne Operations in WWII*, p. 69. **Coyle,** *I was standing*, CR, B7–F50. **Cooperider,** *While talking*, NA, RG 407, E 427, ML, Boxes 24240–42. **HQ/101,** *It had been felt*, NA, RG 407, AOR, 101 AD. **McCarthy,** *Our glider contained*, Koskimaki, *D-Day with the Screaming Eagles*, pp. 274–77.

CHAPTER 10: PROUD OF YOU
Friction of War (pages 290–97)

Roosevelt, *I must have walked* and *The battalion CO*, LC, Roosevelt Papers, Box 61. **746 TB,** *Along the route*, NA, RG 407, E 427, Box 16712. **Reeder,** *We walked out*, Reeder, 6/6/84 article, *New York Times*. **Johnson,** *In his eagerness*, CR, B13–F44. **VII Corps,** *Hedgerow fighting*, NA, RG 407, E 427, Boxes 14423–26. **Gayle,** *The 3rd Battalion*, MHI, Microfilm records, 8 IR/4 ID.

Tough 'Ombres (pages 297–300)

Lynd, *morning of June 6*, MHI, World War II surveys, 90 ID. **90 ID,** *As the boats approached*, MHI, *History of the 90th Division in WWII*, p. 5. **Collins,** *inadequate training*, Collins, *Lightning Joe*, p. 208. **Patton,** *greatest divisions*, Patton, *War as I Knew It*, p. 97.

The Right Place at the Right Time (pages 300–306)

Barton, *June 6 ended*, CR, B13–F7. **Gibbons,** *As we pulled*, CR, B13–F33. **Taylor,** *so few*, Taylor, *Swords and Plowshares*, p. 80. **Taylor,** *reasonably clear*, MHI, S. L. A. Marshall Papers, 2/25/46 letter Taylor to Marshall. **Taylor,** *all dead tired*, CR, B10–F9. **Taylor,** *torture to walk*, Taylor, *Swords and Plowshares*, p. 75.

We Fight Alone (pages 306–8)

Ridgway, *couldn't get in touch*, Ridgway, *Soldier*, p. 9. **Vandervoort,** *stressed the importance*, CR, B9–F1, 3/11/59 letter to Ryan. **Ridgway,** *I am not aware*, MHI, Ridgway Papers, 11/12/48 letter to Chief, Historical Division U.S. Army regarding inaccuracies in *Utah Beach to Cherbourg*. **Wienecke,** *Short 60 percent*, "All-American," *Stars and Stripes*, 1945. **Ridgway,** *Proud of you*, MHI, Microfilm records, 82 AD.

CHAPTER 11: THE FIRST DAY OF A LONG STRUGGLE
The Courage of Two O'Clock in the Morning (pages 309–20)

Collins, *not altogether satisfied*, Collins, *Lightning Joe*, p. 201. **Bradley,** *In contrast*, Bradley, *A Soldier's Story*, p. 275. **Bradley,** *The sudden presence*, Bradley, *A General's Life*, p. 247. **Troop Carrier,** data and casualties, Warren, *Airborne Operations in WWII*, p. 58. **Gavin,** *Moral courage*, MHI, Gavin Papers, 1975 interview, p. 23; also CR, B8–F4, 1958 interview with Ryan, p. 7. **Bidwell,** *Airborne units*, Huston, *Out of the Blue*, p. 186.

Lost Souls (pages 320–25)

Bradley, *piece of cake*, Bradley, *A General's Life*, p. 249. **Gibbons,** *pure relief*, CR, B13–F33. **Casualties,** *less than 200*, Harrison, *Cross-Channel Attack*, p. 329. **U.S. Navy,** *Force U's part*, NHC, *USNA*, p. 493. **Bradley,** *In my opinion*, MHI, General Board USFET Study No. 16, "Airborne Operations." **Casualties,** 82/101 Divisions, Harrison, *Cross-Channel Attack*, pp. 284, 300. **Casualties,** Troop Carrier, Warren, *Airborne Operations in WWII*, pp. 224–25. **Casualties,** overall: If VII Corps casualties in Exercise Tiger are added to its D-Day losses, the human losses suffered by V and VII Corps to train for and execute the Omaha and Utah assaults were roughly equal.

What a Plan! (pages 325–29)

Montgomery, *violence, speed, and power*, Montgomery, *Memoirs*, p. 221. **Montgomery,** *lessons learnt*, Montgomery, *Memoirs*, p. 199. **Churchill,** *I have to announce*, Hansard, *Parliamentary Proceedings*, June 6, 1944, cols. 1209–10.

Bibliography

Autry, Jerry. *Gen. William C. Lee: Father of the Airborne.* Raleigh, NC: Airborne Press, 1995.

Babcock, Robert. *War Stories: The 4th Division from Utah Beach to Pleiku.* Baton Rouge, LA: St. John's Press, 2001.

Bando, Mark. *101st Airborne: The Screaming Eagles at Normandy.* Osceola, WI: MBI, 2001.

———. *Vanguard of the Crusade: The 101st Airborne Division in WWII.* Bedford, PA: Aberjona Press, 2003.

Bass, Richard. *The Brigades of Neptune: U.S. Army Engineer Special Brigades in Normandy.* Exeter, England: Lee Publishing, 1994.

———. *Spirits of the Sand: A History of the U.S. Army Assault Training Center.* Exeter, England: Lee Publishing, 1991.

Berger, Sid. *Breaching Fortress Europe: The Story of U.S. Engineers in Normandy on D-Day.* Dubuque, IA: Kendall Hunt, 1994.

Blair, Clay. *Ridgway's Paratroopers: The American Airborne in WWII.* New York: Morrow, 1985.

Blanchard, W. J. *Our Liberators: The Combat History of the 746th Tank Battalion during WWII.* Tucson, AZ: Wheatmark, 2003.

Bland, Larry, ed. *The Papers of George Catlett Marshall,* vols. 3 and 4. Baltimore: Johns Hopkins, 1991.

Bradley, Omar. *A Soldier's Story.* New York: Henry Holt, 1951.

Bradley, Omar with Clay Blair. *A General's Life.* New York: Simon and Schuster, 1983.

Braim, Paul. *The Will to Win: The Life of Gen. James Van Fleet.* Annapolis, MD: Naval Institute Press, 2001.

Brereton, Lewis. *The Brereton Diaries.* New York: Morrow, 1946.

Brinson, W. L. *Three One Five Group.* Lakemount, GA: Copple House, 1984.

Butcher, Harry. *My Three Years with Eisenhower.* New York: Simon and Schuster, 1946.

Chandler, Alfred, ed. *The Papers of Dwight David Eisenhower: The War Years.* Baltimore: Johns Hopkins, 1970.

Chandler, David, and James Collins, eds. *The D-Day Encyclopedia.* New York: Simon and Schuster, 1994.

Collins, J. Lawton. *Lightning Joe: An Autobiography.* Baton Rouge, LA: LSU Press, 1979.

Craven, Wesley, and James Cate. *The Army Air Forces in WWII.* Vol. 3, Europe: Argument to V-E Day. Chicago: University of Chicago, 1951.

Critchell, Laurence. *Four Stars of Hell.* New York: Berkley, 1987.

Crookenden, Napier. *Dropzone Normandy.* New York: Charles Scribner's Sons, 1976.

Dank, Milton. *The Glider Gang.* Bennington, VT: Merriam Press, 1999.

Davis, Richard. *Carl A. Spaatz and the Air War in Europe.* Washington, DC: Center for Air Force History, 1993.

De Guingand, Francis. *Operation Victory.* London: Hodder and Stoughton, 1947.

D'Este, Carlo. *Decision in Normandy.* London: William Collins, 1983.

Devlin, Gerard. *Paratrooper.* New York: St. Martin's, 1979.

— — —. *Silent Wings.* New York: St. Martin's, 1985.

Ehrman, John. *Grand Strategy,* vol. 5. London: HMSO, 1956.

Eighth Infantry, 4th Infantry Division. *The 8th Infantry Regiment.* Germany: 4th Infantry Division, 1945.

Eighty-Second Airborne Division. *Saga of the All-American.* Chicago: 82nd Airborne Division Association, 1946.

Eisenhower, Dwight. *Crusade in Europe.* New York: Doubleday, 1948.

Elliott, Peter. *Allied Minesweeping in WWII.* Annapolis, MD: Naval Institute Press, 1979.

Eubank, Keith. *Summit at Tehran: The Untold Story.* New York: Morrow, 1985.

Fane, Francis, and Don Moore. *The Naked Warriors: The Story of the US Navy's Frogmen.* Annapolis, MD: U.S. Naval Institute, 1995.

Francis, Devon. *Flak Bait: The Story of the Men Who Flew the Martin Marauders.* New York: Duell, Sloan, and Pearce, 1948.

Freeman, Roger. *UK Airfields of the Ninth: Then and Now.* London: After the Battle, 1993.

Gavin, James. *Airborne Warfare.* Washington, DC: Infantry Journal Press, 1947.

— — —. *On to Berlin.* New York: Viking Press, 1978.

Gawne, Jonathan. *Spearheading D-Day.* Paris: Histoire & Collections, 1998.

Gilbert, Martin. *Winston Churchill: Road to Victory, 1941–1945.* Boston: Houghton Mifflin, 1986.

Greene, Ralph. "What Happened off Devon." *American Heritage* (February 1987).

Hamilton, Nigel. *Master of the Battlefield: Monty's War Years, 1942–1944.* New York: McGraw Hill, 1983.

Harrison, Gordon. *Cross-Channel Attack.* Washington, DC: Chief of Military History, 1951.

Havener, J. K. *The Martin B-26 Marauder.* Blue Ridge Summit, PA: Aero Books, 1988.

Hinsley, F. H., et al. *British Intelligence in the Second World War,* vol. 3, pt. 2. London: HMSO, 1984.

Huston, James. *Out of the Blue: U.S. Army Airborne Operations in WWII.* West Lafayette, IN: Purdue University Press, 1998.

Ingersoll, Ralph. *Top Secret.* New York: Harcourt, Brace, 1946.

Ingrisano, Michael. *Valor without Arms: A History of the 316th Troop Carrier Group.* Bennington, VT: Merriam Press, 2001.

Isby, David, ed. *Fighting the Invasion: The German Army at D-Day.* London: Greenhill, 2000.

Jeffers, H. Paul. *In the Rough Rider's Shadow.* New York: Ballantine, 2002.

Jensen, Marvin. *Strike Swiftly: The 70th Tank Battalion from North Africa to Normandy to Germany.* Novato, CA: Presidio, 1997.

Johnston, Lew. *The Troop Carrier D-Day Flights.* Privately published, copy at AMC Museum, Dover AFB, 2003.

Kimball, Warren, ed. *Churchill and Roosevelt: The Complete Correspondence.* Princeton, NJ: Princeton University Press, 1984.

Koskimaki, George. *D-Day with the Screaming Eagles.* Havertown, PA: Casemate, 2002.

Langdon, Allen. *Ready: A WWII History of the 505th Parachute Infantry Regiment*. Indianapolis: 82nd Airborne Division Association, 1986.

Lewis, Nigel. *Exercise Tiger.* New York: Prentice Hall, 1990.

Liddell-Hart, B. H., ed. *The Rommel Papers*. New York: Harcourt, Brace, 1953.

Lord, William. *History of the 508th Parachute Infantry*. Washington, DC: Infantry Journal Press, 1948.

Lowden, John. *Silent Wings at War.* Washington, DC: Smithsonian, 1992.

Marshall, S. L. A. *Night Drop: The American Airborne Invasion of Normandy.* Boston: Little, Brown, 1962.

McKernon, Kevin. *Corry: The Destroyer that Led the Normandy Invasion.* West Haven, CT: Easy Rudder Press, 2003.

McLaughlin, Jerome. *D-Day Plus 60 Years*. Bloomington: Author House, 2004.

Moench, John. *Marauder Men*. Longwood, FL: Malia, 1989.

Montgomery, Sir Bernard. *The Memoirs of Field Marshal Montgomery.* New York: Signet, 1958.

———. *Normandy to the Baltic*. London: Hutchinson, 1948.

Morgan, Sir Frederick. *Overture to Overlord*. New York: Doubleday, 1950.

Morison, Samuel E. *The Invasion of France and Germany, 1944–1945.* Boston: Little Brown, 1962.

Mowry, George. *Landing Craft and the War Production Board*. Washington, DC: U.S. Government, 1944; copy at MHI.

Murch, David, and Muriel Murch. *The American Forces at Salcombe and Slapton during WWII*. Plymouth, England: PDS Printers, 1984.

Murphy, Robert. *No Better Place to Die*. Croton Falls NY: Critical Hit, 1999.

Oakley, Derek. *Royal Marines and D-Day*. Portsmouth, England: Royal Marines Historical Society, 1994.

Otway, T. B. H. *Airborne Forces*. London: Imperial War Museum, 1990.

Patton, George. *War as I Knew It*. New York: Pyramid, 1966.

Pogue, Forrest. *George C. Marshall: Organizer of Victory, 1943–1945.* New York: Penguin, 1993.

———. *Pogue's War: Diaries of a WWII Combat Historian*. Lexington, KY: University Press of Kentucky, 2001.

———. *The Supreme Command*. Washington, DC: Chief of Military History, 1954.

Price, Scott. *The U.S. Coast Guard at Normandy*. USCG Historian's Office Website, www.uscg.mil, 2003.

Rapport, Leonard, and Arthur Norwood. *Rendezvous with Destiny.* Bentonville, OH: 101st Airborne Division Association, 1948.

Reeder, Russell. *Born at Reveille.* New York: Duell, Sloan, and Pearce, 1966.

———. *Fighting on Guadalcanal.* Washington, DC: Department of the Army, 1943; copy at MHI.

Ridgway, Matthew. *Soldier: The Memoirs of Matthew B. Ridgway.* New York: Harper, 1956.

Roosevelt, Eleanor. *Day Before Yesterday.* New York: Doubleday, 1959.

Roscoe, Theodore. *U.S. Destroyer Operations in WWII.* Annapolis, MD: U.S. Naval Institute, 1953.

Rothbart, David. *A Soldier's Journal with the 22nd Infantry in WWII.* New York: iBooks, 2003.

Rust, Kenn. *The 9th Air Force in WWII.* Fallbrook, CA: Aero, 1970.

Ryan, Cornelius. *The Longest Day.* New York: Simon and Schuster, 1959.

Sampson, Francis. *Paratrooper Padre.* Washington, DC: Catholic University, 1948.

Seventieth Tank Battalion. *History of the 70th Tank Battalion, June 5, 1940 to May 22, 1946.* Washington, DC: Department of the Army, 1950.

Small, Ken. *The Forgotten Dead.* London: Bloomsbury, 1998.

Stanton, Shelby. *WWII Order of Battle.* New York: Galahad, 1984.

Stillwell, Paul. *Assault on Normandy: First-Person Accounts from the Sea Services.* Annapolis, MD: U.S. Naval Institute, 1994.

Taylor, Maxwell. *Swords and Plowshares.* New York: Norton, 1972.

U.S. Army Air Force. *DZ Europe: History of the 440th Troop Carrier Group.* Germany, 1945.

U.S. Army Historical Division. *Utah Beach to Cherbourg.* Washington, DC: Department of the Army, 1947.

U.S. Coast Guard. *The Coast Guard at War,* vol. XI. Washington, DC: U.S. Coast Guard, 1946.

U.S. Department of State. *Foreign Relations of the U.S., Diplomatic Papers: The Conferences at Cairo and Teheran, 1943.* Washington, DC: GPO, 1961.

U.S. Navy. *U.S. Naval Administration in WWII, The Invasion of Normandy,* vol. 5. Washington, DC: U.S. Navy, 1945.

Warren, John. *Airborne Operations in WWII, European Theater.* Washington, DC: USAF Historical Division, 1956.

Wills, Deryk. *Put on Your Boots and Parachutes: The 82nd Airborne Division.* Leicester, England: AB Printers, 1992.

Wilmot, Chester. *The Struggle for Europe.* London: Collins, 1952.

Wilson, Theodore, ed. *D-Day, 1944.* Abilene, KS: University Press of Kansas, 1994.

Wolfe, Martin. *Green Light: A Troop Carrier Squadron's War from Normandy to the Rhine.* Washington, DC: Center for Air Force History, 1993.

Yeide, Harry. *Steel Victory: The Heroic Story of America's Independent Tank Battalions at War in Europe.* New York: Ballantine, 2003.

Young, Charles. *Into the Valley: The Untold Story of USAAF Troop Carrier in WWII.* Dallas: PrintComm, 1995.

Zetterling, Niklas. *Normandy 1944: German Military Organization, Combat Power, and Effectiveness.* Winnipeg, Manitoba, Canada: Fedorowicz, 2000.

Acknowledgments

The American airborne and seaborne assault of the Cotentin Peninsula in Normandy on June 6, 1944, was a military operation of immense complexity. To research and describe this operation in more precise detail than previous D-Day accounts is a monumental challenge to the twenty-first-century historian. The invasion encompassed vast sea, land, and air forces, which planned, executed, and documented their critical roles on D-Day in entirely different ways. As established in my previous book, *Omaha Beach: June 6, 1944,* my methodology depends overwhelmingly on primary source materials drawn as much as possible from military documents produced soon after the invasion. Indeed, I held to that resolve even more firmly in this book than its predecessor. However, the diverse military units that participated in the Cotentin invasion did not document their roles in the invasion with equal thoroughness, and for some outfits, particularly parachute units that did not assemble in reasonably organized shape for days after the invasion, locating pertinent and valuable primary source documents was as difficult as the search for the proverbial needle in a haystack.

I was extremely fortunate to locate and gain the trust of many brilliant archivists and researchers while writing this book, all of whom helped guide me quickly to sources of information that would have taken me months to locate on my own. Richard Sommers and David Keough of the U.S. Army Military History Institute, Tim Nenninger of the National

372

Archives, Mark Reardon of the Center of Military History, Roger Cirillo of the Association of the U.S. Army, Adrian Lewis of the University of North Texas, David Haight of the Dwight D. Eisenhower Library, and Doug McCabe of the Cornelius Ryan Collection at Ohio University were all gracious and patient with me in my difficult search for vital new D-Day archival sources. I am particularly indebted to the Military History Institute for awarding me a Matthew B. Ridgway research grant for the year 2004 to support this pursuit.

My friend Jon Gawne, author of the seminal book *Spearheading D-Day,* was as usual most helpful when any perplexing D-Day research issue cropped up and by opening up his nearly limitless supply of D-Day photographs to me. Tom Bowers, expert researcher and former senior staff member at the Center of Military History, guided me through the complexities of National Archives research, an effort that produced many valuable documents contributing greatly to a deeper understanding of the invasion.

The story of the Ninth Air Force's Troop Carrier Command has been repeatedly overlooked by D-Day historians, and all of the following people helped immensely to rectify that lamentable oversight: Randy Hils, Tony Ingram, Mike Ingrisano, Lew Johnston, Michael Leister (director of the Air Mobility Command Museum in Dover, Delaware), Jerry McLaughlin, Joe Molyson, Donald Orcutt, Adam Parsons (a D-Day Troop Carrier pilot and former 506th paratrooper), and Charles Young Jr.

There is no person alive who knows more about the 101st Airborne Division on D-Day than Mark Bando, and his books on that subject prove it. Whenever a question related to the 101st arose while researching and writing this book, Mark generally knew the answer and was kind enough to send it to me promptly via e-mail. Other experts on American parachute and glider operations in Normandy who were most charitable with their time were Ray Geddes, George Koskimaki (author of *D-Day with the Screaming Eagles*), and Bill Weber (editor of *Airborne Quarterly*).

Dave Berry, a leading expert on D-Day pathfinder operations, provided me with many fascinating details about those daring paratroopers who led the way into Normandy shortly after midnight on June 6, 1944.

I was also fortunate to know those many men who carry the flame of the 4th Infantry Division within their souls: Bob Babcock, Philippe Cornil, Butch Maisel, David Rothbart (author of *A Soldier's Journal*), and Robert Rush (author of *Hell in the Hürtgen Forest*).

Gordon Shelley, Don Jones, and Clive Stevens were extremely obliging in providing their expert knowledge of mine warfare at sea, a subject that I knew little about before embarking on this project. Given that German naval mines inflicted severe damage on Admiral Moon's Force "U" on D-Day, this was a subject I had to master to tell the Utah story truthfully.

Grant Gullickson, Kevin McKernon, and Peter Garay generously imparted to me their considerable knowledge of the U.S. Navy destroyer *Corry,* one of the first Allied warships lost to enemy action on D-Day. After corresponding with Grant and Kevin by e-mail, it was a thrill to meet them on Utah Beach in June 2004 to mark the sixtieth anniversary of the invasion and *Corry*'s loss.

William Gayle, Gordon Harrison, S. L. A. Marshall, Forrest Pogue, and Roland Ruppenthal were all brilliant World War II U.S. Army historians whose early work yielded to later D-Day historians a solid foundation of facts and data, without which this book could not have been written. Similarly, Cornelius Ryan, author of the classic D-Day history *The Longest Day,* had the foresight to preserve his voluminous research materials and D-Day veterans' surveys from the 1950s, all of which are now maintained in scrupulous order at the Ohio University Library in Athens.

I would also like to thank Cal Collier (a Ninth Air Force B-26 pilot), Maryland Governor Robert Ehrlich, Bob Mullauer, Maj. Gen. Bruce Tuxill (Adjutant General of the Maryland National Guard), Maj. Gen. Daniel Long (a former commander of the 29th Infantry Division), Sgt. Maj. Thomas Webb, Fran Sherr-Davino, and Curt Vickery for their constructive advice and unwavering support of this project.

At Stackpole Books, my editor Chris Evans had faith that I could do the job properly and, as usual, did sterling work bringing this book to fruition, supported by his gifted assistant David Reisch and art director Wendy Reynolds.

I will borrow the 4th Division's motto to declare that any historian with supporters as "steadfast and loyal" as my friends listed here is indeed privileged.

Bless 'em all.

Index

abbreviations, xix–xx
Adair, M. C., 191
Adams, Jonathan, 165
Addeville, Haute and Basse (Upper and Lower), 139–40, 259
Ahearn, John, 241
air support, importance and role of, xiii–xiv, 41–49, 83–91
Alexander, Mark, 275
Allen, Richard, 140, 259
Amfreville, 155–56
Andersen, Howard, 215
Anderson, Samuel, xviii, 87
Angoville au Plain, 139
Anti-Aircraft Artillery Battalion, 377th, 35
Anvil, 65
Arizona, USS, 80
Armored Field Artillery Battalion
 29th, 227–29
 65th, 35, 226–27
army organization, xvi–xvii
Audouville, 245
Ausland, John, 228
Azalea, HMS, 61, 62

Bailey, Edward, 227
Bailey, Harry, 191
Ballard, Robert, 139–41, 259
Barber, Henry, xviii, 332–33
Barker, Ray, 7
Barnett, USS, 78, 177, 186
Barton, Raymond O., xvii, 32–33, 179, 230–33, 298, 300–301, 312
Batcheller, Herbert, 146, 165
battalions, xvi

Batte, James, 226
Baumann, Gefreiter, 118
Bayfield, USS, 78
bazooka teams, 157–58
beach obstacles, 52–53, 56, 185, 197, 313
 See also mines
 clearing of, 208–13
 Rommel's asparagus, 95
Beard, Felix, 241
Beaty, Sherman, 89
Beau Guillot, 197
Beauregard, Edward, 112
Beuzeville-la-Bastille, 166
Bidwell, Bruce, 320
Black Prince, HMS, 80
Blakely, Harold, 173
Bletchley Park, Hut 3, 94–95
blitzkrieg, 40–41
bombardment
 air, 83–91
 naval, 77–83, 344–45
Bradley, Omar, xiv, xvii, 70, 311, 316, 320, 323
 Collins, selection of, 28
 Overlord planning and, 14–16, 23
Brandenberger, Elmer, 264, 265
Brannen, Malcolm, 117–18, 165
Brécourt, 251–52
Brereton, Lewis, xvii, 40, 73
Brévands, 133, 136–37
Brierre, Eugene, 243, 244
Brown, M. H., xviii, 77
Browning, Frederick, 47
B-26 Marauders, 87–91, 185
Buckley, George, 143

Burke, Thomas, 273
Burt, William, 264
Butcher, Harry, 14
Butler, John, 144

Caffey, Eugene, xviii, 194, 238
Caloville, 127
Calvados, 5
Camien, John, 264–65
Cardonnet Bank, 217
Carentan, 118
Carroll, Robert, 139
Cassidy, Patrick, 262, 264
Casteel, John, 207
casualties, 186, 322–25, 330–31
Cauquigny, 154–64
causeways
  Chef du Pont, 161–64
  description of, 17–18, 292
  infantry assault on, 221–29
  La Fière, 94, 145, 153–54, 157–58,
    161–163, 164
  number 1, 125–33, 221, 239–45, 246
  number 2, 125–33, 222, 246–56
  number 3, 119–25, 221, 245–46
  number 4, 119–25
  paratroopers assault on, 119–33
  penetration of, by infantry and para-
    troopers, 239–46
C-47s, 23–25, 36–40, 98–106
Chappuis, Steve, 123–24, 261–62
Chef du Pont, 161–64, 307
Chemical Mortar Battalion, 87th, 35,
  225–26
Cherbourg, 12, 291–97
Churchill, Winston, xiii
  Overlord planning and, 1–4, 14, 20
  speech to Parliament, 328–29
Clark, Mark, 27, 28
Cole, Robert, 124–25
Collins, Frederick, 222
Collins, Howard, 121–22
Collins, Joseph L., xvii, 27–29, 67, 96,
  173, 186, 206, 217–18, 246, 267,
  268, 291, 299–300, 310
commanders, list of, xvii–xviii
companies, xvi
Coningham, Arthur, 16
Cooperider, Claibourne, 287–288
Corry, USS, 213–216, 323
COSSAC. *See* Operation Overlord
Cota, Norman, 28

Cotentin Peninsula
  causeways, description of, 17–18
  causeways 1 and 2, 125–33
  causeways 3 and 4, 119–25
  description of shoreline, 52, 54, 57–58
  German deployment, 53–58
Coxon, Donald, 153–54
Coyle, James, 287
Creek, Roy, 163–64
Crete, 41
Crisson, Robert, 191, 192, 199
Cross, Herbert, 211–12
Crouch, Joel, 100–101

Danforth, Virgil, 131–32
Deyo, Morton, xviii, 78, 79
Dickman. See Joseph T. Dickman
Distinguished Service Cross (DSC)
  awards, list of men receiving, 333–34
Dolan, John, 153–54, 157, 158
Dollmann, Friedrich, 51
Doss, Adrian, 139
Douve, 53, 54
  bridges, 133–41
drop zones, 92–114
  See also Landing
Dunn, Edward, 175, 176–77

Eaton, Ralph, 170–71
Eben Emael, 41
E-boats (*Schnellboote*), 59–62, 65
Edelman, Hyman, 180
Église Notre-Dame, 125, 247
Eight Air Force, 85, 87
8th Infantry Regiment, xvi
  landing and initial assault, 184–91
  second wave, 191–200
  3rd Battalion, 221–22, 296–97
  third wave, 218–29
  training, 312
82nd Airborne Division, xvi–xvii, 36–37,
  42–49, 339–40
  drop zones, 92–114
  status of, on June 6th, 267–77, 306–8
Eisenhower, Dwight D., xi–xii, xvii, 40,
  98
  airborne division and, 43
  commander, selection of, 26–28
  D-Day date, selection of, 69
  Overlord planning and, 14, 21
Ekman, William, xviii, 146, 270
Elmira mission, 284–88

Empire Gauntlet, 78, 175, 222
engineer battalions
  237th, 35, 209, 210–11
  299th, 35, 209–10
Engineer Shore Regiment, 531st, 35
Engineer Special Brigade (ESB), 1st,
  34–35, 193–94, 237–39
Erebus, 79
Étienville. *See* Pont l'Abbé
Ewell, Julian, 46, 129–32
Exercise Tiger, 58–64, 65

Fales, Clarke, 298
Falley, Wilhelm, 117–18, 165, 316
Farquharson-Roberts, D. A., 82
Farrell, Lieutenant, 259–60
Farris, James, 64
Ferguson, Robert, 154
Fighting on Guadalcanal (Reeder), 234
Fleet, Burton, 64
Force O, 72
Force U, xviii
  bombardment, 77–83, 344–45
  pre-invasion movement, 64–73
Forthmann, Andrew, 169–70
4th Cavalry Group, 35, 175–77, 279
4th Infantry Division, xvi
  assault by, 184–200
  training, 29–33, 312
Franscioni, Gene, 114

Gage, Phillip, 139
Gainer, Virgil, 165
Garay, Paul, 215
Gavin, James, xviii, 40, 42, 46–49, 92, 95,
  98, 100, 117, 126, 155, 159–62,
  275–76, 319
Geddes, George, 62
Geddes, Raymond, 132
Gerhardt, Charles, 28
Germans
  reaction to assault troops, 184–85
  reaction to landing of paratroopers,
    116–19
Gerow, Leonard, 29
Gibbons, Ulrich, 229, 301–2, 321
Gibson, Glen, 204, 205
glider infantry regiments, 38–39, 42, 92,
  339, 340
  Elmira mission, 284–88
  Keokuk mission, 288–89
  nighttime landings, 141–44, 169–71

325th, xvii, 118
327th, xvii, 136
401st, 278–284
Gold Beach, 5, 118
Grant, George, 134
Gueutteville, 167
Guingand, Francis de, 14, 21

Haley, James, 197–98
Hall, John, 72
Hameau Germain, 253–55
Harmon, Ernest, 28
Harris, Ernest, 121–122
Harrison, Thomas, 233–34
Hayn, Friedrich, 116–17
Hedgerows, use of, 296
Heim, Marcus, 158
Hershner, Ivan, 245
Hester, Clarence, 251
Hiesville, 141–44
Higgins, Gerald, 245
Hill 30, 167–68, 277
Hill 110, 94
Hitler, Adolf, xi
Hitztaler, William, 111
Hobart, Percy, 201
Hoffman, George, 213–15
Hohl, Edwin, 132
Holdy, 249–51
Hughes-Hallett, John, 16

Ile de Terre, 175, 176
Ile du Large, 173, 175, 176
Iles St. Marcouf, 35, 173–77
Infantry Regiment, 12th, xvi
Infantry Regiment, 22nd, xvi
  pre-invasion movements, 69
  training, 29–33
Ingersoll, Ralph, 280, 284
Ingram, Robert, 108
Isle Marie chateau, 163

Johnson, Gerden, 82, 236
Johnson, Howard Ravenscroft, xviii, 49,
  136–39, 256–61, 303, 305
Johnson, John, 64
Johnson, Legrand, 124
Johnson, Orris, 204
Joseph, John, 105–6
Joseph T. Dickman, 78, 186
Juno Beach, 5

Kellam, Frederick, 158, 275
Keokuk mission, 288–89
Killoran, Thomas, 176
Kinzie, Melvin, 176
Kirk, Alan, xvii, 65
Kormylo, Joseph, 156–57
Koskimaki, George, 244
Krause, Edward, 147–48
Krebs, Frank, 134

La Barquette dam, 54, 133, 138–39, 256
La Dune, 196
La Fière bridge, 94, 145, 153–54, 157–58,
    161–63, 164, 275, 307
La Grande Dune, 195
landing
    of first assault troops, 177–84
    by gliders, 141–44, 169–71
landing, by paratroopers
    501st, description of, 129–33, 136–41
    502nd, description of, 119–25
    505th, description of, 146–54
    506th, description of, 125–29, 134–36
    507th, description of, 154–64
    508th, description of, 117–18, 164–68
    German reaction to, 116–19
landing craft
    importance of, 21–22
    types of, xviii–xix
Landing Craft, Assault (LCAs), xix
Landing Craft, Infantry (LCIs), xix
Landing Craft, Mechanized (LCMs), xix
Landing Craft, Tanks (LCTs), xix
    LCT-458, 228
    LCT-593, 204–5
Landing Craft, Tanks (rockets) (LCT[R]s),
    xix
Landing Craft, Vehicle, Personnel
    (LCVP), xix
Landing Ship, Tanks (LSTs), xix
    attack on, 59–62
land obstacles. See beach obstacles
Le Bel Esnault chateau, 138, 139
Lee, William, 43, 44–45, 46
Lees, Howard, 191
Legere, Lawrence, 132
Leigh-Mallory, Trafford, 22, 47, 48, 92,
    96–97
Les Forges, 280–83
Levy, Louis, 156, 157
Lillyman, Frank, 101, 346–47
Lindquist, Roy, xviii, 164, 168
Lyme Bay, 59–64
Lynd, J. Q., 298–99

Mabry, George, 197, 241–44
MacNeely, Carlton, 187, 195–96, 239–41
Maisel, Frederick, 253–55
Maloney, Arthur, 161, 162, 276
Marcks, Erich, 118, 248, 256
Marmion farm, 121–22
Marr, John, 153
Marshall, George C., xii, xvii, 189
Martin Company, Glenn L., 87–88
Mason, Charles, 170
Matheson, Salve, 127
McCarthy, John, 289
McGinity, James, 154, 158, 275
McKnight, John, 134–35
McLean, Kenneth, 8
McNair, Lesley, 44
McRoberts, Neal, 101
Medal of Honor awards, list of men
    receiving, 335
Mendez, Louis, 49, 165
Merderet, 53, 54, 155, 157, 275–78
Mézières, 262–66
Michaelis, John, 120, 265
Millett, George, xviii, 155, 164, 277–78
mines
    See also beach obstacles
    land "S" (Bouncing Betties), 176, 197,
        239, 320–321
    sea, 73–77, 204–5, 216–17, 320
Moench, John, 90
Montgomery, Bernard, xii, xvii, 48
    Overlord planning and, 1–25, 325, 327
Montilio, George, 136
Moon, Donald, xviii, 64–73, 183–84,
    215–18
Moore, Elzie, 239
Moreno, John, 65, 186
Morgan, Frederick, xvii, 5, 9
Morin, Arthur, 130
Moseley, George Van Horn, xviii, 120
Mozgo, Rudolph, 253
Muir, Marvin, 112
Mulberry design, 12, 16
Murphy, Mike, 142, 144

Natalle, Emil, 143–44
Naval Combat Demolition Units (NCDU),
    208–13
Navigation devices, 101
Neil, Don, 204
Nelson, Donald, 21–22
Neuville au Plain, 152, 270–75
Nevada, USS, 79–80, 275
Nimitz, Chester, 80

Ninth Air Force, 87–91, 185
IX Bomber Command, 343
IX Troop Carrier, 37–40, 107–14, 341–42
90th Infantry Division, xvi, 297–300
  359th Infantry, 298–99
91st Air Landing Division (German), 53, 95, 249, 313
Norris, Samuel, 254

Olson, Harvey, 176
Omaha Beach, 5, 118
  air bombardment, 85, 87, 185
  compared with Utah Beach, xiv, 29, 185, 212
101st Airborne Division, xvi, 36, 42–45, 46, 338–39
  drop zones, 92–114
Onken, John, 176
Operation Market-Garden, 94
Operation Overlord
  assessment of, 300–329
  planning, xii–xiv, 1–25
Operation Torch, 34, 278
O'Reilly, Robert, 121
Osprey, USS, 75, 323
Ostberg, Edwin, 161, 162, 163
Owens, William, 157

Parachute Artillery Battalion, 377th, 107, 121
parachute regiments, xvi–xvii, 42–43
  drop zones, 92–114
  501st, xvi, 129–33, 136–41, 256–61, 303, 305, 339
  502nd, xvi, 119–25, 261–66, 339, 346–47
  505th, xvi, 47, 146–54, 305, 340
  506th, xvi, 125–29, 134–36, 249–52, 339
  507th, xvi, 154–64, 276, 277–84, 340
  508th, xvi, 117–18, 164–68, 277, 340
  German reaction to, 116–19
  pathfinders, 99–102, 105–6, 338, 340
  uniform and equipment of, 348–49
Parachute Regiment, German 6th, 53, 248
Parrott, John, 215
Parsons, Adam, 37–38, 125
Patch, Lloyd, 249–51
pathfinders, 99–102, 105–6, 338, 340
PC-1261, 181–82
Peterson, Theodore, 273
Picauville, 166–67
Pile, Malvin, 243
Plymouth, 66–67

Pont l'Abbé, 166
Portal, Charles, 23
Pouppeville, 127, 129, 131–32, 241–44
Pratt, Donald, xviii, 142, 144, 159, 288
Putnam, Lyle, 149

Quartermaster Railhead Co., 557th, 61
Quartermaster Service Company, 3206th, 61
Quincy, USS, 80, 259–60

Rabe, Günther, 61
radio messages, decryption of, 94–95
Raibl, Tony, 285
Ranger outfits, 173, 175
Raff, Edson, 278–84, 286
Raudstein, Knut, 250
Ravenoville, 121
Rebarchek, John, 193
Reeder, Russell, xviii, 233, 234–36, 294–95
Renaud, Alexandre, 145
Ridgway, Matthew, xvii, 27–28, 44, 45, 47, 118, 150, 278, 306, 308
Rogers, Thomas Deforth, 211
Rommel, Erwin, 50–51, 56, 73, 74
Rommel's asparagus, 95
Roosevelt, Franklin D., xii–xiii, 20
Roosevelt, Theodore Jr., xviii, 70, 91, 177–84, 187, 190–91, 192, 193, 219, 231, 255–56, 290–91, 332–33
Roysden, Dale, 158
Rubin, Alfred, 176
Ruge, Friedrich, 74

St. Côme du Mont, 135, 256–61, 305
Ste. Marie du Mont, 125, 127–30, 222, 246–56
St. Martin de Varreville, 119–24, 261, 294–95
Ste. Mère Église, 94, 124–25, 145–54, 271–75, 306–7
St. Sauveur le Vicomte, 94
Saladin, HMS, 61
Sampson, Francis, 260–61
Sampson, Otis, 274
Santarsiero, Charles, 112
Schnellboote, 59–62, 65
Schroeder, Leonard, 187, 196
Schwartzwalder, Ben, 153
Scimitar, HMS, 61
SCR-609, 259
SCR-717, 101
VII Corps, xvii, 26–27

709th Division (German), 51–53, 194–95, 312–14
Shanley, Thomas, 113, 166–67, 277
Shettle, Charles, 135, 136, 256
Sicily, airborne mission in, 36–37
Simmons, Conrad, 199, 245
Singleton, Raymond, 170
Sink, Robert, xviii, 107, 125–27, 249–50
Smith, Walter Bedell, 17
Smith, Ward, 134
Snow, Robert M., 91
Soemba, HNMS, 79
Soldier's Story, A (Bradley), xiv
Sperber, Harold, 103–4
Stalin, Josef, 20
Stark, Harold, xvii
Stopka, John, 121–22
Stoy Hora, 134
Straussler, Nicholas, 201–2
Strayer, Robert, 127–28, 249
Strickland, Erasmus, 222, 252
Summers, Harrison, 264–65
Sword Beach, 10, 12

Tabb, Robert, 210–11
tank battalions
    role and importance of, 201–8
    70th, 34, 204–8, 241
    741st, 206
    743rd, 205–6
    746th, 35, 224, 278–84
tanks, duplex drive (DD), 34, 182, 185, 201–8
Task Force Raff, 278–84
Taylor, Maxwell, xvii, 28, 46, 126, 129–31, 244, 288, 302–3, 305–6
Teague, Arthur, 222, 223–224
Thomas, George, 176–77
Thomason, Joel, 228–29
Tighe, Thomas, 244
Timmes, Charles, 155–56, 276–77
Training for Utah Beach, 29–33, 172–73
Tribolet, Hervey, xviii, 294, 295–96
troop carriers C-47s, 23–25, 36–40
    61st and 442nd, 155
    315th and 316th, 146, 149–50, 152
    434th, 141–44
    pathfinders, 98–106
    serials, 106–14
Truman, Harry, 88
Truscott, Lucian, 27
Turnbull, Turner, 152, 270–75
Turner, William, 127, 249
Tuscaloosa, USS, 80

12th Infantry Regiment, 233, 234–36, 294–95
22nd Infantry Regiment, 3rd Battalion, 222–24, 233–34, 294, 295–96

Utah Beach
    assessment of, 300–329
    bombardment, air, 87–91, 185
    bombardment, naval, 77–83, 185
    compared with Omaha Beach, xiv, 29, 185, 212
    drop zones, 92–114
    first-wave units on, 336–37
    landing of first assault troops, problems for, 180–84
    practice exercises (Exercise Tiger), 58–64
    pre-invasion movement, 64–73
    training for, 29–33
U-2A convoy, 71–72

Van Antwerp, Harold, 134
Vandervoort, Benjamin, 149, 150, 152, 270–74, 307
Van Fleet, James, xviii, 184, 187–89, 182, 300, 312
Vaughn, Wales, 177
vertical envelopment, xiv, 18–19, 37, 314
Vickery, Grady, 222, 252
Von Schlieben, Karl-Wilhelm, 50–53

Warren, John, 63
Warren, Shields, 45–46, 165, 167, 277
Weisberg, Benjamin, 107
Wharton, James, xviii, 237–38
Wienecke, Robert, 308
Wilhelm, Frederick, 106
Willard, Robert, 199–200
Williams, Paul, xvii, 99
Winters, Richard, 251–52
Wolfram, Robert, 196
Wolverton, Robert, 133–34
Wood, George, 152–53
Wood, Wilson, 89
Woodruff, Roscoe, 27

XYZ objective, 261–66

York, Alvin, 44
Young, Charles, 110, 125–26

Zahn, Donald, 136
Zampiello, Anthony, 241
Zanders, John, 176